The Inevitable Guest

Line drawing of Jemima Darby, by James Dance Cawthon, from an 1880 photograph.

THE
INEVITABLE
GUEST

Life and Letters of Jemima Darby

by
JOHN   ARDIS   CAWTHON

The Naylor Company
Book Publishers of the Southwest
San Antonio, Texas

To
the memory of
Maria Elizabeth Kolb **Tooke**

Contents

List of Illustrations

Introduction to the Letters

§

"A half-score of sons and daughters, a tall, lank, and rather weatherworn gentleman, and a slender, soft-voiced weary-looking mother composed the family group, unless one counts the inevitable guest or old maid cousin who, like the furniture or the servants, always formed part of a planter's household."

William E. Dodd, *The Cotton Kingdom* (New Haven, 1919), p. 72.

If a nineteenth century aunt or female cousin did not marry, she lived with her next of kin. She shared vicariously in the mysteries of their birth and mating; she understood somberly the realities of eternity. Children loved and feared her; menfolks paid their respects. She sewed and quilted to earn her living, and for diversion read her Bible or gossiped among the housewives. Jemima Darby was such a relative.

When Miss Darby left Darlington District, South Carolina, in April, 1860, to go to Louisiana to live with her nephew, Dr. Alexander James Kolb, in Ringgold, she carried with her a small package of six letters. Subsequently she selected fifty-two of the letters which she received from South Carolina and two invitations from Ringgold and filed them away in her trunk. According to tradition, she read the letters often.

Upon Miss Darby's death in 1884, her nephew's wife, Amanda Melvina Brinson Kolb, preserved the letters. When Mrs. Kolb died in 1890, she left the letters at the home of her daughter, Maria Elizabeth Kolb Tooke, where they remained until Mrs. Tooke's death in 1935. Miss Darby's great-great-niece, Miss Ida G. Tooke, daughter of Maria Elizabeth Kolb Tooke, brought the letters back to Ringgold when she moved there to live at the home of her sister, Mrs. Ella Tooke Thomas, late in 1935.

In a letter to the writer, a great-great-great-nephew to Miss Darby, Miss Tooke remarked:

> These old letters that we have of Aunt Jemima Darby may interest you. It has been so long since I read them I have forgotten the contents. You . . . likely would find valuable information, especially names, in them, and I am sorry I did not think to offer them to you. . . . Mama used to talk about Aunt Jemima. She was from Society Hill, S. C., you know, and proud as a peacock of her family and family traditions. Grandfather was her nephew and a favorite. He must have been the

last one she had to turn to for a home in her old years. And she never liked it here. Shall I mail the package to you?[1]

To read the Darby letters is to relive thirty years of turbulent American history. Between 1853 and 1883, Miss Darby and her contemporaries witnessed the end of the Cotton Kingdom, the Confederate fighting, the Reconstruction, the birth of the New South, and the opening of the West. Among Jemima's acquaintances, there were no descendants of royalty, nor were there any paupers. Her friends were practitioners of Baptist humility, but they numbered statesmen among their families. Her Southerners had good taste, but very little money. Miss Darby, her relatives, and her friends represent a group whose story has not been told.

This is not a history of great Americans or great Southerners. Jemima Darby's friends admired their leaders, but nearer home were neighbors and kinfolks, of whom they wrote. The index to this volume contains more references to Williamsons of Darlington than to Lees of Arlington.

The letters which Miss Darby received before leaving South Carolina were:

1. Three letters from Mrs. Elizabeth Frances Cannady Vann, of Brookville, North Carolina, to her husband's cousin, Jemima Darby, at Society Hill, South Carolina, January 31, 1854, to March 18, 1855;
2. Two letters from Mary Darby, Society Hill, South Carolina, to her sister, Jemima, at Bennettsville, South Carolina, April 22 and August 14, 1857;
3. One letter from Mary A. Catlett, Darlington, South Carolina, to her friend, Jemima, at Cheraw, South Carolina, July 12, 1856.

During the preparation for the journey to Louisiana and during the twenty-three years when Miss Darby lived in Louisiana, letters were written by:

---

[1] Ida G. Tooke, Letter from Ringgold, Louisiana, to John A. Cawthon, Russellville, Arkansas, September 17, 1952.

Fourteen letters were not addressed to Jemima Darby, but were written during the same period by relatives and friends whose accounts of events and descriptions of people keep the story moving. The supplementary letters were one letter to Mary Ann Charles, Darlington, South Carolina, from Emily King Taylor, Yorkville, South Carolina, which Mrs. Charles had enclosed in a letter to Miss Darby; one letter to Ella Kolb Cawthon, Ringgold, Louisiana, from her aunt, Harriet Brinson Fouts, Sparta, Louisiana, who made reference to some lace which she had purchased for Miss Darby; one letter from William Vann, Leavensworth, South Carolina, to his son, Dr. Alexander Russia Vann, Brookville, North Carolina; four letters from Thomas E. Howle, Leavensworth, South Carolina, to Dr. Vann, Brookville, North Carolina; three wartime letters from T. E. Howle to his wife; one letter from Mrs. A. R. Vann to her sister-in-law, Mrs. Howle; one letter from Bettie Hill, Richmond, Virginia, to T. E. Howle at Manassas; one letter from Mrs. LeGrand, Sumter, South Carolina, to Mrs. Howle; and one note from John K. McIver to T. E. Howle.

Two invitations, both from Ringgold, were sent by Mrs. James Smith and Mr. J. M. Lockett.

Miss Tooke's prediction that the letters were likely to contain "valuable information, especially names," proved to be correct. Among the families whose names appeared in the letters are:

Adams	Crosland	Gregg	McCall	Smoot
Alexander	Culpepper	Griffin	McIntosh	Sompayrac
Andrews	Dabbs	Harllee	McIver	Sparks
Bacchus	Darby	Hart	McLean	Stephenson
Bacot	Dargan	Hartwell	Malloy	Stokes
Baker	Davis	Haynesworth	Napier	Stout
Bealer	DeLorme	Hill	Nettles	Strickland
Beattie	Dorrity	Howard	Norwood	Taylor
Bevil	Douglas	Howle	Orr	Thomas
Bostick	Dove	Hunter	Parnell	Vann
Brearley	DuBose	James	Parrott	Wallace
Burn	DuPre	Keith	Pearce	Watson
Cannon	Eason	Killins	Pegues	Whitner
Catlett	Edwards	Kirven	Phelps	Wilds
Chambers	Evans	King	Player	Williams
Charles	Ferguson	Kolb	Porcher	Williamson
Coggeshall	Flinn	LaCoste	Pressley	Wilson
Coit	Fountain	Lane	Rice	Wingate
Coker	Fraser	Law	Rogers	Winn
Conners	Furman	Lee	Ross	Witherspoon
Council	Gandy	Lide	Sanders	Woods
Crane	Garrison	Lucas	Smith	Zimmerman

The letters to Miss Darby reveal more than names, however; they recount biographical sketches of entire families and of individuals. Jemima and Mary Darby lived in the homes of Catletts, Kings, Williamsons, and Vanns, all related to old Carolina families. Mrs. King was a Bacot; Mrs. Bright Williamson was a Rogers; Mrs. Thomas Williamson was a Wilds. William Vann married Goodson, Jones, and Passmore; his sons married Miss Cannady, and Miss Byrd; his daughter married Mr. Howle. A. P. LaCoste married into the King family; Andrew Charles into the Williamsons. Jemima's sister, Elizabeth, married a Kolb, cousin to the Revolutionary War hero. Closely linked with the lives of Miss Darby and her friends were the Baptist preachers of the region — Dargan, Furman, Beattie, Napier, Burn, Bealer, and Phelps. Mr. Dargan married a Lide; Mr. Bealer, a Bacot. To list Jemima's friends was like alphabetizing a roll-call of the district. The story of Sallie Elizabeth Williams's growth was narrated from the time of her birth until her twenty-second year. Paralleling the lives of South Carolina relatives and friends were the lives of Miss Darby's Louisiana family, to whom frequent references were also made.

And while there are few direct quotations from Miss Darby among the letters, she dominates them all, a symbol of the past and a link between contemporary branches of her empire.

xvi

Writers of the letters made use of the educational opportunities of their day. Spelling was phonetic and sentence structure simple. Punctuation consisted chiefly of periods and semicolons.[2] The Epistles of the New Testament furnished patterns for letter writing in Jemima's South Carolina. To adopt a style of writing which involved the use of Biblical references was easy for regular churchgoers at Black Creek, Darlington, Welsh Neck, and Mispah. Trite and formalized introductory and concluding statements were composed with great care. News was reported and opinion expressed with ease and clarity.

Credit for the photograph of Miss Darby goes to Miss Tooke, who said:

> I am inclosing the picture of Aunt Jemima. She is very stately looking, we think. We decided that she looks very modern with her short curly hair. I am sorry it is fading. I remember Mama saying she did love to wear silk and have some lace somewhere. You can tell that it is silk that she has on.[3]

The editing of the letters was a cooperative enterprise between twentieth century descendants of Miss Darby's relatives and friends in South Carolina and those "out West." Contributions of primary source materials from descendants of Jemima's acquaintances back home made possible the preparation of the South Carolina phase of the story. Special acknowledgements go to the vast number of South Carolinians who, "if not kin, are kin to kin" — to Beulah W. Coggeshall, who, curious because of "Nancy's" name in the letters, became involved in a project which led her far beyond the call of duty as reference librarian in the Darlington Public Library; to Sarah Elizabeth Howle Campbell, whom Dr. Crane, in the letters, would have named "Carolina Secession," and her daughters, Edith, Elizabeth, and Vara; to Eleanor Vann Rose, Franklinton, North Carolina, granddaughter of Dr. Alexander Russia and Frances Elizabeth Cannady Vann; to Eunice Chambers, Hartsville, whose Chambers, Williams-Ferguson ancestors were Jemima's Black Creek and

---

2 Commas and apostrophes, which were used infrequently, have, in some cases, been added editorially. Paragraphing has also been included when necessary.

3 Ida G. Tooke, Letter from Ringgold, Louisiana, to John A. Cawthon, Russellville, Arkansas, October 27, 1952.

Auburn neighbors; to Horace Fraser Rudisill, Florence, who discovered letters by Jemima Darby; to members of the Darlington County Historical Society who, on June 1, 1953, displayed the type of hospitality which should be reserved for homefolks only; to custodians of valuable records at Furman University, the Historical Commission at Columbia, the Courthouse at Darlington, and the University of South Carolina.

Even though Mrs. Charles once said to Miss Darby, "You will have to call to your assistance all of the eyes and spelling talent of your family to assist you in making sense of this . . ." it is not likely that she anticipated the assistance of members of the family three times removed at a time when the letters had lain in an attic for seventy years.

Acknowledgements go to Jemima's twentieth century kinfolks in North Louisiana — to Ida Gertrude Tooke, family archivist and historian; to Ella Tooke Thomas, whose birth was announced in the letters and who lived to see them published; to James Alexander Cawthon, whose first six years were spent in the house with his Aunt Jemima; and to Elenora Albrecht Cawthon, Jemima's great-great-great-niece-in-law, from Texas, whose enthusiasm for the Jemima Darby project has brought her tiresome hours of research and editing and endless tracking through "all of the best graveyards" between Cashaway Ferry, South Carolina, and San Antonio, Texas.

Sweet Gum Leaf — A standard southern quilt pattern which was used for a quilt pieced by Miss Jemima Darby between 1878 and 1884 and given to her nephew, the author's father, sometime before his sixth birthday. The squares, measuring approximately twelve inches, are done in red and green on a white background. The quilt, in useable condition today as a coverlet, now belongs to the author.

First Baptist Church, Darlington, South Carolina.

Woodlawn Green, home of William Vann, near Auburn, South Carolina.

Black Creek Baptist Church, Dovesville, South Carolina.

Model of Fort Sumter, South Carolina.

Catlett House, 463 Pearl Street, Darlington, South Carolina.

Mrs. Thomas F. Howle about 1870.

Captain Thomas F. Howle in 1862.

Ella Caroline Kolb Cawthon, Ringgold, Louisiana, 1875.

Sallie Elizabeth Williams, 1873.

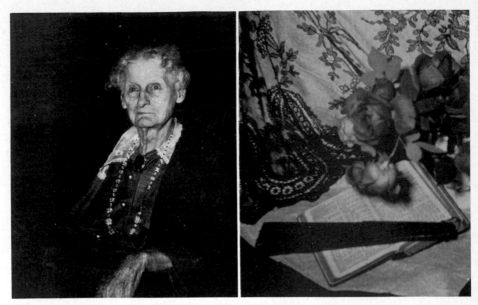

Mrs. William T. Campbell,
Darlington, South Carolina, 1953.

Jemima Darby's fan, lace shawl
and Bible.

Dr. and Mrs. A. J. Kolb and family, Ringgold, Louisiana, circa 1860.

Furman University, Greenville, South Carolina.

Mary Darby's grave, Society Hill, South Carolina.

South Carolina Background
PART I

"Marlboro, Chesterfield, and Darlington Districts became in the middle and latter half of the eighteenth century a melting-pot of five or six races. There came forth from the mint a blended people, bearing an image and superscription that was not to be erased by the flight of time."

Harvey Toliver Cook, *The Life and Legacy of David Rogerson Williams* (New York, 1916), p. 315.

Caught up in the westward movement, Jemima Darby, at the age of sixty-six, found herself moving across the entire expanse of William E. Dodd's cotton kingdom[1] — from her home in South Carolina to an unmarked grave in San Antonio, Texas. Jemima, the sixth child of Owen and Mary Vann Darby, was born in the Pee Dee section of South Carolina on January 30, 1794, and died February 21, 1884.

Owen Darby, who was born in 1733, married Mary Vann in South Carolina in 1782. He owned land "on the Round O in Darlington District which lay on both sides of the Darlington-Society Hill Road."[2] He and Mary Darby had nine children:

1. Elizabeth (November 5, 1783 — August 3, 1853) married Jesse Kolb on October 10, 1810;
2. Benjamin (May 22, 1786 — ?) never married;
3. James Carel (December 28, 1787 — August 17, 1828) never married;
4. William Henry (October 8, 1789 — October 29, 1829) never married;
5. Jacob (February 1, 1792-1823) never married;
6. Jemima (January 30, 1794 — February 21, 1884) never married;
7. Mary (January 6, 1796 — July 18, 1858)[3] never married;
8. Jeremiah (December 20, 1797 — July 31, 1831) never married;
9. Rebecca (June 22, 1800 — November 2, 1821) never married.[4]

Elizabeth, the oldest of the Darby children, was the only member of the family who married. Her husband was Jesse, son of Jehu Kolb, a collateral relative of Abel Kolb,[5] and the son or grandson of Martin, Jacob, or Henry, whose father, Johannes, of Mannheim in the Palatinate, Germany, "came to America in 1707, settled at Germantown, Pa., and came to Pee Dee about 1739 and settled near Cashuway Ferry at Kolb's Neck."[6]

Thus, through Elizabeth, all Darby heirs and Jemima's next of kin in her old age were named Kolb.

Jehu Kolb was a resident of George Town District, South Carolina, when he enlisted in the Army of the United States in March, 1776. He served with the Fifth Rifle Regiment, commanded by Col. Isaac Heyer, until July, 1777.[7] He was discharged in Cheraw District, and obtained land "on the southwest side of Pee Dee river and south of Black Creek, near the Great Cypresses on the head of Long Branch"[8] in 1785. The 200-acre tract which he acquired was bounded "on the east by Josiah Kolb's and vacant land; on the northeast by Christopher Teel's vacant land and on all other sides by vacant land."[9]

Jehu and his wife, Lucretia, were members of Black Creek Baptist Church from the year of its organization, 1803, until their deaths.[10] Jehu served as deacon after his being "set apart" in June, 1811. Lucretia's name disappeared from the church records after 1817, and on January 17, 1827, Jehu married a young woman whose given name was Angelina.[11] At the age of seventy-one, he declared that he owned the following property in Darlington District:

700 acres of poor pine land	
1 horse worth	$40.00
stock of cattle worth	$35.00
stock of hogs worth	$25.00
one negro woman worth	$225.00
The whole valued at	$465.00[12]

In 1829, he had "two in family beside himself, viz: his wife, aged about 38 years, and the negro woman above named, aged about 37 years."[13] Because of a wound in the knee which he received at the Battle of Eutaw, he was not able to perform active labor. He died May 2, 1844, universally respected.[14] In 1855, Angelina was still living in Darlington District, where she was awarded a pension of $80 per annum and 160 acres of bounty land.[15]

Owen Darby owned at least 1,000 acres of land in Darlington District at the time of his death on October 30, 1804,[16] but, with the burning of the courthouse on March 19, 1806, all records of land entries were destroyed. Hence the dates when the Darby family arrived in the Pee Dee region and acquired property are not known.

The Welsh Neck had been settled in 1736. Alexander Gregg summarized the activities of the early settlers:

> . . . a company of the Welch settled on Cat Fish, a stream in what is now Marion District. They remained there a short time, and then moved higher up the river to the neighborhood of the Welch Neck. . . . The lands on the upper Pee Dee seem to have suited their agricultural purposes better. To that rich and compact body of land, embraced in a bend of the river, opposite the present village of Society Hill, and called, from an early period "Welch Neck", the attention of these prudent settlers appears from the first to have been directed. And there they began to gather in a body. The "Welch Neck" extended from Crooked Creek to the Red Bluff below, a distance of about six miles, embracing the rich lands of the swamps several miles across.[17]

In January, 1738, the people of the community were "organized into a society of the Baptist faith, and erected a house of worship on the east bank of the river a short distance above the ferry, now known as Sparks, on the road leading from Society Hill to Bennettsville."[18]

On August 1, 1779, Owen Darby was examined for membership and baptized, and on August 7 was received into full fellowship of Welsh Neck Baptist Church. Earlier in the year, Peggy and Honor Darby had been admitted to the church by baptism.[19] Already a member of the church was Mary Vann, whom Owen married in 1782.

The Darby children were brought up in a home where stern Baptist standards of morality were practiced by their mother, but where, because of the father, church attendance was not compulsory. Records of the Welsh Neck Church are filled "with cases of discipline of their members, for offenses of drunkenness in public . . . of absenting themselves from the Lord's house."[20] According to the church minutes, Owen Darby was a hard man to discipline.[21]

So it was that when "the Baptists of South Carolina entered the new century with a tremendous stirring of their spiritual life and with an equally astonishing increase in their numbers,"[22] Jemima's father was not among them.

The Baptists of Society Hill were firm in their belief that baptism must come only after the individual was positive that he had been saved. Whenever the individual was positive that he could vouchsafe voluntary obedience to the gospel, and not until then, did he profess conversion. A contemporary and friend of Jemima's, who was also born in 1794, was

> . . . often brought under deep religious influences, but it was not until his fortieth year that he made a profession of religion by putting on Christ publickly, in the ordinance of baptism. He united with the Welsh Neck church, at Society Hill. From that time, he became an earnest advocate of the cause of the Redeemer.[23]

Jemima Darby's own conversion took place on September 3, 1825. The account is included in the church minutes.

> The exercises of the day commenced with a sermon from the pastor (John XXI: 3 — 6). It was delivered with encreased animation and produced a corresponding effect. Some of the congregation were softened and came forward requesting prayer to be made for them. After the church met, Miss Jemima Darby related a work of grace on her heart, which was highly satisfactory. And she was received for baptism.[24]

She was baptized by Rev. William Dossey on September 4. Mary Darby was baptized on the first Lord's Day in 1829.

> 1828   Dec   At one of the meetings, Miss Mary Darby was received for baptism upon her profession of faith in Christ.

1829 Jan First Lord's Day. Met at the Water, when Mary
Darby and the ten black persons before received
were baptized. After public worship they were received into fellowship. The supper of the Lord
was administered.[25]

The Welsh Neck Church which Jemima and Mary Darby
joined was not the old church on the east side of the river which
their parents had joined. In 1798, the church was rebuilt at a site
on the west side of the Pee Dee River, where it was described as:

> . . . a plain, substantial square building without a porch in
> front, but with a large addition on one side the whole length
> of the building for the use of the negroes. It was divided from
> the larger part by a low wall about as high as the backs of the
> pews with an aisle extending from their side entrance to an
> open door into the main auditorium. The church was nicely
> furnished inside, with walls ceiled and neat pews. An aisle in
> the middle and one at each side led back to the pulpit and
> lower platform on one side. Several of the pews were square
> with seats on three sides which we as children admired very
> much and wished father had selected one of those, but our pew
> was a long straight one and we could only face the pulpit! Pews
> were rented then and each family had its own.
> The pulpit was a high one with a flight of steps on each
> side and doors which closed. The seat could accommodate two
> ministers, possibly three, quite comfortably. A sounding board
> was over the pulpit. In front of the pulpit and nearly on a level
> with it were two high seats or pews for the use of two excel-
> lent ladies who were almost deaf but loved to attend church
> and were regularly there.
> The lower platform with its reading desk was used for pray-
> er meetings or services conducted by other than the minister.[26]

Jemima Darby counted Elizabeth Witherspoon Williams, wife
of David Rogerson Williams, among her friends. They had grown
up together in the Pee Dee region, were faithful members of the
Welsh Neck Church, and were residents of Society Hill. On October 10, 1830, one week before her famous husband's death, Elizabeth Williams wrote her will; Jemima Darby was a witness.[27] The
will, written at Society Hill on the same day that D. R. Williams,

in a letter to Governor Stephen D. Miller, wrote, "I reached here this evening with my family from the Springs,"[28] stated:

> Feeling the uncertainty of life and not knowing how soon or in what manner I may be called home, I embrace the privilege of declaring my desire representing the property which God in his great mercy has granted me.

The first five items bequeathed Negroes to the children of D. R. W.[29] and Alexander McIver.[30] The next item left ten Negroes, the family silver, the family portraits, her writing desk and traveling trunk to her "dearly beloved grandson, David Rogerson Williams."[31]

> But of everything else belonging to me, I desire to be sold (furniture, carriage, horses, stock which are lawfully mine and the crop of hand) to be divided in three equal parts — one to Welsh Neck Church, of which I am a member; one to Welsh Neck Association; and one to South Carolina Baptist Convention.

She named Dr. Thomas Smith,[32] Brother Alexander Sparks,[33] and her "beloved son, John Nicholas Williams,"[34] executors. The witnesses were Jemima Darby, John McIver,[35] and S. C. Williams.[36]

As the second wife of Mr. Williams, whom she married in November, 1809, Elizabeth Witherspoon was "in every respect fitted to fill the place of wife, mother and mistress in this worthy household."[37] As a widow, during the ten years following Mr. Williams's death in 1830,[38] Elizabeth Witherspoon Williams "entered with all her energy into the beneficent schemes of the neighborhood and state."

The South Carolina of Jemima Darby's day was considered the center of the cultural life of the country.[39] When William Harrison Scarborough, portraitist and miniaturist, selected a home in 1839, he brought his family to Darlington District "where culture, education, wealth and appreciation of art abounded."[40] All of the first families of Society Hill, Darlington, and Cheraw whom Scarborough painted were Miss Darby's friends. The list included James, McIver, Dargan, Evans, Lide,

Wilds, Ervin, Sparks, Jamison, Coggeshall, Flinn, Wilson, Haynes-worth, and Charles. There were two portraits of Darby women, wives of Jemima's cousins,[41] but Jemima did not sit for the artist.

The manner in which Mary Vann Darby and her family supported themselves after Owen's death has not been made a matter of record, nor are the causes of so many early deaths known. First to die was the mother on October 11, 1821, followed by Rebecca, the youngest daughter, on November 2 of the same year; Jacob in 1823; James Carel in 1828; William Henry in 1829; and Jeremiah in 1831. The date of Benjamin Darby's death was not recorded, but he was present when Owen Darby's heirs sold a large part of their property in 1823.[42] Benjamin was thirty-six years old at the time.

During the 1830's, 1840's, and 1850's only Jemima and Mary Darby were left of their family in Darlington. James King bought property from Jemima in 1836[43] and from Mary in 1838.[44]

Elizabeth Darby Kolb and her husband had, in the meantime, reared a family of their own. They had five children: David Cameron, born July 11, 1811; Mary Ann, born April 22, 1814; Jesse, born March 11, 1817; Alexander James, born May 13, 1820; and Carolina Nicholas, born May 29, 1822. Carolina died as an infant in 1822; young Jesse and his sister, Mary Ann, died in 1831. Jesse Kolb's disposal of property inherited by Elizabeth from the Darby estate, with Jemima witnessing the 1822 transaction,[45] would indicate that he left Darlington District during the early part of the 1820's. His first move was into the neighboring district of Marlborough, on the eastern side of the Pee Dee River.[46] From South Carolina, Jesse and Elizabeth Kolb migrated first to Alabama, where David Cameron married Emily Frances, daughter of General Reuben C. and Mary B. Shorter.[47] Emily Shorter Kolb died in 1839 and David C. Kolb died in 1841.

Alexander J. Kolb, the only surviving child of Jesse and Elizabeth, had moved to Florida in 1840, where he clerked for the firm of Dodge, Kolb, and McCoy, in Apalachicola. Later he

. . . read medicine under Dr. Cowen, of Eufaula, Alabama, and attended lectures in Jefferson Medical College in Philadelphia, Pa. In 1844, he entered the practice of medicine near Brown Ferry, Florida, where he practiced for four years. In

March, 1848, he moved with his aging parents to Natchitoches Parish, Louisiana. After a year he moved to Bossier Parish, where his father, Jesse Kolb, died. Dr. Kolb next moved to Sparta, Louisiana, with his aged and afflicted mother who died there, on August 3, 1853.[48]

With Elizabeth Kolb's death, there remained of Jemima's immediate family only herself, her sister Mary, and her nephew, Dr. Kolb.

The matter of Darby finances is mentioned in none of the letters. If the Darby sisters had economic problems, they were too proud to comment, and yet at one time, "the destitute condition of Sister Mary Darby was brought to the attention" of Welsh Neck Church, and "it was resolved to grant her assistance."[49] Mary, who was in extremely poor health, did not always stay with Jemima, but she too seems to have been an "inevitable guest or old maid cousin who . . . always formed part of the planter's household."[50] First she was with one friend or relative, then another.

But the year 1853 found both Jemima and Mary living at Woodlawn Green, near Auburn, South Carolina, with the family of William Vann,[51] the son of William Vann, Sr.,[52] a Revolutionary War soldier.

A sketch of the elder William Vann has been outlined by a great-great-granddaughter:

> In 1780 William Vann left Hertford to go to his brother who was then living on the Congaree River, South Carolina. This man was lame in one leg caused by white swelling. On account of freshets in the Pee Dee River he never succeeded in getting to his brother, but stopped on the Pee Dee and there died.[53]

Further, William Vann's life in Darlington County was described in this manner:

> He was in the Revolutionary War. Endured such hardships that he could not bear the closeness of a house, so he built a log cabin in the yard with a roof, but no door, and slept there. Neighbors asked if he was not afraid of the bears and wolves, and he said, "If a bar can get me before I can get the bar, let him come on."

The country was very sparsely settled. Only means of travel was on horseback or cart.

The Tories destroyed everything that William Vann had. He died soon after the war leaving a large family with no means of support.

His son, William Vann, was bound out by the court to a woman who was very cruel to him. He saved all of his money and gradually bought all of her property.[54]

William Vann's property was on Pollard's Bay, near Black Creek, and was formerly owned by James Dove and William H. Frazier.[55]

William Vann, Sr., had at least three sons, two of whom were referred to specifically as "cousins" in the Darby letters. They were Thomas Vann, who left South Carolina for Georgia and died there about 1890; Mills Vann, who died in 1875 at the age of ninety-three in the Auburn community, whose wife was Clementina Wright; and William Vann (May 29, 1795 — February 25, 1881), who married Sarah Goodson (October 12, 1812), Mrs. Sarah Jones (April 20, 1820), and Louise Passmore (December 19, 1867).

William Vann, the master of Woodlawn Green, and his first wife, Sarah Goodson, were the parents of five children: Margaret H.,[56] Mary Ann,[57] Josiah T.,[58] Alexander Russia,[59] and Sarah Ann.[60] There was one daughter, Elizabeth Sarah (Bettie or Lizzie),[61] by the second Mrs. Vann, Sarah Jones.[62]

By 1853, Mary Ann and Bettie had married and were living in the Darlington neighborhood. Josiah T. (Joe), known as "the old bachelor," resided at home, as did Alexander Russia (Rush). After graduating at Wake Forest College, North Carolina, and at Jefferson Medical College, Philadelphia, Pennsylvania, young Dr. A. R. Vann had married Elizabeth Frances (Fanny) Cannady,[63] daughter of Wyatte and Elizabeth Hockaday Cannady, on April 4, 1850, and had brought her back to live among his kinfolk in Darlington District.

Woodlawn Green was a two-storied frame house with a wide front gallery and with a separate building for a kitchen attached to the main house by an extended hall at the rear. There were four large rooms and the kitchen downstairs and three rooms upstairs. Brick chimneys, with fireplaces on both floors, stood on each end of the house; there was another chimney, with a fireplace, at the rear of the kitchen. Imported wainscoting and mahogany doors were the showy permanent features of the interior of the house.[64]

The Misses Darby did their best to make Rush's wife feel welcome at Woodlawn Green. Both were present when her two sons were born.[65] They helped to prepare little William Wyatte's body for burial in the family cemetery, and then lavished their love upon Samuel Cannady, the second child. But Elizabeth Frances Cannady Vann was not happy in South Carolina. She longed to return to the way of life which had been hers on her father's plantation in North Carolina. And to live in the same house with William Vann, whom later correspondents from the area branded as wilful and bossy, was not always a pleasure. According to a descendant, "Billy Vann was determined to make a lot of money, which he did."[66]

The Vanns belonged to Black Creek Baptist Church. Sarah Jones Vann was "received for baptism" on July 4, 1828, soon after her marriage; William Vann "came forward and offered an experience of grace" on March 4, 1832; Mills Vann was a deacon. A. R. and E. F. Vann presented letters, which were accepted, on March 15, 1851, he from Philadelphia, Pa., where he had been in school, and she from Brassfields, Granville County, N. C., and finally, "Brother A. R. Vann requested letters of dismissal for himself and wife."[67]

Fanny was pleased; she would return to her beloved North Carolina. Rush Vann would go back to his father-in-law's plantation in Granville County and practice medicine there. Apparently Jemima and Mary Darby were Fanny's favorites among the in-laws. "Cousin Jemima" was to be her link with South Carolina. To Jemima, Fanny wrote the first letter which appears in this series. The letter, for which the stamp is hand-canceled at Brookville, Granville County, North Carolina, was addressed to Miss Darby at Society Hill, South Carolina.

Mrs. A. R. Vann, Brookville, North Carolina, to Jemima Darby, Society Hill, South Carolina.

Brookville Jan 31st 1854

Miss Jemima Darby
      Society Hill, S. C.

Dear Cousin

According to promise I have at last found a few minutes
to write to you, but think not that I have not thought of you
in so long a time. Not so. We talk of you often and wish to see
and to know where you are. I do hope that you have found a
good home and true friends. We have had quite a time of
mirth and social glee since our arrival up here   it seems hard
for all hands of us to get regularly to business again   as for
my part I feel quite out of place to be found at work   the
Dr.[68] has some six or seven patients; and has had the misfortune
to loose one or two of that number; which I fear will injure
him; they were both negro children, but still we can but hope
for the better. We are keeping house for brother Samuel;[69]
and will continue with him this year if not longer or rather
how much longer I cant say; possibly always.

You never saw anything grow like the boy has, he is getting to be quite fleshy and talks all the time and about everything, he says you are gone and cousin Mary too. I hope that
cousin Mary's health has improved. I feel anxious about her;
it is a great misfortune that you cant be all the time with her,
I think if you could she would be well again soon. She ought
by all means to be very careful of herself and I know if you was
with her you would have her be, but still cousin Mary must
not think hard of me for saying of this, for she knows as well
as we do that she will be independent sometimes or at least
more so than we would wish to see her.

Well, Cousin Jemima I expect that the anticipated wedding[70] has come off before this; if so let me wish them much
joy   May peace and prosperity attend them threw life, but
is it not a great pity that such a gem should be thrown away
upon such an old creature; I think it is a misfortune for any
person to marry unless they marry their equal; if equally
matched everything glides sweetly and softly along, if not you
know it cant.

How long did you stay with the old folks after we left; I
hope that you stayed in peace. We have not had a line from
any of them since we left; I suppose they dont care anything
more for us. The Dr. wrote his father some three weeks ago;
but I have not written to any of them and dont think I shall

unless they write first to me; as they promised to do it. You must write me all the news. All the connections send their love to you; the Dr. says take care of yourself and dont forget to exercise in the open air; give our love to cousin Mary and all of the connections; Goodbye, excuse all mistakes and write soon.

Ever your cousin,

E. F. VANN

* * * * *

At the beginning of 1853, Governor John L. Manning of South Carolina congratulated the state upon its momentary political calm.[71] When the Legislature met early in November, the newly elected governor's message recommended "the re-chartering of all private banks," suggested "further attention to the school system," and advised "the appointment of a commission to revise the criminal law." In spite of the current calmness on South Carolina's political front, Mr. Manning predicted that "the North would speedily renew its acts of hostility against slavery," and expressed the hope that "the Southern States would unite to force the rights of the States to be respected, or else that they take their place as a Southern Confederacy among the nations of the earth."[72]

South Carolina was advertised as "a very healthy country . . . with regard to her white inhabitants."[73] Just prior to leaving office in 1850, Governor Whitmarsh Seabrook had indicated that "the entire sand-hill and pine lands, as well as the towns and villages, furnished the most signal evidence of the salubriety of their atmospheric influence."[74]

Negroes were, however, not so healthy. Speaking for the South as a whole, Dr. Cartwright of New Orleans addressed the Louisiana Medical Association in 1852 on "The Diseases of Negroes."[75] He listed as common diseases: pulmonary congestion, bilious and adynamic fever (remittent and intermittent), scrofula, frambesia (commonly mistaken for syphilis), Negro consumption, drapetomania and dysaesthesia. "Drapetomania" was described as a "disease which caused negroes to run away," and "dysaesthesia" was sometimes known by the overseers as "rascality."[76]

⊰{ 14 }⊱

At Woodlawn Green, life on the farm was complicated by the fact that slaves must be bought and sold; horses sickened and died. Alone now, except for Josiah and Cousin Mary, William and Sarah had waited anxiously for news from North Carolina. Motivated by filial concern for his son's welfare and grandfatherly affection for young Bob, William Vann replied to Rush's letter almost immediately.[77]

William Vann, Woodlawn Green, Auburn, South Carolina, to Dr. A. R. Vann, Brookville, North Carolina.

Woodlawn Green
February 10th, 1854

Dear Son,

Yours of the 17th came to hand a few days ago, which afforded us a great pleasure to hear from you, that you & family were well with the exception of coals, which has been the case in my family. I have been quite unwell with a coal & cough for some time, but it is getting better & I hope soon to be entirely well. Lewis[78] is still no better, and has been under Dr. Dargan[79] ever since you left but he dont seem to improve only the swelling has nearly left him & I think it very doubtfull whether he will ever get well or not. I have sold Wily[80] since you left, for 500 $ to a man in Sumterville, & bought a negro girl from Steven Cater & gave 725 $ for her, and Mr. Wilkins[81] is selling out to start to Ilinois the first of March & I bought a negro fellow from him & gave twelve hundred & sixty five dollars for him & Josiah bought a *yellow* negro woman & gave eight hundred & fifty dollars for her, negroes are selling very high & I have sold all of my crop of cotton & gave it for two negroes. Cousin Polly Darby[82] says that she is still in the land of the living, but a little better than when you left. Mills Vann[83] has moved to the Latta place[84] & the old folks have turned almost young in their old age. William Vann[85] from Orangeburg is in with his daughter Mary. William has fattened up very much, since he was out before & Mary is nearly grown & she will spend this year with Mills and go to school to Jerry — We have received a letter from Billy and Patsy Hall and family had arrived there safe, & Caroline Wright and Lige Damshear married a few weeks ago.

Their have been several deaths in this neighborhood since you left. Dr. Tim Dargan[86] died a few weeks ago, with the Consumption, or some lingering disease and Noel King[87] died a few weeks ago, and old Jesse died a few weeks ago, and Forman that married a Wingate[88] is also dead. Dr. Wilson[89] has been quite sick with a coal, has been confined to his room for three weeks, but his health is improving again, — Henry and Mary Ann[90] are quite well, & Mahala[91] and her family were well a few weeks ago.

Mr. LaCoste and Sallie Ann King[92] were married last Thursday night, had quite a nice party. Cousin Polly went up[93] to it & enjoyed herself finely. Well, I believe that I have told you all the news, in the family, only I have not told you that I have had the misfortune to luse *Downin* since you left. Josiah's horse beat him to death in the lot the very day that you started to N. Carolina, or injured him so that he died that night, it was a great loss, & I never expect to own another such a horse, or one that I think as much of as I did *Downin*. I want to know in your next whether you have bought land or not, and what arrangements you expect to make, & want you to say something about *Bob*,[94] for this was the very one that I wanted to hear from, & you did not even say that the child is well. Betsy's little Willie[95] is growing finely, can sit alone, & is very smart, but he has been quite unwell for the last week, nothing but teething we are in hopes. We have just heard that Robert Vann's[96] wife had another *air*, but we dont know what it is, the family all join me in love to you & family. You must write soon. Your *true* father

WILLIAM VANN

P. S. If you & Fanny cant write something about Bob I don't want you to write at all.

* * * * *

T. E. Howle, Bettie Vann's husband, operated Wilson's store at Leavensworth, about five miles from Woodlawn Green, and cultivated a tract of land belonging to his father, James Howle.[97] The community's name came from Nathaniel Leavensworth to whom the land had been granted in 1786, but the Wilson family had owned the site of the store since 1819. John F. Wilson and family[98] moved to Leavensworth in 1850 and lived in a house with a latticed piazza.

Across the road from the Wilson house was the store, first run for a long time by Mr. J. P. Wilson, later by Mr. John F. Wilson, grandson of John Flavel Wilson, and Mr. Evander McIver Griffin. It was a typical country store with everything the surrounding farmers needed.[99]

From Mr. Howle went a letter to his brother-in-law, Rush Vann, on February 16, 1854, with news of his having purchased an interest in the store. The letter, sealed with wax, carried no postage stamp. In the upper right-hand corner of the sheet which had been folded into the form of an envelope, Tom Howle had written "T. E. Howle, PM." with the word "FREE" above this signature.[100] The outside address read: "Dr. A. R. Vann, Brookville, Granville County, N. C."

Thomas E. Howle, Leavensworth, South Carolina, to Dr. A. R. Vann, Brookville, North Carolina.

Leavensworth, Febry 16, 1854

My dear brother

After a delay of many days longer than intended or thought of, I have taken my seat to write you a few lines, in answer to your letter received some time ago, and I am satisfied if you knew how busy I have been you would readily excuse the long silence that has intervened since the reception of your favour.

Trade has been brisk this last few months and a great many settlements to make with our customers have kept me about on a stretch. Joshua Smoot[101] left us about the 5th January without a days warning, which threw everything in my hands for about two weeks which gave me but little leisure time, and that of course had to be spent with my little family. I have my brother James[102] with me now, and am but little better off, as he has not got in use of things yet. I have purchased Mr. Wilson's[103] interest in the store and am now on my own hook, root little pig or die and I am afraid it will be root a while and die for good. I came to the conclusion that it would be as good a time as ever would get to begin. Mr. Wilson was anxious to sell out on account of bad health, and offered me his interest at cost and gave me five years to pay him, with interest from the first of January last, which was the time that we dissolved. There are several advantages that I have here, that I could not have in another place in a long time. One is that I am generally well acquainted with the people of this neighborhood and know their means for paying debts. Another is — a good many of them are indebted to the late firm of J. P. W. & Co.,[104] and will of course trade with me as I am also interested in that concern and may perhaps secure both the customers to the old firm of J. F. W. & Co.,[105] and that of the late J. P. W. & Co., and perhaps have the chance of selecting my customers, yet the place is not without disadvantages, and I suppose there is no location without them. A good many men I will have to indulge untill another year from the fact that they will have to pay their debt to J. P. Wilson & Co., next fall, this is the most serious of all as money with its present stringency is worth more to me than 7 per cent interest. However, I hope I can indulge and survive too but I assure you I feel very gloomy sometimes when I think of the liabilities that must hang over me to keep up a regular and full assortment of goods. You have no idea of the capitol that is required where this credit system is carried to such lengths as it is here, but if I have to give long credits I must have long percents from the fact that there is a great deal of competition and prompt men will be the boys that can buy goods at short per cents, but enough of that.

Our neighborhood are in enjoyment of peace and health, nothing new transpiring. A few weddings a few deaths and a few births. Mr. LaCost is married. Miss Julia Wright is to be married soon to a Sumter man by the name of Laws. The Misses Nettles[106] are all at home this year. Our old friend J. A. Williams[107] is still on the *props.* A. L. Williams[108] is flourishing and his wife is flourishing too, and looks as if the pumpkin seed has begun to swell a little, or as you would say "looks as if she was bee stung" (this is private). Bettie is well and health good. Our little boy is growing. Can sit alone. Bettie writes with love to you Fannie and the little boy and all the family. Write soon and give us an account of yourself. Excuse all errors.

As ever yours,

T. E. HOWLE

* * * * *

When six weeks passed without a reply to his letter of February 16, Mr. Howle wrote a second letter to his brother-in-law, in which he again discussed business matters and described activities of planting time in South Carolina. The lively interest shown in Rush Vann and his family by both Mr. Howle and William Vann must have quieted Fanny Vann's fears that her husband's family in South Carolina "dont care anything more for us."[109] Mr. Howle's letter, which was mailed free at Leavensworth, was hand-canceled.

Thomas E. Howle, Leavensworth, South Carolina, to Dr. A. R. Vann, Brookville, North Carolina.

Leavensworth
March 24, 1854

Dear Rush

I wrote you some six weeks ago and not having heard from you concluded to write you a few lines again thinking that it would be gratifying to hear from your old native place, but at the same time am at a loss to know the reason you have not written to us. I cant think you have forgotten us all so soon, but must conclude until I hear from you that my last letter never reached you.

Well, we have every prospect for an early spring   the weather has been very mild for the season   vegetation is making rapid strides   the bud of yesterday is today the leaf and the small petal is decorated around its slender stem with the ful blown flower, planters are now very busy — and a good many of them are through planting corn and making preparations to begin to plant cotton. The guano[110] fever is raging here extensively. Almost every planter is trying it this years and if it proves satisfactory there is no telling the quantity that will be bought next year.

Well, Rush I hope you are well and enjoying good health and that you are making money which I assure you is a very scarce article here. Money has not been so tight in a great while as it has been for the past few weeks. The Banks have been buying up Southern paper[111] at a shave of 1½ per cent per month, which is equal you will see to 18 per cent a year, this being better business than loaning money at 6 per cent.

That the consequence is a very little has been put out among us but a great deal sent off to buy up paper as above stated.

My little family are all well. Our little boy is growing fast. Bettie writes with me in love to you Fannie and the boy — and all acquaintances and friends. Hope to hear from you soon. The mail has come and I must close.

Your father and sisters families are well.

As ever yours,

T. E. HOWLE

* * * * *

FOOTNOTES

[1] "The region which in the middle of the last century was known as the Cotton Kingdom extended a distance of more than a thousand miles from South Carolina to the Neighborhood of San Antonio, Texas." Opening sentence in William E. Dodd's *The Cotton Kingdom* (New Haven, 1919).

[2] Jesse and Elizabeth Kolb, Deed to Samuel Bacot, November 8, 1808, State of South Carolina, Darlington County Deed Book H, 1806-1898, p. 208.

[3] Mary Darby's grave at Welsh Neck Baptist Churchyard, Society Hill, South Carolina, is marked. If other members of the family are buried with her, there are no markers.

[4] Darby family records are taken from Jemima Darby's Bible, in the possession of Ida G. Tooke, Ringgold, Louisiana, June, 1953.

[5] Alexander Gregg, *History of the Old Cheraws* (San Antonio and Columbia, 1867 and 1905), p. 83.

[6] Kolb Family Chart, prepared by Thomas Evans Wilson, Darlington, S. C., July, 1932.

[7] Jehu Kolb, Application for Pension for Revolutionary War Service, South Carolina, October 14, 1832, Files of the Government Pension Records, Washington, D. C.

[8] Survey of Alexander Craig, District Surveyor, February 24, 1786, Recorded in Book No. 1, p. 288, Bundle 103, Plat No. 198, South Carolina Historical Association Files, Columbia, S. C.

[9] *Ibid.*

[10] "Black Creek Church Book, A. D. 1798," pp. 18-78.

[11] Angelina Kolb, Application for Widow's Pension (Revolutionary War Soldiers), South Carolina, May 30, 1853, Files of the Government Pension Records, Washington, D.C.

[12] Jehu Kolb, Application for Pension for Revolutionary War Service, South Carolina, October 21, 1829.

[13] *Ibid.*

[14] Gregg, *History of the Old Cheraws*, p. 84.

[15] Angelina Kolb, Acceptance of Widow's Pension Award, October 24, 1855, Files of the Government Pension Records, Washington, D. C.

[16] Owen Darby Heirs, Records of sale of land, March 11, 1807 — October 1, 1838, State of South Carolina, Darlington County Grantor Index A-E, 1806-1898.

[17] Gregg, *History of the Old Cheraws*, p. 52.

[18] *Ibid.*, p. 53.

[19] "Minutes of the Welsh Neck Baptist Church, Society Hill, South Carolina," p. 1.

[20] Edward D. Coker, "County History — Sketch of the Early History of Society Hill," paper read before Darlington County Historical Society on April 4, 1938; preserved by Darlington County Circulating Library.

[21] "Minutes of the Welsh Neck Baptist Church, Society Hill, South Carolina," April 6, 1782, June 5, 1784, and July 31, 1784.

[22] Leah Townsend, *South Carolina Baptists* (Florence, South Carolina, 1935), p. 305.

[23] William E. Paxton, *A History of the Baptists of Louisiana* (St. Louis, 1888), pp. 576-577. Mr. D. R. W. McIver, whose first wife was Carolina Wilds of Darlington District, moved to Alabama and finally to Louisiana, where he died at Kingston, DeSoto Parish, February 10, 1863.

[24] "Minutes of the Welsh Neck Baptist Church, Society Hill, South Carolina," September 3, 1825.

[25] *Ibid.*, December, 1828 — January, 1829.

[26] Jane Lide Coker Wilson (Mrs. Furman), *Memories of Society Hill* (Pee Dee Historical Society, South Carolina, 1909-1910), p. 8.

[27] Elizabeth Witherspoon Williams, Will of October 10, 1830, Recorded January, 1841, State of South Carolina, Darlington County. *Darlington County Wills Collection*, Darlington Public Library.

[28] Cook, *The Life and Legacy of David Rogerson Williams*, p. 337.

[29] The Reverend D. R. W. McIver was the son of Mary Ann Williams McIver, D. R. Williams's sister who lived in her brother's home after the death of her husband in 1808.

30 Alexander McIver, lawyer and judge, a brother to D. R. W., lived in Society Hill and married Mary Hanford.

31 David Rogerson Williams II, the son of John Nicholas Williams and his first wife, Mary Chesnut, was the grandson of Elizabeth Witherspoon Williams's husband and his first wife, Sarah Power.

32 Dr. Thomas Smith was the husband of the widow of Judge Samuel Wilds.

33 Alexander Sparks (September 27, 1780 — January 29, 1857), her brother in the church, was a prominent Society Hill resident, the son of Captain Daniel Sparks, and one of Marion's men.

34 John Nicholas Williams, the son of David Rogerson Williams and his first wife, Sarah Power, was born at Society Hill, July 2, 1797, and married (1) Mary Chesnut, and (2) Sarah Canty Witherspoon.

35 John H. McIver, oldest son of Alexander and Mary Hanford McIver, was a great-nephew to David Rogerson Williams.

36 Sarah Canty Witherspoon Williams, daughter of John D. Witherspoon, Sr., was the second wife of John Nicholas Williams, and a niece of Elizabeth Witherspoon Williams.

37 Cook, *The Life and Legacy of David Rogerson Williams*, p. 180.

38 David Rogerson Williams died November 17, 1830, of wounds received while erecting a bridge at Witherspoon Ferry on Lynch's Creek. William Dossey, who baptized Jemima Darby in 1825, officiated at the funeral.

39 Helen Kohn Henning, *William Harrison Scarborough, Portraitist and Miniaturist: A Parade of the Living Past* (Columbia, 1937), p. 4.

40 *Ibid.*, p. 6.

41 Mary Eugenia Thomson Darby was the wife of Artemus Burnham Darby; Margaret Elliott Darby was the wife of James Darby.

42 Darby heirs, Deed to Samuel Bacot, January 4, 1823, State of South Carolina, Darlington County Deed Book H, 1806-1898, p. 209.

43 Jemima Darby, Deed to James King, November 15, 1836, State of South Carolina, Darlington County Deed Book N, 1806-1898, p. 267.

44 Mary Darby, Deed to James King, October 1, 1838, State of South Carolina, Darlington County Deed Book N, 1806-1898, p. 213.

45 Jesse and Elizabeth Kolb, Deeds to (1) Jordan Sanders, September 9, 1822, and (2) Samuel Bacot, November 8, 1822, State of South Carolina, Darlington County Deed Book H, 1806-1898, pp. 202 and 208.

46 A mathematics drill book prepared by the oldest son, "David C. Kolb, 1827, Marlborough District, S. C., November 23rd, April 17; David C. Kolb was born July 27, 1811," was in the possession of Annis Cawthon, Ruston, Louisiana, in 1964.

47 Dumas Malone, (ed.), *Dictionary of American Biography* (New York, 1933), X, p. 492.

48 Ida G. Tooke, "Some North Louisiana Pioneers," unpublished manuscript, Ringgold, Louisiana, 1952.

49 "Minutes of the Welsh Neck Baptist Church, Society Hill, South Carolina," October 31, 1857.

50 Dodd, *The Cotton Kingdom*, p. 72.

51 William Vann (May 29, 1795 — February 25, 1881), of Darlington District, South Carolina, was the son of William Vann and his wife, a Miss Hamilton of Virginia.

52 William Vann's wife was a Miss Hamilton of Virginia.

53 Eleanor Vann Rose, Letter from Franklinton, North Carolina, to John A. Cawthon, February 9, 1953, quoting "Notes on an envelope made by Samuel Cannady Vann, 1892, while talking to his father, Alexander Russia Vann."

54 *Ibid.*, quoting from notes taken while talking to her father, Samuel Cannady Vann, in 1924.

55 Eleanor Vann Rose has a map showing the property which William Vann bought from Elizah Goodson. This map shows that William Vann owned property adjoining it. The recording of the deed was witnessed by Josiah Vann in 1847.

56 Margaret H. Vann was born November 8, 1816.

57 Mary Ann Vann (October 14, 1818 — October 10, 1892) married Henry King.

58 Josiah T. Vann (July 29, 1820 — January 7, 1892) married Sallie C. Byrd October 21, 1886.

59 Alexander Russia Vann (May 5, 1822 — October 22, 1892) married E. F. Cannady April 4, 1850.

60 Sarah Ann Vann was born September 11, 1824.

61 Elizabeth Sarah Vann (November 25, 1833 — January 15, 1913), daughter of William and Sarah Jones Vann, married Thomas Epathraditus Howle, son of James Howle, November 19, 1852.

62 Sarah Jones Vann (October 27, 1796 — October 3, 1866) was the daughter of Jeremiah and Elizabeth Mercer Jones.

63 E. F. Vann (1824-1884), daughter of Wyatte and Elizabeth Hockaday Cannady, married A. R. Vann April 4, 1850.

64 The William Vann house faced northwest and was located about a mile southwest of Auburn, South Carolina. On May 31, 1953, it was occupied by Negroes.

65 William Wyatte Vann (January 20, 1851 — June 12, 1851) and Samuel Cannady Vann (July 27, 1852 — November 11, 1924).

66 Recollections of Sarah Elizabeth Howle Campbell, daughter of Thomas E. and Bettie Vann Howle, widow of William T. Campbell, 524 Cashua Street, Darlington, South Carolina, May 30, 1953.

67 "Black Creek Church Book, A. D., 1798," pp. 77-167.

68 A. R. Vann was one of the 1,266 doctors in the state of North Carolina, according to the U. S. Census Office, *Population of the U. S., 1860*, p. 363.

69 Samuel Cannady was a Granville County planter.

70 The marriage referred to cannot be identified positively. In later letters, correspondents spoke of the marriage of A. P. LaCoste, who was fifty years old, to Sarah Ann King, the twenty-eight-year-old daughter of James and Hannah Bacot King. Mr. LaCoste had grown daughters; Harriet, the wife of George McIver, had several children. Harvey T. Cook, in *The Life Work of James Clement Furman* (privately printed, 1926), p. 321, stated that J. C. Furman was allowed to go from Welsh Neck to Cheraw once a month to supply the pulpit. "In this way," Mr. Furman is quoted as saying, "we formed the close fire-side intimacy with A. P. LaCoste — with a Napoleonic form, with the French mercurial temperament, and an energy that sprang like whalebone from any pressure, with strong religious convictions and emphatic expressions of them, he was a man whom no good man could know without valuing and loving. His good wife, the mother of his three daughters, . . . was calm and quiet and deeply pious."

71 *Harper's New Monthly Magazine*, VI (December, 1852 — May, 1853), p. 261.

72 *Ibid.*

73 J. D. B. DeBow, *Industrial Resources Etc., of the Southwest* (New Orleans, 1853), Volume III, p. 138.

74 *Ibid.*

75 *Ibid.*, Volume II, p. 318.

76 There is nothing in the article to indicate whether the humor was contributed by editor DeBow or Dr. Cartwright.

77 Eleanor Vann Rose, Franklinton, North Carolina, is the owner of the original copy of her great-grandfather's letter to her grandfather, 1854.

78 Lewis was a valuable slave whose symptoms suggest that he might have been suffering from some form of kidney ailment, probably chronic nephritis, or Bright's disease. Since kidney ailments were not considered common among Negroes, no treatment was suggested. Dr. Dargan probably diagnosed Lewis's ailment as one of the many forms of fever and sought to eliminate the cause of the swelling.

79 Theodore Alonzo Dargan (August 15, 1822 — September 10, 1881), the son of Timothy and Lydia Keith Dargan, married Maria Louisa Bacot.

80 A slave.

81 Samuel B. Wilkins (April 11, 1802 — April 11, 1879), one-time lawyer, became a Baptist minister.

82 Mary Darby was called "Polly" by the family.

83 Mills Vann (1782-1875) was the son of William and _____ Hamilton Vann and a brother to William Vann, the writer of the letter.

84 William Latta was the Revolutionary War hero who was responsible for the establishing of a Latta home in the Pee Dee region.

85 William Vann of Orangeburg was a nephew to William Vann of Auburn, probably Mill's son.

86 Timothy J. K. Dargan, son of Timothy and Lydia Keith Dargan, who married Louisa L. Wilson, died in 1853.

87 "Minutes of the Welsh Neck Baptist Church, Society Hill, South Carolina," September 6, 1845. "Mr. Noel King who many years ago was excluded for joining the Methodist church, having acknowledged his error and professed a desire again to unite with us was received into the fellowship." September 30, 1849, "Noel King was dismissed from us to join Black Creek church."

88 Later there is a reference to a Cotys Wingate Furman.

89 Dr. Furman E. Wilson (February 17, 1826 — January 31, 1897) married Jane Lide Coker on June 20, 1850.

90 Mary Ann Vann (October 14, 1818 — October 10, 1909), daughter of William and Sarah Goodson Vann, married Henry King.

91 On Mills Vann's home place, near Auburn, South Carolina, there stood (May 31, 1953) one marker, which read:

In Memory of

MRS. ANN MAHALA HOLLOMAN

daughter of Mills Vann who died in May 1856
Aged 44 years

She embraced religion in early youth and adorned
her profession until death; she departed in peace.

92 A. P. LaCoste (December 18, 1803-1862) married Sallie A. E. King (April 23, 1825 — May 10, 1857), daughter of James and Hannah Bacot King, in 1854. Mr. LaCoste, who had been born in Charleston, first married Margaret Dawson Fort, the mother of three daughters who were now grown.

93 The Kings lived in Society Hill.

94 Samuel Cannady Vann (July 27, 1852 — November 11, 1924), A. R. Vann's son, born at Woodlawn Green, was about eighteen months old.

95 William James Howle (August 21, 1853 — June 30, 1935), oldest son of Thomas E. and Bettie Vann Howle, was about six months old.

96 "Black Creek Church Book, A. D., 1798," p. 153, "Nov. 15, 1851 — Church met to attend upon examination of Brother Robert R. Vann preparatory to his ordination to the Gospel Ministry. Sister Charlotte W. Vann being present, presented a letter of dismissal from Wateree Baptist church in Fairfield District." This was the same date that Mrs. Elizabeth Cannady Vann presented her church letter from Brassfields, Granville County, North Carolina.

97 Edith Campbell, Letter from Darlington, South Carolina, to John A. Cawthon, Russellville, Arkansas, May 21, 1953. "This was not Great-grandfather Howle's home place, but land adjoining, or near Black Creek Church property. We have no record of this, but it is information handed down from one generation to another."

98 John Flavel Wilson's second wife was Hannah Kolb Evans, daughter of Enoch and Ann Kolb Evans. Mr. Wilson died in July, 1851, and his wife died about three years later. James P. Wilson was John F. Wilson's son by his first wife, Elizabeth DeLesseline. John Flavel Wilson II, the son of Dr. Furman and Jane Lide Coker Wilson, was the grandson of John F. Wilson I and his second wife.

99 Julia Ervin, "Old Houses in Leavensworth," *Darlington County Historical Society Records and Papers, 1938-1944* (October 28, 1941), p. 118.

100 DeBow, *Industrial Resources Etc., of the Southwest,* Volume II, p. 360. "*Franking Privileges.* Certain officers and citizens are entitled to freedom of postage on their letters and packets; among these are Mrs. Harrison, Mrs. Taylor, any person who has been President of the United States, Vice-President, members of the Congress, delegates from the territories, the Governors of the States, the three Assistant Postmaster Generals and certain postmasters, each, however, under certain given restrictions." Anna Symmes Harrison, widow of President W. H. Harrison, lived at North Bend, Ohio, until 1855 and died on February 25, 1864. Margaret Smith Taylor, widow of President Zachary Taylor, lived at Pascagoula, Mississippi, until her death on August 18, 1852.

101 Joshua Smoot was later Orderly Sergeant in Company M, Eighth South Carolina Regiment, Captain T. E. Howle commanding.

102 James F. Howle (March 25, 1837 — ?), son of James and Mary Jane Kirven Howle, married Mary House. James, Jr., was the first son of James and his second wife, whom he had married May 19, 1836. James, Jr., and Thomas E. were half-brothers; Thomas's mother, Margaret A. Keith Howle, died on July 23, 1833.

103 James P. Wilson.

104 James P. Wilson and Company.

105 John Flavel Wilson and Company.

106 Louise, Alice, and Annie Nettles were daughters of General Joseph B. and Hannah Blackwell Nettles of Darlington.

107 James A. Williams (September 3, 1825 — February 2, 1886) married Caroline Williamson.

108 A. Linton Williams's second wife was Martha Harriet Fort (October 29, 1829 — November 20, 1858), daughter of Josiah and Ann E. Fort.

109 E. F. Vann to Jemima Darby, January 31, 1854.

110 United States Department of Agriculture, *Yearbook* (Washington, 1900), p. 337. "Guano was used for its ammonia. It was introduced into the United States in 1842 where it spread in popular favor. It was the only source of phosphoric acid until the South Carolina rock phosphates were introduced in 1867."

111 Funk and Wagnall's *Encyclopedia* (New York, 1952), Volume IX, p. 3365. "During the three decades following 1833, sometimes referred to as the dark decades of American banking, abuses of sound banking practices multiplied and assumed scandalous proportions, and speculators . . . flourished."

South Carolina Background
PART II

After six months, Fanny Vann again wrote to Miss Darby. Her letter, addressed to Society Hill, was forwarded to Leavensworth, where Miss Darby was staying with the Howles.

During the first half of the year 1854, the Vanns in North Carolina had established a routine which was pleasing to Fanny. She kept busy at home and there were social activities within the community which she enjoyed. North Carolina's public schools were more progressive than those of neighboring states. In 1854, Calvin H. Wiley had been state superintendent of education for two years and had begun to organize an educational program which was to gain national fame. With both public and private schools conducting public examinations, the doctor and his wife were kept busy during the spring. Rush Vann, as one of the most highly educated citizens in the community, was invited to act as a member of many of the examining committees. Mrs. Vann enjoyed the excitement of the celebrations which followed at night.

Dr. Vann's practice was that of a country physician who went from house to house to care for the sick. He visited both Negroes and white patients. Women found him exceptionally capable. The recent visit of Joe Vann, Rush's brother, to North Carolina prompted Fanny to assure Miss Darby that she too would receive a cordial welcome at the Vann home.

Mrs. A. R. Vann, Brookville, North Carolina, to Jemima Darby, Society Hill, South Carolina.

Miss Jemima Darby
    Society Hill, S. Carolina

Dear Cousin

After so long a silence I have again attempted to address
you by letter; hopeing that you will forgive me for not writing
before this; do not I beseech you charge me with wilful
neglect; but rather with anything else; you have no idea how
busy I have been since I received your epistle; so much sewing
and housekeeping to attend to, lots of parties to prepear for;
I know I never heard of so many during any one season in my
life; every school of any note for 30 miles had an examination
and gave a large party at night; I believe the last one came off
last week; and now I am in hopes that the excitement will subside;
but I don't know why I should for it seems to be the life
of the country.

We are being cheered this evening by a delightful rain after
a considerable drough; and I would enjoy it much more if my
dear husband was not out in it; he has two patients to see who
are excessive ill; only under such circumstances would I consent
to let him go; he has just about had his hands full for the
last eight weeks; and has been very successful so far; Sam has
a great joke on the Dr. for being such a great woman's man;
he says that the Dr. has not attended a woman who does not
extoll him to the skies   Dr's reply is: that is all he wants;
as the women rule the nation. The Dr. sends his respects to you
and cousin Mary; we often talk of you both and wish to see
you; how is cousin Mary's health? Samuel appears to have forgotten
all or nearly all about S. C.   he has seen so many
new things since; he grows very fast and talks almost as plain
as I do; Cousin Jemima notwithstanding he is my child he is
beyond a doubt the most intelligent child I ever saw; he begins
to converse very well and will sit and tell you about things;
the only fault is he is spoilt; considers it quite an insult not
to command the first respect etc., but for this he is not to blaim
as he has always had it, he sends a kiss to you and cousin Mary.

I wonder if cousin Mary is at the Dr's father yet; do tell me
how the old folks are getting along since we left. Where and
how is Jo[1] getting along   we have never heard a word from
him since he left here; he promised great things but has never

fulfilled them; I have never received the scratch of a pen from any of them; only the few lines of Mary Ann's in your letter and that I answered pretty soon after received

Cate[2] and myself are buisy prepareing Father and Mother[3] to go to Alum Springs in Va;[4] they will start in a few days and if Father improves will be gone at least two months. Oh! how anxious we all feel about him; how thankful we will feel if he can only be restored to health again   such a dear Father as he is   how hard it would be to give him up; during there absence we will have to quit home[5] and spend our time with the children[6] but one consolation is it is nearby and can soon get from one place to the other. I wish we could have the pleasure of your company; we would enjoy it so much and I think you would enjoy it too. If you ever see any of our kinfolks in S. C. give our love to them and tell them to write to us; remember us kindly to our friends; excuse all; and write us as soon as you get this.

Ever yours affectionately,

E. F. VANN

* * * * *

During the period between July 5, 1854, and March 18, 1855, there had been an epidemic of typhoid fever in Granville County, North Carolina. Dr. Vann himself had been ill but had managed to attend to his patients "with the exception of some few days." Josiah Thomas, Rush and Fanny's third son, was born November 8, 1854.

Miss Darby was back at Society Hill. Mary Darby was not with her.

Mrs. A. R. Vann, Brookville, North Carolina, to Jemima Darby, Society Hill, South Carolina.

Brookville   March 18th   55

Miss J. Darby
    Society Hill
        S. Carolina

Dear Cousin

Owing to circumstances unavoidable I have been detained from answering your long received letter; circumstances too of a rather deplorable nature; indeed it is a thing I hope that we will never have to content with again; I have reference to the Typhoid Fever; one of the most appaling diseases among the mountains; nearly everyone of our family has had it and several of Father's and several of Brother William's.[7] Brother William had the misfortune to loose a negro boy with that exception we have been very fortunate. The Dr. has had the care of them all besides other practice in the neighborhood; all of them now appear to be considerably on the mend; I hope that it will stop here but it rearly appears that it will go threw the whole family as some fresh cases occasionaly break out yet; and first that took it are just getting out   tho not able to do anything.

The Dr. himself has had a considerable attact of it   tho was able to go with the exception of some few days; he is now able to attend to his business; I felt as if it was a breaking up affair when he took it; so I took my seat by his bead and began to shed tears; it rearly appeared as it was all that I could do; as he would not consent to have another Dr. This fever and the pneumonia are rageing considerably threw this country at this time. Father's health is very bad at this time   we are fearful that he will not stand the spring out. Oh! you know how we are distressed as you have experienced the loss of a dear father; it seems hard yes very hard to give him up; it grieves my heart to think of it. But alas! we all must die sooner or later and our greatest thought should be to be in readiness. Well, cousin Jemima it realy appears like a long time since we parted and it may be still longer before we meet again for all we know; unless you will come up to see us; tho the Dr. has been invited back by the people of Swift Creek with the assurance of 2000 or 1500 dollars per year; he has a little mind to go but I tell him it is folly unless his father will give us a home.

Well, well cousin what do you think. Still I know you have long since heard of it but you have not seen him; no, no, you have not seen our little black-eyed jewel[8]   he is a rare little jewel; there is not his equal on earth except in his buddy; he is a hale hearty fellow just like his mother; the Dr. calls him his Cannady boy with his black eyes ruby lips and rosy cheeks; we have named him Jo   cant you give us a fancy name to go with it. Our oldest boy has grown a great deal both in size and smartness; there are but few such; I wish you could see them; tell cousin Mary about them   she loves them I know.

Give our love to her when you see her and tell her that we are anxious to see her; the little boys send a kiss to you both; cousin you must excuse me for not writing more. I declare I never did have such a job before. I have just got me a box of new pens and have used nearly everyone trying to write this letter; my patience is exhausted with them   our love to all. Write soon and let me hear from you all.

Goodbye

Ever your cousin,

E. F. VANN

* * * * *

By May, 1855, there was a steady stream of correspondence between Mr. Howle and Dr. Vann. William Vann, in the meantime, had gone up to Brookville for a visit with his son. Fanny's father, Wyatte Cannady, whose poor health had been mentioned in her letter to Jemima on July 5, 1854, had died. Mr. Howle expressed the sympathy of his family.

Thomas E. Howle, Leavensworth, South Carolina, to Dr. A. R. Vann, Brookville, North Carolina.

Leavensworth, S. C.
May 29, 1855

Dear Rush

Your last favour came to hand, and I would have replied sooner but knew that your Father was going up, and he would give you all the news. We were sorry to hear of the death of Mr. Cannady, and sympathize deeply with the family in the loss of a kind Parent and the community in such a citizen, at the same time we have no doubt but he is at rest, and with him that it has only been a change from pain and suffering to that of peace and happiness —

We have had a very long drought here. No rain of consequence since September last. The farmers have just got a stand of cotton. We had a little rain here last week and some three miles below there was a good rain. The last three days there has been every appearance of wet weather, but no rain up to this time. Corn is scarce here now. And would sell at about any price. Provisions of all kinds are high and scarce. Cotton is going up with everything else. It is worth from 10 to 11 cents. I have yet about 70 bales unsold which I hope to get a tall price for. I enclose a letter for you — and regret very much not sending you the fish bob you requested. I have it made but forgot it. I hope you are all well and that Mr. Vann got on safe. Tell him all is well. Write soon.

Yours as ever,

T. E. HOWLE

* * * * *

On his return to Leavensworth from New York, where he had been to purchase merchandise for the store in September of 1855, Tom Howle stopped off at Brookville, North Carolina, to visit Rush Vann. It was possible to make the greater part of the trip from North Carolina by train. Yet, to make the journey from Brookville, through Raleigh, via Florence, South Carolina, and back northward toward Darlington, it was also necessary to ride over some of the North Carolina plank roads which had been chartered by the Legislature of 1852.[9] Upon his return from the trip, the last lap of which occupied the greater part of two days, Mr. Howle wrote to announce his safe return to Leavensworth.

Thomas E. Howle, Leavensworth, South Carolina, to Dr. A. R. Vann, Brookville, North Carolina.

Leavensworth, S. C.
Sept. 21, 1855

Dear Rush

I arrived home on Wednesday at 3 o'clock after leaving your home on Tuesday morning. We got to Florence about 3 o'clock in the morning and got on a Freight train the next day. I found several acquaintances and we had quite a lively time of it. Yet very unpleasant. The weather being so warm and so very dry that we got as black as smoke and dust could make us.

On reaching home, I found our baby[10] much better. In fact, he has quite recovered from his attack but has suffered a great deal with soar eyes which is going all about over the country among children. I was fearful at one time that our little boy would lose his sight, but is better now. Bettie and Willie are quite well. Willie[11] says that he is going to New York himself before long.

I have seen your Father and Brother.[12] They were both glad to hear from you and Fannie.

We have nothing new here. Cotton has commenced coming in slowly and selling at 9 cents, which is an outside price. The crop in this state will undoubtedly be a short one, or everybody will be mistaken. The cotton looks well on the flat lands and is growing faster than it has at any time this year but is too late unless frost stays off until the first of November. The sandy land is done, the rust has stopped the growth and the late stands in the spring will cause short crops.

The health of the neighborhood was never better. The Doctors have but little to do. Mrs. Mary D. Chambers[13] has a fine son[14] "destined for Congress, a young Statesman in embryo." Her health is rather bad.

I have made arrangements to get the millet seed for you and Prof. W. G. Walters[15] and will send them by mail ere long if no other opportunity offers.

You must come out this winter if you can and bring Fannie and the boys with you. We would all be glad to see you again in South Carolina.[17]

The old bachelor's[18] health is good. Sends his respect to you and Miss Kate[19] and wants to know what Miss Kate has done with all the Saddle bags preachers. Bettie writes with me in love to you and Fannie   Mrs. Cannady and all the family. Write us when you can.

As ever,

T. E. HOWLE

* * * * *

Jemima's friends were scattered throughout the Pee Dee region. Even though she had been a resident of Society Hill for many years, she had been on extended visits to homes in Darling-

ton, Bennettsville, Leavensworth, Auburn, Hartsville, Springville, Mechanicsville and Cheraw. The summer of 1856 found
her in Cheraw, Chesterfield County, at the home of a Mrs. Watson and her two daughters, Mrs. Pegues and Mrs. Malloy. Mrs.
Pegues was probably the wife or widow of Thomas Pegues, one-
time teacher at Society Hill. Mrs. Malloy was the mother of Mary
Malloy, about whom Miss Darby inquired many years later, who
had married David Coit, the son of Maria Campbell Coit, the
nationally famous beauty from Marlboro County, who, it was al-
leged, had been courted by Sam Houston.[20]

Writer of the ninth letter in the series was Miss Mary Ann
Catlett,[21] of Darlington, who, with her sister, Mrs. Sarah Catlett DuPre,[22] operated a private boarding school for girls.[23] Miss
Mary, who wrote a bold business-like hand, had a hearty sense
of humor, but the implications of her innuendoes are not always
clear to the reader who might not know the people and situa-
tions which made for a jest between her and Miss Darby. In a
will dated February, 1834, Sarah T. Catlett left all of her property to her two daughters, Mary and Sarah.[24] Mrs. Catlett died
in 1838 at the age of seventy and was buried at Society Hill,[25]
where Thomas Catlett was one of the original subscribers to St.
David's Society in 1778.[26] Jemima's and Mary Ann's friendship
dated back to Welsh Neck days where Mary Ann had been "an
humble and faithful member of the church from early life."[27]

Mary Ann Catlett, Darlington, South Carolina, to Jemima
Darby, Cheraw, South Carolina.

> Saturday 12 July 1856
> Darlington

Miss Jemima Darby
Cheraw

To the care of Mrs. Dunkin Malloys[28]

Thank you dear Miss D for your communication of the 3rd
from Mrs. Pegues. Sarah and myself have often thought and
spoken of you since you left us but not one word have we been
able to hear from you except that you were assisting some lady

in Chesterfield,[29] to prepare for traveling. Now you may just believe us or not when I tell you that we were very glad this morning to receive your letter and also gratified to learn you were with those of whom I have so often heard you speak in terms of such warm affection as you did of Mrs. Watson and daughters.[30] I thought and do not believe I was mistaken that you really loved them as sisters. Do remember us affectionately to them and thank Mrs. P. for her invitation to visit her and would certainly do so were we to go to the neighborhood. We hope they will at some day not far distant visit their Darlington friends and consider us among the number.

You wish to know how we have gotten along since you left the news of the place etc., etc. Well so far as our outgoing, incoming, uprising, downsitting has been concerned most of it pretty much the same until the carpenters commenced upsetting and in that department will leave you to judge our every day sensation from that time which I think began in May. What with the carpenters, bricklayers, painters, it has not been an Oasis but knowing it was work which was obliged to be done we made up our mind to wade through the hammering, etc., the best we could in a quiet way, looking forward to the time should we live that we will once more be clean and comfortable. The last day in June the school and boarders closed much to our gratification. In May the week previous to the commencement of the work, Mrs. DuPre Mrs. Bentley and little Hettie came.[31] Spent only a week. Mrs. DuPre has gone to Mrs. Bentley's. In very feeble health and the old lady who is no better says she will go after awhile. Brother[32] was in Wilmington last week. The Dr. came up soon after you left and Cornelius speaks of coming the last of this week. Some disposition to dirrhea   otherwise it is pretty healthy in this place. Mrs. Foman[33] (alias)[34] Cotys Wingate lost her oldest and youngest daughters with it and she herself is now quite sick. Mrs. Terril[35] and C. both indisposed. Mr. Dargan's[36] health some better. He has just returned from Alabama with Mrs. Harrison[37] his wife's sister. Mrs. Law[38] is traveling   her health much worse. Good night

Saturday

I did intend to have finished this and sent it to you some days ago but you know that each day generally brings its attendant and various duties even in small families   therefore hope to be excused by Miss Darby for this seeming neglect to her request saying "do write very soon." There is nothing of much interest in town except that the inhabitants keep pretty healthy in a general way. Mrs. Foman is still alive but do not think the Dr. has much hope for her if any. Mrs. Terril is better. Mrs. Jossey[39] lost her infant at the time. She is pretty well now. Suppose you have heard of the marriage of James McCall[40] to a niece of Haynesworth also of Charlie De Lorme[41] and Miss (Samuel) Dove.

Understand Mrs. Conners has returned to the Hotel. Carrie has been with them mostly since she left school. We are having many nice flowers, apples and watermelons as we know what to do with. Mrs. Julius DuBose[42] is the only one who has moved to Springville. Olivia Wingate has gone to her brother Manley at Wake Forest.[43] Miss Susan Orr[44] went with her, made a few days visit, caught a widower[45] and returned with Alonzo. Mrs. Flinn[46] and Ellin[47] are spending the summer thus far at home. "Mother Remiar" says your pastor[48] is quite pleased with Miss Mary C,[49] the Col daughter. He comes down pretty often and makes Dr. Flinn's headquarters. Mrs. Bacotts[50] brother Tom Dyer and his daughter of Louisiana spent some days in this place last week. They are traveling for the benefit of his health. Poor man he does not look as if he would stand it long. Mrs. Bacot and Mrs. Bealer[51] have been to Sullivan Island. The latter has been too poorly since her return to attend church. L and Sallie[52] are engaged in making sweet pickle. How many children will you have this summer?[53]

Wish you would write occasionally and always tell us just how you are getting along. Mr. Tom Wilds preparing to go up the country to spend the summer. The carpenters are there getting ready for their new house. Sarah has just come in and sends her love and says "do tell you to write for she can read your writing like a book. She was wishing the day previous to getting your letter that you would write." I cannot give you all the messages now that my sheet is so nearly filled. Her love to Mrs. Watson and Mrs. Pegues.

Your friend,

MARY

* * * * *

From one hospitable Pee Dee home to another went the Darby sisters. Now, Mary was with her relatives on Black Creek; then, Jemima was in Cheraw, Darlington or Society Hill. In the spring of 1857, Jemima was in Bennettsville, Marlboro County; Mary was in Society Hill. On April 22 and again on August 14, Mary Darby wrote to her sister. The first letter came from the home of the Kings:

> On the hill opposite this place (the Edwards house) there was once a house, small but beautifully situated which was built as a home for the manager of Dr. John K. McIver's plantation. For several years this was the home of an excellent family, Mr. and Mrs. James King and their children. Mrs. King was Miss Hannah Bacot of Darlington, a sister of Mrs. Sarah Bacot McIver, wife of Col. Thomas McIver, who moved to Alabama, and a half-sister of Mrs. H. L. Charles, Mrs. Serena Dargan, and others. Mrs. King and her daughters were models of neatness, industry, thrift, highly esteemed and useful members of our church, as was Mr. King also. Miss Sarah Ann King, well educated, taught school for some years until she became the second wife of Mr. A. P. LaCoste of Cheraw. She lived only a few years . . . .[54]

Mr. and Mrs. King died[55] only a short time after their daughter, Sarah Ann, married Mr. LaCoste, who was a widower.[56] Sallie's oldest child, a boy,[57] lived only four days. When Mr. LaCoste was away from Society Hill on business, his wife and youngest child lived with the King sisters, Eliza, Hannah, Emily and Josephine.

Mary Darby, Society Hill, South Carolina, to Jemima Darby, Bennettsville, South Carolina.

Society Hill
April 22, 1857

Miss Jemima Darby
Bennettsville, Marlboro

My dear sister

I came up to a church meeting and have not returned yet. The first week I suffered a good deal with rheumatism, but I am better. The Misses Williamson[58] came up yesterday, and informed me that my bonnet was at Mrs. B. Williamson's.[59] I was afraid you might think me sick if you did not hear from me soon. Emily[60] has been in bed a week with rheumatism. She was entirely helpless awhile. Could not move hand or foot until it was moved for her but she is a good deal better.

Sallie's baby was born the 10th of March.[61] She has recovered slowly. The little babe has been very healthy up to this time. The other children[62] are well.

Mr. T. Williamson[63] *has sold his place at last, there is not the least doubt about it.* Did you ever see such weather? Mrs. Tullis left the week before Court. Lowndes[64] has come and is knocking about home. I have not paid out any money since I saw you, only for medicine. I expect to go down in a few days and will get Caroline[65] to write and let you know how I am pleased with my bonnet.

Mr. LaCoste[66] left the 23rd of March. Sallie has had 3 letters. The last was written the first day of April. He had intended to leave the next day for Leavensworth City, Kansas. He was at St. Louis.

You ought to see the little babe. It would remind you of old times. She is such a sweet little thing. Sallie does not make any fuss about it. She leaves it for the rest. I received your letter dated March 16. I got Sallie to write this and she is very tired, writing on her lap, so you will please excuse the scrawl.

I think we shall all have to go to a new country soon. Cousin Jacob Bruce[67] and his wife are expected out this summer. Mrs. Tullis is ver anxious for me to go and live with her.[68] She wrote back that David's son[69] was at college.[70] The girls send love to you. Give my love to Mrs. Crosland.[71] And I am your affectionate sister

MARY DARBY

{ 42 }

P. S. I spent two nights with Eliza Evans,[72] since I came up. She is quite well.

* * * * *

When Mary Darby wrote to Jemima in August, 1857, her letter was sent from the Black Creek home of Thomas[73] and Sarah Wilds Williamson.

After Mr. Williamson's death in 1858, Mrs. Williamson, her daughter, Sarah, and their servant, Elzy, requested letters of dismissal from Black Creek Church[74] and were received into the Mispah Church,[75] which was situated in a woodland about two miles from the old Marion highway and about five miles from Florence.

Mary Darby, Society Hill, South Carolina, to Jemima Darby, Bennettsville, South Carolina.

Postmark: Society Hill, Aug. 14

Springhill, Aug 57

Miss Jemima Darby
Bennettsville, S. C.

Dear Sister:

I would have written but Hannah was busy while I was there.[76] I suffered a great deal but feel better today than in a long time. This is my first visit down to Mr. Williamson's.[77] His health is failing   cannot eat but little. I suppose you would like to know where they will go but have not determined yet. Miss Mary Rogers[78] and Lou[79] are over also. Lowndes[80] is gone.

I went to Lizzie's[81] a short time before Cousin Clemmie[82] died. She seemed glad to see me   had a good talk with her   was resigned to the Lord's will   Lizzie has not named her babe[83] nor Mary[84] neither   fine boy   I suppose you have heard of Augustus and Albert Forts[85] death. Friends have hope in their deaths. Mrs. Fort takes it very hard.

Lizzie Bealer[86] was sick 3 weeks   was resigned   Mrs. Hunter[87] has the babe   they call it Eugene since her death as her name was Eugenia. Serena[88] has been sick sometime bowel affliction. Robert Woods Mr. Sam Woods[89] son died recently. Miss Sims[90] has been very low. Mrs. Duprey[91] and family have gone to Virginia   Mary Lucas married Parrott[92] — a steady man is taking care of the house while they are gone.

Emily King is improving   has been at Mr. Cyrus Bascots[93] trying sulphur water   is at her Aunt E's[94] today spent one week at Mr. Williamson's[95]   Dr. Bascot's girls[96] at home   Miss her[97] very much   take in some work but E[98] cannot go any yet. Mr. LaCost[99] is there   will go merchandising in Cheraw next month. Mrs. Edwards[100] lost a brother recently   not Bordman[101]   In deep black Robert has been quite on Black Creek this week.

Mr. Wilkins[102] preached for us last Sunday "Come see where the Lord lay." I could not hear him well and Eliza could not hear[103] any more than she does Mr. Phelps.[104] He has been at Greenville[105]   returned Saturday.

Jane[106] is at her fathers[107] while her mother[108] is traveling. Mr. Peats and Rev. Edwards[109] Mr. Tom Lide and family[110] are with her. I wore my bonnet Sunday   it feels comfortable   Mrs. McIntosh[111] seldom goes out   James[112] health about the same. Dr. Porcher's daughter in bad health.[113] She Mary Rogers[114] Mary Jane Gregg[115] have gone off to the Springs. I have been sewing a little for Eliza   do not trouble myself so much about affairs passing on   Jim[116] has a fine crop on the place   My love to Mrs. Crosland.

Girls[117] join me in love to you

Your sister

MARY

P. S. Mrs. Edwards called to know if I would stay with Miss Charlotte[118] while they are gone. I will go tomorrow and think it will be a pleasant change. Sallie Griffin[119] is going to stay with Eliza.[120]

* * * * *

Mary Darby lived almost a year after writing the 1857 letter. She died on July 18, 1858, and was buried in Welsh Neck Baptist Churchyard, Society Hill. Jemima had this inscription carved on the stone:

MISS MARY

Daughter of Owen and Mary Darby

Died July 18, 1858

Aged 62 years, 1 mo., 12 days

This stone is reared by an only sister
whose heart breathes the following sentiment:

" 'Tis sweet to think when virtue dies
When sinks her lovely form to rest;
How soon that form shall lovelier rise,
To join the parted spirits blest."[121]

Years later, Bettie Wilds Lide, of Springville, sent word to Miss Darby that she "kept up her sister's grave."

Jemima was now alone in South Carolina; her next of kin was her nephew, in Ringgold, Louisiana. She could remain among distant relatives and friends, or she could go out to the "Far West" to live with her own flesh and blood. She elected to go out.

FOOTNOTES

1 Josiah Vann was known as "Joe" by his family.

2 Catherine Cannady was Fanny's sister.

3 Wyatte and Elizabeth Hockaday Cannady were Fanny's parents.

4 Bedford Alum Springs, Bedford County, Virginia.

5 The Vanns were living in the house with her brother Samuel, a short distance from her father's home.

6 The children were Mrs. Vann's younger brothers and sisters.

7 William Cannady was Mrs. Vann's brother.

8 Josiah Thomas Vann was born November 8, 1854, Brookville, North Carolina.

9 Guion Griffis Johnson, *Ante-Bellum North Carolina, A Social History* (Chapel Hill, 1937), pp. 26-27. "The railroads, however, still left a large portion of the State with no better transportation facilities than it had during the Revolution."

[10] Thomas E. Howle, Jr. (July 18, 1855 — January 20, 1926) was the second son of T. E. and Bettie Vann Howle.

[11] Willie Vann was now two years old.

[12] William Vann and Josiah T. Vann.

[13] Mary Deborah Ferguson Chambers (1835-1917) was the daughter of Alexander and Elizabeth Williams Ferguson, and the wife of Benjamin Wesley Chambers.

[14] This son lived only a short time. There is no marker over his grave in the Williams-Chambers-Baker cemetery, near Auburn, South Carolina.

[15] W. G. Walters was a professor at the college, Wake Forest, North Carolina.

[16] Samuel Cannady was three; Josiah Thomas was one year old.

[17] In a letter to Jemima Darby, March 18, 1855, E. F. Vann wrote, "Well, cousin Jemima it realy appears like a long time since we parted and it may be still longer before we meet again for all we know; unless you will come up to see us."

[18] Josiah Vann was thirty-five years old.

[19] Catherine Cannady was Dr. Vann's sister-in-law.

[20] D. D. McColl, *Sketches of Old Marlboro* (Bennettsville and Columbia, 1916), p. 106.

[21] Mary Ann Catlett (January, 1800 — December 15, 1861) was the daughter of Sarah Catlett.

[22] Sarah Catlett DuPre (June 9, 1809 — February 28, 1867) was the wife of the Reverend Mr. L. DuPre.

[23] Beulah W. Coggeshall, Darlington, South Carolina, in a letter to John A. Cawthon, Russellville, Arkansas, February 19, 1953, cites records of the Darlington County Historical Society, p. 39. "It is unusually interesting to note that the house in which Mrs. Skinner now lives was in by-gone days a private school operated by the Misses Catlett who taught exactly *four* pupils. . . . This house was also known as the DuPre house in the 70's (463 Pearl St.)."

[24] Sarah T. Catlett, Will of February, 1834, recorded in Will Book 10, p. 29, Darlington County Wills, *County Wills of South Carolina* (Columbia, University of South Carolina Library, 1939).

[25] Tombstone inscription in Welsh Neck Baptist Churchyard, Society Hill, South Carolina, May 31, 1953.

[26] Coker, "County History — Sketch of the Early History of Society Hill," p. 7.

[27] Tombstone inscription in Baptist Churchyard, Darlington, South Carolina, June 1, 1953.

[28] Duncan Malloy (November 26, 1803 — September 15, 1877) married his cousin, Mary Ann Malloy (October 14, 1815 — June 12, 1885), daughter of Charles and Catherine Malloy.

29 Chesterfield County, South Carolina.

30 "Minutes of the Welsh Neck Baptist Church, Society Hill, South Carolina," March 5, 1842. "Lucy (Sister Watson's) was dimissed to join the church at Cheraw." Mrs. Watson, her family, and her slaves left Society Hill about 1842 to go to Cheraw. On March 31, 1849, Mrs. Watson was visited by J. E. Kirven and Robert G. Edwards, an official committee from Welsh Neck Church who were appointed to investigate her failure to attend church. Their report, March 31, 1849, read: "From sickness and other unavoidable causes she had not been able to attend church and but seldom the church at Cheraw, and from the uncertainty of living longer than one year at Cheraw, she had not asked a letter of dismissal from us and that it is still her desire to continue a member with us, which is satisfactory, and feeling a deep interest and sympathy in her destitute condition, it was ordered that our church furnish her with a letter of *recommendation* to the church at Cheraw." This letter of recommendation placed her "under the watchcare" of the Cheraw church but left her membership at Welsh Neck.

31 The mother of Lewis DuPre, Mary's brother-in-law, lived in Virginia. Mrs. Bentley was Lewis's sister; Hettie was her daughter.

32 Lewis DuPre was the husband of Mary Ann's sister, Sarah.

33 Apparently this was a misspelling of Furman.

34 Miss Catlett referred to Cotys Wingate Furman; she confused the term with *nee.*

35 Ann Allison Terrel (August 4, 1790 - ?), wife of John Terrel.

36 Julius Alfred Dargan, son of Timothy and Lydia Keith Dargan, married Martha Woods. He died in March, 1861.

37 Elizabeth Woods, sister of Mrs. Julius A. Dargan, was the wife of John Morrison.

38 Elizabeth McIver Law (April 3, 1815 — June 28, 1885) was the wife of Augustus Law.

39 The wife of J. Josey, Baptist minister.

40 James Sanders McCall (October 14, 1833 — August 15, 1870), the son of James Sanders and Elizabeth Ellison Lucretia (Muldrow) McCall, married Elizabeth Earl on June 26, 1856.

41 Charles H. DeLorme (July 25, 1835 — November 27, 1907) married Anna Dove.

42 Margaret E. DuBose (1812 — July 10, 1862) was the widow of Julius DuBose, a minister.

43 Manly Wingate was associate pastor at Darlington until he became president of Wake Forest College, Wake Forest, North Carolina.

44 Susannah E. W. Orr, signer of the Covenant of Ebenezer Church, January, 1823, was a consistent attender of conferences at Ebenezer, 1823-1838. After her dismissal by letter from Ebenezer to join Darlington Church in January of 1838, she became the organizer of the first Missionary Society in the Darlington Church, and was a faithful church member there until her death in November, 1883.

45 This was one of Miss Catlett's jokes; Miss Orr had no beau.

46 Amelia Eliza Zimmerman Flinn (? — March 14, 1866) was the wife of Dr. T. Flinn.

47 Ellen Flinn, the daughter of Dr. and Mrs. Flinn, married A. B. Lamb of Charleston.

48 J. C. Phelps was the unmarried pastor of Welsh Neck Church at Society Hill.

49 Mary Ann Charles, daughter of Colonel Edward W. and Sarah Lide Charles, married W. F. B. Haynesworth of Sumter.

50 Mary McIver Bacot, wife of Dr. Henry H. Bacot, was the daughter of D. R. W. McIver and his first wife, Caroline Wilds, who was the mother of six children. D. R. W. McIver's second wife was Martha Elizabeth Screven Grant, whom he married in 1838 at Society Hill. In 1843, the McIver family moved to Alabama, and in 1856 to Louisiana.

51 Lissie Bacot Bealer (June 21, 1827 — July 8, 1857) was the wife of George B. Bealer, pastor of Darlington Baptist Church, 1851-1865.

52 Slaves.

53 Sunday School students.

54 Wilson, *Memories of Society Hill,* p. 37.

55 James King (1800-1856) married Hannah Bacot (1804-1855).

56 Augustus P. LaCoste (December 18, 1803-1862), born in Charleston, married Margaret Dawson Fort (1797 — ?).

57 Furman Hart LaCoste (December 15-19, 1855).

58 Sarah Wilds, Caroline Matilda, and Mary Ann Williamson, daughters of Thomas and Sarah Wilds Williamson.

59 Jane Rogers Williamson (September 23, 1788 — February 7, 1867), daughter of Colonel Benjamin Rogers, married Bright Williamson on December 24, 1812. Mr. Williamson died November 20, 1854, and was buried in the Presbyterian Churchyard, Darlington, South Carolina.

60 Emily King was then twenty-seven years old.

61 Margaret Dawson LaCoste was born March 10 and died May 5, 1857.

62 The youngest members of the King family were Hannah and Josephine.

63 Thomas Williamson (January 20, 1785 — December 27, 1858) married Sarah Wilds.

64 Lowndes Williamson was the son of Bright and Jane Williamson.

65 Caroline Williamson was the daughter of Thomas and Sarah Wilds Williamson.

66 A. P. LaCoste (December, 1803-1862) married (1) Margaret Dawson Fort, (2) Sarah Ann King, and (3) Eliza King.

67 Jacob Bruce was listed as one of the first subscribers to St. David's Society. He owned land between Society Hill and Darlington, but had, by 1857, moved farther west to Alabama. His exact relationship to the Darbys is not known.

68 Mrs. Tullis was also a former South Carolina resident who had moved on to Alabama. In 1856, Thomas E. Tullis purchased a lot in Clayton, Alabama, about 20 miles from Eufaula, where Reuben Francis Kolb lived with his Shorter kinfolks.

69 David Cameron Kolb (July 11, 1811 — August 11, 1841), son of Jesse and Elizabeth Darby Kolb, married Emily Frances Shorter (1816-1839), Eufaula, Alabama. They had one son, Reuben Francis Kolb (April 15, 1839 — March 23, 1918), who married Mary Caledonia Cargile of Barbour County, Alabama.

70 *Dictionary of American Biography*, Volume X, p. 492. "He [Reuben Francis Kolb] was educated in the public schools of Eufaula and at the University of North Carolina, graduating from the latter institution in 1859, at the age of 20." *Memorial Record of Alabama* (Madison, 1893), Volume II, p. 705. "He was educated at the schools of Eufaula until he went to Howard College at Marion, Alabama, remaining there until the winter of 1857 when he went to Chapel Hill, North Carolina, where he graduated in June, 1859."

71 Gregg, *History of the Old Cheraws*, p. 99. "Edward Crosland married a daughter of Samuel Sneed . . . settled on the Pee Dee, near Gardiner's Bluff, in what is now, 1867, Marlborough District, where he reared a large family. His sons were John, Samuel, Daniel M., Israel, David, George, Philip and William." Miss Darby's friend was Ann Thorpe Crosland (1822-1893), wife of Dr. William Crosland (1800-1865), Bennettsville.

72 Eliza Evans (1807 — December 9, 1878) was the daughter of Samuel and Catherine McIver Evans. Wilson, *Memories of Society Hill*, pp. 49-50. "The daughters of Evander McIver were Miss Ann James McIver (Aunt Nancy); Catherine, who married a Mr. Evans and had two children: Mr. Samuel Evans, who removed and married in Mississippi, and Miss Eliza Evans who never married. She became entirely deaf, but was quite an intelligent lady, a great reader and reciter especially of poetry of which she was very fond; and entertaining in conversation, but eccentric in some respects, probably owing to her deafness . . . She owned considerable property, was generous in her gifts to the church and the benevolent objects which she left, and left a good portion to Furman University and a legacy to our church for purposes specified in her will . . ."

73 The brothers, Bright and Thomas Williamson, were the sons of Thomas Williamson, Senior. Bright (July 12, 1778 — November 20, 1854) married Jane Rogers; Thomas (January 20, 1785 — December 27, 1858) married Sarah Wilds.

74 "Black Creek Church Book, A. D. 1798," March 5, 1859, p. 188.

75 "Mispah Church Book," March, 1859, p. 161.

76 Mary Darby had been visiting in the home of the King sisters in Society Hill during the early spring.

77 Thomas Williamson's home at Black Creek was called Springhill.

78 Mary Rogers (May 10, 1797 — August 28, 1879), a daughter of Colonel Benjamin Rogers, was a sister to the widow of Bright Williamson.

79 Martha Louisa Rembert (June 12, 1831 — August 5, 1899), the daughter of Colonel James and Sarah George Martin Rembert, married Lucius Alexander Williamson, March 19, 1851. Lucius Williamson was a son of Bright and Jane Rogers Williamson.

80 Bright and Jane Rogers Williamson had a son named Lowndes; Thomas Charles Williamson also had a son named Lowndes.

81 Lizzie Vann Howle lived at Leavensworth.

82 Clementina Wright was the wife of Mills Vann, cousin to the Misses Darby.

83 Lawrence Keith Howle (April 6, 1857 — August 6, 1936), son of T. E. and Bettie Vann Howle, married Mary Ella Campbell.

84 Mary Vann, daughter of Mills and Clementina Wright Vann, married Ladson Dorrity.

85 John Adger Law, (ed.), *Citadel Cadets, The Journal of Cadet Tom Law* (Clinton, 1941), reported that while on a visit to his home in Darlington, Tom Law went to the home of Mr. and Mrs. Fort on December 22, 1856, and referred to his hosts as Albert and Margaret Norwood Fort "who had several children."

86 Elizabeth Eugenia (Lissie) Bacot Bealer, who was born June 21, 1827, died July 8, 1857.

87 Emilie Bacot Hunter, wife of Andrew Hunter, was Mrs. Bealer's sister.

88 Serena Bacot Dargan (January 3, 1833 — November 7, 1910) was the widow of Charles A. Dargan and a sister to Mrs. Bealer and Mrs. Hunter.

89 Samuel A. Woods, son of Andrew and Mary Dargan Woods, married Martha DuBose. He was a charter member of the Darlington County Agricultural Society, and served on committees which studied "Meadows and Grasses" and "Gardening." His home was in Springville. Robert was a young man, unmarried, probably a teen-ager.

90 Gertrude Lydia Sims (December 6, 1839 — October 2, 1891) was the daughter of A. D. and M. A. P. Sims of Springville. Sue Flinn James in "His Springville," *Darlington County Historical Society Records and Papers,* p. 61, speaks of ". . . the distinguished Miss Sims who was held in awe by them all."

91 Sarah Catlett DuPre, wife of Lewis DuPre, was a sister to Miss Darby's friend, Mary Ann Catlett, of Darlington.

92 Mary Lucas Parrott, the wife of John Parrott, was a sister to George Washington Lucas, whose wife was also named Mary Ann. Mrs. Parrott joined Black Creek Church September 5, 1856.

93 Cyrus Bacot, son of Samuel Bacot I, was Emily King's great-uncle.

94 Emily Leslie Bacot, wife of Samuel Bacot III, was Emily King's aunt by marriage.

95 Although they were only distantly related, the Thomas Williamsons and the Kings always referred to each other as "Cousin."

96 Dr. Henry H. Bacot, who married Mary McIver in 1841, had three daughters: Carolina, born in 1843; Harriett, born in 1844; and Mary Eliza, born in 1850.

97 "Her" refers to Emily King.

98 Emily was still not well enough to work. The King sisters were seamstresses.

99 A. P. LaCoste (1803-1862) was the Cheraw merchant whose second wife, the former Sallie Ann King, sister to Eliza, Hannah, Emily and Josephine, died on May 10, five days after her little girl died. Within a short time, Mr. LaCoste married Eliza King.

100 Ellen Hartwell Edwards (April 10, 1828 — July 24, 1902), daughter of the Reverend Jesse and Margaret Hartwell, was the wife of Robert G. Edwards.

101 J. Boardman Hartwell was born in Darlington in 1835 and was for fifty years a Baptist missionary to China. Paxton, *A History of the Baptists of Louisiana,* p. 514. "During his long and laborious life, Jesse Hartwell was an active promoter of Foreign Missions, and gladly gave up to this work his gifted son, J. Boardman Hartwell, D.D., late missionary to Tung Chow, China, and now laboring with the Chinese in California." John T. Christian, *A History of the Baptists of Louisiana* (Shreveport, 1923), p. 234. Jesse Boardman Hartwell, the seventh child and first son of Rev. Jesse and Margaret F. Hartwell, did not leave for China until 1858. Converted at the age of six, Boardman had been a student at Howard College, Marion, Alabama, and, later, a professor of mathematics at Mt. Lebanon University, Bienville Parish, Louisiana. He married Eliza H. Jewett, of Macon, Georgia, who accompanied him from Louisiana to China. They arrived in Shanghai, March, 1859.

102 Samuel B. Wilkins (April 11, 1802 — April 11, 1879) was pastor at Ebenezer Baptist Church, 1856-1857, and was serving as supply pastor at Society Hill while Mr. Phelps was in Greenville.

103 Wilson, *Memories of Society Hill,* p. 8. "In front of the pulpit and nearly on a level with it were two high seats or pews for the use of two excellent ladies who were almost deaf but loved to attend church and were regularly there."

104 J. A. Phelps, a bachelor, came to Society Hill from the North to be pastor of Welsh Neck Baptist Church in 1855.

105 Greenville, South Carolina, was the center for all Baptist activities within the state. Furman University was located there and many of the church leaders lived near the University.

106 Jane Lide Coker (August 16, 1831 — November 22, 1920), daughter of Caleb and Hannah Lide Coker, married Dr. Furman E. Wilson on June 20, 1850. They lived in the Wilson family home, Society Hill.

107 Caleb Coker (September 14, 1802 — July 17, 1869) married Hannah Lide October 14, 1830, and brought her to Society Hill to live. In 1857, however, the Coker family lived at Camp Marion, two miles west of Society Hill.

108 Hannah Lide (March 3, 1812 — May 19, 1900), daughter of James and Jane Holloway Lide, married Caleb Coker. As a young married woman, she made a trip to Virginia for her health, and in 1843, she and Mr. Coker went to Carow-

ville, Alabama, for a visit with her parents. She liked to travel and the changes seemed to improve her health.

109 Peter C. Edwards, son of Peter Kolb and Jane Draughon Edwards, was a brother to Robert G. Edwards. He married Anne McIver, daughter of the Reverend D. R. W. and Carolina Wilds McIver. Mr. Edwards was a professor at Furman University. Mrs. Edwards's father and stepmother left the neighborhood of Carowville, Alabama, in 1856, and moved to De Soto Parish, near Shreveport, Louisiana.

110 Thomas P. Lide (December 8, 1812 — September 8, 1878) was a wealthy landowner whose home, White Plains, was in Springville, near Darlington. His wife was Elizabeth Sparks (July 10, 1810 — July 23, 1882). Mr. Thomas Lide and Mrs. Hannah Lide Coker were first cousins, their grandparents having been Major Robert and Sarah Kolb Lide.

111 James H. McIntosh's mother was Margaret Lucas prior to her marriage. She lived to an advanced age, according to Wilson, *Memories of Society Hill*, p. 68.

112 James H. McIntosh (September 19, 1800 — October 24, 1858), prominent citizen and merchant of Society Hill, lived near the old Witherspoon house. Mr. McIntosh married Martha Gregg, daughter of David Gregg.

113 Dr. Peter C. Porcher (March 3, 1814 — January 25, 1853) practiced medicine in Kentucky before coming to South Carolina. His daughter, Belle, who was in extremely poor health, married Tom Gregg in 1861.

114 Mary Rogers, daughter of Colonel Benjamin Rogers, was a sister to Mrs. Bright Williamson.

115 Mary Jane Gregg was a sister to Tom Gregg, who married Belle Porcher.

116 James King had bought property from Mary and Jemima Darby in 1836 and 1838.

117 The Williamson daughters, Mary Ann, Caroline and Sarah, were all at home in 1857.

118 Miss Charlotte Kirven, who became a member of Welsh Neck Church in 1816, died at an advanced age in 1867. "Minutes of the Welsh Neck Baptist Church, Society Hill, South Carolina," November 4, 1843. "The case of Sister Charlotte Kirven was reported as requiring the aid of the church and referred to the Deacons." On January 6, 1849, a committee was appointed to attend to the repairing of the baptismal font, the churchyard fence and the removal of Sister Charlotte Kirven's house. After this, Miss Kirven began to "board" with various members of the church and considered the Robert G. Edwards home her own. On February 2, 1861, "It was resolved that the balance due the Poor Fund and whatever more be given by the members of the church be applied to the Board of Miss Charlotte Kirven."

119 Sallie Griffin was Eliza Evans's second cousin. Wilson, *Memories of Society Hill*, p. 50. "Eliza Evans was very fond of my little friend and playmate, Sallie Griffin, 'adopted' her for awhile, and took her with her when she traveled."

120 Evidently Mary Darby regarded Miss Evans's house as her home when she was in Society Hill. Both were deaf; Miss Evans was wealthy; Miss Darby was poor

and sewed in order to earn her keep. When Miss Evans traveled, Miss Darby spent the time with other friends or relatives. Her visit to the Williamsons was a temporary arrangement, as would be her sojourn with Miss Charlotte Kirven in the Edwards's home.

[121] Inscription on tombstone, Welsh Neck Baptist Churchyard, Society Hill, South Carolina, read by the author on May 31, 1953.

Journey to Louisiana

"To leave one's native state is a sad
thought . . ."

Mary A. Catlett to Jemima Darby, March
11, 1860.

Early in 1860, Jemima Darby, who was now sixty-six years old, made her decision to leave South Carolina and go to Louisiana. To seek a new home in the northern section of Louisiana was no new experience for citizens of Darlington District. In 1854, Boykin Witherspoon[1] and his wife, Elizabeth,[2] established a home in De Soto Parish. Friends spoke of them as being residents of "some western state." D. R. W. McIver[3] had been preaching in Louisiana since 1856. His daughter, Flora, who married Dr. William J. Frierson,[4] native of Charleston, lived near Gloster, De Soto Parish. John J. Marshall and his sons, Oliver H. and James G.,[5] natives of Darlington, were living at Stonewall, Louisiana. Dr. Jesse Hartwell,[6] prominent Baptist leader who had helped establish both Furman University at Greenville, South Carolina, and Howard University at Marion, Alabama, died in 1859, while serving as president of Mount Lebanon University, a Baptist school in Bienville Parish. Mrs. Hartwell[7] was still living in Louisiana.

Yet Jemima's friends were alarmed when she announced her plans to leave South Carolina. Mary Ann Catlett hastened to express her family's regrets over Jemima's leaving. "Try to keep a cheerful heart in leaving your friends," she admonished.

Jemima was in Leavensworth with the Howles when she received Mary Ann's letter which brought an invitation to visit the Catletts in Darlington before her departure for Louisiana.

Miss Catlett had been invited by Miss Darby to join the party going to Louisiana. She decided not to accept her friend's invitation. To go to Louisiana required more planning, and perhaps more courage, than to go down to Charleston. One of Miss Catlett's visits to Charleston in 1858 was recorded by Tom Law.

May 3, 1858. This afternoon, I went again to the Depot to meet those expected friends. And was happily not disappointed again. I found in the car, Aunt Elizabeth, [Elizabeth McIver

Law (April 3, 1815 — June 28, 1885) was the wife of Tom's uncle, Ezekiel Augustus Law.] Mrs. McIver, [Sallie Ervin Mc-Iver (June 30, 1826 — October 30, 1897) was the wife of Allen McIver.] and Miss Mary Catlett, all of whom put themselves under my care. After getting the baggage, etc. (by the assistance of Dr. Johnson, of Marion, who came along on the train with them) we repaired to Miss Cabnett's Boarding House, where they put up.

May 7. I went out this afternoon to see my lady friends off. We got to the Depot some time before the cars left, so I had time to get them and their baggage on, get tickets and chat awhile and see them off.[8]

Mary Ann Catlett, Darlington, South Carolina, to Jemima Darby, Leavensworth, South Carolina.

Darlington, S. C.
March 11, 1860

Miss Jemima Darby
Leavensworth, S. C.

Yours Dear Friend I have received by tonight's mail saying you expected to leave soon for Louisiana. Well if it were not for two things I think that I should most certainly accept your urgent request that of joining the party.[9] 1st it is now so late in the season that my stay would have to be too hurried wishing to spend not less than 6 or 7 months when I went. 2nd I could not very pleasantly take such a trip and leave Sarah in the school room with the addition of the household cares from garrett to cellar. I hope you will find the change a pleasant one. We have been wishing to hear from you not knowing *where* you were.[10] We have been closely confined to domestic cares all winter. Sallie's[11] death made a serious loss. One we fear that will never be filled by us. Her two little girls Hettie and Sallie are doing very well. Our brother Thomas the minister spent two months with us since we were here.[12] We have only two boarders this winter.

With the exception of colds we are as a family in usual health. The death of Mrs. Chancellor Dargan[13] was quite unexpected to us although her health had not been good for months. Mrs. Samuel Wilds[14] has recently been to Charleston to obtain medical advice of the celebrated Dr. Hunter. Do not mean (not the would-be sheriff).[15] Wish I could assist you in preparing for your journey. Brother[16] I dare say will be ready to meet a *certain* claim with you when you come.

Accept much love from Sarah and kindest regards from brother. Except to have *your wishes* on the subject gratified neither of us rejoice at the idea of your leaving South Carolina. To leave one's native state is a sad thought however pleasant and profitable the change may be and in going into the family of your nephew, Dear Friend may every blessing both temporal and spiritual be yours and should I be permitted to visit my friends in Jackson,[17] I hope to meet you.

Will be glad to hear again from you. Try to keep a cheerful heart in leaving your friends.

Yours truly,

M. A. CATLETT

Dear Jemima

You must not come to stay only an hour or two. Make us a visit. Do not fail.

Yours truly,

S. C. D. P.

Come anytime after this week as we can enjoy your visit better.

* * * * *

Jemima did not disclose to her friends, the Catletts, the date when she would be leaving South Carolina. At Saturday meeting, March 31, 1860, she obtained a letter of dismissal from Welsh Neck Church "to join some church in Louisiana."[18] In all probability she left Darlington early the next week — April 2 or 3. On April 22, she reported a safe arrival in Louisiana. There are three established facts about the trip: (1) the route covered about 1,200 miles; (2) the trains passed through many places of note during the night; (3) there was no opportunity to visit Miss Catlett's relatives in New Orleans.

"Miss Darby embarked on this long and, at that time, hazardous journey from the home of Captain Thomas E. Howle,"[19] of Leavensworth. She left Darlington by train and made a large portion of the trip by train. By 1860, it had been recognized that the building of railroads was a vital part of the spread of the Cotton Kingdom.

The tapping of the cotton belt was also carried on by railroads which were built during the two or three decades preceding the Civil War. The mother-road of all was the Charleston and Augusta Railway, which was the first to tap the Georgia cotton belt.[20]

More details about specific route were:

One might journey in comfort . . . directly to the head of the railroad at Cheraw, proceeding via Florence, Manchester, Branchville, and Augusta, to Atlanta, direct; or via Millen to Macon and thence to Columbus and Montgomery.[21]

Jemima did not go by way of Charleston, which would have been a longer route than to have gone through Kingsville.[22] To reach Atlanta, she probably traveled over four separate railroads in this order:

Darlington District, S. C., to Florence, S. C. — Cheraw and Darlington Railway;

Florence, S. C., to Kingsville, S. C. — Wilmington and Manchester Railway;

Kingsville, S. C., to Augusta, Ga. — South Carolina Railway;

Augusta, Ga., to Atlanta, Ga. — Georgia Railroad.[23]

From Atlanta, there were three routes to Louisiana: Route 1, through Mobile, Alabama; Route 2, through Chattanooga, Tennessee; and Route 3, which moved directly west. It is assumed that Jemima traveled over Route 3, which involved a certain amount of stagecoach travel as well as numerous changes of trains and hindrances due to roadbed construction. Jemima's most direct route from Atlanta would have been:

Atlanta, Ga., to West Point, Ga. — Atlanta and West Point
 Railway;
West Point, Ga., to Montgomery, Ala. — Montgomery and
 West Point Railway;
Montgomery, Ala., to Selma, Ala. — Stage (Alabama and Mis-
 sissippi Rivers Railway under construction);
Selma, Ala., to Uniontown, Ala. — Alabama and Mississippi
 Rivers Railways;
Uniontown, Ala., to Forest, Miss. — Stage (Alabama and Mis-
 sissippi Rivers Railway and Southern Mississippi Rail-
 way under construction);
Forest, Miss., to Vicksburg, Miss. — Southern Mississippi Rail-
 way;
Vicksburg, Miss., to Louisiana shore — Ferry:
Louisiana shore to Monroe, La. — Vicksburg, Shreveport and
 Texas Railway.[24]

To reach Ringgold, Miss Darby again traveled by stage. The
Vicksburg, Shreveport and Texas Railroad had not been ex-
tended past Monroe in April, 1860. Her route from Monroe to
Mount Lebanon was identical with the one described by Longino:

> At Monroe we again found the familiar old stage coach,
> and at once engaged passage. . . . We fared very well until we
> reached old Vienna, where we had supper and changed horses.
> . . . Ever and anon, we would reach open country. . . . Along
> about one o'clock, our driver sounded the bugle for the old
> college town of Mount Lebanon, and soon our coach was stand-
> ing in front of a store and post office, while the post master
> crawled out of his warm bed, to receive and deliver the mail.[25]

Mount Lebanon was the point 28 miles from Ringgold where
Jemima was delayed two days. How far Dr. Alexander Russia
Vann, his brother Josiah, and Mr. Byrd accompanied Miss Darby
is not known. Like many Carolinians, they had left home to
study conditions in Louisiana with an eye toward moving there,
but decided to return to their homes after five weeks. If they
visited their relatives in Ringgold, they probably did not spend
the entire time there.

Upon her arrival in Ringgold, Jemima went directly to the
home of her nephew, where she received a "cordial welcome."[26]

At the time of his aunt's joining his household, A. J. Kolb was forty years old. He had not seen Jemima since he was a boy in South Carolina.

Kolb had been a resident of Ringgold for about five years, having come there from Sparta, where he had had the distinction of being the first physician to practice medicine in Bienville Parish.[27] When his mother, Elizabeth Darby Kolb, Jemima's sister, died on August 3, 1853, at Sparta, Dr. Kolb had been married to "Miss Mell,"[28] a daughter of Philip[29] and Maria Brinson,[30] for about a month.[31] Their first child, Charles Francis, was born at Sparta on April 12, 1854, but died at Ringgold on January 28, 1855. There were three young children at the Kolb home when Jemima arrived: Ella Caroline, born on September 9, 1855; Thomas Haywood, born June 4, 1857; and Maria Elizabeth, born May 30, 1859.[32]

To Jemima, who was accustomed to splendid Pee Dee houses, her nephew's durable frontier-style cottage, which had been constructed with no attempt at ornamentation, must have seemed starkly plain. There were six rooms and a lean-to at the back, with a dogtrot running the full length of the house from front to back. Across the front, facing south, was a porch. As the family had increased in size, two rooms of equal size had been added to the front portion of the house where they jutted out from the corners at the southwest and southeast ends of the porch. Built in a grove of oak and pine trees, to which some cedars were later added, the house stood a little apart from, and to the rear of, the few stores which made up the business district of Ringgold.[33]

In the Ringgold to which Miss Darby came in the spring of 1860 were a Baptist church, three stores "kept by Philip Eldridge, R. C. Whitten and W. J. McKee,"[34] a Masonic lodge, a school house, and a dozen or more dwelling houses.[35]

The Baptist church at Ringgold had been admitted to the Red River Association when the organization met at Minden on September 23, 1854,[36] but in 1861 the Association reported that the Ringgold church did not have a pastor.[37] During the time when there was no pastor at the Baptist church, the more devout citizens attended Hardshell Church, about a mile east of the community. Upon the return of the Kolb family from a service in this church early in October, 1862, their young son, Thomas

Haywood,[38] aged five, announced to his mother, "I am going to die." To her reply of, "Some day, of course, you will die," the boy answered, "Yes, I am going to die. Uncle Zackie[39] told me today in his sermon; so I am going to die." He died that week.

Mackey Lodge No. 131, A. F. and A. M. was chartered in 1854.[40] Dr. A. J. Kolb, a visitor from Sparta, was present at the organizational meeting. On January 20, 1855, members of the lodge were: J. D. Cawthon,[41] James Bryan, J. B. Thomas,[42] H. M. Prothro, B. F. Allums,[43] W. M. D. Cawthon,[44] S. F. Snell, J. B. Stanland, John Tooke,[45] E. W. Davis,[46] James Monroe, G. W. Cawthon,[47] and Dr. Kolb.

Church, lodge, and school were all housed in the same building.

A two-story building was erected at the intersection of Military Road and Hall Street, for the lodge building and the lower floor for religious services of all denominations. A school was also started and the lower floor used for that purpose.[48]

The town's cemetery was at New Providence, the Hardshell Church on the Sparta road. The Kolb children, Charles Francis and Thomas Haywood, were buried there.

Ringgold's location on the Military Road,[48] which, after 1828, ran through the heart of North Louisiana from Campti to the Arkansas boundary at Haynesville, added some importance to the village. Soldiers moving to and from Fort Jessup, near the Texas border, chose a camp site near Ringgold for regular use. The main artery of north-south traffic traveled through the center of the little town.

Sparta was 15 miles east of Ringgold. J. W. Dorr, the tourist who described Louisiana for the New Orleans *Crescent* in 1860, reported that Sparta was "smartly in the woods, having been unhappily located far from any navigable watercourse." Merchants hauled their merchandise from Lake Bistineau, 18 miles away, where boats landed at Port Dolivar. "Sparta is a serious little place of about 225 or 50 inhabitants," Dorr reported.[50] Of the site chosen for Sparta,[51] he said:

It is unfortunately located in a regular old-fashioned sand-bed, the base of which could scarcely be reached by an artisian bore, though the pedestrian thinks he is going to the bottom at every step. It would not be surprising if, two or three generations hence, Spartans were born splay-footed — nature compensating in their physical conformation the disabilities under which this heroic people labor as a consequence of the character of their abiding place.

Regardless of the nature of the town, Jemima was, no doubt, gravely concerned with affairs at Sparta, the seat of government for the parish where she had elected to live. Mount Lebanon, the first town in Bienville Parish that Jemima had seen, was of greater concern to her because Baptists from her own South Carolina had created a religious and cultural environment there which reminded her of home.[52]

If Jemima read Dorr's comments on Bienville Parish, she agreed with his statement that "the parish is very much in the woods and everything is in keeping with that style."[53] Of the soil, terrain, slaves, and vegetation, he wrote:

> There is every variety of soil, from very fertile to very barren, . . . The great body of the lands is still untilled, and there are many tracts as desirable as any which are now held in private hands that are still open to entry. There are but few large planters in the parish, the people being mostly small farmers with but few slaves. . . . The cotton lands yield an average of rather less than half a bale of cotton to the acre.
>
> The forest growth of the parish is magnificent. The pine, the cheapest, most common and useful among woods, as iron is among the metals, grows to large size; the sassafras becomes a stalwart tree, from eight to twelve inches in diameter, and the beech, white ash, sweet gum, hickory and several varieties of oak, all flourish exceedingly.

Among the heads of families who were called "large slave owners,"[54] and who lived near enough to Ringgold for Jemima to make their acquaintance were A. Cawthon,[55] K. P. McDaniel,[56] Simeon Theus,[57] John Tooke,[58] D. K. Thomas, Zack Thomas, J. J. Vickers,[59] and J. L. Vickers.[60] By South Carolina standards, however, these men were not considered "large slave owners," the numbers of their slaves ranging from twenty-six to sixty-three.

After meeting her nephew's family, where she had a cordial

reception, and her new neighbors, in what Mary Ann Catlett had judged to be a "sociable place," Miss Darby was introduced to Mrs. Kolb's relatives, the Brinsons.

James Brinson, a pioneering Baptist preacher, had been Mrs. Kolb's grandfather.[61] Of James Brinson, Paxton wrote:

> He was born in Tennessee, and came to Louisiana in 1821 and settled not far from the present town of Vienna; and being a Baptist minister, he gathered a church called Pine Hills, in 1822, made up at first chiefly of members of his own family, who accompanied him from Tennessee. So far as I have been able to ascertain, he is the first Baptist preacher who labored in the region between the Ouachita River and the Dorchete. He gathered a few churches. He died in what is now Claiborne Parish, September 5, 1831.[62]

James Brinson reared a large family. Among them was a son, Philip Purser, who married Maria Theresa Nelson, daughter of Major John Nelson,[63] a Revolutionary War soldier, and his wife, Nancy Ware Hunter, whom he married in North Carolina, where their daughter was born. Mrs. Brinson was in Bienville Parish when Miss Darby arrived; her husband was not. Mr. Brinson, having been "influenced by infidels, had strayed from the church, wandered around and had gone to South America,"[64] where he remained until 1864, when he heard a missionary preach, became remorseful, and returned home. On the voyage back to the United States, there occurred an incident which has been related by J. F. McFarland, a nephew of Philip Brinson.

> He was quite an old man when I first saw him. He was, to me, a hero. It seems that he sailed on a ship to South America. While his ship was on the sea, they were overtaken by a storm, and almost despaired of being able to save the ship or themselves. As the story was told to me and the other members of our family, it appeared that Uncle Philip looked on himself as the Jonah that brought the storm upon them.[65]

McFarland indicated that he knew other members of the Brinson family also:

Dr. T. J. Fouts, Mt. Lebanon, La., married Miss Harriett Brinson, with whom I became acquainted when I attended Mt. Lebanon University; her brother, Haywood Brinson, resided in the village of Sparta, where, as a member of a brass band, I had the pleasure of meeting his family.[66]

Miss Julia Ann Brinson, oldest daughter of Philip Purser and Maria Theresa Brinson, never married. Miss Darby came to know her quite well because, in her old age, Miss Brinson spent a part of her time at the Kolb home. Beulah Brinson Wilson, daughter of Haywood and Olivia Watkins Brinson, recalled that she remembered both her Aunt Julia and Miss Darby.

> She did not know how the two get along but was sure it was all right as Aunt Jemima got along well with everybody and Aunt Julia demanded, and got, the best. If there was one beautiful cup in the house, she had her tea or coffee in it. If she had to sleep with someone, which was not often, she always put a bolster pillow down between them, or else, slept on the top sheet to separate herself from the other person. But she was very smart, and knew it, and was good in her own way.[67]

Legends about Julia Brinson abound among descendants of the Brinson family: how she prophesied; how she was swindled by a lawyer who claimed to have legal access to a vast legacy left for her family through the estate of Major John Nelson; how she always washed her hands after shaking hands. For several generations, nephews and nieces knew what their parents meant by "as peculiar as Aunt Julia Brinson."

As time passed, Dr. and Mrs. Kolb had other children: Mary Harriet, born August 12, 1861; David Alexander, born July 1, 1863; Lee Jackson, born August 31, 1865, and named for Generals Robert E. Lee and Stonewall Jackson; and Edwin Kirtley, born March 13, 1868.[68]

Jemima's arrival in Ringgold injected a strong South Carolina influence into a frontier Louisiana village. To each of the Kolb children, their aunt was distinguished and wise; to the citizens of Ringgold, Miss Darby represented gentility and culture. Her opinions were respected; her way of life was emulated. Two letters from South Carolina in reply to Jemima's account of her journey to Louisiana reveal some of the details of the trip and indicate her friends' attitudes toward her decision to leave home. Miss Catlett wrote from Darlington on May 18, and Mrs. Howle wrote from Leavensworth on June 4. All efforts to locate Jemima's "long interesting narrative of her journey" have failed.

Mary Ann Catlett, Darlington, South Carolina, to Jemima Darby, Ringgold, Louisiana.

Darlington, S. C.
May 18, 1860

Yours Dear Friend postmarked April 22nd is at hand and knowing your anxiety to hear from South Carolina I most cheerfully grant your request which was "Do write soon." We are indeed glad to hear of your safe arrival in Louisiana. How you were blessed. Just to think of your going I suppose considerably over twelve hundred miles and "kept perfectly well all the way and not in the least fatigued." How much you have to be thankful to your Heavenly Father but how often we are unmindful of all His mercies. So sorry you could not have stopped a few days in New Orleans[69] to see our niece, Mrs. Flora White (sister-in-law of Capt Hooper of that city) (by the way did we give you Flora's address?) Fully intended to do so, but think in the multiplicity of things we had to *talk* about the *last day*[70] it was forgotten. It must have been a privation to you having passed so many places of *note* in the *night*. The two days you spent in 28 miles of Ringgold must have appeared a long time. So much for your being arrived in a land of *carriages* for had you been a *horseback* rider you might have found a more ready conveyance.[71] I could almost imagine just how you felt in reaching the Drs[72] particularly at your cordial reception. From the calls made so soon think it must be a sociable place. Never mind about the *church* for awhile. You can have a spice of Tedoe[73] in your sisterly feelings toward the strange brethren of Louisiana. You know popularity does much for a body in these days of religious as well as political strife.[74] Hope you will assist in the S. School. While I feel that you are a true Baptist, yet would just as soon teach a Sabbath School in the Pres. or Methodist congregation as in the Bap[75]

The exact day of your leaving Darlington must be our excuse for not seeing you at the Depot. I am sorry you felt so much disappointed. Miss Cotys says had she known when you started she would have met you there. As you said nothing of it, I suppose Mr. Ourl's[76] servant was faithful to trust *committed* to his *care* from *here.* Thank you for your long interesting narrative of your journey but still (Mother Eve-like) there are many more things we would have liked much if you had told us about. Did you order the *Darlington Flag* sent to you? If so suppose you have ere this heard of the heartrending catastrophe of 22 persons being drowned in Boykins Mill pond 10 miles of Camden. I saw the "Southern Baptist" had been sent you. How far is Ringgold from Jackson? With whom did you go except Dr. Vann? Have not heard a word about how you got off. The event no doubt dear Friend has cast a sad very sad gloom over poor brother L[77]   True his *new* black hat is quite a shiney one but he has on it a new crape which bespeaks the sorrowful feelings of his heart. He made a call soon after he got it and an apology for keeping it on while he sat there. A new one was more unpleasant than the old one because it did not set so well to the head. Now, do you not think that one crape could have done? Well, enough of Brother L you will say provided your mind has changed.

A little revival in the Limestone School.[78] Margarett Dargan[79] and Lavinia McIver[80] — among the converts and Bettie Dargan[81]   Quite a prominent one holding prayer meetings among the school girls. Brother Dargan[82] went up there the past Wednesday. We were all invited to Ellen Flinn's[83] wedding but did not go. Brother was in Charleston a week during the Convention and left town the day of the wedding. He called a few moments to see Mrs. F. Says she "looked badly." The dr. is very kind. Goes to see her generally once in 2 or 3 weeks and was there nearly a week at the time of the wedding. Two boxes (tiny ones) of cake was sent us done up in *Bride* like manner — with Mr. and Mrs. Lambs name on the inside. Lizzie Wingate only daughter of William Wingate is also married to Mr. Wearing of Columbia, a widower (but no children). Said she has done very well.

Mr. George Williamson's[84] two daughters are here at school, Virginia[85] and Kate.[86] They seem to have missed a mother's training.[87] Mrs. Andrew Charles[88] sends for them every Friday evening. Andrew[89] told me two weeks ago they had not heard from you and wished they could as they wanted very much to hear. Suppose you have written to some of the family.[90] I have nothing special in the way of news. Brother says if you will have him called to that place[91] and give him $15.00 he will go out to preach for you a year.

Accept very much love and many good wishes from Brother Lewis and Sarah. Indeed Sarah has been very sick nearly a week but better the past few days (dyarrhea). She says she would have written some in this had it not been for her sickness. How large is Ringgold? Miss Cotys has been very sick (a few days) since you left but is about again. Did you hear that Caroline Jossey[92] has a living child at last? The Methodist Church has been handsomely repaired. Wish you would have Mr. Bealer called somewhere out there and then this church could have the monotony broken by getting somebody else.[93] We will be pleased at any time to hear from you and will occasionally take pleasure in letting you hear from me and *mine* if you will just accept the hurried scribble in which I am often as in this case obliged to write. Our regards to the family.

Your unalterable friend,

M. A. CATLETT

* * * * *

While Jemima and Mary Darby were visiting in the home of William Vann, Bettie Vann Howle and her brothers developed a considerable fondness for their maiden cousins. Upon her arrival in Louisiana, Jemima wrote a number of letters. The one to Bettie Howle was answered promptly. Mrs. Howle was the only member of the Vann family to correspond with Miss Darby in Louisiana.

Mrs. Thomas E. Howle, Leavensworth, South Carolina, to Jemima Darby, Ringgold, Louisiana.

Leavensworth, So. Ca.
June 4, 1860

Dear Cousin,

Your communication came to hand a few days ago. Was glad to hear that you had arrived safely at your Nephew's in good health and well pleased with the country, and I do hope that you will continue to be pleased, and never have cause to regret leaving S. Ca. I have thought of you a great deal since you left, and trust that the Lord will ever be your friend, in time of need and will guide and protect you in your lonely *condition.* I am sorry to hear that you have no Baptist preaching in your little village or in the neighborhood. I should think that you would find it poor living without an opportunity of hearing preaching on the Sabbath, being accustomed to attending Baptist preaching. You must go to work and try to build up a church now that you have gone to a new country. You must work hard and produce preaching in your village.

Our church and Sunday School[94] seem to be in a **very** flourishing condition at this time. We have an interesting school in the morning for the whites and after service we have a very large school for instructing the blacks. Mr. Howle[95] is the Superintendent, and we have about a hundred and fifty pupils. All the church seem to take an interest in it, and I hope that it will result in much good.

Well, Cousin Jemima I have nothing new or interesting to write. Captain Bob Edwards[96] has sold out his plantation and was to leave last Friday for Louisiana in company with Mr. Witherspoon.[97] I hear that the idea of leaving So. Car. has gone very hard with him. He is in very poor health and low in *flesh.* I am very sorry that he was compelled to leave for they will be greatly missed by the community at large.

We have not heard a word from Rush since he left Jo at Kingsville on his return home. They were gone about 5 weeks. They made quite a short stay. They became homesick and made their way back as fast as possible. Mr. Byrd told some big tales about the rich lands of Louisiana. I think that persons were disposed to doubt his veracity. Jo is not disposed to bragg on the fine lands and crops but to tell the plain simple truth. Cousin Jemima I do not think that they are at all contented now to remain in South Carolina. I mean when I say all (Rush, Jo and Mr. Howle)   Of course they are not all the people but they are the ones that had the Louisiana fever when you left. I think that Mr. Howle has cooled off for I never hear him speak of it now. Do tell me earnestly if you think that Lou. will compare with S. Ca.

We have had a great deal of rain here for the last few weeks. Crops though are looking very well, and my garden you would not know it. The corn is getting up in the apple tree and the vines are running over the fence   we are eating cabbage, Irish potatoes, beets, squash, beans and will soon have tomatoes.

My little chaps are getting on pretty well. The little boys[98] have had very bad colds but they are better and little sis[99] is too   do wish you could see her   she is now running all over the house and yard and trying to talk. She gets more interesting every day. You must write soon and tell me all the news about your new country and what you are doing. The children join me in love to you and your nephew's family.

Your affectionate cousin,

B. H.

* * * * *

Bettie's letters were mailed at Leavensworth, the post office for people living in the Black Creek neighborhood. Dargan described the area in its geographical relationship to Darlington in these words: "Harmony Hall . . . was situated in a region of Sandy pine and oak lands about five miles to the north of the county town of Darlington, called in accordance with old Southern custom 'Court House.' "[100] Of Springville, he wrote:

Rising from the left bank of Black Creek lies the neighborhood known as Springville, not at all a town or even a village. There was no postoffice or store. It was only a scattered neighborhood of homes placed in that locality because of its healthfulness and convenience.[101]

And, at last, he located the community known as Black Creek:

Black Creek, which followed its winding course through the swamps at the foot of these hills, is also closely associated with the memories of boyhood. . . . Across the creek on the corresponding high lands were several homes in close touch with Harmony Hall, though not reckoned as a part of Springville; and still further beyond, and near the dear old stream from which its name was taken, stood the Black Creek Baptist Church in a neighborhood of its own.[102]

Since 1856, committees had been at work on a new church at Black Creek. James Howle, William Vann, A. L. Williams, and J. A. Fort were members of the first building committee. Added to the committee on December 6, 1856, were T. E. Howle, James A. Williams, John Gandy,[103] and the minister, J. O. B. Dargan.[104] On January 8, 1860, the new church was dedicated. The program for the service was:

Scripture	Rev. J. C. Phelps, Society Hill
Prayer	Rev. L. DuPre, Darlington
Sermon	Rev. G. B. Bealer, Darlington
Dedicatory Prayer	Rev. Phelps
Statement	Rev. J. O. B. Dargan[105]

In a column at the western corner of the church was a niche where records were to be preserved for posterity.[106]

Undoubtedly, the most forceful character within the Springville-Black Creek community was John Orr Beasley Dargan, whose pastorate lasted forty years and about whom his son wrote,

His life-work revolved about Springville as his home and Black Creek as his church. Various offers and calls came to him as he grew in years, in pulpit power, and in influence, but that home ever held him in its tender embrace and we could never get his consent to move.[107]

And it was under Mr. Dargan's spiritual guidance that Thomas E. Howle and James A. Williams came to be prominent laymen participating in the work of the local church, the Welsh Neck Association, and the State Convention. Named to be the delegate from Welsh Neck Association to attend the State Convention at

Greenville in 1860 was Thomas E. Howle,[108] who also served as chairman of a committee on education and missions.

Bettie Vann Howle loved her church and home community, but her social activities were not limited to Black Creek and Leavensworth. One of her visits[109] to Charleston has been described:

> March 26, 1858. This evening at parade I had the pleasure of meeting Mrs. Swinton, Mrs. John DeLorme, Mrs. Thomas Howle and Miss Anna Maria Nettles, the latter being just from Darlington. Presented Ralph Nesbit to them.[110]

Mrs. Thomas E. Howle, Leavensworth, South Carolina, to Jemima Darby, Ringgold, Louisiana.

Leavensworth, S. Ca.,
July 21, 1860

Dear Cousin

Your welcome letter came to hand a few days ago. The contents read and appreciated. Although it is not answered as soon as I intended doing it for I have been so *busy* for the last two or three weeks that I could not find time even to write a letter (which you know is quite a *job* for me). Well Cousin Jemima I am so lonely that I can scarcely live. I have not seen my *husband* since last *Wednesday*. He has gone to Greenville to attend the Convention which is now in session. There has quite a crowd gone up from Darlington and Society Hill. I do hope that Mr. Howle will be home Thursday night for when he is gone I feel like everybody is gone, and I am left alone in the wide world which is quite a deplorable condition for one to be placed in, but I must not fret, for he can't always be with me.

Well, to change the subject   we had quite a fine rain yesterday evening which was very much needed. Farmers had almost despaired of making bread, the drough continued so long and I am afraid that it is now too late as to do the corn much good for the crops are nearly made. I don't think that I have ever heard so much complaint of dry weather in my life, and it is not only this place, but it is the world over, but we ought not to complain for we have much better than we deserve.

We have nothing new or interesting in the neighborhood. There has been but very little sickness this summer. Linton Williams'[111] two oldest boys have been quite sick but are better. Lint is not *married* yet[112] but I think that he and *Jane Fort*[113] will make it *out* soon. Mrs. Dr. Crane had another fine daughter, two weeks old, and is quite sick.[114] Mary Chambers[115] had another daughter and Caroline Williams[116] expects to have *one* in *about* four *months*. Did you ever hear the like? Everybody has got a baby or expects to have one, *but me*. You must not let Caroline know that you have heard about her situation. She says that her health never was better than at the present time and I do hope that she will get on well and have a *living* child. Cousin Mary[117] has been complaining for several days *but done* nothing yet. They are getting on as usual.

Captain Robert Edwards and his family left for Louisiana two or three weeks ago. It was thought here that his *mind* was very much impaired in consequence of his finding himself so much behind, and finally being compelled to sell out and look for a new country. His great trouble seems to have been that in consequence of his situation, he became wordly minded and it went very hard with him. He started with B. Witherspoon and got as far as Columbia and was taken sick and came back and stayed about a month and started again with his wife and Dr. Pressly[118] went with them part of the way but don't speak of what I have written for it will be a great mortification to his family. It is thought here that they will not return any more.

Miss Nancy McIver[119] died a few weeks ago. Didn't learn what was the matter. Mrs. Griffin[120] and Sallie[121] are gone to live with Mrs. Coker.[122] Old Mr. Winn died suddenly last Tuesday night. He was found dead between Mr. Coker's[123] store and his own house.

It seems as if the Society Hill Church is getting very weak. Our Church seems to be in a flourishing condition. We have prayer meeting and Sunday School besides preaching. We had an excellent sermon yesterday from Mr. Bealer.[124] His wife is in a *situation* that he could not leave her to go to the Convention. Mr. Napier preached for us on the Sunday before. Mr. Dargan has been absent for three weeks. He went up to Lime Stone[125] to see his daughter Bettie[126] *graduate* and from there to the Convention. Well Cousin Jemima I believe that I have told you all the *dry* news that we have. My children are quite well. The little boys are as bad as can be. Little *sis* is running all over the house and yard and trying to talk. She is decidedly the most interesting child that I have ever had. I don't say so because she is a *girl* but because it is really so.

I forwarded the turnip seed about a week ago in three bundles. Hope that you will receive them and make some *big* turnips in your *rich* lands. Give my kind regards to your nephew and niece and tell them that I would like very much to see them. Write soon and tell me all the news.

Your affectionate cousin,

BETTIE S. HOWLE

* * * * *

Edwin Charles Dargan, the son of the Black Creek pastor, J. O. B. Dargan, has left a record of his boyhood in the Black Creek neighborhood, where he was a contemporary of the Howle boys. Adults were distressed, he related, over the serious problems which faced the nation at the beginning of the 1860's, but the younger boys and girls were not affected. He explained:

> We had our school days, our picnics, our plays and games, our visits to each other. The boys had their fishing and bathing, and young life had to find its expression notwithstanding the sorrows and anxieties of our seniors, with which we of course sympathized in our childish way, but could not so fully understand.
>
> The religious life of the community kept on its way. We went to church and Sunday School. Father preached every other Sunday at Black Creek. The other two Sundays the family usually went to Darlington where Mr. Bealer was the beloved pastor all during the war. . . .[127]

But the times were unsettled; people moved about. From Black Creek, letters of dismissal were sought by staunch supporters of the church. Mrs. Deborah Baker[128] asked for a letter because she "contemplated leaving the state."[129] Mrs. Sarah W. Williamson, her daughter, Miss Sarah, and their servant, Elzy, requested letters of dismissal in order to unite with Mispah Baptist Church, near Florence.[130]

There are more than a hundred references to the Thomas Williamson family in the Darby letters. Actually, about 75 per cent of the letters were written by Williamsons. Mary Ann Williamson Charles, who outlived all of her sisters, was the most faithful correspondent, but both Sarah Williamson and Caroline Williamson Williams seemed to enjoy writing to their old friend. It was not surprising that Mary Ann, Sarah, and Caroline all referred to Jemima as "Miss Darby," who was a contemporary of their mother, Sarah Wilds Williamson.

Sarah Wilds,[131] the daughter of Samuel[132] and Nancy Ann Lide Wilds,[133] married Thomas Williamson[134] in 1811. Her mother was a member of the South Carolina branch of the distinguished Kolb family, being the daughter of Major Robert[135] and Sarah Kolb Lide.[136] Sarah Kolb's parents, Johannes and Sarah Kolb, from whom Jehu was also descended, were born in Mannheim and came to America in 1707.

Thomas and Sarah Williamson had ten children: Samuel Thomas,[137] George Lawrence,[138] Sarah Wilds,[139] Caroline Matilda,[140] Ann Elizabeth, Mary Margaret, Robert Lide,[141] Joseph Wilds,[142] Horace,[143] and Mary Ann.[144]

When Jemima left for Louisiana, Mrs. Williamson was a widow, living at her home, Orangedale, near Florence, South Carolina, the post office, and Mispah, the Baptist Church. With her were her unmarried daughter, Sarah, aged thirty-nine, and her son, Wilds, aged thirty-five. Samuel's daughter, Jane, was married,[145] and his daughter, Mary,[146] and son, Edwin,[147] were grown. George's wife, Catherine,[148] was dead; his son, Thomas,[149] was almost grown; his daughters, Virginia and Kate,[150] were in school. Horace and his wife had one daughter, Theodosia.[151] Mary Ann, who had married Andrew B. Charles but had no children, was, later in the year, to live at Stony Hill, near Cashaway Ferry on the Pee Dee River. Caroline Williamson Williams, wife of James, lived in the Black Creek neighborhood, where the Williams family attended church with Miss Darby's relatives, the Howles.

Carrie Williams sprinkled gossipy little news items about all of Miss Darby's friends throughout her letters. On June 9, 1860, she wrote from her own home, Hickory Grove, at Leavensworth, where Thomas Howle was postmaster.

Mrs. James A. Williams, Leavensworth, South Carolina, to Jemima Darby, Ringgold, Louisiana.

Hickory Grove
June 9, 1860

Miss Jemima Darby
    Ringgold, La.

My dear friend,

Your letter arrived during my absence; made a visit of near three weeks to mother. Sister[152] nursed and stuffed me so much that I feel much better, hope now that my strength will continue to increase. Dr. Crane[153] advises a trip to Calvota Springs, Georgia. I dislike leaving home and feel little like being in company, but think Jim's health requires change more than mine, therefore expect we will go if I can make up my mind to start sometime next month. Mother's health is as usual. Spends much time with poultry and garden   has a fine one and fruit a plenty   Sister is teased about their pastor[154] as he visits them occasionally but does not mind it. I dont think he has any idea of matrimony. Mr. Wilkins[155] has struck up again. Visited Mag Fort and she did not treat him with respect   hear he intends calling on Mary Norwood[156] again   how strange for a smart man to act so silly. Mary Chambers has a daughter[157]   better time than ever. Mr. Parnell[158] is not expected to live. Dr. C. is busy all the time. Mrs. Fort keeps very feeble. Mrs. John Fort is spending the summer here; I have not seen her   have not been out of a Sabbath in five weeks   attended church meeting.[159] We are to have 2 deacons elected next time   hope I can attend at that time.

You are a long distance from Baptists[160] but I think there are many good Methodists and can join with them in good works   hope all unite and you may have a fine school[161]   much good may redound to the glory of God although present prospects appear gloomy   good seed may spring up after many years. Our school is still flourishing   its a source of much regret that I am compelled to cease attention to it   found such a great pleasure in the task. You did not mention if the Doctor's family were Baptists[162] shall hope they are anyway.

Mrs. DuPrey has been quite sick. Both attend High Hill church   keep a school every Sabbath and Mr. D.[163] preaches once a month   I have not seen Mrs. Lucas[164] since you left   seldom gets up to church; attends Darlington

Sister M.[165] spent two days while I was at Mother's   had been quite sick previously   ate a big dinner at Aunt Jane's[166] and paid a severe penalty   Mr. Wallace and Jane have been over   quite a nice gentleman[167] J. said they have a fine garden and what is better kept it in order themselves   Mary[168] is on a visit now   looks much better.

Mrs. Wilds[169] is improved but poorly. Sallie[170] cannot stand alone a minute. Betty and Mollie[171] look delicate   have lost so many negroes[172]   think they cannot travel this summer. Alonzo Dargan[173] will reside in Mrs. Wingate's house   had a large party   hear of no other weddings   but Julia Porcher[174] and Mr. Ashley near Mother's will come off next week. Wilds[175] takes out looking at the ladies   think surely this year he must get him a wife. I received a letter from Cousin E. Evans.[176] Inquired about you and I was so provoked when Sallie said you did not take a silk dress; she is very well pleased and thinks to remain there.

Dr. Vann said if Fanny would consent he would go   do not think any of the crowd[177] realized their expectations. Jo not pleased. Mary Parrott[178] called here and paid her subscription   had chills   looks very feeble. I thought Mr. Dabbs[179] would die recently but has got better   does not sit up much. A Lide[180] and wife I expect have gone west for a long visit   think she might have remained with her mother   I have another supply of geraniums growing nicely and some beautiful roses   think you wish some musk seeds   sent them and phlox   Thank you for those you sent. I feel you will have to work to read this but do not feel like writing it over. J. joins me in love to you.

Your friend,

CARRIE WILLIAMS

P. S. Mary Player[181] no better but her mother tries to think she will get well.

* * * * *

Carrie Williams, whose "situation" had been revealed to Jemima by Bettie Howle in July, was still not willing to admit the cause of her serious illness when she wrote to her friend in September. Death, for her, was imminent, she believed, but she was not afraid.

The Baptist church was the center of all activity at Black Creek. Jim Williams and Tom Howle, Bettie's husband, had been ordained as deacons. Dargan's report of the ceremony was supplementary to Carrie's. "One of the young deacons of my father's Black Creek church was Thomas E. Howle. I remember seeing him and the beloved James Williams standing arm in arm as they were ordained deacons in that dear old church."[182] According to Mrs. Williams, Mr. Bealer, pastor of the Baptist church at Darlington, who preached the ordination sermon, made the deacons' duties "almost as responsible as his own." The text of the sermon was "Paul and Timotheus, the servants of Jesus Christ, to all the saints in Christ Jesus which are at Philippi, with the bishops and deacons."[183] It was altogether fitting that the Black Creek pastor, Mr. J. O. B. Dargan, give the charge to the young deacons.

Mrs. James A. Williams, Leavensworth, South Carolina, to Jemima Darby, Ringgold, Louisiana.

Hickory Grove
Sept 12, 1860

My dear friend

I had almost given up hearing from you   glad you've kept well   my health would not admit traveling   Returned from mother's first of June and have not gone as far as the depot since   have increased in strength and if spared through next month hope to enjoy better health. If not, hope to be prepared for the last hour which must come sooner or later. Never thought I would look forward to such an event with so much composure. Feel little dread although friends appear anxious and uneasy for me.

Mother and sister came up for the ordination of T. Howle and Jim.[184] Hoped she could stay but two nights was all; in usual health and sister fattens. She would like to correspond with you. Reports are sometimes untrue. Don't think your friend[185] has any notion, know she has not the least idea of undertaking such a charge. Some have Brother Wilds engaged to Martha[186] but he has never made the first call there. Mother wished the parson would call oftener than he does.[187] Had several blacks baptized, church[188] more prosperous than ever.

Oh! you cannot guess who Mr. Dargan dipped last Sabbath   Amasa Adams, wife and two daughters.[189] Now you may take credit of doing a good work starting the girls to church. L and Jim,[190] the parents. Quite a reformation since the first call there, house and yard clean   five regular Sabbath scholars   parents in good order and regular church going folks; there seems to be more zeal in our church than I've ever known   most are roused up to try to do something   had no protracted meeting   Mr. Dargan had to ride on an agency this month   came very near losing him but suppose you see in the *Baptist* how they kept him   some have to pay more than they are able, others fall short   Mr. Vann got up to one hundred   Abel Gandy[191] only sixty.

I hope the new deacons will prove faithful   know Jim is too timid to do as much good as he otherwise would. Mr. Bealer[192] preached Whilden[193] prayed and Dargan gave the charge   an interesting time   text: Philippians 1st verse, 1st chapter. Brother B made their duty almost as responsible as his own.[194] We've collected all but $4.50 cts for the carpet $25 for the communion set   Suppose Tom[195] will get it and trust us for the balance. I don't know.

Cousin E's postoffice is Cooperswell[196] last I heard in bad health. Misses King were well   have not seen them   Sallie Griffin is in Springville[197]   spoke of visiting me but has not come yet. Aunt Nancy[198] died in July   All stay with Rachel[199] who got Dr. F. Wilson's place[200] Peter[201] sleeps at his office but eats with them   I have not heard if Mrs. DuPrey went off but think she did. Mary Ann Lucas[202] has been quite sick   too late moving   one of the girls had fever[203]   prospects of another *heir*   expect she regrets it   persons do not respect her as much since her village exposure.

It is generally known that Mr. E.[204] had almost lost his mind before he left here   sold to Wilbur Evans   all but his house and lot   kept that   don't know what Mrs. Kirven[205] will do.

I've never got to Lizzie[206] yet. She called here with Mrs.

John Fort and I thought to go down but could not   Indeed home suits me best. Poor Jim is often sick that he cannot nurse quite as much as he wishes. He is very tender and careful of his Carrie and confines himself to the house a great deal.

Mrs. Dabbs[207] is still alive   a mere skeleton   only speaks a few words at a time. I must close for a long time, if ever again. Had to rest since I began this. Hope we shall meet in Heaven. Mary Dorrity had a son Friday week.[208] How is your S. School?

Your friend,

CARRIE WILLIAMS

* * * * *

In spite of her doleful predictions, Carrie Williams did not die; she had a baby. Shortly after the birth of James Leonidas Williams, to be called Leon, Miss Darby received two letters which reported his arrival and mentioned many other matters. Carrie wrote on December 4, and Sarah wrote on December 14.

The Negro problem had moved nearer the Williamson family. Their own cousins, the Misses King, at Society Hill, had begun to have servant trouble. Yankees, too, were becoming a nuisance. Mrs. Baker, who had returned to Black Creek from "the North," brought disturbing reports.

Mrs. James A. Williams, Leavensworth, South Carolina, to Jemima Darby, Ringgold, Louisiana.

Hickory Grove
Dec. 4, 1860

My dear friend

As sister was so busy nursing the blue-eyed boy who came to town on the first of November[209] I could not get her to write. Have had a good recovery and feel better than in a long time. I call him James Leonidas   mother's great name has come at last   will call him Leon   weighed nine pounds and Jim thinks him a none-such. Mrs. H.[210] has her fun laughing at us   says he is too fine looking for us   everyone admits

◄{ 81 }►

he is pretty   Moll[211] laughs at his big nose. Sister and mother left yesterday   seemed loth to leave me but I must try to get a little stronger.

The Association[212] passed off pleasantly   I had some company although Dr. Flin[213] forbid it. The next one will be at the Hill[214] Moll went to see the girls last week   E[215] does not look well   Joe[216] a grown lady. Robert Edwards has returned   almost restored now   Mrs. Sparks[217] worried herself. Mr. Lide's[218] been sick ever since the Association. Mary Ann Lucas[219] has a daughter. Jane Wallace a son[220]   Will come over as soon as the babe can ride. I will write more next time.

Your friend,

CARRIE

* * * * *

Late in 1860, Andrew and Mary Ann Charles completed their new home near Cashaway Ferry, which was considered an old community.

> Journeying from the beautiful village of D_____ to a well-known ferry upon the Great Pee Dee, we go down a steep hill (just before we enter the low lands of the river), that is known as "L_____ Hill." Upon the top of this hill and on both sides of the public highway there may be seen an old, neglected graveyard, which has been the burial place of the people in that neighborhood for more than a century past. . . .
> This was the original site of an old church, in which the early settlers on the river, mostly of the Baptist faith, worshiped. The old meeting house has long since been removed to a more convenient locality, and time has made some sad changes about the place. . . .[221]

Obviously, Darlington was the village to which the novelist referred in his 1870 romance, and Lowther's Hill was the cemetery[222] at the side of the road. Cashaway Neck was the church.[223]

"Stony Hill," the Andrew Charles home, was located somewhat northwest of Lowther's Hill Cemetery and two miles northeast of Mechanicsville Church, on land which had once been a part of the Thomas Williamson estate.[224] The house was a twin of the Hugh Lide Charles[225] house in Darlington.

Andrew Charles and his wife were distant relatives, having descended from the Peter Kolb family. Andrew was the oldest son of Colonel Edgar W. Charles and his first wife, Sarah Hugh Lide, and was reared in a home where the father was "a patriot, patron of the arts and sponsor of education."[226] Andrew himself was "a man of very striking personality, tall and spare, with a great big forehead and strong blue eyes." Like his father, he was "very fond of literature . . . and his fresh and original comments on men and things were entertaining and bright."[227] When she was asked, late in life, why she had married Andrew Charles, Mary Ann has been quoted as saying "For the *name*, child, for the name."[228]

Sarah included a report on her two sisters, Mary Ann and Caroline, and her cousins, the Kings, in her letter to Miss Darby on December 14, 1860.

Jemima knew that Sallie King LaCoste had died on May 10, 1857, and was buried beside her two infants at Welsh Neck Churchyard. Mr. LaCoste moved on to Cheraw to keep his store there, but soon came back to Society Hill to court and marry Sallie's sister, Eliza. On December 3, 1859, "Sister Eliza LaCoste, formerly King, was dismissed by letter to join the Baptist church at Cheraw."[229] Their first child was named Florence.

Sarah Williamson, Orangedale, South Carolina, to Jemima Darby, Ringgold, Louisiana.

Orangedale, S. C.
Dec. 14, 1860

Dear Miss Darby

I expect you think I have given out ever writing to you and will be surprised when you receive this. I spent one month with sister. Have been home one week. She is with us now. The little boy is growing fast. Is a sweet little fellow and pretty and you know that is something unusual for me to say of a young baby.

I attended the Association[230]   there was a very large congregation Sunday   had better preaching than usual   Dr. Curtis[231] of Limestone   Mr. Bostick[232] of Cheraw   Mr. Prichard[233] of North Carolina delivered some excellent sermons.

We had Mr. Duncan[234] at Mispah last Saturday and Sunday   gave us a fine sermon about the rich young man in the gospel   He is agent for Furman university   I am afraid he didn't get much from our little church. We have had several additions to our church this year, none during our meeting. We have a small Sabbath school   large Bible class when all are there. Mr. James is our teacher. I expect you have heard of the death of Mrs. Billy McCall's[235] son.[236] It was a great loss to her. He was very much liked by all that knew him. She attends church more than she did when we first came down. Has never been to see us yet. Old Mrs. James[237] died last month. I sat up with her two nights before I went to sisters. Was perfectly resigned and waiting the Lord's time   what a happy state to be in the last moment.

William Napier[238] is in from Florida to be married to Jane Bostick.[239] Our pastor is to preach two sundays next year for us. I haven't treated him coldly.[240] Don't hear of his addressing any one. I think he acts as he should do.[241] Has the rheumatism so badly can't preach sometimes. Martha has the asthma frequently. Mrs. Rogers is trying to cure Mary Player of dropsey. The physicians seem as if they can't do it   I called to see her last week   she looks like she was dead now   hasn't the least colour   is low-spirited and has been very cheerful.

What do you think? Rosannah Johnson[242] went to the Association[243] went home with Elizabeth Fountain[244] tuesday night   played the piano until two o'clock and had a babie before day   had her mother[245] and doctor brother with her; sent to Mrs. William Fountain[246] for clothes to put on it. Hannah[247] says she is very glad it happened there for she can never get them to stay with her until it is over.

Sister Mary Ann has moved to her new house. I was there last week. They are well. Andrew has been better this part of the winter than he was last year. If a nice comfortable convenient house will add to ones happiness they have it. She went up to see the Kings before they moved. Found them well. Says Joe has grown and improved very much   puts up her hair   they make a dress a day[248]   get as much as they can do. Cant do anything with the trifling servant they have. Sometimes there are 20 negroes in the kitchen. Told the Patrol about it. I expect they keep them out now. Has no fastening on her doors except a button   has no garden   no milk   very poor cooking   Moll thinks she is a bad manager. Eliza[249] has spent a week with them. Say she has fattened. Is very healthy. Her little girl[250] suckes yet. Is the most active child ever was   loves to go to auntie   always sleeps with Emily.

Robert Edwards has returned   his mind has improved since he got back. Mrs. Hartwell[251] came with them. He is going to sell his land, stock and provision. Have the negroes and place on the Hill left. Lafayette Gandy[252] is going to marry Bettie Smoot[253] and live at the Harlee place near Mrs. Dabbs. Mrs. Baker is coming to spend the winter with Mrs. F.[254] I expect she is tired of the Yankies.

Brother Horace's little girl[255] has had soar throat. I am afraid they cant raise her. Think too much of her. Mrs. Tom Fountain has the eighth daughter.

How do you get along? Do you ever hear Baptist preaching? How many children has the doctor?[256] Do you teach the children?

Mother's health is as good as usual. Has a stiff knee often. Brother Wilds said he had a great notion to surprise me with a wife when I came home, stayed away so long. Virginia and Kate are going to school to Mrs. DuPre. Like it very much. Mother and Sister join me in love to you. Do write soon.

Yours affectionately,

SARAH WILLIAMSON

* * * * *

FOOTNOTES

1 Boykin Witherspoon (1814 — ?), son of John D. and Elizabeth Boykin Witherspoon, married Elizabeth Edwards in 1841 in Darlington District, South Carolina.

2 Elizabeth W. Edwards (1822 — ?), daughter of Peter and Jane Draughon Edwards, was the mother of twelve children.

3 David Rogerson Williams McIver (December 8, 1794 — February 10, 1863), son of John and Mary Ann Williams McIver and nephew of Governor David Rogerson Williams, for whom he was named, married (1) Caroline Wilds, and (2) Martha E. Grant, in 1838. He moved to Carowville, Alabama, in 1843, and to Kingston, Louisiana, in 1856.

4 William S. Frierson (1834 — ?), son of Dr. George P. and Mary A. Scriven Frierson, was born in Charleston. His wife, Flora McIver, was born in Darlington District. They were married in Kingston, Louisiana, where both families had migrated after having lived first in Alabama.

5 Colonel John J. Marshall (1807-1877), son of Adam Marshall, married Maria Hawes in Darlington District, where their sons, Oliver H. and James, were born. The family moved to Montgomery County, Alabama, in 1843, and to Florida, where Mrs. Marshall died in 1852. In 1854, Colonel Marshall and the sons moved on to Louisiana.

6 Jesse Hartwell, son of Jesse Hartwell, Buckland, Massachusetts, went to Charleston in 1822, and moved from there to Society Hill. His grave marker, a tall obelisk, at Mt. Lebanon Cemetery, near Gibsland, Louisiana, states: "Sacred to the memory of Jesse Hartwell, D. D. — born in Buckland, Mass., May 2, 1795; baptized, September 15, 1815; ordained, Providence, R. I., 1821; died in Mt. Lebanon, Bienville Parish, Louisiana, Sept. 16, 1859. This monument was placed over his remains by the board of trustees of Mt. Lebanon University (of which institution he was President at the time of his death) by the Rehoboth Church of which he was pastor, by the students and other friends. He was learned without ostentation, pious without austerity, gentle in disposition, yet uncompromising in principles and in his life most beautifully exemplified the doctrines which he so seriously taught."

7 Margaret F. Hartwell (1810 — November 19, 1880), the wife of Jesse Hartwell, was born in Charleston, South Carolina. She died in Society Hill, but her body was returned to Mt. Lebanon for burial.

8 John Adger Law, (ed.), *Citadel Cadets, The Journal of Cadet Tom Law* (Clinton, 1941), p. 231.

9 Dr. A. R. Vann, his brother Josiah, and a Mr. Byrd went along to investigate conditions in Louisiana. The letters do not reveal the other members of the party.

10 Jemima moved about so often that her friends could not be certain of her whereabouts.

11 Sallie DuPre Bentley, sister to Lewis DuPre, Mary Catlett's brother-in-law, had died, leaving two little daughters, Sallie and Hettie.

12 When Sarah Catlett, mother of Mary and Sarah, made her will in 1838, she left all of her property to her daughters. In the Catlett lot in the Baptist Church-yard, Darlington, are the graves of Reuben, William, Robert, and Kemp Catlett, all of whom died in the 1820's and 1830's. There is no marker for Thomas.

13 Chancellor G. W. Dargan (April 3, 1802 — June 12, 1859) married (1) Mary Adeline Wilson (June 29, 1810 — March 4, 1843). In 1846, he married Mrs. Elizabeth M. Player Wilson, whose grave is not marked in the Dargan lot, Baptist Churchyard, Darlington.

14 Anne Ellison Wilds was the wife of Colonel Samuel Wilds and a cousin to the Misses Williamson.

15 Andrew Hunter, Darlington, married Emilie Bacot.

16 Lewis DuPre, Mary's brother-in-law.

17 Jackson, Mississippi.

18 "Minutes of the Welsh Neck Baptist Church, Society Hill, South Carolina," March 31, 1860.

19 Darlington, South Carolina, *News and Press*, June 11, 1953, p. 13.

20 William E. Dodd, *The Cotton Kingdom* (New Haven, 1919), p. 36.

21 Ulrich Bonnell Phillips, *A History of Transportation in the Eastern Cotton Belt in 1860* (New York, 1908), p. 364.

22 On their return trip, Dr. Vann and Josiah Vann used the Kingsville route; it is assumed that they had gone out the same way.

23 T. J. Sinclair, Personal letter from Manager, School and College Service, Public Relations Department, Association of American Railroads, Washington 6, D. C., to John A. Cawthon, Russellville, Arkansas, January 26, 1953, based on research by Mr. Stephenson of the Public Relations Office and referring to Appleton's *Illustrated Railway and Steam Navigation Guide* for May, 1860, pages 24 and 245-255.

24 *Ibid.*

25 Luther Longino, "Travel: Yesterday, Today and Tomorrow," Minden, Louisiana, *Signal-Tribune*, Historical Edition, Volume 70, Section 2, December 31, 1934.

26 Letter from Mary Ann Catlett, Darlington, South Carolina, to Jemima Darby, Ringgold, Louisiana, May 18, 1860.

27 "Slabtown, Ringgold . . . and Now," Ringgold, Louisiana, *Press News*, Progress Edition, July 28, 1950, p. 8.

28 Amanda Melvina Brinson (November 15, 1832 — May 25, 1890) was the daughter of P. P. and Maria T. Nelson Brinson.

29 Philip Purser Brinson (December 31, 1802 — May 24, 1882) was a son of James Brinson, "the first Baptist preacher who labored in the region between the Ouachita and Dorchete."

30 Maria Theresa Nelson Brinson (December 8, 1793 — December 29, 1878) was the daughter of Major John and Nancy Ware Hunter Nelson of Virginia.

31 A. J. Kolb and Melvina Brinson were married at Sparta, Louisiana, July 5, 1853.

32 A. J. Kolb family chart.

33 In 1954, the basic part of the house, with an accumulation of renovations essential to upkeep for low-income renters, was still standing on its original site on a busy street in the town. In 1918, Edwin Kirtley Kolb and James A. Cawthon, son and grandson of Dr. Kolb, visited their birthplace and explained the various features of the house, which at that time was in an excellent state of repair and unoccupied, to the writer, who was eleven years old. By 1964, the house had been completely demolished.

34 Walter Prichard, (ed.), "A Tourist's Description of Louisiana in 1860," *Louisiana Historical Quarterly*, XXI, Number 4 (October, 1938), p. 1188.

35 "Slabtown, Ringgold . . . and Now," p. 8.

36 William E. Paxton, *A History of the Baptists of Louisiana* (St. Louis, 1888), p. 312.

37 *Ibid.*, p. 321.

38 Thomas Haywood Kolb (June 4, 1857 — October 11, 1862).

39 Zachariah Thomas (March 28, 1813 — May 1, 1879), a Baptist preacher, bought land in Township 16, Range 9, near Ringgold, in Bienville Parish, about 1850.

40 *Biographical and Historical Memoirs of Northwest Louisiana* (Chicago, 1890), p. 161.

41 Joseph Dabney Cawthon (September 21, 1825 — October 4, 1905), son of Ashley Claiborne and Catherine McDuffie Cawthon, married (1) Susan Newsom, and (2) Sallie Jones, and is buried at Summer Grove, Caddo Parish, Louisiana.

42 James Bryant Thomas (August 9, 1831 — September 17, 1862), who married Telitha Ann Missouri Nix (February 25, 1838 — May 15, 1862), was killed in the Battle of Sharpsburg, Virginia.

43 Benjamin Franklin Allums (December 24, 1844 — June 20, 1928), son of Floyd Allums, a native of Alabama, married Margaret Lucy Conley (August 20, 1847 — November 26, 1906), daughter of Thomas Conley, of Bienville Parish. Both Mr. and Mrs. Allums are buried in Springhill Baptist Cemetery, Bienville Parish, Louisiana.

44 William McDuffie Cawthon, son of Ashley Claiborne and Catherine McDuffie Cawthon, never married.

45 John Arthur Tooke (August 11, 1815 — January 12, 1888), son of John and Mary (Polly) Jones Tooke, married Anna Nixon Vickers, and is buried at the Tooke family cemetery, near Ringgold, Louisiana.

46 E. W. Davis (May 1, 1831 — July 7, 1899) and his wife, E. B. Davis (May 24, 1837 — September 8, 1894), are buried at Providence Cemetery, Ringgold, Louisiana.

47 George W. Cawthon (1832-1887), son of Ashley Claiborne and Catherine McDuffie Cawthon, married Emily Pior and is buried at Springville Cemetery, Coushatta, Louisiana.

48 "Slabtown, Ringgold . . . and Now," p. 8.

[49] Lilla McClure, "Old Military Road Once Vital to U. S. Defense," *Shreveport Times*, May 3, 1953, p. 6-B.

[50] Prichard, "A Tourist's Description of Louisiana in 1860," *Louisiana Historical Quarterly*, XXI, Number 4, p. 1188.

[51] Work Projects Administration, *Louisiana: A Guide to the State* (New York, 1941), p. 633. "Today nothing remains of the old town, and prickly pears grow in the deep white sand."

[52] Roy T. Sessums, *Bienville Parish: Resources and Facilities* (Baton Rouge, 1952), p. 14. "In 1836, settlers arrived in the vicinity of Mt. Lebanon from the southern sea-board states. Many were from South Carolina.... Many were of the Baptist denomination. . . . In 1853, Mount Lebanon University was founded, receiving endowment from the Baptists of Louisiana and other states."

[53] Prichard, "A Tourist's Description of Louisiana in 1860," pp. 1188-1189.

[54] *Biographical and Historical Memoirs*, pp. 153-155.

[55] Ashley Claiborne Cawthon was the grandfather of James Ashley Cawthon, who was to marry Ella Kolb.

[56] K. P. McDaniel (February 20, 1811 — April 30, 1865) and his wife, Susan W. (August 29, 1819 — March 29, 1880), are buried at Mount Lebanon Cemetery, Louisiana.

[57] Simeon Theus (1797 — March 12, 1868) and his wife, Mary Ann (1814 — April 2, 1886), are buried at Mount Lebanon, Louisiana.

[58] John Arthur Tooke was the father of Henry Jones Tooke, who was to marry Maria Elizabeth Kolb.

[59] James Jackson Vickers (September 9, 1806 — June 22, 1866) was the father of Margaret Hunter Vickers, first wife of Ashley Thomas Cawthon, and mother of James Ashley Cawthon.

[60] John L. Vickers, a brother to James Jackson Vickers, married Jane Thomas.

[61] Ida G. Tooke, Letter from Koran, Louisiana, to John A. Cawthon, Baton Rouge, Louisiana, November 14, 1934, reporting that her mother, Maria Elizabeth Kolb Tooke, daughter of Dr. A. J. and Melvina Brinson Kolb, "says that James Brinson was our ancestor, my great-grandfather, your great-great-grandfather."

[62] Paxton, *A History of the Baptists of Louisiana*, p. 515.

[63] John Nelson (March 30, 1753 — July 20, 1819) married Nancy Ware Hunter (July 19, 1754 — January 11, 1813).

[64] Obituary from Sparta, Louisiana, *Rural Times*, May 24, 1882.

[65] J. T. McFarland, Letter from Mansfield, Louisiana, to John A. Cawthon, Russellville, Arkansas, October 17, 1952.

[66] *Ibid.*

[67] Ida G. Tooke, Letter from Ringgold, Louisiana, to John A. Cawthon, Russellville, Arkansas, December 7, 1952.

68 Edwin Kirtley Kolb was named for E. N. Kirtley, teacher and preacher at the Baptist Church, Ringgold, when the baby was born.

69 Mary Catlett was probably not aware of the route which Jemima had taken. There was never a possibility of her going through New Orleans. As a matter of fact, Miss Catlett admits that she probably forgot to give Miss Darby her niece's address.

70 The *last day* here refers to the last day of Jemima's visit with the Catletts, not to her last day in South Carolina.

71 Miss Catlett enjoyed making jabs at the frontier conditions in Louisiana.

72 Dr. Alexander James Kolb (May 13, 1820 — May 6, 1886) was Miss Darby's nephew.

73 A corruption of "Te Deum," Miss Catlett's way of saying "Thankfulness."

74 Miss Catlett referred to the agitation in the South over the slavery question, which was particularly significant to people of South Carolina where the Democratic National Convention, meeting at Charleston on April 23, had witnessed the withdrawal of Southern delegates who had reconvened in Richmond on May 1. Church people were deeply embroiled, regardless of the stand that they took on the issue.

75 There was a community meeting house, but no Baptist church building, in Ringgold in 1860. While the Ringgold Baptist Church had been organized and admitted to the Red River Association in 1854, the church was without a pastor in 1860. Baptists, Methodists, and Presbyterians used the lower floor of the combination church-lodge hall-school building for their Sunday School and church services. Paxton, *A History of the Baptists of Louisiana*, pp. 312 and 321.

76 Jemima had begun her journey to Louisiana from the home of T. E. Howle, of Leavensworth.

77 Lewis DuPre, Baptist minister, and brother-in-law to Mary Ann Catlett.

78 Limestone was founded in 1845, at Gaffney, South Carolina, according to the Charlotte *Observer* of November 16, 1952.

79 Margaret Lydia Keith Dargan (1844-1911) was the daughter of the prominent Baptist minister, J. O. B. Dargan, and his wife, Jane Lide Dargan.

80 Lavinia McIver (September 26, 1845 — September 12, 1929), daughter of Allen E. and Sallie Witherspoon Ervin McIver, was the second wife of William Caleb Coker.

81 Elizabeth Pugh Dargan (1842-1883) was the daughter of Mr. and Mrs. J. O. B. Dargan.

82 John Orr Beasley Dargan.

83 Ellen Flinn, daughter of Dr. and Mrs. Thomas J. Flinn, married Augustus B. Lamb, of Charleston, South Carolina, in 1860.

84 George Lawrence Williamson (August 25, 1818 — February 18, 1871) was the second son of Thomas and Sarah Wilds Williamson.

85 Virginia Ella Williamson, oldest child of George L. and Catherine Williams Williamson, was almost thirteen years old.

86 Katharine Caroline Williamson, daughter of George L. and Catherine Williams Williamson, was ten years old.

87 Catherine Williams (December 26, 1822 — October 8, 1859), who had married George Williamson in 1846, was a sister to James A. Williams, who had married Caroline Williamson, George's sister.

88 Mary Ann Williamson Charles (August 28, 1829 — February 17, 1889), wife of Andrew Charles, was a sister to George Williamson, and therefore an aunt to Virginia and Kate.

89 Andrew Charles (July 10, 1827 — February 15, 1891) was the son of Colonel Edgar W. and Sarah Lide Charles.

90 The Thomas Williamson family.

91 Ringgold, Louisiana, a place upon which the Catletts and the DuPres did not place great value.

92 J. Josey was a Baptist minister in the Pee Dee region.

93 This is a strange statement. Generally, Mr. Bealer was admired and respected. Yet, Miss Catlett was undoubtedly a nonconformist.

94 The Black Creek Baptist Church.

95 The name Howle was pronounced *owl.*

96 Robert G. Edwards, son of Peter Kolb and Jane Draughon Edwards, and grandson of Joshua and Ann James Kolb Edwards, married Ellen Hartwell, daughter of Jesse Hartwell, prominent Baptist minister. After preaching in the Pee Dee section, Dr. Hartwell took an active part in establishing both Furman and Howard Universities. He was a leader in the movement to organize the Southern Baptist Convention and was one of its first secretaries. In 1857, he became president of Mt. Lebanon University, Mount Lebanon, Louisiana, and died there on September 16, 1859. Paxton, *A History of the Baptists of Louisiana,* p. 512.

97 Boykin Witherspoon (1814 — ?) married Elizabeth Edwards (1822 — ?), Robert's sister.

98 William, T. E., and Lawrence Keith, sons of Thomas E. and Elizabeth Vann Howle.

99 Maggie J. Howle (April 24, 1859 — November 13, 1937) married her cousin, Josiah T. Vann, Jr., March 4, 1878. She is buried in Troy, Alabama.

100 Edwin C. Dargan, *Harmony Hall* (Columbia, 1912), p. 6.

101 *Ibid.*

102 *Ibid.,* p. 9.

103 John Gandy was the youngest brother of Abel Gandy, who inherited the home place.

104 "Black Creek Church Book, A. D. 1798," October 4, 1856, and December 6, 1856, p. 187.

105 *Ibid.,* p. 196.

106 *Ibid.,* p. 190.

107 Dargan, *Harmony Hall,* p. 15.

108 *Minutes of Welsh Neck Association,* 1832-1871 (Greenville).

109 In the group were Mrs. William Swinton, wife of a lumber factor in Charleston; Mrs. Anna Nettles DeLorme, cousin of Anna Maria Nettles; Anna Maria Nettles, daughter of General J. B. Nettles, Darlington; and Mrs. Howle.

110 Law, *Citadel Cadets, The Journal of Cadet Tom Law,* p. 210. Ralph Nesbit, from Georgetown, was a cadet at The Citadel.

111 A. Linton Williams was the son of David and Elizabeth Williams and brother of James A. Williams.

112 Linton Williams married (1) Martha E._____, (December 15, 1823 — September 2, 1851), and (2) Martha Harriet Fort (October 29, 1829 — November 20, 1858), daughter of Josiah and Ann E. Fort.

113 Linton Williams's third wife was not Jane Fort, Martha Harriet Fort's sister; he married Mary A. Norwood, daughter of Joseph and Sarah McIntosh Norwood.

114 Mrs. James B. Crane was the wife of the doctor who had come to Darlington from Georgia in 1859.

115 Mary Deborah Ferguson Chambers, daughter of Alexander and Elizabeth C. Williams Ferguson, was the wife of Benjamin Wesley Chambers. The baby's name was Mary T. Chambers, born May 14, 1860.

116 Caroline Williamson Williams, daughter of Thomas and Sarah Wilds Williamson, was the wife of James A. Williams.

117 Mary Vann Dorrity, daughter of Mills and Clementina Vann.

118 Dr. S. H. Pressley, whose first wife was Jane Edwards, Robert's sister.

119 Ann James McIver (March 24, 1785 — July 2, 1860), who never married, was the oldest daughter of Evander and Sarah Kolb McIver.

120 Eliza McIver Griffin (December 3, 1803 — November 10, 1876), youngest daughter of Evander and Sarah Kolb McIver, was the wife of Thomas Griffin.

121 Sallie Griffin (October 9, 1828 — June 1, 1894) was the daughter of Thomas and Eliza McIver Griffin.

122 Mrs. Sarah Rachel Holloway Coker, the widow of Thomas Coker and niece of Mrs. Griffin, was Sallie's first cousin.

123 Lewis M. Coker (October 15, 1819 — February 26, 1889) was a Society Hill merchant.

124 George B. Bealer, pastor of the Baptist Church at Darlington, married (1) Lissie Bacot, who died in 1857, and (2) Emily Winkler, Charleston.

125 Limestone was a girls' school, founded by the Baptists in 1845, at Gaffney, South Carolina.

126 Elizabeth Pugh Dargan (1842-1883) was the daughter of J. O. B. Dargan.

127 Dargan, *Harmony Hall,* p. 35.

128 Deborah S. Williams Dove Baker (December 28, 1807 — February 5, 1865), daughter of David Williams, married (1) James Dove, and (2) Baker.

129 "Black Creek Church Book, A. D. 1798," November 1, 1856, p. 178.

130 *Ibid.,* March 5, 1859, p. 188.

131 Sarah L. Wilds Williamson (August 7, 1793 — March 2, 1871).

132 Samuel Wilds (February 13, 1751 — April 24, 1803).

133 Nancy Ann Lide Wilds (June 16, 1765 — October 21, 1814).

134 Thomas Williamson (January 20, 1785 — December 27, 1858) was the son of Thomas Williamson.

135 Robert Lide (May 17, 1731 — March 12, 1802), Major of the Militia of the Revolution; Deacon, Baptist Church.

136 Sarah Kolb Lide (September 26, 1736 — September 24, 1789), second wife of Robert Lide.

137 Samuel Thomas Wilds Williamson (November 6, 1811 — April 5, 1877) married Sarah Terrel, of Marlboro.

138 George Lawrence Williamson (August 25, 1818 — February 18, 1871) married Catherine Williams, sister of James A. Williams, who married Caroline Williamson, in 1846.

139 Sarah Wilds Williamson (March 5, 1821 — June 14, 1865) never married.

140 Caroline Matilda Williamson (December 19, 1822 — August 10, 1863) married James A. Williams.

141 Ann Elizabeth, Mary Margaret, and Robert Lide Williamson all died young.

142 Joseph Wilds Williamson (June 16, 1825 — May 6, 1864) never married.

143 Horace Williamson (February 20, 1827 — July 17, 1895) married Theodosia Green, of Sumter County.

144 Mary Ann Williamson (August 28, 1829 — February 17, 1889) married Andrew Charles.

145 Jane Valinda Williamson (August 4, 1836 — May 26, 1894) married Thomas Wallace.

146 Mary Williamson married Charles Brown and moved to Texas. They had no children.

147 Edwin Pembroke Williamson (? — 1917) never married.

148 Catherine Williams Williamson (December 26, 1822 — October 8, 1859).

149 Thomas W. Williamson (October 11, 1848 — November 22, 1910) married Jennie Mary Wallace.

150 Virginia Ella (August 25, 1847 — October 8, 1909) and Katharine Caroline Williamson (November 10, 1849 — May 12, 1909) never married.

151 Theodosia Green Williamson (April 8, 1857 — July 12, 1946) married John J. Dargan (October 10, 1848 — March 8, 1925).

152 Sarah Williamson lived with her mother and brother at Orangedale, near Florence, where Carrie had visited.

153 Dr. James B. Crane, Darlington, who moved from Georgia in 1859, was elected an elder in the Presbyterian Church in 1865. He later moved to Searcy, Arkansas.

154 Robert Napier (February 21, 1806 — April 19, 1891), pastor at Mispah, was a widower. Shortly after becoming pastor at Mispah in 1834, he married Elizabeth B. Lane, daughter of T. and Martha Lane. Mrs. Napier (1816-1858) left a son, William, and two daughters, Martha and Sarah.

155 Samuel B. Wilkins, Baptist minister, aged fifty-eight, had been a widower since 1849.

156 Mary Norwood, daughter of Joseph and Sarah McIntosh Norwood, became the third wife of A. Linton Williams.

157 Mary T. Chambers (May 14, 1860 — October 9, 1862) was the new baby.

158 Carma Parnell (October 4, 1804 — March 24, 1894) lived to be ninety. According to the "Minutes of the Welsh Neck Baptist Church, Society Hill, South Carolina," March 24, 1894, "Our aged brother Mr. Carmel Parnell died today."

159 Church meetings for transacting matters of business were held on Saturdays.

160 The nearest active Baptist Church was at Mount Lebanon, 28 miles from Ringgold.

161 Sunday School.

162 At the time, Dr. Kolb's interest in the Baptist Church was lukewarm; Miss Mell was a consistent Baptist.

163 Between the years 1860 and 1863, Mr. Lewis DuPre was pastor at High Hill Church, between Darlington and Timmonsville.

164 Mary Ann Lucas, aged thirty-three, was the wife of George Washington Lucas, an overseer on a plantation.

165 Mary Ann Williamson had married Andrew Charles.

166 Jane Rogers Williamson (September 25, 1788 — February 7, 1867), widow of Bright Williamson.

167 Thomas S. Wallace (December 6, 1828 — February 20, 1896) was Jane Williamson's husband.

168 Mary Williamson married Charles Brown and moved to Cleburne, Texas.

169 Julia Terrel Wilds (June 27, 1813 — October 21, 1876) was the wife of Peter Wilds, brother to Carrie's mother.

170 Sallie Williamson Wilds (September 27, 1845 — June 19, 1892) was the invalid daughter of Peter and Julia Wilds.

171 Julia Elizabeth Wilds (June 24, 1839 — January 11, 1915) and Mollie D. Wilds (November 23, 1841 — March 24, 1890) were the unmarried daughters of Peter and Julia Wilds.

172 Even though the year was 1860, this was the only reference that Carrie made to the grave problem of slavery in South Carolina.

173 Colonel Alonzo Dargan, son of Julius Alfred and Martha Woods Dargan, married Jennie Quigby in 1860. He was killed at Petersburg while leading his regiment.

174 Julia Porcher (February 25, 1837 — April 6, 1873) married Thomas Ashley in 1860.

175 Joseph Wilds Williamson was thirty-five years old.

176 Eliza Evans, Mary Darby's old friend, had gone for a visit to her brother's home in Cooper's Well, Mississippi.

177 The men who went to Louisiana with Miss Darby's party — Dr. A. R. and Josiah Vann, and Mr. Byrd.

178 Mary Lucas Parrott was a member of the Black Creek Church from September 5, 1856, when she was baptized, until October 17, 1869, when she requested a letter of dismissal to unite with the Darlington Church.

179 Samuel Dabbs, son of Joseph and Hannah Kolb Dabbs, married Sarah L. Grove.

180 Alexander Lide, son of Thomas and Elizabeth Sparks Lide, moved to Mississippi in 1860.

181 Mary Wilson Player, aged twenty-four, was at the home of her mother, Sarah Witherspoon Wilson, Darlington.

182 Dargan, *Harmony Hall*, p. 33.

183 Phil. 1:1.

184 "Black Creek Church Book, A. D. 1798," June 30, 1860, p. 199. "T. E. Howle and J. A. Williams were elected to serve as deacons."

185 Miss Darby had heard, through Mrs. Williams, that Mr. Napier had called on Sarah Williamson and that she was teased about him.

186 Martha Napier (April 23, 1840 — September 2, 1893) was the daughter of Pastor Robert Napier. She was baptized at Mispah in September, 1852.

187 Mrs. Williamson looked with favor upon the attention which Mr. Napier showed Miss Sarah after his wife's death.

188 Mispah was the name of the church near Florence for which Mr. Napier served as pastor.

189 "Black Creek Church Book, A. D. 1798," September 1, 1860, p. 201. "Doors of the church were opened for new members. Mrs. Sarah Adams and two daughters, Miss Mary and Amanda came forward and were received for baptism." September 9, 1860, p. 202. "Mr. Amasa Adams received the ordinance of baptism."

190 Linton and Jim Williams had persuaded Mr. and Mrs. Adams to go to church.

191 Abel Gandy, son of Booker and Delilah Gandy, married Lavinia Johnson.

192 Mr. Bealer was the pastor at Darlington, but came out to Black Creek to preach at the ordination of the new deacons.

193 R. F. Whilden, Baptist minister from Charleston, came to participate in the service.

194 P. E. Burroughs, *Honoring the Deaconship* (Nashville, 1929), p. 24. "Combining the New Testament references to the deaconship we have full references as to the character of the men who fill the office. Deacons were to be business men . . . . These things were assumed. They were passed without mention. A first and chief concern was felt as to their spiritual and moral qualifications. . . . The Holy Spirit has honored the deaconship by imposing high standards for those who are to fill the office. These standards embody the highest ideals of Christian character. They are so high and so exacting that men must pause in reverence as they contemplate them."

195 As the merchant at Leavensworth, T. E. Howle had agreed to order the communion set for the committee.

196 Cooper's Well, Mississippi, was a small village about 15 miles southwest of Jackson.

197 Springville was the region east of Black Creek; Leavensworth was on the west side of Black Creek.

198 Ann James McIver (March 24, 1785 — July 2, 1860), daughter of Evander and Sarah Kolb McIver, was called "Aunt Nancy" by all her relatives and friends. She was Eliza Evans's own aunt, Eliza's mother having been Catherine McIver, also a daughter of Evander and Sarah Kolb McIver.

199 Rachel Holloway Coker was also Aunt Nancy's niece. After the early death of Rachel's mother, Rachel McIver Holloway, the child had gone to live with her aunts. She spent the greater part of her time with Aunt Nancy. In 1843, Rachel Holloway married Thomas Coker, who died in 1846. Rachel lived with Caleb Coker's family until she moved into Dr. Wilson's house in Society Hill in 1860.

200 Jane Lide Coker Wilson, *Memories of Society Hill* (Pee Dee Historical

Society, 1909-1910), p. 8. "In January, 1860, we moved from our home in Society Hill to Hartsville."

[201] Dr. Peter Griffin, son of Thomas and Eliza Griffin, was Sallie's brother and a nephew to Aunt Nancy McIver. After graduating from college and medical school, Peter Griffin continued his study of medicine in Paris, France, and came back to practice in Society Hill.

[202] Mary Ann Lucas was the wife of George Washington Lucas.

[203] The Lucas family had twin daughters, M. J. and S. M., aged nine.

[204] Robert G. Edwards had gone to Louisiana earlier in the year.

[205] Charlotte Kirven, who was granted assistance by the Society Hill Church, made her home with the Edwards family as long as any of its members were in Society Hill.

[206] Lizzie was Miss Darby's cousin, Mrs. Thomas E. Howle, a neighbor to Mrs. Williams.

[207] Sarah L. Grove, who married Samuel Dabbs, was the mother of Quincy Dabbs. She was a daughter-in-law of Joseph and Hannah Kolb Dabbs.

[208] Ladson and Mary Vann Dorrity's son was born August 31, 1860.

[209] James Leonidas Williams was born November 1, 1860.

[210] Mrs. Howle was the wife of Jim's good friend and fellow deacon, Tom Howle.

[211] Mary Ann Williamson Charles was Carrie's youngest sister.

[212] Black Creek Church entertained the Welsh Neck Association, November 10-13, 1860.

[213] Dr. Thomas J. Flinn, Darlington physician, had attended Mrs. Williams.

[214] Society Hill was frequently called "The Hill."

[215] Emily King was about twenty years old.

[216] Josephine King was the youngest of the King sisters.

[217] Jeannette McKarrley Sparks (1791-1871), wife of Alexander Sparks, was the mother of Mrs. Thomas Lide.

[218] Thomas P. Lide (June 10, 1810 — July 23, 1882) married Elizabeth Sparks.

[219] Mary Ann Lucas was the wife of G. W. Lucas, plantation overseer.

[220] The oldest son of Thomas and Jane Williamson Wallace, Carrie's niece, was Joseph Wilds Wallace.

[221] T. W. Hart, *Robert Sanders* (New York, 1897), p. 60.

[222] Buried at Lowther's Hill were Mary Ann Williamson Charles's ancestors, the Lides and Wildses. Her father, mother, brothers, sisters, nieces, nephews, husband, and she were eventually buried there.

223 "Church Book, Records, 1756-78, Cashaway Neck Pee Dee South Carolina," p. 1. "The church at Cashaway Neck on Great Pee Dee River was constituted by the Rev. John Stephens, the Rev. Mr. John Brown, the Rev. Mr. Joshua Edwards on the 28th day of September Ano:Domm: 1756 consisting of 14 members — male and female."

224 Mary Ann Williamson Charles, Will of January 5, 1889. State of South Carolina, Darlington County. Probated May 18, 1895. "I give and devise all my land, houses and real estate consisting of the Stony Hill place to Thomas W. Williamson in trust for the following purposes to wit: To hold the same for the sole use of my husband, Andrew B. Charles and my niece, Sallie Charles Williams during their joint lives and then for use of survivor during his or her life and after the death of both to convey the said land to the child or children of said niece ..."

225 Robert Ervin Coker, "Springville: A Summer Village of Old Darlington District," *South Carolina Historical Magazine*, LIII, Number 4 (October, 1952), p. 207. "Hugh Lide Charles married Caroline Bacot. Misses Leslie and Lalla Charles, the daughters of Maj. Hugh and Caroline (Bacot) Charles, lived long in the old Darlington home of Hugh Charles." Hugh Lide Charles (March 18, 1830 — June 20, 1911) was a brother to Andrew Charles.

226 Helen Kohn Henning, *William Harrison Scarborough, Portraitist and Miniaturist: A Parade of the Living Past* (Columbia, 1937), p. 6.

227 Dargan, *Harmony Hall*, p. 103.

228 Beulah Walden Coggeshall, Letter from Darlington, South Carolina, to John A. Cawthon, Russellville, Arkansas, October 22, 1952. "Nina Coggeshall (almost ninety — born November, 1862) remembers some of the 'girls' asking Cousin Mary Ann 'Why' she married Andrew Charles and her reply — 'For the *name*, child, for the name' — Now whether name meant 'Mrs' or Charles is anybody's guess." Familiarity with the ready wit revealed by Mary Ann Williamson Charles in her many letters might offer another explanation for her reply: "Ask an impertinent question, get an impertinent answer!"

229 "Minutes of the Welsh Neck Baptist Church, Society Hill, South Carolina," December 3, 1859.

230 Welsh Neck Association met at Black Creek, November 10-13, 1860.

231 Thomas Curtis, D.D., was principal at Limestone College, Gaffney, South Carolina.

232 James M. Bostick married (1) Helen (1837-1867), and (2) Anna McIver (1828-1869), daughters of Alexander and Mary Hanford McIver.

233 Dr. T. H. Prichard.

234 Robert Norman Daniel, *Furman University, A History* (Greenville, 1951), p. 47. "James C. Furman, J. Culpepper, R. Furman and H. D. Duncan, were made agents to solicit contributions."

235 Eliza Miller Allsbrook McCall was the widow of William McCall.

236 William Thomas McCall (February 25, 1839 — July 31, 1860) killed himself accidentally.

237 Among the prominent citizens of the Mispah community were several branches of the James family.

238 William Napier was the son of the Mispah pastor, Robert Napier. He was baptized at Mispah in August, 1851. Apparently he had gone to Florida to be with his Lane relatives there.

239 Jane was the daughter of Eli M. Bostick of the Mispah community.

240 Miss Darby had been chiding Miss Sarah for having treated the pastor coldly, using as a basis for her reprimand the news which Carrie Williams had written.

241 Mr. Napier went to Mispah as pastor in 1834 and remained there for forty-five years.

242 Rose Culpepper Johnson was the daughter of the Reverend and Mrs. John Culpepper.

243 The Association met at Black Creek in November, 1860.

244 Sue Flinn James, "His Springville," *Darlington County Historical Records and Papers, 1938-1944*, p. 63. "Two or three hundred feet farther on the Springville thoroughfare was the residence of the Misses Elizabeth, Sarah, Mary and Fannie Fountain, sisters of Mrs. Hart, for whom John Lide Hart had very graciously built a home."

245 Rose Johnson's mother was the wife of the minister, Mr. John Culpepper.

246 Mrs. William Fountain was the wife of a brother to the Misses Fountain.

247 Hannah Fountain Hart, wife of John Lide Hart, and sister to the Misses Fountain, lived in the house next to her unmarried sisters.

248 The Misses King were seamstresses.

249 Eliza King (June 15, 1831 — September 3, 1869) had married A. P. LaCoste, her sister's widower, and was living in Cheraw.

250 Florence LaCoste was less than a year old.

251 Margaret F. Hartwell was the widow of Jesse Hartwell, Baptist minister who died while serving as president of Mount Lebanon University, Louisiana, shortly before Jemima reached Louisiana.

252 Lafayette Gandy was the son of Abel Gandy.

253 Elizabeth Smoot was the daughter of Thomas W. and Sarah Thomas Smoot.

254 Elizabeth Williams Ferguson (January 16, 1807 — May 6, 1885) was a sister to Mrs. Baker.

255 Theodosia Green Williamson (April 8, 1857 — July 12, 1946) was the daughter of Horace and Theodosia Green Williamson.

256 There were three Kolb children at the time: Ella Caroline, aged five years; Thomas Haywood, three years; and Maria Elizabeth, eighteen months.

The War 1860-1865

PART I

"The event was hastened by a real
difference in character between the
people in the north and those in the
south, and this difference made them
dislike each other."

James Wood Davidson, *School History of
South Carolina* (Columbia, 1894), p. 240.

The Ordinance of Secession was adopted by the South Carolina Convention on December 20, 1860. Bettie Howle, writing to her Cousin Jemima on December 27, assumed that the news had already reached Louisiana and hoped that Louisiana would "come out and let old Lincon see that they will not be governed by him and his northern *Fanaticism.*" J. O. B. Dargan, pastor at Black Baptist Church, was "preaching political sermons every Sunday" and everybody seemed "to be warm in the Cause." If Mrs. Howle knew that United States troops, under the command of Major R. Anderson, had been transferred from Fort Moultrie to Fort Sumter on December 26, she did not refer to that fact. Certainly she had no way of knowing that Castle Pinckney and Fort Moultrie had been seized by state troops that very day.

War had not touched the private lives of Miss Darby's South Carolina relatives. At the end of 1860, Mrs. Howle was more concerned with the recent Association at Black Creek Church, with Rose Culpepper Johnson's baby, and with neighborhood gossip than she was with the problems of secession.

The first letter to be written after the secession of South Carolina was mailed at Leavensworth.

Mrs. Thomas E. Howle, Leavensworth, South Carolina, to Jemima Darby, Ringgold, Louisiana.

Leavensworth, So Ca.,
December 27, 1860

Dear Cousin Jemima

Your letter came to hand a few weeks ago, and I must say that it has been a much longer time unanswered than I intended when it was received, but important business has so occupied my time that I could not find time to drop you a line, and I know that you will excuse me for you know that I have my hands full of *children*. In the first place the Association[1] coming on hurried me very much to try to get a few garments made for the children and get the house *in order* but I felt fully paid for my trouble for I enjoyed it very much. Everything seemed to get on very smoothly. We had a very pleasant crowd of twenty-five and thirty all the time.

Mr. Culpepper[2] and wife and Rose[3] stayed with us and seemed to enjoy it very much and on Tuesday night (the last night of the meeting) Rose and her mother went home with Lizzie Fountain[4] to spend the night, and there she gave *birth* to a *daughter*. Now don't you think that is more than you ever heard of. Ladies going to the Association and having *babies*. Well I am truly thankful that it didn't happen at my house. The old bachelor[5] says that will do for him to talk about as he dont believe in ladies attending Associations. Well we had a very pleasant meeting. It was very largely attended and every person seemed to enjoy themselves. The next Association is to be held with the Society Hill Church.

You wished to know something about Robert Edwards' circumstances. The impression here now is that he will save all of his negroes independent of his debts. They are back here now[6] and pretty much the same as when they went off. They will hire out their negroes for the next year, and remain at the same place. They are greatly missed at Society Hill. This church is almost broken up without them.

The Union meeting commences there[7] today, but it is so very cold that they will have a very small congregation.

Christmas holidays are just over. I am truly glad of it for the white folks have had a dry time of it but I guess the darkies kept up the times. There have been several weddings in the neighborhood for the last two or three weeks. Lu Frazier married a Sumter man and left last week, and Mrs. Tedder's third daughter and that Mr. Hogg married last week. They had quite a *big party*. Jim DeLome[8] was to be married this week to a lady in N Carolina. Mary Wilson[9] is to be married very soon to a Sumter gentleman. It seems as if the people have got in a marrying notion about Christmas time. There has been several other marriages among the poorer class of people and some the very lowest.[10] It really looks like starvation. Well I believe that is all the news.

Old Grandmother Howle[11] died last night and is to be buried at Black Creek church. Cousin Mary[12] and family are getting on as *usual*. She lost another baby about a month ago. It seemed to go the same way that her other baby died at just one month. Lizzie[13] is nearly grown and not going to school but we think that there will be a school in the neighborhood next year and we will all send. My boys are growing very fast and little *sis* is a very smart little girl. She talks and seems to understand everything that is said to her.

Well, Cousin Jemima, how do you get along in all this Political excitement? You have seen that our state has ceseded and I do hope that your state and all the southern states will come out and let old Lincon see that they will not be governed by him and his northern *Fanaticism*. Mr. Dargan is preaching political sermons every Sunday and everybody seems to be warm in the Cause. I must close. All join me in love to you.

LIZZIE H.

* * * * *

Important events happened in South Carolina during the early weeks of 1861. On December 30, 1860, the United States Arsenal at Charleston was seized by state troops; a few days later, Fort Johnson was seized. Friends and relatives of Jemima Darby who went into the army belonged to one of the three companies which became part of the Eighth Regiment, a distinctive Pee Dee organization. Among the first of the companies to be mobilized was the Darlington Riflemen, which Coker described:

Early in the year 1861 . . . there were in Darlington District, two such volunteer companies besides the eight or ten of regular militia. The volunteer companies existing at that time were, in order of seniority, first: the Darlington Riflemen, under Capt. A. J. Hoole; second, the Darlington Guards, under Capt. F. F. Warley; third, the Hartsville Light Artillery. The first is the only one that comes within the scope of this sketch.

The Darlington Riflemen had been in existence for many years. It was made up of citizens living mostly in the Swift Creek section, who were riflemen in fact as well as in name — could shoot a squirrel through the eye or bring down a wild turkey or any other game with the old-fashioned long-barreled rifles which were much in favor as sporting guns in that day.

They drilled in the skirmish and rifle drill of the old tactics, hardly known to military men of the present day, but one of the most interesting features in the general musters which were held annually at a point near the court house.

The third company in order of seniority in the Darlington companies of the Eighth Regiment was the "Darlington Grays," under Capt. William H. Evans. The company was organized especially for the war, and was composed of active and intelligent young men, who realizing the gravity of the situation, responded to the call of the State for volunteers. They were for the most part residents of the northern part of the county — from Society Hill to Lynches Creek and the surrounding country — with a small number from near the court house. The first meeting of the organization was held at the old Camp Marion muster ground, near Society Hill, when officers were agreed upon and measures taken to complete the enrollment to the number of about 90 men. At a second meeting, held at the Elior Old Field, near Mount Elon, a full company was present and organization completed. Officers: Capt. W. H. Evans, First Lieutenant, Thomas E. Howle, Second Lieutenants John J. McIver and J. W. Ferguson, Orderly Sergeant, John K. McIver. The Company was designated as Company "F" of the 8th Regiment.[14]

The departure of the Darlington Guards, one of the companies which was quickly mobilized to see immediate action, has been described also:

This company was composed of the flower and chivalry of the land; brave, patriotic and true to principle, they were indeed a corps the State might well be proud of. Anticipating the action of the Convention, Capt. Frederick Warley tendered his services and that of his Company to Governor of the State, F. W. Pickens, even before the Ordinance was passed. The call, however, was soon made and the summons reached Capt. Warley by telegraph at 9 o'clock on the morning of the second of January, 1861.

The members of the Company being scattered throughout the County, it required no small amount of labor and energy to notify them all in time to reach the depot at 9 o'clock AM, the following day, prepared to take the train for Charleston; nevertheless, they were on hand at the proper time. . . . Notwithstanding the short notice, every man was at his post.

Rallying around the beautiful flag — which we all so well remember, was presented by the patriotic ladies of Darlington, through J. A. Dargan, it was received by Capt. Warley, who, in turn committed it to the keeping of the Color Bearer, Sergt. E. B. Brunson, charging him to protect and defend it with his life — they boarded the train for the front. . . .

Farewells were said. Mothers, with their faces bathed in tears, imprinted the last kisses, perhaps, upon their Benjamins, and bade them go forth in discharge of their duty.

Arriving in Charleston in the forenoon of the same day, the Darlington Guards was the first Company to reach the city.[15]

The first expedition for the relief of Fort Sumter sailed from New York harbor on January 5, and the steamship *Star of the West* was fired upon by state troops on January 9. The surrender of Fort Sumter was demanded of Major Anderson by Governor Pickens, and refused, on January 11.

Miss Darby's first letter from South Carolina in 1861 came from Mary A. Catlett, who had not written during the latter part of 1860 because she had been to the springs in Virginia for her health. The political situation was dismissed on the basis of Miss Darby's unquestioned familiarity with national affairs through the press.

But the reality of the War had come home to Darlington. The Baptist minister, Mr. Bealer, talked of going to war as a chaplain, if not as a common soldier. Many Darlington boys, including Quincy Dabbs, had already gone to Sullivan's Island.

Mary Ann Catlett, Darlington, South Carolina, to Jemima Darby, Ringgold, Louisiana.

Wednesday, January 23rd 1861

Miss Jemima Darby
    Ringgold, La.
Care of Dr. Cobb

I feel sorry Dear Friend that all your correspondents have been so remiss of late and myself among the rest. Yours of the 8th came to hand last night which made the 2nd I have received from you since my return from the Virginia Springs in Oct. Well Postmasters have often much to bear as well as other publick officers but so far as I am concerned I must take some of the blame for delinquency on myself. Having made several pleasant Spring acquaintances to whom I promised to write after coming home besides having so many old correspondents including my brothers[16] must be my excuse for not answering your last. However would have done so had I not thought others were punctual in writing.

As regards the *non-going* of the Southern Baptist. We understand for want of funds it has been stopt being published. Do not know what they intend doing with the money in hand due some subscribers. Think it had become a rather poor paper anyhow. I suppose the Dr.[17] takes one of the Darlington papers. I see you are quite a politician. However as you hear so much through various papers you will excuse my not dwelling on the subject.

This has been a dark rainy freezing day. This night week ago, Mrs. Law's[18] mother died (Mrs. McIver).[19] She died at Mr. Frank Williamson's[20] after an illness of 2 weeks most of the time in a stupor, age 65. And on Sunday night last, Mrs. Mary Player[21] died at her mothers.[22] Had been sick you know for a long time. Poor Mary's death was no doubt happy release. And Mrs. Fisher Killins was buried here in the Presbyterian church yard 2 weeks ago. Mr. Player has not been here that I know since the past summer. Is still in Louisiana.

Understand that Mr. Beler[23] has offered his services as Chaplain to the Darlington Volunteers[24] but says he "prefers going as a common soldier." Now dont say you do not believe him. Understood yesterday that he intends making a higher strike in the church. Says he cannot live on the $1000 which the church is now giving him. Some are very much in hopes he will refuse to preach again until they offer him 2000. Oh by the by forgot to tell you that there is a young Mr. B., nearly 2 months old   have not seen him. Suppose you have not heard that Caroline Williamson has a son also a few months old. Mr. Robert Edwards health is bad. Hear nothing from the Misses King these days.

Mr. Samuel Gains Society Hill killed instantly a valuable manservant of Dr. Presleys[25] by accidental discharge of a rifle a few days ago. Understand that he (Gains) is in deep distress about it. Was on horseback going home.

Old Mrs. Dabs[26] is dead. Her son Quincy[27] has gone off as one of the Volunteers to Sullivan Island and Aunt Eliza[28] is staying at Mr. Thom Lides.[29] Dr. Norman who married Louise Nettles[30] has come back from Virginia and will settle permanently in Darlington. For the present will occupy Mrs. Wingate's[31] house. And Mrs. Wingate will board with them. Miss French the musick teacher who was here last year boards this year at Dr. Dargans[32]   Sarah has a good school   6 boarders.

Sally's[33] two little girls are still living and have good health thus far. We have not as yet been able to supply Sally's place and indeed hardly think we ever shall. Hettie[34] is still very smart and a good child. She would surprise you in waiting on the table. Hands the plates around with quite a grace and ease. Mr. Washington L[35] came not long since to enquire the terms of board and schooling for the twins[36] but when he went home and set his wife to counting up the cost suppose he concluded *Fatherlike* that he could not afford it. Mr. John Parrott[37] is in bad health. Farewell.

Yours as ever,

MARY

P. S. Mr. and Mrs. Porter have moved to Alabama. Our overseer for the year is Mr. Langston. My cough is much better. After writing to you at the Springs, I had a very pleasant time. My general health is good.

* * * * *

Enclosed in Miss Catlett's letter was a short letter from Sarah Catlett DuPre, who wasted no time describing national events which Miss Darby was sure to read in the newspapers. The letter is not dated.

Mrs. Lewis DuPre, Darlington, South Carolina, to Jemima Darby, Ringgold, Louisiana.

Dr Friend

When your *note* of inquiry arrived last night I thought I would write to you today and when this morning it was raining and sleeting, I thought I certainly would, but at dinner I found that Sister was doing the deed herself and now I am reading hers. I think she has given you all the news. But now I tell you the next time you send a *note* from Red River to Darlington, you may expect to receive a regular *scold*. You can't think how disappointed I was on opening the envelope to see that it did not contain a *letter*.

Last summer I determined not to leave home, but in Sept. I found that I would be obliged to make a change. Mr. D.[38] was going to Williamstown in the upper part of the state to hold a meeting. I went with him. Both improved very much. Mr. D. had been without his shoe 6 weeks from running an iron hook into the side of his foot. He was at first entirely disabled, but he moved on crutches and finally got to walk. We had a very interesting meeting. There is good mineral water in the place, so altogether it was a pleasant trip. Found on returning carpets down, yards clean and everything really well taken care of. I was at home nearly two weeks before Sister. She is looking better than I had seen her in several years. I have no doubt she went to the right place for her. Roanoke Red.

We all read and think so much about national affairs that really find it is an absorbing theme with me. Suppose Dr. Cobb takes a Charleston political paper. I have all the time had a great fear of Fort Sumter being attacked. But they now say that the wall next James Island is only (according to some) 4 point according to others and that a 90 pound Armstrong gun is placed on that point. I do hope and pray that there will be no blood shed.

Have you heard of the death of Mr. James McCall[39] at the Hot Springs, Va? Mrs. McC was with him. Mr. Earl[40] James[41] Muldrow[42] are among the guards at Charleston. Ida Hunter and George (Edwin) Dargan[43] were married at 12 night and next morning he left. She has been down. It is said that Mollie Wilds[44] and Hartwell Hart[45] are engaged. Also Edd Nettles[46] and Gertrude Sims[47] Both gentlemen and also Robert Nettles[48] have gone. Mr. D. had a note from Capt. Warley[49] last night acknowledging a box of eatables which Mr. D. had sent them.

Andrew C[50] went but has returned. Was sick. Present me very kindly to your niece and nephew. L. Fraser is married. I remain and believe me as ever your affectionate friend,

S

Mr. D's regards and wishes you had a good husband. Sister forgot to tell you that Mrs. Lucas[51] has a baby, daughter. She says the old man has not been to see her since her return.

* * * * *

On January 26, 1861, Lizzie Howle's wish was granted. Miss Darby's Louisiana seceded from the Union and thus declared herself against "old Lincoln." When the Convention met on January 23, 1861, at the state capitol at Baton Rouge, former Governors J. L. Manning of South Carolina and J. A. Winston of Alabama were present as guest speakers. From the reminiscences of William H. Scanland, senate clerk from Bossier Parish, which were reprinted as "a personal record of this memorial session" in the Shreveport *Times,* seventy-eight years later, came an eyewitness description of the session:

> One of the first moves of the convention was to give them the floor. In view of the prevailing strong sentiment in favor of the Union, the Secessionist leaders had issued a call for help and these distinguished citizens from states which had already seceded very probably contributed largely to the result.
> Leaders on both sides vied with each other with persuasive oratory. It was a period when political oratory flourished and the voters were swayed largely by its influence. At times anger blazed threateningly, again tears flowed freely, and throughout the history-making session, agitation was at white heat.
> . . . The announcement that the Secessionists were victorious was greeted with deafening applause and the booming of captured cannon, and for a time pandemonium swept the convention hall.[52]

Back in South Carolina, people read with enthusiasm that the Government of the Confederate States had assumed control of military affairs at Charleston, and that on March 3 Brigadier

General P. G. T. Beauregard, a native of Louisiana, was placed in command.

Patriotic fervor exhibited itself among the women of Darlington District. Unless Sam Bacot joined the Guards, Elma Law would not marry him. Andrew Charles, who had been in poor health for years, enlisted, but after finding army life too strenuous, he received a "good discharge." To the women of his family, he had done his part nobly. There was still hope that there would be no lives lost.

Wartime brought a noticeable increase in engagements and marriages; and, in the meantime, life moved along. Babies were born; the dead were buried. Leadership must come from the women in the community. The role of the church was still to comfort and inspire.

Carrie Williamson Williams was back at her home near Leavensworth when she wrote to Miss Darby on March 22, 1861.

Mrs. James A. Williams, Hickory Grove, South Carolina, to Jemima Darby, Ringgold, Louisiana.

Hickory Grove
March 22, 1861

My dear friend

I am a little surprised that you did not get my letter written as soon as I could do so after the birth of my dear little boy which great event occured on the first day of Nov and Sister wrote on my first visit there last of Dec   was wondering why you did not reply. Lizzie told me she received a letter recently.

Mr. Ben Lucas[53] died suddenly in Florence. Charles[54] lives with Wash. Mag[55] is going to school to Mrs. Dupre. Kim[56] had built near the church[57]   Attends to the business this year.[58] Mary Ann attends church regularly. Children[59] all at home. Have not seen the infant.

Mr. Julius Dargan[60] died on Saturday week. Darlington has met with a great loss as well as his friends.

I called at Mrs. Dupre's. She has a fine school. Miss May[61] is as cheerful as ever. Female prayermeeting every friday in the school room.[62] Tuesday meeting is well attended. I went with

Bettie Wilds[63] last week. Enjoyed it very much. Wish it was a little nearer but can't stand to ride that distance very well, now. I think I shall go sometimes.

Mary Player[64] is at rest at last. Was quite resigned either way. Mr. P.[65] only made a short visit to Darlington. Did not come to see her (Mary) buried. Informed of increasing debility and pain. She was ever anxious to see Jim[66] but his Ma[67] did not think to telegraph to Selma and letters failed to reach him. Is still teaching[68] in Alabama. Mrs. Wilson takes a few boarders. Lives at Dr. New's place. No change in Elly.[69] Tried to have M. buried at the Presbyterian church but Elly insisted and her Ma promised to put her at the Baptist. I visited her grave. Twas decorated with evergreens and flowers.

Mrs. Evander McIver[70] took billious colic   was very ill ten days   Died with Margaret[71] who has had a son since[72]

Ida Hunter and Mrs. Edwin Dargan's George[73] were married in Darlington. Also Gertrude and Edward Nettles[74] Bettie Wilds and Late Lide[75] will be one as soon as he returns. Will leave directly for his farm in Missi. Alexander[76] is 30 miles from him. Sorry to lose them.

Mrs. McIver tis said will give Bettie to Mr. William Frazier[77] very soon. Lou Frazier married Mr. Lowery of Sumter.[78] Fine looking and wealthy but rather wild. Mary Wilson[79] married Mr. Deschamps of Sumter. Did well. Had no party. Fannie will miss her. Lost her cook also.

Cousin Eliza is so delighted with her sister and little nephew will hardly return here.[80] Mrs. Griffin and Peter and Sallie[81] live with Rachel.[82] Evander[83] in Springville. Mr. Phelps[84] is soon to marry Flora Burn[85] if report is true. The Misses King are doing as well as usual.[86] Joe, I hear, makes a good looking lady. Do not hear of any beaux. Their house not covered yet. Mrs. Hartwell's[87] youngest daughter is married. She spent the winter with Mrs. Edwards.[88] Suppose her time will be divided. Robert is about the same. Mrs. Fort[89] staid there with Miss Charlotte[90] while they were gone. Expect she is now at Dr. Pressley's.[91] Lucy McIver[92] married a gentleman from Fairfield. Don't know if she gave up Aunt Kate or took her off.[93] I heard Elma Law[94] told Sam Bacot[95] if he did not join the Guards she would not marry a gent who would not defend his country. So he put off forwith.[96] Hope they return without any life lost. Andrew[97] went but was too feeble. Returned with a good discharge. Moll is nicely fixed in her new home[98]   made them a visit. We had snow Monday six inches deep　　farewell to the gardens and fruit except apples. Hope they are safe yet. I forgot to mention Lafayette Gandy's[99] marriage to Bettie Smoot, Tom's daughter.[100] Not grown. His parents much displeased. Lives at C DeLorme's place.

Aunt Jane[101] is much the same. Mrs. Council[102] resides with her. Mary[103] spent last week with me　　health better. Jane's boy[104] grows finely. Jacky has son, very cross. Mr. Byrd[105] and J. Hart[106] are not going to move. I call my boy Leon. Can almost sit alone. Is blue-eyed and rather good looking. Some think him very much like his Pa. Our school kept up all winter. Cough makes it thin at present. Remember me to Mrs. K. Would like to make her acquaintance. How are the little folks? Forgot the number.[107]

Your friend,

CARRIE

The ladies through Mr. Howle,[108] got a beautiful Communion set for forty dollars, nearly paid for it. It is not often that I feel so much like scribbling. Must get a longer sheet next time. Mrs. Baker[109] is here but will return North soon. Mr. William Vann[110] gives her some plain talk. Mr. Dorrity's father bought him a place in Sumter. Mary[111] did not like to go. No school there and none about here. Sorry to see it so neglected.

* * * * *

After Abraham Lincoln's inauguration on March 4, 1861, and the publication of his inaugural address, which showed that he was determined that there should be no recognition of secession, but that the South was to be forced, by military might, to continue its relationship with the United States government, the Confederate government, which had been organized in February, took possession of all forts along the coast. At Charleston, General Beauregard was ordered to reduce Fort Sumter. The attack began early in the morning of April 12, 1861.

Sarah Williamson, writing on May 4, gave a detailed account of events as they affected the lives of the people whom Miss Darby knew.

Sarah Williamson, Florence, South Carolina, to Jemima Darby, Ringgold, Louisiana.

Florence, S. C.
May 4, 1861

Dear Miss Darby

I received your letter this week and am truly glad to hear from you, and that you are so pleasantly situated and pleased with your relatives. I have been very lazy or would have written to you again knowing you would have replied if you had received it.

I attended the Sunday School celebration at Black Creek on the 23rd. There were nearly 200 children. The long table was filled with girls. Teachers and pupils marched from the old church to the new. They were addressed by Mr. Rice[112] Mr. Edwards[113] and Mr. McIver[114]   Bettie Hart's husband[115]   I am not so pleased with him as Anna's;[116] Mr. R. said he had not seen such a large number of children at any of the places he attended; had one at Willow Creek last Sunday. I hope we will not have one at our church   have so few schollars and very irregular. Mr. James[117] has the Bible class. Only a few study their lessons at all. Mr. Napier[118] often says all the classes he hears have their lessons well. If Mr. J. would get up and say only a few of his know theirs it would do some good.

We called at Mrs. DuPre's for the children[119]   Found them as well as usual. Miss Mary told me she had received a letter from you. She had offered to send you a preacher. I guess it was Mr. Wilkins.[120] She never said who. Have you heard he is going to marry Mrs. Bryant of Cheraw. Surely he will get a wife at last. Your friend[121] has only been to see us once this year. Came then with Mr. Duncan,[122] the agent for the University. I expect he has heard the report   makes him shy; Brother Wilds has never called on the girls[123] yet. I have never spent a day there. They have spent two with me. Sarah is a very pretty nice young lady. Martha has frequent spells of asthma. Mrs. Lane[124] their grandmother has spent the winter with them. Is going back to Florida this month.

Neither of the Misses Harlee[125] are married. It was reported that Lou[126] was engaged to William Thomas McCall.[127] You heard he killed himself accidentally last summer. Mrs. Macantire (Addie McCall that was)[128] was married last week to Mr. Frierson, the Presbyterian preacher. Dont you think she has a good resolution to undertake with 6 or 7 children beside her one and her health poor. Her mother[129] hasn't joined the Presbyterians yet. Comes occasionally to Mizpah. They have a nice church at Florence. Mr. Frierson preaches there once a month and other ministers. Very seldom get to hear him. Preaches the same day we have it at our church.

I saw Mr. and Mrs. Vann[130]   They were busy about the dinner   Lizzie was looking out every day[131] and much distressed about Tom's going off in the Company to Charleston.[132] Linton[133] Jim[134] Jeff[135] Eddie Fort[136] John Fraser[137] Fayette[138] and David Gandy[139] all went. You can imagine there were vacant seats on the men's side.[140] Mother went up with me. I left her with Sister[141]   Expect they will come down Tuesday. Leon has whooping cough. Has not hurt him much. Is a fine fat little fellow sitting alone   Has dark blue eyes, high forehead and brown hair   Sister Mary Ann[142] thinks he is the sweetest little fellow   loves to make him laugh

She paraded him about the churchyard. He looked quite pretty in the white dress she made him. New hat with blue ribbon in the cap. He was so tired at night could not rest.

Carrie has another son.[143] Nancy[144] had one[145] Tuesday night at Aunt Julia's.[146] Betsy was married to Ladin Lide Thursday night.[147] Ellick and wife and daughter are out.[148] Don't know how long they will stay, owing to how the War will be. Said if he has to go, he wishes to go from his native state.[149] Were you not ashamed for your state to be so long coming out?[150]

Quincy Dabbs[151] Frank Williamson[152] and others of our acquaintances have gone to Virginia.[153] Wilds was at Florence when the cars came. Says there are about 200 going out from Georgia every night and morning. They are loaded with them. Looks as if there will not be one man left to protect the females. The Darlington Guards have returned.[154] They were not in the midst of the battle. Were stationed on Morris Island to prevent vessels from landing. Could see the balls pass by them. Had a severe battle of 38 hours and what is remarkable not a life was lost nor one seriously wounded. Anderson[155] in firing the salute to his flag had one of his men killed, two badly wounded, one died soon after.[156] Mel Howard's husband[157] was in the city at the time. Said it was the grandest sight he ever witnessed.

Col. Cashe's Regiment[158] has arrived. Are camping in the old field near Cusacks Mill about 4 miles from us. I expect you know where it is. When Sister comes we will go out to see Jim. I wish you could be here to go with us. E. and P. Griffin[159] both of Society Hill and John McIver[160] are there. 1000 men in all. Surely that will look like war to us. To see them parading. I hear they have offered their services to V.

I have no apple geranium. Sister has one. Will get some seed when they are ripe. Please send me any little seed you can. Sister gave me one that you sent. Not one came up. I wish I had some of your fine soil and roses. Mine are looking pretty. I have to work hard to get them to do so. Wilds says I have put five dollars worth of manure on them. Have a mound with verbenas. I am afraid you cant read this. Wilds and Edwin[161] send their respects to you. Give mine to your niece.

Yours,

SARAH

Heard from the Kings. Were well and get as much work as they can do.

* * * * *

On May 4, Sarah Williamson had written to tell Miss Darby that her sister, Carrie Williams, would soon come down from Leavensworth to visit her family and to see her husband, James, who was among the soldiers in Colonel E. B. C. Cash's regiment whose camp was about four miles from the Williamson home, near Florence. On May 24, Carrie wrote from Orangedale, her mother's home, to give Miss Darby the latest news.

Mrs. James A. Williams, Florence, South Carolina, to Jemima Darby, Ringgold, Louisiana.

Orangedale, May 24, 1861

My dear friend

I received your letter and was pleased to hear of good health and fine spirits. I've been on the path for some weeks past. Suppose you heard nearly all our gentlemen have volunteered, Jim and T. Howle among the rest. Col. Cash's Regiment of near one thousand have been stationed near mother's for some weeks. Expect to leave for Virginia and other places soon. Jim's health has failed and friends have finally persuaded him to apply for a discharge. Dr. Wallace (Sergeant of the Regiment) recommends. Dr. Crane[162] tried to prevent his going at first but he was anxious to assist in the work. Stood it one month. Looks badly. Hope he can get an honorable discharge. All the company have given themselves to the Confederate States.

Lizzie made a great fuss about Tom. Has a daughter 2 weeks old. Dr. Crane named her Carolina Secession.[163] It is very small but pretty. Mrs. Van[164] has been sick. Mr. William Vann says he intends to bear his own expense to go to Virginia to see the fight and help if needed to assist[165] one poor family left alone.

Leon can sit alone. Looks very much like his father. Is a great pet and good child. Cough hurt him a little. Jane is here with her fat boy.[166] Has the measles at present. Very light kind. Expect Leon will take them now.

We will stay next week then return to dear quiet home and try to live nearer to a throne of grace for surely in these times we all need much prayer. Mr. Brayerly[167] visited the soldiers and his wife says they are now constantly remembered by him. Many brave youths are in the number. Mrs. Tom Haynesworth died recently. Oldest son at Fort Sumter.[168] Wish you could have seen the paper with the particulars, but was too much trouble at the time to send it. "The Darlington Grays"[169] were ordered down that day. Mrs. Davis[170] is in bed. Says it will kill her for Johnny to go off and he is determined to go. Mrs. Fort[171] is in trouble about Eddie. Indeed there are few houses where a loved one is not missing. Mrs. Ferguson grieved about Jeff. Health so delicate. Crops are not good and gardens were seldom so poor. Persons generally planted more provisions but not enough yet. Sister is busy with flowers and down goes the steps with her. Boxes so heavy. Made a crash. Watering them. A few beautiful ones. I will send some apple seed. Left my cactus in full bloom and other beauties. Find flowers something to divert my attention. Cannot sew much and feel more feeble since the weather is warmer. Sister sends you a piece of poetry. Mother sends much love. So glad to hear of your contentment.

Misses King are as usual. Eliza has another daughter.[172] I expect old Mrs. McIntosh[173] is troubled. Three grandsons gone.

All very fine gentlemen. Cousin Eliza Evans is still pleased in Missi. I think I told you Mrs. Katie Fort went to live with Lucy who married a gent from Fairfield. Mary Dorrity visited her father recently. Did not see her. The old man is very feeble.[174] Remember me to Mrs. K. Sister joins me in love.

Your friend,

CARRIE WILLIAMS

* * * * *

FOOTNOTES

1 The Welsh Neck Baptist Association met with Black Creek Church on November 10-13, 1860.

2 John Culpepper was pastor at Ebenezer Baptist Church in 1860. George R. Pettigrew, *Annals of Ebenezer, 1778-1950* (privately printed, 1952), p. 55. "John Culpepper and William Lunn were called for the year 1860, and accepted, one preaching on the first Sunday and the other on the third Sunday each month." *Ibid.,* p. 46. "John Culpepper served the church during the war years . . . . and was a fearless champion of State Sovereignty under the Federal Constitution. A Southerner by birth, he was a man of profound and settled convictions, and his voice was often heard in vindication of Southern rights. With tongue and pen (he seems to have been a poet of parts), he defended the South and encouraged her embattled sons. Withal, he was a great preacher, like Apollos 'mighty in the Scriptures.' "

3 Mr. and Mrs. John Culpepper were the parents of Mrs. Rose Johnson.

4 Elizabeth Fountain and her sisters, Sarah, Mary, and Fannie, lived in Springville, near their sister, Mrs. John L. Hart.

5 Josiah T. Vann was regarded as a confirmed old bachelor by his married relatives.

6 The Edwards family remained in Louisiana about six months.

7 The union meeting was about to begin in Society Hill.

8 James E. DeLorme was a student at The Citadel until July 28, 1857. He was killed during the Civil War.

9 Sue Wilson, Letter from Society Hill, South Carolina, to John A. Cawthon,

Russellville, Arkansas, August 10, 1953. "The Wilsons of Sumter were not of our branch."

10 This is the only reference to classes. Tom Howle, merchant, postmaster, and planter who could speculate on seventy bales of cotton for one year might not have been considered a big planter; neither would he have been considered among the "poorer class of people."

11 Edith Campbell, Letter from Darlington, South Carolina, to John A. Cawthon, Russellville, Arkansas, May 21, 1953. "Old Grandmother Howle must have been James Howle's mother (Thomas E. Howle's grandmother) as dates below show that none of James's wives died in 1860: Margaret A. Keith Howle died July 23, 1833; Mary Jane Howle died December 2, 1857; Penelope Howle died November, 1908."

12 Mary Vann Dorrity was Mrs. Howle's first cousin.

13 Mary Dorrity's oldest daughter was named Elizabeth.

14 W. C. Coker, "Sketch of the Organization of the Darlington Companies in the Eighth Regiment, S. C., Volunteers of the Confederate Army," *Treasured Reminiscences,* collected by John K. McIver Chapter, U. D. C. (Columbia, 1911), p. 19.

15 W. E. Charles, "Sketch of the Darlington Guards," unpublished manuscript prepared in 1901 and preserved by Beulah Walden (Mrs. Robert) Coggeshall, Darlington, South Carolina.

16 Early in 1860, Miss Catlett's brother, the minister, had visited them; there are no other references to the other brothers.

17 Dr. Kolb had been away from Darlington District since his boyhood. It is doubtful that he continued to subscribe to a Darlington paper.

18 Elizabeth McIver Law (April 3, 1815 — June 28, 1885) was the wife of Augustus Law, Darlington.

19 Eliza Cowan McIver (April 17, 1795 — January 16, 1861), wife of Evander R. McIver, was buried in the Presbyterian Churchyard, Darlington; Mr. McIver died in Talledega Springs, Alabama, June 26, 1837, and was buried at Tuskegee, Alabama.

20 Benjamin Franklin Williamson (February 3, 1814 — October 20, 1887), son of Bright and Jane Rogers Williamson, married (1) Martha Lenora Wilson, and (2) Margaret McIver, daughter of Mrs. Evander McIver and sister of Mrs. Law.

21 Mary Wilson Player, who was twenty-four years old, died at Darlington on January 13, 1861.

22 Sarah A. E. Wilson and her daughter, Mary Player, lived together in Darlington in 1860-1861.

23 George B. Bealer was pastor of the Baptist Church at Darlington.

24 Darlington Riflemen, Darlington Guards, and Hartsville Light Infantry.

25 Dr. S. H. Pressley, Society Hill, married (1) Jane Edwards, and (2) Sarah McIver.

26 Sarah Grove Dabbs had been seriously ill for several months.

27 J. Quincy Dabbs (1825-1880) married Eufronia Hoole.

28 Quincy's sister, Ann Eliza Dabbs, was a distant cousin to the Lide family.

29 Thomas P. Lide lived at White Plains, Springville, where all relatives, even distant ones, were made welcome.

30 Louise Nettles, daughter of General Joseph B. Nettles, married Dr. B. C. Norment.

31 Mrs. J. E. Wingate was the mother of Manley Wingate, president of Wake Forest College, North Carolina.

32 Dr. Theodore A. Dargan married Maria Louisa Bacot.

33 Sally DuPre Bentley, sister of Lewis DuPre, Mary's brother-in-law, died in 1860.

34 Hettie and Sally were the daughters of Sally DuPre Bentley.

35 George Washington Lucas, aged thirty-five, was a plantation overseer.

36 M. J. and S. M. were nine years old in 1860.

37 John Parrott was the husband of G. W. Lucas's sister, Mary.

38 Lewis DuPre, Sarah Catlett's husband, was a Baptist minister.

39 James Sanders McCall, Sr. (October 18, 1798 — August 25, 1860), son of George and Elizabeth Sanders McCall, married Elizabeth Ellison Lucretia Muldrow, September 22, 1825.

40 Private George W. Earle married Anna Elizabeth McCall, daughter of James S. and Elizabeth Muldrow McCall, December 9, 1858.

41 William E. James, Jr., was the son of W. E. James, Darlington.

42 Private Elihu Muldrow was the son of Samuel and Ursula W. Muldrow of the Ebenezer community.

43 George William Dargan (May 11, 1841 — June 29, 1898), son of William Edwin and Sarah DuBose Dargan, married Ida Louise Hunter (May 3, 1841 — February 11, 1919), daughter of Andrew and Emilie Bacot Hunter.

44 Mary D. Wilds (November 23, 1841 — March 24, 1890), daughter of Peter and Julia Terrel Wilds, never married.

45 Jesse Hartwell Hart (January 19, 1836 — July 8, 1864), son of Thomas and Hannah Lide Hart, and Miss Wilds's families were interrelated.

46 J. Edward Nettles (August 24, 1836 — June 21, 1899), son of General Joseph Nettles, married Gertrude Lydia Sims.

47 Gertrude Lydia Sims (December 6, 1839 — October 3, 1891), daughter of A. D. and M. A. P. Sims, married J. E. Nettles.

48 Robert Nettles married Eugenia Mochelle McCall (February 11, 1837 — February 24, 1898), daughter of Moses Sanders and Mary Elizabeth Gregg McCall.

49 Captain Frederick F. Warley, graduate of The Citadel, lawyer from Darlington, was in command of the company at Charleston.

50 Andrew Charles was married to Mary Ann Williamson.

51 Mary Ann Lucas was the wife of George Washington Lucas.

52 Mary Scanland Jones, "Secession Day in Louisiana," Shreveport *Times*, January 26, 1939, p. 2.

53 Benjamin Lucas, member of Black Creek Church for many years, was sixty-five years old when the census was taken in 1860. He was listed as a planter who gave Darlington Courthouse as his post office. He must have died while on a visit to Florence for his home was in the Black Creek Church neighborhood.

54 Charles Lucas, Ben's unmarried son, was listed as thirty years of age in 1860.

55 Margaret Lucas, Ben's eighteen-year-old daughter, had joined Black Creek Church on July 20, 1856, when she was approximately thirteen years old.

56 Kim Lucas married a Miss Bell.

57 "Black Creek Church, Dovesville," *The Baptist Courier*, Volume 85, No. 47 (Greenville), December 3, 1953, p. 13. "Brother B. Lucas donated the land" on which the church "was built in 1856."

58 According to the census records for 1860, Ben Lucas's property was valued at $22,320. Mr. Lucas turned over the management of the estate to his son, Kim.

59 George Washington Lucas and his wife, Mary Ann, had a son, John, aged twelve, twin daughters nine years old, and an infant daughter born in 1860.

60 Julius Alfred Dargan, son of Timothy and Lydia Keith Dargan, married Martha Woods. He was a Darlington lawyer, a member of the Secession Convention and a signer of the Ordinance of Secession.

61 Mary Ann Catlett and her sister, Mrs. DuPre, were deeply religious.

62 "Minutes of the Welsh Neck Baptist Church, Society Hill, South Carolina," July 4, 1817. "Sister Catlett was received in the fellowship." November 8, 1823. "Sisters Sarah Catlett and her daughters, Mary and Sarah Elizabeth, they being about to remove from the country, were granted letters of dismissal." They moved to Darlington where they continued their interest in church business.

Minutes of Welsh Neck Association, 1832-1871. (Greenville) p. 9. "Contributions: Education, Miss S. Catlett $1; Home Missions, Miss S. Catlett, $2, Mills Vann, $1; Foreign Missions, Mrs. Catlett, $2, Miss S. Catlett, $2, Miss M. Catlett, $2."

When the mother died in 1842, the Baptist Association, meeting at Mt. Zion Church, Marion District, eulogized her, saying: "Have experienced sore afflictions. In passing through a season of unexampled sickness and mortality, we were called to exceptional losses, first, in the death of Mrs. S. Z. Catlett, a venerated and exemplary member; and second, that of their faithful and beloved pastor, Rev. Josiah B. Furman, besides some others."

Miss Mary Catlett was on the Associational pay roll in 1848. "Nov. 16. By due bill of Financial Committee on Miss Catlett — $49.00."

It is not surprising that the Catlett sisters would use their class room as a prayer room.

63 Julia Elizabeth Wilds (June 24, 1839 — January 11, 1915) was the daughter of Peter and Julia Terrel Wilds. She was Carrie Williams's first cousin.

64 Mary Wilson Player was the daughter of Sarah A. E. Wilson, a native of Darlington District, South Carolina. Mary was born in 1836. In 1860, Mary and her mother were living at Darlington Courthouse. According to the United States Census Record, their household consisted of themselves, one ten-year-old male, John, who was listed as "nameless," and a twenty-three-year-old male, W. D. Lewis. Mary had been ill of dropsy for several years.

65 Mr. Player was Mary's husband, who lived in another state.

66 *Memorial Record of Alabama*, Volume 2 (Madison, 1893), p. 349. "Dr. James C. Wilson was born in Tuscaloosa, Alabama, May 15, 1828 . . . the son of David Wilson, native of South Carolina, who came to Alabama in 1820 and was a farmer by trade. . . . His wife was Sarah Witherspoon, also of South Carolina. They were the parents of 10 children, of whom only the doctor survives. . . . Dr. Wilson was educated at Green Springs, under Henry Tutwiler and received his medical training at Charleston, graduating in 1851. . . . He married Susan, daughter of James Jones, Greene County, Alabama, in 1854, and was the father of 12 children . . ."

67 Dr. Wilson's mother, Mrs. Sarah Wilson, was also Mary's mother, who lived in Darlington.

68 Dr. Wilson lived in Carthage, Alabama, for fifteen years after his graduation from medical school. There is no record of his having taught school though he may have done so before he began to practice medicine.

69 Mrs. Elly Wilson was a staunch Baptist; the members of Sarah Wilson's family were Presbyterians.

70 As a young woman, Mrs. McIver had been Eliza Cowan, daughter of John and Elizabeth Salter Cowan, of near Elizabethtown, North Carolina. Evander McIver had gone to Fayetteville to be best man at the wedding of Peter Kolb Edwards and Eliza's cousin, Jane Draughon, when he met Eliza, whom he married in 1814. They had seven children.

71 Margaret McIver was the second wife of Benjamin Franklin Williamson, son of Bright and Jane Rogers Williamson. Harvey Toliver Cook, *The Life and Legacy of David Rogerson Williams* (New York, 1916), p. 301. After Frank Williamson's graduation from the state college in 1833, his father presented him "with a half interest in two farms, one a fine one on the Pee Dee River, the other on Black Creek called Oaklyn Plantation, the place of his birth. After disposing of the river lands, he concentrated his interests on the latter plantation, where he built a modest home and began the foundation of a career that made him a planter of recognized ability and success. . . . Oaklyn became so productive and remunerative that at the beginning of the War between the States, he was accounted one of the most successful planters in the state and had accumulated a goodly fortune."

72 Mr. and Mrs. Williamson's oldest son was Bright Williamson, who was born March 4, 1861.

73 Ida Hunter, daughter of Andrew and Emilie Bacot Hunter, married George William Dargan, son of William Edwin and Sarah DuBose Dargan.

74 Gertrude Lydia (December 6, 1839 — October 3, 1891), daughter of A. D. and M. A. P. Sims, married J. Edward Nettles (August 24, 1836 — June 21, 1899).

75 Leighton Wilson Lide (October 8, 1838 — August 24, 1910), son of Thomas P. and Elizabeth Sparks Lide, married Bettie Wilds. They moved to Mississippi immediately after the wedding.

76 Alexander Lide, also a son of Thomas P. and Elizabeth Sparks Lide, had already married and moved out to Mississippi.

77 The only McIver daughter who married a Fraser was Sarah Margaret, daughter of Abel and his second wife, Rachel Love, who married Judge Thomas Boone Fraser of Sumter. Mrs. Abel McIver was a widow for a period of time before she married a Mr. Cooper. Judge Fraser's second wife was Mrs. Elizabeth James Witherspoon, known as "Bettie." She was Mrs. Abel McIver's niece. Parents of Judge Fraser were Ladson and Hannah Boone Fraser. He had a brother, William Fraser, who married Martha McCutcheon, of Williamsburg. It appears that Carrie Williams was mistaken about who would marry whom.

78 Lou Frazier was a member of the old Scottish family of Fraziers who lived in the Black Creek neighborhood.

79 Sue Stout Wilson, Letter from Society Hill, South Carolina, to John A. Cawthon, Russellville, Arkansas, August 10, 1953. "I do not know whose daughter the Mary Wilson was who married Mr. Dechamps of Sumter, neither do I know *his* given name. . . . The Wilsons of Sumter were not of our branch."

80 Samuel and Catherine McIver Evans had two children: Eliza, who never married, and Samuel, who moved to Mississippi, married, reared a family, and never returned to South Carolina. Samuel Evans's home was at Cooper's Well, Mississippi.

81 Eliza McIver Griffin (December 3, 1803 — November 10, 1876) was the widow of Thomas Griffin. Dr. Peter Griffin and Sallie were her children.

82 Rachel Holloway, the daughter of Jesse and Sarah McIver Holloway, was Mrs. Griffin's niece, who, in 1843, married Thomas Coker. Mr. Coker died in 1845.

83 Evander Griffin was the oldest son of Thomas and Eliza McIver Griffin. He never married.

84 J. C. Phelps, the pastor at Society Hill, did not marry Miss Burn.

85 Flora Burn, daughter of the Reverend Mr. J. W. Burn and his wife, Susan, married Mr. Hubbard, and died in February, 1888.

86 There were three King sisters at home in Society Hill at the time — Emily, Hannah and Josephine.

87 Margaret Hartwell, widow of the prominent Baptist minister, Jesse Hart-

well, had returned to Society Hill after her husband's death in Mount Lebanon, Louisiana.

88 Mrs. Robert Edwards of Society Hill was Mrs. Hartwell's daughter.

89 Mrs. Catherine M. Fort, widow of Moses Fort and daughter of the Reverend Mr. Edward Botsford, was a cousin to Dr. John K. McIver, to whom he was engaged at the time of his death. She had promised that she would take care of his children and he had made her one of the beneficiaries of his will.

90 Charlotte Kirven was at least as old as Jemima, perhaps older, having joined the church by letter in 1816.

91 Dr. S. H. Pressley's second wife was Sarah McIver, one of the daughters of Dr. McIver.

92 Lucy McIver, daughter of Dr. McIver, married Colonel R. B. Watson, of Fairfield.

93 Mrs. Fort went with Lucy and Colonel Watson to Fairfield.

94 Elma Law, daughter of E. Augustus and Eliza McIver Law, was born August 28, 1834.

95 Private Samuel H. Bacot was on the roll of the Darlington Guards which had just left for Charleston.

96 Miss Law did not wait for Private Bacot; she married Dr. William Player.

97 Andrew Charles was Carrie's brother-in-law.

98 Andrew and Mary Ann Charles had moved into their new home near Cashaway Ferry, on the great Pee Dee River.

99 Lafayette Gandy was the son of Abel Gandy, who lived in the Black Creek neighborhood.

100 Elizabeth Smoot was the daughter of Thomas W. and Sarah Smoot.

101 Jane Rogers Williamson was the widow of Carrie's uncle, Bright Williamson.

102 Mrs. Addie Council was a relative of the Williamson family through the Terrels.

103 Mary Williamson Brown, who was on a visit from Texas, was Mrs. Williams's niece.

104 Joseph Wilds Wallace, son of Thomas and Jane Williamson Wallace, was born late in 1860.

105 Mr. Byrd, along with others of the neighborhood, had considered moving to Louisiana.

106 John Lide Hart lived in Springville.

107 Dr. and Mrs. Kolb had three children: Ella, five and one-half; Thomas, almost three; and Maria Elizabeth, almost two. Mary was born on August 12, 1861.

108 Thomas Howle, Leavensworth, was both a deacon in the Black Creek Church and a merchant.

109 Mrs. Deborah Williams Baker traveled a great deal.

110 William Vann and Mrs. Baker were not related, but they had known each other for enough years to enable them to speak freely to each other. Mr. Vann disapproved of Mrs. Baker's living in the North.

111 Mary Vann Dorrity, a daughter of Mills Vann, was Miss Darby's cousin.

112 W. D. Rice came originally from Barnwell County in the southern part of South Carolina, but later became pastor at Society Hill and Sumter.

113 P. C. Edwards (1819-1862), one-time pastor at Welsh Neck, and professor at Furman University, married Anne McIver, daughter of the Reverend Mr. D. R. W. McIver and his wife, Caroline Wilds McIver.

114 D. R. W. McIver, of Kingston, De Soto Parish, Louisiana, must have been to Darlington for a visit, perhaps his last. He died on February 10, 1863.

115 Sarah Elizabeth Hart, daughter of Thomas E. and Hannah Lide Hart, married Capt. A. F. Edwards, Conway, South Carolina, in 1858. Law, *Citadel Cadets* (Clinton, 1941), pp. 277-278, gives this account: "December 29, 1858. Today, Bettie Hart ended her career of 'single blessedness' and entered upon the responsible relations of married life. Her consort is Augustus F. Edwards, Esq., a young lawyer, at present of Conwayboro, whither he carried her immediately upon their marriage. The wedding was a very private one, took place in the daytime after which they set right off. Such is the account given by those present."

116 Anna Maria Coker (May 5, 1834 — September 2, 1899), daughter of Caleb and Hannah Lide Coker, Society Hill, married Colonel B. W. Edwards, Darlington, brother to Captain A. F. Edwards. Miss Coker was Miss Hart's distant cousin and schoolmate at the Misses Bates's school in Charleston.

117 "The History of Mispah Baptist Church (1834-1934)," unpublished manuscript in Furman University Library, Baptist Collection, p. 2. "Many wealthy slave owners worshipped at the church. . . . They were the very pillows of the organization. Some of them were: Napiers, Williamsons, Wallaces, . . . James."

118 "Mispah Baptist Church Book. 1834-1862," p. 5. "Rev. Robert Napier was called in 1835." He remained pastor for forty-five years and he and his wife are buried in the churchyard.

119 Virginia Ella and Katharine Caroline Williamson, daughters of George Lawrence and Catherine Williams Williamson, were attending Mrs. DuPre's school for girls in Darlington.

120 Miss Catlett had offered to send Mr. Bealer, not Mr. Wilkins, out to Miss Darby; she had thought in terms of supplying a pastor, not a beau.

121 S. B. Wilkins, representing the local churches and the association, frequently went out with representatives of Furman University to solicit funds. His wife had been dead about ten years.

122 Robert Norman Daniel, *Furman University, A History* (Greenville, 1951), p. 47. "On June 25, 1850, James C. Furman, John Culpepper, R. Furman and H.

D. Duncan were made agents to solicit subscriptions. They were to give all their time, if possible, and were to receive $3 a day, except for Sundays, while at work."

123 Sarah and Martha Napier were the daughters of the pastor, Robert Napier. Sarah was the younger, having been baptized in September, 1854.

124 T. Lane and his wife, Martha E. Lane, were members of Mispah Church when Robert Napier became pastor in 1834. Mr. Lane died before 1842, and, in the meantime, Elizabeth B. Lane married Mr. Napier. Mrs. Lane accompanied her sons to Florida during the 1840's, but came back to Florence to spend some time with her Napier grandchildren following their mother's death during the late 1850's.

125 Harllee was an old Pee Dee name. Alexander Gregg, *History of the Old Cheraws* (San Antonio, 1867 and Columbia, 1905), p. 622. "Peter Harlee was the first of the name to come to America. . . . He came to Virginia, where he settled. He married Anne Leake and died when quite old, soon after the close of the American Revolution. His family moved South and settled in Marion County. His only son married Elizabeth Stuart. . . . There were born to Thomas and Elizabeth Harlee nine children who lived to maturity."

Of Thomas Harllee's children, three were contemporaries and friends of Jemima Darby: Harriett Harllee McCall, General William W. Harllee, and Dr. Robert Harllee. After Robert Harllee graduated in medicine, he settled at Marion Courthouse. He married (1) Ann Gurdy, and (2) Amelia Cannon Howard. The reference here is to Sallie (December 8, 1840 — April 28, 1879) and Louisa (June 12, 1839-193___), daughters of Dr. and Mrs. Robert Harllee.

126 Louisa Harllee.

127 William Thomas McCall (February 25, 1839 — July 31, 1860), son of William and Eliza Miller Allbrooks McCall, never married. William McCall's family and the family of George McCall, who married Elizabeth Sanders, were related, but the relationship had not been established, according to Harllee, in *Kinfolks*. (William Harllee, *Kinfolks*. New Orleans: Search and Pfaff Ltd., 1934.)

128 Adaline Allbrooks McCall (May 2, 1834 — March 17, 1891) married (1) Richard F. McIntyre, in June, 1854, and (2) David E. Frierson, a Presbyterian minister, in 1861.

129 Eliza Miller Allbrooks McCall, wife of William McCall, was the mother of Mrs. Frierson and of William Thomas McCall.

130 In local and Associational work, William Vann was regarded as a leader. As a deacon at Black Creek, he and his wife were expected to take an active part in the preparation of entertainment for the hundreds of guests who had come for the Sunday School convention on April 23rd.

131 Lizzie Vann Howle was expecting a baby. Sallie Elizabeth Howle was born May 5, 1861. Sallie Elizabeth Howle married William Timmons Campbell, son of Peter Edwin Campbell and Elizabeth K. Campbell.

132 Thomas E. Howle was First Lieutenant in Company F of the Eighth South Carolina Regiment, which had left for Charleston.

133 A. Linton Williams was a brother to James Williams.

134 James A. Williams, Sarah's brother-in-law, was Carrie Williamson Williams's husband, young Leon's father.

135 Jefferson W. Ferguson (January 7, 1838 — September 4, 1909) was a son of Alexander and Elizabeth Williams Ferguson.

136 "Black Creek Church Book, A. D. 1798," p. 207, records a Resolution of Sorrow over the "loss of our Brother J. Edwards Fort who died in the Army in Virginia with typhoid fever July, 1861. He was born February 5, 1838, Baptized September 15, 1856, and died at Germantown, Virginia, July 8, 1861." He was the son of Josiah and Anne Fort.

137 The mention of John Frazier with other members of Black Creek Church leads to the assumption that he was a member of this church also, though no mention has been found of him in the church records. It may be that this is John Fraser, son of William H. Fraser, a resident of the Auburn community.

138 Lafayette Gandy, the son of Abel and Lavinia Johnson Gandy, had recently married Bettie Smoot.

139 David Gandy was a brother to Lafayette, son of Abel and Lavinia Johnson Gandy.

140 Men sat on one side of the church; women sat on the other; slaves sat in the galleries.

141 Sarah referred to Carrie Williams as "Sister." Carrie, in turn, called Sarah "Sister."

142 Mary Ann Charles was known as "Sister Mary Ann" or "Moll."

143 The identity of this Carrie has not been revealed; certainly, Sarah did not refer to her sister, Carrie Williams, Leon's mother, nor did she refer to the Wilds family whose daughters are mentioned in the next sentences.

144 Nancy Lide Wilds Coggeshall (August 7, 1835 — November 8, 1916), daughter of Peter Abel and Julia Terrel Wilds, married Peter Collin Coggeshall II (May, 1830 — July, 1892) in 1854.

145 Alva C. Coggeshall (April, 1861 — July, 1932) was Peter and Nancy's third child.

146 Julia Terrel Wilds was Nancy Coggeshall's mother. She lived at "Wilds Hall," in the Springville area.

147 Elizabeth Wilds and Leighton Lide both appear on the Kolb family chart, having as their common distant ancestor, Major Robert Lide, who married Sarah Kolb. Leighton and Bettie were married May 2, 1861.

148 Alexander Lide and his family had come to South Carolina from Mississippi.

149 Edwin C. Dargan, *Harmony Hall* (Columbia, 1912), p. 101. "Cousin Alex lived in Mississippi during my recollection and I knew him only slightly."

150 South Carolina seceded on December 20, 1860; Louisiana on January 26, 1861.

[151] J. Quincy Dabbs (1825-1880) was the son of Samuel and Sarah L. Grove Dabbs.

[152] Benjamin Franklin Williamson (1814-1887), husband of Margaret McIver, was one of the older men who volunteered to go into service.

[153] There were three South Carolina regiments, which contained most of the soldiers mentioned in the letters — the First, under Colonel Maxey Gregg; the Eighth, under Colonel E. B. C. Cash; and the Twenty-First, under Colonel R. F. Graham. All went to Virginia, in time.

[154] The Darlington Guards, after the fall of Fort Sumter, were confronted with two choices: (1) they might continue in the service as part of the First Regiment, under Colonel Maxey Gregg, who proceeded directly to Virginia, or (2) they might return to Darlington with Captain Warley. Very few of the men who had been members of the Darlington Guards terminated their services with the Confederate Army. They were soon all absorbed in one or another of the local units which eventually were attached to either the Eighth or Twenty-First South Carolina Regiments.

[155] Major Robert Anderson (1805-1871) was commander of the United States troops at Fort Sumter.

[156] Sarah Williamson's account of the battle of Fort Sumter is remarkably accurate. The official records are cited in *War of the Rebellion*, Series I, Volume I, p. 309:

Charleston, April 13, 1861

Hon. L. P. Walker, Secretary of War:
We take possession of Fort Sumter tomorrow morning. I allow him the privilege of saluting his flag. No one killed on our side.

G. T. BEAUREGARD

Charleston, April 14, 1861

Hon. L. P. Walker, Secretary of War:
I have possession of Sumter. Anderson and garrison on *Isabel* going in the morning. One killed; two wounded. Quarters in ruins. Interior of fort damaged. Armament still effective against entrance to channel.

G. T. BEAUREGARD

Headquarters Provisional Forces
C. S. A.
Charleston, April 15, 1861

The commanding general directs that the commanding officer of the garrison of Ft. Sumter will bury the unfortunate soldier who has been accidentally killed by explosion of misplaced powder while saluting his flag. He will be buried with all the honors of war in the parade of the Fort.
By order of Brigadier-General Beauregard:

W. H. C. WHITTING

P. S. The wounded will receive the best attention, and will be placed in the State hospital.

157 Melvina Howard married Joseph Newton Whitner (November 4, 1831 — July 19, 1881) on November 14, 1855.

158 Colonel E. B. C. Cash, of Cheraw, and his regiment were encamped at Florence, where on May 31 they were mustered into Confederate service and on June 1 left Florence for Virginia.

159 Evander M. and Peter E. Griffin were the sons of Thomas and Eliza McIver Griffin.

160 John K. McIver, the son of James Kolb and Sarah Marshall McIver, was born at Society Hill and married Hannah Wilson in 1858. He soon became Captain in Company F of the Eighth Regiment.

161 Edwin P. Williamson was the son of Sarah's brother, Samuel Thomas, and his wife, Sarah Terrel.

162 Dr. James B. Crane was a Darlington physician.

163 This was Dr. Crane's joke. The baby's name was Sarah Elizabeth Howle (May 5, 1861). She married William T. Campbell and in January, 1954, was living in Darlington, still small but pretty.

164 Mrs. William Vann was sixty-five years old.

165 William Vann was sixty-six years old.

166 Mrs. Thomas Wallace and her son, Joseph Wilds, were visiting at her grandmother's house.

167 William Brearley (November 30, 1801 — January 8, 1882), pastor of the Presbyterian Church, Darlington, married (1) Jane B. English of Sumter, and (2) Mary DuBose of Darlington.

168 Private M. S. Haynesworth, Darlington Guards, was the son of Mr. and Mrs. Tom Haynesworth.

169 "The Darlington Grays" was a company known as "F" under the command of Colonel E. B. C. Cash, which had been called to Charleston on April 13, reaching there after the fall of Fort Sumter.

170 Jane DuBose Davis was the mother of John M. Davis, Jr., and daughter of "Aunt Jane" DuBose, who lived at Society Hill.

171 Ann E. DuBose was the wife of Josiah Fort and mother of J. Edwards Fort (February 5, 1838 — July, 1861). Mrs. Fort and Mrs. Davis were sisters.

172 The second daughter of A. P. and Eliza King LaCoste was named Georgia.

173 James H. McIntosh, whose mother's maiden name was Margaret Lucas (October 9, 1783 — November 5, 1862), married Martha Gregg. James and Martha McIntosh had three sons who served in the war: David Gregg McIntosh, Dr. James H. McIntosh, and Edward McIntosh.

174 Mills Vann had been reported old and infirm in 1860.

The War
PART II

By mid-year of 1861, South Carolina troops had begun to move into Virginia. Colonel E. B. C. Cash's Eighth Regiment of South Carolina Volunteers left Florence on June 1 and arrived in Richmond a few days later. While in Richmond, Lieutenant Thomas E. Howle had been entertained in the home of the Hill family, and their daughter, Bettie, wrote a letter to Lieutenant Howle on June 22, after he had arrived at Manassas.

Bettie F. Hill, Richmond, Virginia, to Thomas E. Howle, Manassas.

Richmond, June 22, 1861

Honoured Friend: —

I received your welcome missive last evening and we were indeed quite glad to learn of the safe arrival of your regiment, and also that you are well. You can not imagine my delight on the reception of it, for though I had waited quite patiently to hear from you, yet I never despaired knowing that your various duties must keep you quite busily employed. The weather here has been and is at present very oppressive, in consequence of which many families are leaving the City, and were it not for the many military to be seen, our town would present a some-what lonely appearance, contrasted with its usual gaiety. There is not much news current here at present; I suppose you have heard ere this of an engagement of our forces with the fed-eral troops numbering about two hundred and fifty men, a few miles west of Cumberland, near New Creek Depot; the enemy after firing a few random shots broke and fled; one man was wounded on our side, but the enemy's loss is not accurately known, several of them being killed. Our troops captured two guns and a stand of colors.[1] There arrived in this City, on yesterday, two prisoners of war, one a Lieutenant Col. of a Pennsylvania regiment, but after being conveyed before the Secretary of War, they were discharged on parole of honor.

Thus far "victory" has attended us, and Providence has wonderfully interposed to shield our heads in the day of battle, and unto His Great Name be all the praise for our success. May His smile cheer us in this dark and gloomy hour.

I hope you have received ere this the box of lint; Father sent it up by a gentleman, who intended going straight to Manassas   for though it was a very small quantity yet we will send more shortly together with another box, the contents of which may perhaps prove more acceptable at the present time.

My thoughts often recur to the pleasant time passed during your recent visit to our City, but we sincerely hope that we may not be deprived of the pleasure of spending many more joyous hours in your company, for I can assure you *we* arrived at Manassas in imagination much earlier than *you* did in reality. You fear that you may not be able to visit your family in July; I sincerely hope you may for I know it would afford you so much pleasure. Present our compliments to all our friends; we anticipated seeing them in our City ere this, but nevertheless hope to do so soon. My cousins are yet with us; they are much pleased at the conduct of *"Our Lieut."* in reading his Bible daily, and urge him to continue it. As I have written much more than I intended and as I fear I may weary you with the perusal, I must conclude. Excuse all imperfections such as the handwriting etc., as our family is not generally distinguished by the beauty of their penmanship. Write often for we are always delighted to hear from our friends.

May success and happiness attend you all, and may Heavens brightest blessings ever be showered on those who have gone forth to sacrifice everything for the liberties of their dear country, is the fond wish of

Your attached friend

BETTIE F. HILL

N. B. Father intends leaving for Manassas tomorrow morning, but your regiment being at Centerville, as it is uncertain about seeing you, so I will send this by mail. Mother requests me to tell you that you may expect a box for you all of etc., sometime next week.

* * * * *

At Manassas, Colonel Cash's regiment joined General Beauregard's army, where it was assigned to the First Brigade, commanded by Brigadier General M. L. Bonham.[2] On July 17, according to Lucy Davis King, the regiment, "by order and as part of the plans, retreated to the face of the army and fell back to Bull Run, where it held the crossing at Mitchell's Ford."[3]

Official records cite Colonel Cash's report to General Bonham.[4]

Hdqrs. Eighth Regiment South Carolina Vols.,
Camp Victory, July 31, 1861

Early on Sunday morning, the 21st instant, heavy cannonading and rapid discharges of musketry were heard about two miles to my left, and about 11 o'clock A.M. I received orders through Colonel Kershaw to move forward and engage the enemy. . . . The two regiments proceeded rapidly to the scene of action, were formed in order of battle some two or three hundred yards from the ground which afterwards proved to be to us the main point of battle.

. . . . Advancing I found a considerable force fronting my line and concealed by a rail fence. For a time, we supposed them to be our friends. Captain Pawley, of my staff, boldly moved forward with a view to ascertain the real character of those thus concealed. He had advanced some twenty paces when he was fired upon. Escaping uninjured, he immediately returned the fire, killing one of the enemy, as they now proved to be. I at once ordered the firing from my line. After several well-directed volleys had been delivered the enemy (zouaves) were driven back. Falling back in great confusion, they were rallied in a valley some distance in the rear, where the enemy was posted in great numbers. From this point they returned my fire, killing five of my men and wounding several.

. . . . After a short delay, I was ordered by Colonel Kershaw to follow his command in the direction of the stone bridge. While executing this order I was met by General Beauregard, who ordered me to dislodge a body of the enemy supposed to be in the wood to my left. . . . After continuing the pursuit for some two and a half or three miles we came in full view of the heavy columns of the retreating enemy. The regiments were halted, and Captain Kemper commenced a rapid and well-directed fire upon them, which caused them to abandon their guns wagons &c., and completed the defeat.

. . . . My officers and men behaved gallantly during this trying ordeal, displaying that heroism and bravery which have ever characterized southern troops. Where all behaved so well I would do violence to my own feelings were I to institute any comparisons by individualizing any as particularly distinguished for meritorious conduct.

. . . . Annexed to this report is a list of the killed and wounded of my regiment.[5]

By July 23, 1861, when Sarah Williamson wrote her next letter to Miss Darby, the nation was engaged in grim devastating war. Boys from the Pee Dee had fought and died at Bull Run in Virginia. Back home, people were troubled with runaway slaves; bodies of their young men were being brought home for burial; patriotic groups were leaving for the front. Sarah's report was on conditions at home.

Sarah Williamson, Florence, South Carolina, to Jemima Darby, Ringgold, Louisiana.

Orangedale
July 23, 1861

Dear Miss Darby

I received your welcome letter. Have been slow to answer waiting for some news from the Creek.[6] Mother went up to Molls.[7] Met sister there. Found her and the little boy much improved since they were here. Said Lizzie[8] was at her own home. The clerk[9] stays with her. And her mother[10] spends some time with her. Is much distressed about Tom.[11] Thinks she will never see him again.

I expect you have heard Eddie Fort[12] was brought home *dead*. His father went on but got there after he was dead. Linton[13] nursed him. Said he was affected as the others were. Poor Mrs. Fort. I am truly sorry for her. Jane[14] married Evander White the week before. Have gone to Cheraw. Clearks for John Evans, I think and poor business these hard times. Vanderford had not returned the last I heard.

Havent heard from the girls[15] in some time. Dont see them any more than if they were in Texas. Mr. Phelps[16] is not married yet. His congregation must be thin now. Several have gone to Virginia.

James Napier[17] Robert James[18] and two of Henry Cannons[19] sons are to go with McIntoshes company[20] in a few days. I spent last Tuesday with the Miss N[21]   They were quite busy getting James ready. The parson was very polite. Dont hear anything about his getting married. Has not taken off crape yet. Bell Porcher[22] married Tom Gregg a few weeks past. Her health is still poor. Have gone to the Springs.

The children[23] spent last week with us. V is better than K. Just as careless as ever. Mrs. DuPre has not improved them in neatness as I expected she would knowing they had no mother. Seems to have given it up altogether. I would be glad if they could go to Lime Stone. Think it would be better for them. Have such a long vacation to stay at home. No persons fit for them to associate with. I cant keep them or stay there all the time.

Crops are fine here this year, particularly corn. Peter says Wilds has the best he ever saw him have anywhere.[24] Have very little fruit. No peaches   no plums. I hear you have fine ones.[25] Do send me over a basket full. I have made black berry cordial and jelly. Got some pears at Mr. Napier's. Made some preserves. Charles[26] spends most of his time here. His health is bad. Is very low spirited. You know what a talker he used to be. Scarcely says a word now without you speak to him. Will catch fish. Had some fine trout last week.

Leonard Dove[27] spent a week with us. Is looking well. A nice young man. Is trying to get an office in some of the companies. Has not succeeded yet. George Dargan[28] Johny Lide[29] and Oliver C[30] have gone to the Cavalry company;[31] we hear that Beauregard has got Scott[32] in a tight place. Am afraid it is too good to be true.

Aunt Julia[33] has been ill for two weeks. Dr. Flinn[34] and Hart[35] attending her. Has typhoid fever. Was delirious some time. Much distressed about Sallie[36]   Has given her up. Has become perfectly resigned. Thinks she will die and cant raise her head without causing sick stomach. Has fainting spells. Has to be fanned all night. Scarcely sleeps unless she is under the influence of anodyzne. Dr. H. says she may get well with strictest attention. I sat up with her Sunday night. Mary Rogers[37] has been with her all the time. Sister Mary Ann[38] is with her a good deal. Likes to have her fix the pillows. Just telegraphed to Betsie[39] last week. Hope she will get to see her. She dreamed that B. had come. Spoke to everyone in the room but her. Went and knelt at her feet crying. Said Dr. Flinn was telling it everywhere that her going off was the cause of her sickness.

Mrs. McCall and Sallie[40] called on us a few Saturdays ago on their way to church for the first time, do you think we ought ever to return it? Says Addie[41] finds it hard to keep a nice house with so many children. One of their servants set the house on fire in the day. Found it before it burned much.

The neighborhood has been in commotion for the last fortnight trying to catch runaways. Caught three. Say there are 50 out near us. The swamp is a great place for them. Tom and Sack[42] had been out more than two months. Went without a word. Caught Tuesday night. Had to shoot him. The wounds are not severe. She had a gun. Got it from Tarver,[43] near Elly Wilson's.[44] Were going to shoot brother Wilds Thursday night as he came from Florence. Just caught them in time to save himself. They expected Lincon to set them free on the 4th July. I suppose as he didn't do it they would kill Massa and be free anyhow. I am more afraid of the negroes than of the Yankees. I have finished my paper. All are well. Mother is singing. All send respects to you,

Yours,

S. L. WILLIAMSON

* * * * *

Although they were situated some distance inland,[45] natives of the Pee Dee region were alarmed when Union forces organized expeditions against seacoast towns in South Carolina late in 1861. Charleston and Beaufort were targets for attacks and Georgetown had been set up as a training center for troops. Hence, civilians at home were alerted for news from these three areas. Some Darlington men were in Virginia, but, during the middle weeks of December, there were no major operations which included their regiments. Unaccustomed to the hardships of army life, the men were often sick. Frequently, they died of natural causes. In a short letter from Camp Bonham, Thomas E. Howle described conditions to his wife, Bettie, in Leavensworth.

First Lieutenant Thomas E. Howle, Camp Bonham, Virginia, to Bettie Vann Howle, Leavensworth, South Carolina.

Camp Bonham[46]
Nov. 25, 1861

My dear wife

I have just got in Camp from pickett and find P. W. Boze- man[47] with his discharge and ready to leave for home. We have had an awful wet cold time. It has snowed or sleeted every day while we were out. I tell you we had a time but have come through right side up and all well. I think I can stand almost anything now. We are looking to Pensacola[48] with a great deal of interest. The snow is very pretty on the mountains. The ground was covered here last night.

James[49] is still sick and Dr. Griffin[50] thinks he is a great deal better. If he does not improve fast I will get him off to the Hospital. Tell Father[51] if he gets seriously sick I will send him off to a good hospital and while he is in Camp I will at- tend to him in person.

Yours of the 18th and 21st is at hand. I am not sending clothes and you can send my suit by some safe opportunity. I send you one hundred and twenty dollars $120 by Bozeman. You can do as you like about subscription to the church. Re- tain Mr. Dargan[52] if possible. We all will have to make sacrifices now. Preachers as well as other people. Good-bye dear wife. Write often to

Yr devoted husband,

T. E. HOWLE

* * * * *

Federal troops who captured Port Royal Ferry and Beaufort, South Carolina, were unable to carry out orders. "Seize or destroy all cotton," the order read. "Employ negroes in picking cotton, collecting, packing cotton, who on your vouchers, properly made out and certified to, will be paid by the Quartermaster's Depart- ment."[53] The Confederates, whenever possible, burned their own cotton as they deserted their homes. The Negroes "rendered but little assistance. Many came in and ran off. They had not yet been organized. . . . The large families that they brought in made a great many useless mouths."[54] The climate was not healthy; malaria was deadly.

But the citizens of South Carolina were not aware of these obstacles to their enemy's progress. Nor did they know how United States forces planned to attack their Charleston.

> I believe that the South Carolinians are under the conviction that we are about to strike their center by Port Royal Ferry. We want to keep up the delusion, and if I only had some cavalry would feel justified in moving the bulk of our force to the southern end of the railroads and shutting off South Carolina from Savannah, and preparing the way to effectually take the city by the southern route.[55]

Conditions at home were disturbing. Refugees were pouring in from the low country.[56] Prices were high; commodities not available. Women lived in terror of Negroes, who, never certain of their status, roamed about with no sense of security and no proper sense of loyalty. Mrs. Witherspoon[57] of Society Hill had been murdered[58] by her own slaves in September, 1861.

> For some years after their children had all married the old people resided alone, though often the house was filled with children and grandchildren visiting them. Old Mr. Witherspoon died suddenly although he had been in failing health for some time. His widow's death was most tragic, murdered by her own trusted servants in the first year of the Civil War. The shock of this most distressing event was terrible and will never fade from the memory of those who once knew and esteemed her.[59]

Sarah Williamson, Florence, South Carolina, to Jemima Darby, Ringgold, Louisiana.

Florence
December 16, 1861

Dear friend

I almost imagine I hear you say, Sarah has forgotten me. I think and speak of you often though I am lazy about writing. Thomas[60] asked at breakfast about you. So you may be sure you are not forgotten by any of us; all are glad to hear from you. Mother has been suffering with rheumatism in her right arm. Was so she couldn't use it, but very little. I rubbed it with red pepper and compor bound it up with flannel. It is better. She has her hymn book singing merrily. Brother Wilds left the first of Nov for the coast[61] in Cousin Tom Wilds company. They are stationed near Georgetown. Have not had anything but drilling to do yet.

I expect you have heard the Yankees have Beaufort, S. C. All of the citizens left. Burnt up their houses and as much cotton as they could but the Yankees have a great many negroes. Took the organ out of the church. Had musick and danced with the negro women. We hear they are very hard on them. Some have run away. Say they chain them to wheelbarrows to haul dirt. Are picking out the cotton. Created quite a panic. Many of the planters have sent the negroes up in the country.

Sarah McCall's husband[62] has taken some. A good many Florence families from Charleston are trying to get board at Darlington. Mr. DuPre has Mr. Henning's family. The president of the Georgetown bank charges 20 dollars apiece for the whites, 10 for servants. Says he can promise only plain fair at that; dont you think he will get rich. Mrs. DuPre has some schollars. Her prices are so high; the times so hard Virginia and Kate are not going now. Bettie Dargan[63] took Furman's[64] school in Springville when he left. I hear she is getting on well with it. Hope she will teach next year if the Yankees do not have possession by then. I am afraid they will be in our midst. A great part of Charleston was burnt last Wednesday.[65] Suppose it was done by some Yankee. They threaten to lay it in ashes.

We feel the hard times now. Had to give 20 cents for cotton Osnaburgs[66] for the darkies. Could not get wool. Cant get flannels for the soldiers. Salt is selling at 15 dollars a sack. Some persons have gone to the sea shore to make it. Say it cost them 10. How are you doing for coffee? We have tried potatoes and rye. Think the rye best. I hear it fattens people. I am sure I ought not drink it though I like it with nice cream in it. Better than rio coffee.

Andrew and Moll were here last week. He is very thin. Has asthma often. You never saw anyone fatten as M. has. She used to laugh at me. She is a great deal larger than I am now. Martha Sanders has a daughter. Are going to live in the Goodwin house next year.

Robert James[67] came from Virginia last week. Has been sick. Cant stand the cold climate. Ground covered with snow when he left. Has a discharge. Says he is going on the coast when he gets well. Laden Lide[68] has recovered. Is at home now. Bettie is looking well since her trip to Richmond. Hartwell Hart[69] was very ill but is recovering. A great number of the soldiers are sick. It would be dreadful if the Yankees were to attack them now.

Margaret Fort[70] went to the Association at the Hill. Dined at the Kings. Said they are all well and cheerful. Eliza was not down. Mr. LaCost[71] had another attack not long before. His mind was affected. I suppose he is better; heard he bought all the cards in town at 37 cents and sold them at a dollar; and that is the way most of our merchants are doing. As mean as the Yankees. I am dreading Christmas as all of our best men are gone. I hear the darkies have threatened to take Darlington. William Stokes went with Brother Wilds. You know we feel like we are broken up, but the enemy is at our door, as it were, so we have to do as best we can.

The Witherspoon negroes[72] were hung in the field in front of where Mr. King[73] lived. Hung until nearly dead, cut down in a hole and covered up to feel something their mistress[74] felt.

Mrs. Baker[75] came the last of Oct. Had to go to Scott[76] to get a passport and had her trunk examined. Jeff[77] is at home. Has improved. Resigned in Virginia. Will go in his own state.

Aunt Julia has got so she has been to church a few times. Mr. Douglas[78] had soar throat for more than a week. Had the doctor. Is better today. Mr. Vann went to Virginia after his grandson. Has been sick since his return. Sisters little angel boy[79] winged his way to heaven the 5th of November. Was taken the night he was a year old with spasms and had them until he died. It was almost heart-rending to see him suffer and not be able to relieve. Complained very little. His head was affected. He was beautiful in death. Sister has a cough. Looks badly. Mother sends her love.

SARAH

Jim went to make salt. Sister came stayed with us more than a week. How we missed the babe.

* * * * *

Late in 1861, Confederate officers faced the problems of supplying replacements for the South Carolina troops whose terms of enlistment expired on April 18. Writing from camp in an undated letter[80] to his wife, Thomas Howle revealed his opinion of how to cope with the situation.

Lieutenant Thomas E. Howle, Centreville, Virginia, to his wife, Lizzie Vann Howle, Leavensworth, South Carolina.

No. 2

Dear Wife

Mr. Frazer[81] did not leave this evening and as I filled up my sheet I concluded to add another line. The weather is now fair and cold and I hope will continue fair. Your letter of the 19th is just at hand. I am glad to hear you continue well. My health is good. I can eat almost anything and at any time. I suppose you will think this nothing strange as I was always fond of eating. I think it would be hard for me to get satisfied on Spare Ribs or sausages. We have been putting up beef, and now have as good corn beef as can be had anywhere. To-day I eat a tremendous dinner — Pork and Cabbages. Jno. Jr. and Jno's wife[82] sent him some cake, catsup, etc., which we enjoy very much. J. I expect will leave for home soon. He is among the Lieutenants that has applied for a Forlough. I am sorry to hear that Dr. Griffin is improving so slowly.[83] We miss him very much here especially when everyone is sick. There is some talk of revolunteering here. I don't know whether our men will reenlist here or wait untill we all go home. It will never do for South Carolina troops to back down at this time and neither will it do to go home the 18th April and leave this line exposed. It will then be the season for the Campaign to open. The only way to remedy the matter that I can now conceive will be to disband us two months before the time and then for the President[84] to make a requisition before the Governor[85] for as many troops as he wants the state to furnish to have them in service about the middle of April — and say nothing about bounties — if the men are not paid as much as the Federal Government may think they ought to have — raise the pay per month — or reorganize here and form the nueclus of a Regiment and then send them home for sixty days to recruit. It is getting a little late at night and I must close. I hope you are all well.

Yr husband,

T. E. H.

(Tuesday, 24th)[86]   All is well this morning. I hope you will have a Merry Christmas. Tell Julia[87] that I gave one pair of her gloves away and will give the other pair to another young man in a few days. Of course they will think and believe that they were knit by her. We got out on picket tomorrow and will not return untill Saturday. We have solid cold weather this morning. The wind blew a perfect hurricane all night. I hope you are well.

Yr husband

T. E. HOWLE

* * * * *

"We are all distressed," wrote Sarah Williamson on March 6, 1862. Troops who had been engaged in drilling for several months had been moved up to the front. Appeals for recruits were being made by military leaders and civilian administrators. From South Carolina, there were 9,636 troops in service "beyond the state," and 21,271 "within the state."[88] Sarah's brother, Joseph Wilds, was among them.

Charleston was vulnerable to enemy attack, as were all South Carolina coastal cities. The chief of the United States Army engineers had already drawn up a detailed plan for the attack on Charleston,[89] and Confederate commanders were confident that "the enemy would soon attack Savannah or Charleston, directly or by the shortest land approach, especially if their generals have a proper appreciation of a moral effect of a victory."[90]

Edisto Island, South Carolina, had been occupied by federal forces on February 11. Colonel Henry Moore, commander of the post, believed that the position which he occupied represented the key to Charleston.[91]

Hatred for the Yankees ran high in South Carolina by 1862.

Bad weather added to the discomfort of soldiers and brought fears to the hearts of the women at home. Sarah's morale was low.

Sarah Williamson, Florence, South Carolina, to Jemima Darby, Ringgold, Louisiana.

March 6, 1862

Dear Miss Darby

Your welcome letter was received some time ago. I have been so busy getting Virginia ready to go to Lime Stone have delayed answering. Bettie Dargan has a school in Springville.[92] Kate is going to board at Cousin Thomas Lide's[93] and go to her.

We are all distressed. Brother Wilds and Mr. Douglas[94] are to leave this week for the war.[95] I don't know what is to become of the poor females. No man in the neighborhood but Mr. H. Cannon.[96] His health so bad he can't go out at night. I am afraid we can't keep hogs or chickens. A great many negroes from the low country at Florence.[97] William Stokes is here on furlough. Left Edwin[98] well. Cousin Sam Wilds[99] came home last night. Sick. Bad cough. Is afraid it will settle in his lungs. A great many cases in the hospital. Two die a day in Georgetown.

We have had rain for the past two months. Made it worse for the soldiers. Keep a guard at Pee Dee bridge. 500 men are ordered to be ready in Darlington Monday. It is a dreadful time. Who knows what is to be the end of this war. Mother thinks she won't live to see it. Her health has been very good this winter. Has been gardening. Planted all kinds of seed. Peas are stuck. Growing finely. Plants nearly large enough to set out. Trees are very backward. I hope we will have peaches this year. Have a nice orchard.

T. Howle is at home[100] getting recruits for the war.[101] I expect you have heard he is captain since Evans resigned.[102]

Sister was at the Hill for a few days a few weeks back. Went to see the girls; they were well. Cant get much sewing. Times too hard. Have the same servant they had last year. Think her very good. Let her iron. Saw Eliza's oldest girl[103]   didn't find her as pretty as she expected; her father had another attack. Was not expected to live. William[104] died in Virginia; they all took it very hard. Emily is afraid she will never see me. Mr. Phelps[105] has gone to Columbia. Mr. Dargan preaches for them once a month. Robert Edwards gets worse. Cant bear for Miss Scharlotte[106] and his wife to talk or leave him any time; Mr. Adams[107] has bought Mrs. Witherspoon's house.

Cornelia and Lucy[108] are at Mr. Pressley's. L. has a son. Quite a pet for Aunt Kate.[109] Jeramie Thomas is a boarder from Georgetown not a schollar. Mrs. DuPre has 19 schollars. Margaret Bristow and girls. She has Miss Tompy Hamilton keeping house[110] for her.

Since I commenced writing, Cousin Jane Dargan,[111] Hannah Dabbs[112] and sister came and spent two nights and day. Left this morning for Andrews. It was a treat to have them. It reminded us of old times at Spring Hill. How sad it is to think we shall never see the old associates again in this life; Cousin J and H. are looking as well as I ever saw them. H. is living at Cousin Evans.[113]

Mr. Dargan went to see Mr. LaCoste a few days before. As soon as he entered the room he said "Here lies an old man waiting for the Lord's time." Appeared to be in a happy frame of mind. Two of his toes had dropped off, mortefied. The doctor wished to cut off the foot. He would not consent. Mr. D. said Eliza looked haggard and pale. The room was so offensive. Enough to make her so. I expect Eliza will come to live with her sisters.

Cousin Joseph Lide[114] married Carrie McIver.[115] I hear Aunt Jane[116] is pleased at it. She read a great deal for Aunt Jane. Who would have thought that gay girl would have fancied such a sober-sided man? Mr. Wilkins is getting along finely with his new wife.[117] Mrs. Baker is at Mrs. F.[118] Talks very hard about the Yankees. Never wishes them to conquer us. Says it will be dreadful times if they do, and I think they will. I am almost out of heart since their last victory.[119] Our people have no arms. What can they do? Wilds says I must practice shooting so I could kill some if they come to the house. I think I can use the old sword better.

Mrs. James, Martha Sanders and Amelia spent the evening with us. M. has a fine, large daughter. Looks very much like Henrietta. She is going to stay by herself. Says she is not afraid.

Mr. Culpepper[120] has been confined to bed several weeks. Has breaking out on the leg. Discharges a pint at a time. I am afraid he will never get well. He is missed by the soldiers. He would go frequently to see and preach to them. Mr. Thomas[121] has a company. Is near Georgetown.

Paper is getting scarce. Calico is selling at 37 cents. Such as we gave 12 for. Shirting 40; salt at a dollar a pint at the Hill. I see no way for poor people to live. Molasses 75 a gallon. Meat 25 cts. A great many persons are spinning and weaving.

Mr. and Mrs. Killings[122] are dead. Mrs. Nesmith lives with Mrs. Fisher. Our pastor has not been to see us this year. Does not visit us as often as he did when we first came down. Mrs. Lane[123] is there. Can't get to Florida.

I hear Aunt Jane[124] is failing fast and can scarsely walk. Mrs. Council[125] is with her. Sister is looking badly. I am afraid she can't stand it long. Jim is thinking of going to war. She sends love to you. Mother says she would like to see you. Remember me to your niece.[126] Write soon.

Yours,

SARAH

* * * * *

By June of 1862, citizens of South Carolina were concerned with the enemy's position within the Southland. It appeared that the Yankees had gained control of a significant number of Southern towns and railroads.

On April 10, 1862, Colonel Graham[127] was ordered to move "all troops and public stores under his command from Georgetown to Charleston."[128] For a month, the men camped near the old South Carolina Railroad depot, after which they were assigned to Morris Island where "thorough discipline was the order of the day."[129] Early in June the siege of Charleston began. The United States transport *Flora* reached James Island on Monday, June 2, and troops of the First Brigade, Second Division, Department of the South, under Brigadier General Isaac I. Stevens, were landed. There followed a skirmish in which Union forces advanced rapidly upon a masked battery of Confederates while the gunboat *Unadilla* directed fire from the water.[130]

Four companies of the Twenty-Fourth South Carolina Regiment (Infantry), the Marion Rifles, Pee Dee Rifles, Evans Guard, and Colleton Guard participated in the fighting and were responsible for the capture of twenty-two prisoners before the Federals were driven back to their "support," but not from the island. A list of the casualties showed one officer, Lieutenant A. J. Mims, and eight men wounded.[131]

New Orleans, having "surrendered to the combined naval and land forces of the United States," and "having been evacuated by the rebel forces," was proclaimed in a state of martial law by Major General Benjamin Franklin Butler on May 1, 1862.[132] Fifteen days later, General Butler, a New England Democrat whose father had fought under General Andrew Jackson against the British at New Orleans in 1814, issued his infamous "Woman Order," declaring that any woman who insulted or showed contempt for United States soldiers would be "regarded and held liable to be treated as a woman of the town plying her vocation."[133]

Stonewall Jackson was in the midst of his Valley Campaign. During the four battles of Kernstown (March 23), Winchester (May 25), Cross Keys, and Port Republic, he so frightened the government officials at Washington that necessary reinforcements were not sent to the Union army near Richmond. There was occasion for rejoicing back in South Carolina.

Pee Dee men whom the Williamsons and Miss Darby knew had arrived in Virginia in time for the Battle of Seven Pines on May 31 and June 1. William Augustus Law reported:

> We were stationed on Green Pond, between Charleston and Savannah, on the coast, and were there about six months, guarding the coast. Then we were sent to Columbia, where our troop was reviewed. We were sent to Richmond, a journey of twenty-one days. After resting a few days, we were ordered to the front in a big Battle at Seven Pines.[134]

Women of Sarah Williamson's and Jemima Darby's station were in no wise sand-hill tackeys. Although devout Baptists, they were not brush-arbor illiterates with preachers who exhorted. The Williamsons and Darbys represented the middle class of South Carolinians, who owned only a few slaves and to whom religion was dignified, but vital. They sent their daughters to boarding schools and academies; their men fought as company grade and non-commissioned officers. To them war meant privations and insecurity. Unlike Mary Boykin Chesnut,[135] kinswoman to Darlington citizens, and Varina Howell Davis, who followed their distinguished husbands to Richmond and continued to hold court in traditional fashion, Sarah Williamson went to no balls, wore no imported lace, and listened to no scandalous gossip. Her garden and church and the sick and the dying occupied her time. She feared that her letter of June 9 would never travel all the way from South Carolina to Louisiana during such perilous times.

Sarah Williamson, Florence, South Carolina, to Jemima Darby, Ringgold, Louisiana.

Florence, S. C.
June 9, 1862

Miss Jemima Darby
    Ringgold, La.

Dear Miss Darby

Your welcome letter came to hand more than a month after it was written. I dont know that you will ever receive this as the Yankees have so many of our towns and railroads. Their gunboats are near Charleston.[136] Have been fighting several days.[137] 400 landed on James Island. Our men drove them off. Took a good many prisoners.[138] A few of our men were killed.[139] We are all anxiety. Brother Wilds[140] and Peter Coggeshall[141] are there and a great many of our acquaintances. Edwin[142] is at home sick. Very willing to be this far from our enemies. I do pray that they may not kill our earthly dependances nor take one city.

Do you not pity the ladies of New Orleans? I fear our country is to be overrun by such miserable beings as Butler[143] Then what is to become of us? None but the Allwise God knows. They are fighting near Richmond. Stonewall Jackson has gone over to Maryland.[144] Doing wonders. T. Howle is at home sick. Linton has been sick. Got a discharge. Is at home improving. Jeff has gone to Virginia. Mrs. Ferguson and Mrs. Baker are both feeble. Cousin Nancy Dubose[145] has been crippled. Cant walk. Cousin Jane[146] has been in bed most of the time since Johny died.[147] Eliza LaCost stays at Cheraw. Is to keep Harriet McIver's[148] children[149] when she goes in camp with George.[150] She spent most of her time with him in Geotown. They sold out Mr. L's store[151] at a very high price. I have never heard how much E got. I have not heard from the girls in some time.

Every house on the Hill is occupied. Several families in the Witherspoon house.[152] Everyone in Darlington and Springville has refugees. Sallie McIver[153] has several boarders. Mrs. DuPre still keeps school and takes boarders. Mr. Belar has moved to Mr. James house. Rented his out. His wife[154] had chills. Mr. William James[155] died a few weeks back of measles. Robert died in Virginia soon after.[156] John DeLorme[157] died of typhoid fever. Had only been there two months. Addie is at his father's There are two families in the Wickam house from near Geotown. I expect they find it a dull place. I dont expect many persons have called to see them. Hannah Waring has her house full.

Everything to live on is very scarce except corn. Butter cant be had for 50 cents. Small chickens for 15; bacon 37½ a pound; salt, 60 dollars a sack; coffee, 75 cents a pound. I dont know how people are to live if the war continues much longer.

I received a letter from sister. Says she is fattening on Whiskey and sweet milk. I think it is the wrong way. Her cough is better. Cant ride farther than the church. Said they had 30 sunday school schollars. I haven't been there since February. I dont feel like getting so far from the office.[158] Virginia[159] is getting uneasy. Anxious to get home. Is afraid the Yankees will take the railroad, and she cant get back. Mr. Curtis[160] is afraid he will have to give up the school. Finds it hard to get provisions. I should be very sorry. I think V. is improving. Kate is studying well with Bettie. She has 25 schollars. Too many I think. Mr. Dargan is to spend tomorrow with us on his way to Marion. Preaches there Sunday.

We went to Florence Sunday. Heard Tom Law[161]   His subject was God's Special Providence. He explained it well. We were much pleased with him. Think he will make a fine preacher.

Mr. Wilkins married Mrs. Brown Bryant. Children are pleased. Even his gold negro, Hiam, is pleased. Dont you think it fortunate for her. Mrs. Fort says she has everything unquiet about her.

Mother is out attending her poultry. Has 15 turkeys, 5 goslings. She has not been so well for some time. Has a fine garden. We have had rain all the spring. Suits this garden. My yellow multiflora and Persian honeysuckle have been beautiful. Are more than half way up the piaza post. I have a cloth of gold at one. Will bloom soon. We have ripe apples. The peach trees are full. I am afraid I shall get so fat I cant walk much.

Carrie is looking out.[162] Hannah is with her. Has two pretty boys. Looks very healthy. Paper is scarce. I am going to write to sister on yours and she will have the pleasure of two. Edwin sends his respects. Sister M sends hers. Left here today and looks badly. Mother joins me in love to you and Mrs. K.

Yours,

SARAH

*　*　*　*　*

According to the terms of their re-enlistment, South Carolina Volunteers were granted extensive furloughs during which they were free to visit their families. Thomas Howle, who had been promoted from first lieutenant to captain late in 1861, spent about four months at his home in Leavensworth, during which time he recruited about seventy-five or eighty men.[163] He left Darlington District to return to Virginia about the middle of June, accompanied by Captain John K. McIver,[164] a friend of long standing from Society Hill.

Captain John Kolb McIver, Society Hill, South Carolina, to Captain Thomas E. Howle, Leavensworth, South Carolina.

Society Hill
June 16, 1862

Dear Capt

I have just received your note by Charles and wish very much that I had known two days earlier that you would be going on so soon. I have made all arrangements to start this afternoon and have promised to take a negro for Mr. Coker and several bundles which are to meet me at the Depot and I cant well get word around in time to have them stopped. I

however will wait until tomorrow Tuesday as I am anxious
to have your company and so I will expect to meet you at Dove
tomorrow afternoon.

Very truly yours,

J. K. McIVER

＊ ＊ ＊ ＊ ＊

When Captain Howle returned to Virginia, he was assigned
to General Stonewall Jackson's forces, which, while operating in
the Shenandoah Valley, had held back a large Union army under
General McDowell and had prevented their joining McClellan's
forces for an attack on Richmond. On June 25, with McClellan's
outposts only about four miles from Richmond, General Lee attacked. In the Seven Days Battle, June 26 to July 2, Lee succeeded
in stopping McClellan's advance, but could not prevent the
Union forces from establishing new bases on the James River.
On June 28, Howle wrote to his wife directly from the battlefield.

Captain Thomas E. Howle, Camp Hoole, Virginia, to Bettie
Vann Howle, Leavensworth, South Carolina.

Camp Hoole
June 28 62

Dear Wife

The Battle is going on[165]   Our plans are working well
The enemy are routed   on their right wing. Jackson
has got in the rear and is said has possession of the Rail Road.
We now have the Grand Army in our power; and will soon
have them completely so. We have been under three fires but
have not fought yet. Our men are all safe, for which we are
thankful to the Ruler of the Universe. We ran in their pickets
yesterday and our position is in front of Richmond. We hold
them in check (in prospect). Hill[166] and Longstreet[167] is on
their right and Jackson in the rear. We will close the matter
in all probability today and tomorrow. I narrowly escaped
yesterday   a ball came in six inches of me and a slug nearly as near. We have captured artillery and other baggage. The

fight is now going on on the Right. Jackson has cut off their supplies and has possession of their transports and Railroad at Pamenky River.[168] Do write me and pray for my safety. And rest assured dear wife that if I fall it will be in the leading my gallant little company who behaved themselves well in the skirmish yesterday. My prayer is that this conflict will soon be over and that the Army of Rebellion will soon seek shelter on their own soil.

Your aff. Husband,

T. E. HOWLE

* * * * *

FOOTNOTES

1 "Report of Col. A. P. Hill, 13th Virginia Infantry," June 19, 1861, *War of the Rebellion*, Series I, Volume II, pp. 130-131. "Col. J. C. Vaughn, Third Tennessee Regiment, with two companies of his own and two Regiments from the Thirteenth Virginia Regiment, proceeded to New Creek Depot, 18 miles west of Cumberland, on the line of the Baltimore and Ohio Railroad and bring the two pieces of artillery and burn the rail road bridge." The orders were executed in meticulous detail.

2 *Treasured Reminiscences,* collected by John K. McIver Chapter, U. D. C. (Columbia, 1911), p. 10.

3 *Ibid.*

4 "Report of Col. E. B. C. Cash, Eighth South Carolina Infantry, of Operations, July 18 and 19," *War of the Rebellion,* Series I, Volume II, pp. 531-533.

5 The list shows: killed, five privates; wounded, three commissioned officers, four non-commissioned officers, sixteen privates; total killed, five; total wounded, twenty-three. Total killed and wounded, twenty-eight.

6 James and Carrie Williams, Tom and Lizzie Howle lived at the "Creek" (Black Creek neighborhood).

7 Mary Ann Charles's home was near Cashaway Ferry.

8 Bettie Vann Howle had the choice of remaining at Leavensworth or moving over to Auburn, near her father's home.

9 Tom Howle had left his store at Leavensworth in custody of the clerk.

10 Sarah Jones Vann, second wife of William Vann, had only one child, Elizabeth, called Lizzie or Bettie.

11 First Lieutenant Thomas Epathraditus Howle was with the Eighth South Carolina Regiment at Manassas, Virginia.

12 J. Edwards Fort (1838-1861), son of Josiah and Ann E. Fort, died of typhoid fever in July of 1861, while serving with the army in Virginia.

13 Linton Williams's second wife was Eddie's sister, Martha Harriett Fort, who died in 1858.

14 Jane Fort, daughter of Josiah and Ann E. Fort, married Evander White, Cheraw. She, too, was Eddie's sister.

15 The Misses King, Society Hill, were referred to repeatedly as "the girls."

16 J. C. Phelps, pastor of the Welsh Neck Baptist Church, Society Hill, was described by Mrs. Furman Wilson, *Memories of Society Hill* (South Carolina, Pee Dee Historical Society, 1909-1910), p. 10. "He was a diligent student, prepared fine sermons which he read very closely, and made a good impression as a preacher. Being a Northern man, peculiar in his manner and appearance, tho affable and desiring to be friendly, he found it impossible to adapt himself to our people and customs, especially being an unmarried man who had no one to help him in overcoming his awkwardness and mingling unreservedly with his people."

17 James Napier was the son of the Reverend Robert and Elizabeth Lane Napier.

18 Robert Ervin James was the son of William Elias James, Darlington.

19 William Henry Cannon was a son of Henry and Mary Ervin Cannon, Springville.

20 David Gregg McIntosh commanded Company B of the First South Carolina Regiment.

21 Martha and Sarah Napier were the unmarried daughters of Robert Napier.

22 Belle Porcher, daughter of Dr. Peter C. Porcher, married Thomas Gregg in 1861.

23 Virginia and Kate Williamson were teen-age daughters of George Williamson.

24 Peter Collin Coggeshall was a Williamson relative by marriage. Joseph Wilds Williamson operated a farm near Florence.

25 R. B. Howell and W. U. Richardson, *Bienville Parish, Louisiana* (New Orleans, 1885), p. 5. ". . . plum is a fruit common in every household."

26 Charles Andrews's mother, Mrs. Nancy Andrews (December 20, 1775 — April 5, 1856), a relative of the Wilds family, was buried in the family plot at Lowther's Hill Cemetery.

27 J. Leonard S. Dove, cadet at The Citadel, from Darlington, was graduated in

1861. He received his commission as lieutenant in the Palmetto Light Artillery in 1861.

28 Timothy George Dargan (1840-1881), son of the Baptist minister, J. O. B. Dargan and his wife, Jane Lide Dargan, graduated from The Citadel in 1861, married his cousin, Louisa Dargan, and enlisted in Hampton's Legion, Bonham's Regiment, for service in the cavalry at Manassas, Virginia.

29 John Miller Lide, son of Evan and Martha Miller Lide, George Dargan's cousin, married Eliza Edwards.

30 Oliver Coggeshall was the son of Peter Collin Coggeshall I and Ann Shorey Pawley. He (1832-1888) was the younger brother of Peter Collin Coggeshall II, the Williamson relative by marriage who, with his wife, Nancy, was mentioned so often by Mrs. Charles.

31 Colonel Wade Hampton organized "Hampton's Legion," composed of South Carolina men, early in 1861 and moved the group on to Virginia in time for the Battle of Bull Run.

32 The Battle of Bull Run had just been won. General Winfield Scott was in command of the troops around Washington; General P. G. T. Beauregard was in command of the Confederate forces across the Potomac.

33 Julia Terrel Wilds was the widow of Peter Wilds.

34 Dr. Thomas J. Flinn, Darlington, a native of Ireland, married Amelia Eliza Zimmerman, Darlington.

35 Dr. Robert Lide Hart (1816-1879) married Elizabeth A. Flinn (1822 1867), and settled in Darlington as a practicing physician in 1840.

36 Sallie Wilds was Mrs. Wilds's afflicted daughter.

37 Mary Rogers, a practical nurse, worked with the sick among her relatives and old friends. She was a sister to Mrs. Bright Williamson.

38 Beulah W. Coggeshall, Letter from Darlington, South Carolina, to John A. Cawthon, Russellville, Arkansas, November 30, 1952. "Mary Ann Charles must have been a woman of force — the sisters (Misses Nina and Clara Coggeshall and Mrs. Mamie Coggeshall Lide, Wilds Hall) say that in Grandma's last illness, she was in full charge at Wilds Hall."

39 Elizabeth Wilds had recently married Leighton Lide and moved to Mississippi.

40 Eliza Miller Allbrooks McCall was the mother of William Thomas McCall, who died in 1860 of an accident, and of Sarah Delphina (December 20, 1842 — December 7, 1902), who married Robert Pickett Hamer in 1861.

41 Addie McCall McIntyre Frierson was the wife of David E. Frierson, the Presbyterian minister, and a daughter of Mrs. McCall.

42 Tom and Sack were slaves, male and female.

43 Miss Williamson's statement that Sack "got the gun" leads one to the conclusion that this was a stolen gun, rather than one supplied to the runaways.

[44] Mrs. Elly Wilson was related to Mary Player, who had died in Darlington.

[45] Beaufort is 162 miles from Darlington; Charleston, 120; and Georgetown, 82.

[46] Headquarters, Third Brigade, under the command of Brigadier General M. L. Bonham, consisting of four South Carolina regiments.

[47] P. William Bozeman joined Black Creek Church on September 5, 1856.

[48] "Report of M. Lovell to Hon. J. P. Benjamin, Secretary of War, from Headquarters Dept., No 1, New Orleans, La.," November 19, 1861, *War of the Rebellion*, Series I, Volume VI, p. 769. "We have made steady progress in our preparation for defense. Six tons of powder have been made and distributed to the various works. I have increased the Armament of Fort Pike . . . Fort Macomb . . . Fort Livingston . . . Fort Jackson . . . and Fort St. Philip. . . . The Raft will stop a fleet under close fire of more than 100 guns." Also, "The arrival of a regiment of Mississippians gave us now 4 new regiments, 3000 men at least. . . . We will put them to a rigid course in instruction."

[49] James F. Howle, Jr., (March 25, 1837-1919), a half-brother to Thomas, married Mary House.

[50] Dr. Peter Griffin, son of Thomas and Eliza McIver Griffin of Society Hill, married Emma Mauldin.

[51] James Howle (August 23, 1799-1878), father of Thomas and James.

[52] At this time, J. O. B. Dargan, pastor of Black Creek Baptist Church, was receiving offers to go elsewhere in the state at a better salary.

[53] "Orders of T. W. Sherman, Brig. Gen., Commanding, Headquarters, Expeditionary Corps, Port Royal, S. C.," December 3, 1861, *War of the Rebellion*, Series I, Volume VI, p. 201.

[54] "Report of T. W. Sherman to General M. C. Meigs, Washington, D. C.," December 10, 1861, *ibid.*, p. 202.

[55] "Report of T. W. Sherman, Port Royal, S. C., to General George B. McClellan," December 23, 1861, *ibid.*, p. 210.

[56] "Orders of R. S. Ripley, Brig. Gen., Commanding, Headquarters, Provisional Forces, Sept. S. C., Fulafinny, S. C., to Col. William E. Martin, Commanding Mounted Regiment," November 16, 1861, *ibid.*, p. 34.

[57] Elizabeth Boykin Witherspoon was the widow of John D. Witherspoon.

[58] John Witherspoon DuBose, "The Witherspoons of Society Hill," *Bulletin* of Pee Dee Historical Association (Hartsville, 1910), p. 21. "Mrs. Witherspoon died an unnatural death, at home in Sept. 1861, age 75 years, in full possession of all her mental and physical faculties."

[59] Wilson, *Memories of Society Hill*, p. 57.

[60] Thomas Williamson, son of Miss Williamson's brother, George, who had come to live with his grandmother and aunt during Wilds Williamson's absence, was thirteen years old.

61 The coast of South Carolina was being guarded against an inevitable attack.

62 Sarah McCall (December 20, 1842 — December 7, 1902) married Robert Pickett Hamer in 1861.

63 Elizabeth Pugh Dargan (1842-1883), daughter of Reverend J. O. B. Dargan and his wife, Jane Lide Dargan, graduated from Limestone Academy in the spring of 1860.

64 James Furman Dargan (1838-1907), son of J. O. B. and Jane Lide Dargan, was named for Dr. James C. Furman, lifelong friend of the Dargan family and an instructor of the sons. James Dargan married Mary Atmar Smith of Charleston.

65 This fire was accidental; no official notice was taken of the act. Miss Williamson had probably heard rumors that the Federal forces had already made their attack.

66 Osnaburg was a coarse linen originally made in Osnaburg, Germany.

67 Robert James, son of W. E. James of Darlington, had been granted a sick leave.

68 Leighton Lide, husband of Elizabeth Wilds, returned from Mississippi to enlist in South Carolina and became ill while serving in Virginia. Bettie had gone up to nurse him.

69 Hartwell Hart, son of Thomas E. and Hannah Lide Hart, was engaged to Mollie Wilds.

70 Margaret Norwood Fort was the wife of Albert Fort.

71 A. P. LaCoste, Cheraw merchant, married (1) Margaret Dawson Fort, (2) Sallie Ann King, and (3) Eliza King.

72 Slaves belonging to the John D. Witherspoon, Sr., estate.

73 James King, father of Eliza, Sallie, Hannah, Josephine, and Emily King, owned a house opposite the Edwards house, near Welsh Neck Church, Society Hill.

74 Elizabeth Boykin Witherspoon, widow of John Witherspoon, Sr., was murdered by her own slaves in September, 1861.

75 Mrs. Baker left Black Creek neighborhood in 1856, returned in 1860 and went back north in 1860.

76 General Winfield Scott, Washington, D. C., was in command of the Union forces.

77 Jefferson W. Ferguson was Mrs. Baker's nephew.

78 Archibald Douglas (November 8, 1817 — December 19, 1861), Society Hill hotel keeper, was a native of Scotland.

79 James Leon Williams, one-year-old son of James A. and Caroline Williamson Williams, died November 5, 1861, and was buried in the Williams family cemetery, near Auburn, South Carolina.

80 The postscript to the letter is dated December 24; the body of the letter was probably written a day or two earlier.

81 John Frazier was an acquaintance from the Black Creek neighborhood.

82 Mrs. Frazier had sent food to the men.

83 Dr. Peter Griffin had returned to Society Hill to recuperate.

84 Jefferson Davis (1808-1889), president of the Confederacy.

85 Francis W. Pickens (1805-1869), governor of South Carolina.

86 The postscript was written across the upper part of the body of the letter.

87 Julia King, the daughter of Henry and Mary Ann King, and Mrs. Howle's niece, stayed with her aunt during the war. Julia later married William Croswell.

88 "Report of Adjutant General's Department, State of South Carolina, to Hon. James Chesnut, Jr., Chief of Military Department, Executive Council of South Carolina," *War of the Rebellion*, Series I, Volume VI, p. 404.

89 "Notes Relative to an Attack — Charleston, prepared by D. F. Woodbury for General J. G. Barnard, Army of the Potomac, February 18, 1862," *ibid.*, pp. 227-235.

90 "Correspondence from Headquarters, Military District, South Carolina, R. S. Ripley, Brig. Gen., Commanding, Charleston, February 18, 1862, to Capt. W. H. Taylor, Assistant Adjutant-General, Savannah, Georgia," *ibid.*, p. 391.

91 "Report of Col. Henry Moore, 47th New York Infantry, Edisto Island, February 15, 1862, to L. Thomas, Adjutant General, Washington," *War of the Rebellion*, Series I, Volume VI, pp. 89-90.

92 Robert Ervin Coker, "Springville: A Summer Village of Old Darlington District," *South Carolina Historical Magazine*, LIII, Number 4, (October, 1952), p. 190. "It was simply the region east of Black Creek from about Hood's Bridge, a couple of miles from Darlington, S. C., northward to about a mile beyond Lide's Bridge; and thence westward across Black Creek, to include the residences of T. P. Lide, William Charles and others."

93 *Ibid.*, p. 205. "Thomas P. Lide, who, with his wife, Elizabeth Sparks, of Society Hill, had the home called White Plains across Black Creek."

94 Archibald Douglas had two sons who fought in the war, Hugh and Robert. According to Wilson, *Memories of Society Hill*, p. 46, "Mr. Hugh Douglas, a very fine young man, volunteered at the outbreak of the war and died in the service of his country. Mr. Robert Douglas was also a soldier throughout the war, and afterwards married a Miss Terrel."

95 The men would leave for the front; they had been training at Georgetown for several months.

96 Henry Cannon was then about seventy-nine years old.

97 "General Orders No. 9, Headquarters, Expeditionary Corps, United States Army, Hilton Head, S. C., February 6, 1862," *War of the Rebellion*, p. 222. "The

helpless condition of the blacks inhabiting the vast area in the occupation of the forces of this command calls for immediate action on the part of the highly favored and philanthropic people."

98 Edwin Williamson, Sarah's nephew, son of her brother, Samuel Thomas, and his wife, Sarah Terrel, had entered service only recently. William Stokes and he were stationed at Georgetown, South Carolina.

99 Samuel Hugh Wilds, son of Jesse and Mary Ervin Wilds, entered State and Confederate service as captain of a choice company of men from around Darlington Courthouse, known as Company B of the Twenty-First South Carolina Regiment, Volunteer Infantry. He married Anna Ellison.

100 Thomas E. Howle, with Company F of the Eighth South Carolina Regiment of Volunteers, left Florence on June 1, 1861, took part in the Battle of Manassas Junction, and spent the most of the following summer at Flint Hill, near Fairfax Courthouse, and the winter at Centreville, Virginia.

101 *Treasured Reminiscences*, p. 10. "Early in the winter of 1862, the Confederate Congress passed an act granting to all officers and men who had enlisted for a limited period furloughs with transportation to their homes, provided they would re-enlist for the war. Captain Howle got about one-half of Company F to re-enlist, and they left for home. Taking this as a nucleus, he recruited the company and returned to the regiment with 75 or 80 men."

102 Captain William H. Evans resigned his commission during the winter of 1862.

103 Florence LaCoste, oldest daughter of A. P. and Eliza King LaCoste, was about two years old.

104 Archives of the state of South Carolina, *Roll of Honor*. William King, Pvt., First Rifles, Company E, died of disease at Richmond, Va., December 13, 1861.

105 J. C. Phelps had been pastor at Welsh Neck for five years.

106 Charlotte Kirven was the Edwards's sister in the church.

107 Wilson, *Memories of Society Hill*, p. 57. "Mr. E. L. Adams purchased the place and his family had their home here until his death."

108 Cornelia and Lucy McIver were daughters of James Kolb and Sarah Marshall McIver. Cornelia married Zimmerman Davis; Lucy married R. B. Watson.

109 "Aunt Kate" was Mrs. Catherine Fort, a cousin to Dr. James K. McIver, to whom he became engaged after the death of his first wife, Sarah Marshall McIver, and who promised to look after his children. When Lucy married, Aunt Kate moved with her to Ridge Springs, where she lived the remainder of her life.

110 Mary Ann Catlett, who had supervised household affairs at the school kept by her sister, died December 15, 1861.

111 Jane Lide Dargan (November 10, 1815-1886), daughter of Hugh and Elizabeth Pugh Lide, married Pastor J. O. B. Dargan on June 13, 1837; she was a first cousin to Sarah's mother, Sarah Wilds Williamson.

112 Hannah Dabbs (1814-1893), daughter of Samuel and Sarah L. Grove Dabbs, maiden cousin of many Pee Dee families, was noted as a genealogist.

113 Evan J. Lide (March 18, 1802 — September 9, 1882), son of Hugh and Elizabeth Pugh Lide, brother to Mrs. J. O. B. Dargan, married (1) Margaret Ervin, (2) Martha Miller, sister to Miranda Miller, wife of the artist, W. H. Scarborough, and (3) Mrs. Lavinia Eason.

114 Joseph Mark Lide, son of James and Jane Holloway Lide, married Caroline Wilds McIver early in 1862.

115 Caroline Wilds McIver (born in 1837) was the daughter of Thomas Edwards and Sara Allston Bacot McIver.

116 Jane Holloway Lide was Joseph's mother.

117 Samuel B. Wilkins, Baptist minister (April 11, 1802 — April 11, 1879), married Mrs. M. Bryant of Cheraw, in 1862.

118 Elizabeth Williams Ferguson (1807-1885) lived in the Black Creek neighborhood.

119 Edisto Island, South Carolina, was occupied February 11, 1862, by Federal troops.

120 John Culpepper, many times moderator of Welsh Neck Association, was said to have been proud of his noticeable resemblance to John C. Calhoun.

121 J. A. W. Thomas (December 31, 1822 — August 21, 1896), husband of Margaret Spears (April 29, 1824 — April 27, 1895), was captain of Company F, 21st South Carolina Volunteers. He was a seventh descendant of Tristram Thomas who came to Maryland before 1664 from Wales.

122 The death of Mrs. Fisher Killens was reported at Darlington early in 1861.

123 Mrs. Martha Lane was the mother-in-law of Pastor Robert Napier.

124 Jane Rogers Williamson was the widow of Sarah's uncle, Bright Williamson.

125 Mrs. Addie Council was distantly related to the Williamson family.

126 Amanda Melvina Brinson Kolb, Ringgold, Louisiana, had been described in complimentary terms by Miss Darby in letters to South Carolina.

127 Colonel Robert F. Graham was in command of the 21st Regiment, South Carolina Volunteers.

128 "Special Orders No. 20, Hdqrs., Dept., S. Carolina, Georgia, etc. Pocotaligo, April 10, 1862, by order of Major General John C. Pemberton: J. R. Waddy, Assistant Adjutant General," *War of the Rebellion*, Series I, Volume VI, p. 433.

129 Henry Kershaw DuBose, *History of Company B, 21st Regiment (Infantry), South Carolina Volunteers* (Columbia, 1909), p. 17.

130 "Report of Lieut. Orran H. Howard, Acting Signal Officer, U. S. Army, Signal Station, Beaufort, S. C., June 23, 1862," *War of the Rebellion*, Series I, Volume XXVI, p. 27.

131 "Report of Lieut. Col. Ellison Capers, Twenty-Fourth South Carolina Infantry, Camp 24th S. C. Volunteers, Regt., Advance Forces, James Island, S. C., June 10, 1862," *War of the Rebellion*, Series I, Volume XXVI, p. 29.

132 "Proclamation, Headquarters, Department of the Gulf, New Orleans, May 1, 1862," *War of the Rebellion*, Series I, Volume VI, p. 717.

133 "General Orders No. 28, Hdqrs., Department of the Gulf, New Orleans, May 15, 1862, by command of Major General Butler," *War of the Rebellion*, Series I, Volume XV, p. 426.

134 *Treasured Reminiscences*, p. 35.

135 Mary Boykin Chesnut, *A Diary from Dixie*, edited by Ben Ames Williams (New York, 1949).

136 The gunboats *Unadilla, Pembina, Henry Andrews, Hale*, and *Ellen* were anchored at Charleston harbor.

137 The fighting had gone on since June 3.

138 Twenty-two prisoners were taken on the first day of fighting.

139 From June 3 until June 16, there were four officers (Capt. Samuel J. Reed, 1st S. C. Artillery; Capt. Henry C. King and Lieut. John J. Edwards, 1st S. C. Batallion, Charleston; and Lieut. Richard W. Greer, 24th South Carolina) and forty-one enlisted men killed at James Island.

140 Joseph Wilds Williamson was a private in Company B, 21st Regiment, South Carolina Volunteers.

141 Private Peter Collin Coggeshall, Company B, 21st Regiment, South Carolina Volunteers, was the husband of Nancy Wilds Coggeshall and father of six children.

142 Private Edwin P. Williamson, Company B, 21st Regiment, South Carolina Volunteers, was Sarah's nephew, the son of her brother Samuel.

143 General Benjamin Franklin Butler (1818-1893) was in command of Union forces that took New Orleans on May 1, 1862, and issued the "Woman Order" on May 15, 1862.

144 Actually Jackson was busy with the Shenandoah Valley Campaign in Virginia, and did not cross over into Maryland until September 4. The Battle of Fair Oaks had been fought on May 31.

145 "Aunt" Nancy DuBose was the mother of Jane DuBose Davis.

146 Jane DuBose Davis was the second wife of John Davis, Sr., of Society Hill.

147 John Davis, Jr., died in Virginia soon after entering service in 1862.

148 Harriet LaCoste McIver (July 19, 1826 — September 14, 1903), daughter of Eliza's husband, A. P. LaCoste, married George Williams McIver on October 31, 1845.

149 There were three McIver children: Alexander Markland, aged eleven; George Walter, seven; and Flora, two.

150 George W. McIver (June 1, 1825 — July 31, 1896), son of Alexander and Mary Hanford McIver, married Harriet LaCoste.

151 A. P. LaCoste died March 29, 1862, and was buried beside his first wife in St. David's Churchyard, Cheraw.

152 Wilson, *Memories of Society Hill,* p. 57. "Old Mr. Witherspoon's house was a large building facing due north, in accordance with his original idea, thus having a corner of the house toward the street giving it a somewhat awkward appearance." After Mrs. Witherspoon's murder by her slaves, ". . . the house and offices were filled with refugees driven from their homes in Charleston and elsewhere."

153 Sarah Ervin McIver (June 30, 1826 — October 30, 1897) was the wife of Allen McIver, Society Hill.

154 Mr. Bealer's first wife, Elizabeth Eugenia Bacot Bealer, died in 1857; his second wife, whom he married prior to July, 1860, was Emily Winkler, Charleston, sister of Dr. Edwin Theodore Winkler, pastor of the First Baptist Church of Charleston from 1854-1868.

155 William Elias James (April 7, 1784 — March 7, 1862) was buried in the Presbyterian Churchyard, Darlington.

156 The body of Robert Ervin James (? — March 10, 1862), oldest son of William E. James, was brought home for burial by his brother, W. E., Jr., ten days after their father's funeral.

157 John DeLorme, son of Charles and Elizabeth Britton DeLorme, married Anna Nettles.

158 Sarah disliked being away from the post office; there was always a chance that Wilds might have written.

159 Virginia Williamson was in school at Limestone College, Gaffney, South Carolina.

160 Thomas Curtis, D. D., was principal at Limestone College.

161 Thomas Hart Law (1838-1923), son of Thomas Cassels and Mary Westfield Hart Law, whose days at The Citadel are recounted in *Citadel Cadets, The Journal of Cadet Tom Law,* married Anna Elizabeth Adger, of Charleston, in 1862.

162 Carrie was expecting a baby. This is the unidentified Carrie, not Carrie Williams, whom Sarah called "Sister."

163 *Treasured Reminiscences,* p. 10.

164 Captain John K. McIver (September 1, 1835 — October 13, 1863) married Hannah Wilson in 1858.

165 Spencer Glasgow Welsh, *A Confederate Surgeon's Letters to His Wife* (Marietta, Georgia, 1954), p. 15. "Next morning (28th) the battle began anew, but there was not nearly so much cannonading because our men rushed upon the Yankees and took their cannon. The musketry, though, was terrific. It reminded me of myriads of hailstones falling upon a house top. I could see the smoke and the bombs burst in the air, and could hear the shouts of our men as they could capture the Yankee batteries."

166 Major General Ambrose Powell Hill (1825-1865), C. S. A.

167 Major General James Longstreet (1821-1904), C. S. A.

168 Pamunkey River.

The War
PART III

Nine companies of the Twenty-First Regiment, South Carolina Volunteers, were stationed on Morris Island, Charleston, in October, 1862.[1] Many men from the Pee Dee region, including Miss Williamson's relatives, were members of the regiment.[2] Service on the coast was monotonous, rather barren of stirring events. Illnesses in the camps caused more concern than enemy attacks. Malaria, long a source of dread in the lower regions of South Carolina, was prevalent among the troops where protection from mosquitoes was virtually impossible. "Fever" symptoms were chills followed by fever as high as 105°, and then by profuse sweating. Chronic malaria resulted in emaciation, muscular weakness, mental depression, and poor soldiering. Diarrhea was caused as frequently by nervous shock and tension as by unsanitary conditions.

At Harper's Ferry, West Virginia, General Stonewall Jackson captured the garrison on September 15, after a bombardment of two days. Federal loss in killed and wounded was 217, with 12,250 taken prisoner. The Confederate loss in killed and wounded was 288.

The Confederate forces had driven back the enemy at Sharpesburg on September 16 and 17, and General Lee wrote to his troops:

> On the field of Sharpesburg, with less than one third his numbers, you resisted from day-light until dark the whole army of the enemy, and repulsed every attack along his entire front of more than four miles in extent. The whole of the following day you stood prepared to resume the conflict on the same ground, and retired next morning without molestation across the Potomac. Two attempts subsequently made by the enemy to follow you across the river have resulted in his complete discomfiture and being driven back with loss. Achieve-

ments such as these demanded much valor and patriotism. History records few examples of greater fortitude and endurance than this army has exhibited, and I am commissioned by the President to thank you in the name of the Confederate States for the undying fame you have won for their arms.[3]

But Captain Tom Howle, Leavensworth merchant and Black Creek deacon, whose wife, Bettie, had been so lonely that she could "scarcely live" when her husband attended the Baptist Association at Greenville in 1860,[4] was not present to hear Marse Robert's commendations. He had been shot down during the hottest part of the battle, while his brother, James, "besought him that they might change places, for Tom was married and Jim was not."[5] He was buried temporarily on the battlefield.

Black Creek church records dedicated a page of tribute to Tom's memory, saying:

> Thomas E. Howle of this community fell mortally wounded on the bloody field of Sharpesburg, Maryland on 17 September, 1862 and died during the ensuing night. Thus one of the noblest, purest and best of men has fallen in the service of his country. Another victim of the wicked, relentless and cruel warfare now being waged against us unoffending Southerners by the Northern states of this Continent who with barbarous and fiendish ferocity seem determined upon our utter ruin and extermination as a people. Among the lamented heroes who have fallen around the blood stained shrine of liberty whose names will be recorded in lines of light and honour upon the historic pages for the admiration of future generations was Tom Howle, who was born August 19, 1825 and died September 17, 1862. He professed religion in September 1842 and became a Deacon of this church September 2, 1860.[6]

At Corinth, Mississippi, Grant reported:

> Yesterday, the rebels, under Van Dorn, Price and Lovell, were repulsed from their attack . . . with great slaughter. The enemy are in full retreat, leaving their dead and wounded on the field. . . . Rosecrans pursued the retreating enemy this morning. . . . From 700 to 1,000, besides wounded, are left on our hands.[7]

Denying that the retreat from Corinth had been "a rout, as has been industriously reported by the enemy,"[8] Van Dorn admitted a victory for the Federal forces.

When Miss Williamson wrote to Miss Darby on October 16, she had only the poorest quality of paper and ink. Her words were crowded into narrow lines on a small sheet of paper on which the ink formed heavy smudges. Miss Darby received the letter several weeks later.

Sarah Williamson, Florence, South Carolina, to Jemima Darby, Ringgold, Louisiana.

Florence
Oct. 16, 1862

Miss Jemima Darby
Ringgold, La.

Dear Miss Darby,

I received your letter the ninth of the month. Was truly glad to hear from you. Had begun to think you had not got the one I wrote you. I have been waiting to get a letter from sister and from Lizzie to tell you about her. Poor Tom's presentiment has been realized. He was killed at the Battle of Sharpesburg. Nothing but bad news to communicate.

Old Mrs. Wilson[9] died last Monday. She requested Brother Horace[10] to carry her to Williamsburg.[11] Went down Tuesday night. He could pass near the church. The children[12] went with him. I don't know where they will live. They have lost their best earthly friend. She wished them to keep house. Get Mrs. Council[13] to stay with them. I don't think Aunt Jane[14] will let them do so. Mrs. W. never got over the death of her son. Her mind was not so good after. There was no one better prepared for a change than she was. She has passed through many trials in this life. Julia Green[15] was with her most of the time. Not there when she died. Her uncle[16] moved to Arkansas. She had to return to the children. Her brother[17] is in the Army. No relative near to assist her.

Mary Chambers lost two children last week with Scarlet fever. I have not heard which ones.[18] I am uneasy about sister. So many children there have it.[19] She expects to be confined the first of November. She has spells of coughing at night when she gets up. There are heat sweats after. They are very weakening. If it werent for that, her health would be better this time.

Theodosia[20] was down last week and has a fine large boy three months old. Is sick often. Mother thinks she will not raise him. Theo[21] is a very nice sweet child. Growing fast. More like her mother.

Sister Mary Ann has dispepsia. Looks as yellow as a pumpkin. Has severe pains in her stomach. Seems as if it will kill her. Has fallen off. Andrew is in usual health. Have not been there in a month.

Brother Wilds had a severe spell of fever. Was confined to the house four weeks. Went back to camp too soon. Has had diarhea most of the time. Is at home now. Has improved. Is to leave next week. The water on Morris Island is very bad. Does not seem as if he can stand it.

Edwin has been home nearly two months with chills and fever. Dreadful cough. Dont you think I have enough soldiers to nurse. We have a wayside hospital at _____. Mr. Benton Prince[22] of Cheraw has charge of it. Mrs. Freer and Mrs. Brown are nurses. Jack Brunson was killed at Harper's Ferry. George and Tom Jinks died in the hospital. Quince Hill died of wounds. James Wilson was wounded in the knee. Is at home. Cant walk without crutches. Expects to teach school at Darlington.

Aunt Julia's health is not good. Bettie and Mollie are thin. Lou Bird's husband was killed. She has four boys.

The last news is bad. The enemy were victorious at Corinth.

Our Association is at Bennettsville. I hope we will be able to go. We have a paper printed in Columbia. *Confederate Baptist* Two dollars. Have the first numbers. Not as good as the old one.

Old Mrs. Croslands[23] oldest son is in the Army.

The people at the Hill got tired of Mr. Phelps. He married a rich old maid. Is in Columbia studying the last time I heard of him.

Mr. LaCost left Eliza all he had.[24] Is keeping house. I saw a lady from there last week. Said she is well. The children[25] are very attentive to her. The girls[26] are getting along in the old way.

Mrs. Baker went on to the Charlottesville hospital. Couldn't stand it at Mrs. Ferguson's. Intends to go to Jeff.[27]

Mrs. Lane[28] and Sabrina Long leave next week for Florida. Have been here nearly two years.

Mr. Dargan preaches twice a month at the Hill. Aunt Nancy DuBosc made Mrs. Fort a visit.[29] Think it is the last. Is very feeble. Cousin Eliza Evans has not returned yet. Cant get any person to come with her. Her brothers son was killed in the first battle of Corinth.

We have to give thirty dollars a sack for salt. Thirty for a barrel of flour. We made wheat.

Edwin sends his respects. Mother joins in love to you. Wishes she could see you.

Your friend,

SARAH

* * * * *

During the fall of 1862 when nine companies of the Twenty-First Regiment, South Carolina Volunteers, were stationed at Morris Island, the company to which James A. Williams, Carrie Williamson's husband, and Josiah Vann, their neighbor, belonged, was left to guard the Pee Dee bridge.[30]

To Carrie Williams, writing on November 24, 1862, the war was of less significance than the birth of her daughter, Sallie Elizabeth Williams, on October 23.[31] From this date forward, all else was to become second in importance to Mrs. Williams and her sisters; Sallie was to be the consistent topic of the letters for the next twenty-one years.

Mrs. James A. Williams, Florence, South Carolina, to Jemima Darby, Ringgold, Louisiana.

Orangedale
November 24, 1862

Dear friend

Sister[32] found your letter waiting. As she is busy nursing J's[33] babie suppose you will not object to my answering it. I have so many correspondents and health so feeble is why I've neglected you so long, but think I wrote you last.

I have a daughter five weeks old. Had an easy time and good recovery but suffer a great deal with soar throat. Call the baby Sallie Elizabeth. She is very cross. Dont know what I shall do without sister when I return home. We all want her. Mother cannot spare her.

Jim has been gone a month. Stationed at Pee Dee Bridge. Finds Joe Vann[34] a clever helpmate. First time Joe's been in service. One of the reserves. The old man[35] stirs about the home   attends to his business. Think his wife enjoys life a little more recently. Mr. Wilson[36] promised Tom if he died to take care of his family. They remain at the same place[37] and he will settle up and attend to everything. Not many meet with such a friend.

Lewis[38] stole meat and insulted Mrs. Boseman.[39] Was tried and convicted. Some thought he was turned loose on the road to jail. No news of him in more than a year now.

Henry King's oldest daughter[40] married Mr. Thomas, raised by Mr. Privet. Has a daughter. One of the girls[41] have staid this long with Lizzie. She speaks of getting Betsy Tedder next year. Took T's death very hard at first but I hear is very cheerful again. Has three boys and two girls.[42] Mr. Dorrity[43] moved to his place on Sumter river. Dont see them now. Poor old man[44] has a lonely time. Attends church. Expect he misses Mary. The scarlet fever got into our neighborhood[45] and four of Mary Chambers children were laid to rest in one week.[46] Lela was sick only a few hours. She and little Mary died the same day. I cannot realize they all have passed away. She bears it well and I hope it may bring her into the church.

Mr. Wilkins had a revival in his church.[47] Bettie Nettles and Charlie Wilkins[48] were baptized. Also George Norwood[49] who is at home on sick furlough. Mr. Dargan's health is failing rapidly. Not able to preach frequently. Expect a disappointed congregation met today (fast day). Had published he would be there but has been very sick. The next Association will be at B. C. It was well attended and how I should have liked to have been there. Mr. Richard Furman[50] preached one night. Houseful of ladies to hear him. And Mr. Culpepper[51] got up. Poor Mechanicsville was not represented. T. Fountain[52] was sick.

Cousin Eliza Evans has got back at last.[53] Overjoyed. Came on the Express train. Have not seen her yet.

Ann Maria Fort has a daughter. Mrs. Dubose and Davis made Mrs. Fort a visit.[54] Both very feeble. Sick after they got home. Mrs. Fort hoped Johnie's death would convert his father and she thinks there is some chance until he mentions Yanky. Looses it all.

Emily and sisters were well. Hear often but seldom see them as I've not been able to ride. Mary Ann Lucas has some peace at home. W. is in the service now. Her youngest is a pretty child. I am sorry to see that she is not so punctual at sabbath school and church since she got near it. I suppose you heard Kim[55] shot himself in Virginia. Had fever. Was delirious. His wife Miss Bell that was has two daughters.

All wish to be remembered to Mrs. K. I can sympathize with her in her hour of trial.[56]

Your friend,

CARRIE

* * * * *

The Union general, Ambrose E. Burnside, who had been appointed to succeed General George B. McClellan in November of 1862, pushed his advance in Virginia, but was badly defeated by Lee in the Battle of Fredericksburg on December 13.

In western Kentucky and Tennessee, there had been active campaigning throughout the year. General Bragg had advanced into Kentucky hoping to compel the withdrawal of Federal troops in the North. He threatened Cincinnati, but the Kentuckians failed to support him. He was retreating southward when he met the Federal army of General Rosecrans in the Battle of Murfreesboro on Stone River, December 31, 1862 — January 3, 1863.

With all these stirring events, Elizabeth Frances, wife of Dr. A. R. Vann, Brookville, North Carolina, was not concerned when she wrote to her sister-in-law, Bettie, widow of Thomas E. Howle, on February 19. Dr. Vann had been to Darlington District to attend Howle's funeral at Black Creek Church.[57] Mrs. Vann was prompted by her concern for Mrs. Howle to suggest that they arrange to live near one another. Without an appreciation of Mrs. Vann's love for her native North Carolina, her gesture toward her sister-in-law cannot be appreciated.

Mrs. Alexander Russia Vann, Brookville, North Carolina, to Mrs. Thomas E. Howle, Leavensworth, South Carolina.

Brookville, Feb. 19, 63

My dear sister

We received your last letter on Friday evening last, and was glad to hear that you and the children were well. This leaves our family in usual health. Walter[58] has had diphtheria since his Pa got back from South Carolina.[59] He had it severe for two or three days, more than any of our children. We have all had it now except George which is a gratification to me. In some families in Granville this disease has proved very fatal, but we have had the good luck not to loose a single one, which is a rare circumstance. Brother John[60] has been suffering severely with neuralgia of the head this week. It looks as if that boy will never see another well day. I dont think that he has seen one since last May. This war has destroyed his constitution I do believe. It looks as if it will kill Mother[61] He is her baby and I fear her idol for that cause I fear he will be taken from her. Rush doubtless wrote to you about the death of Brother Macon[62] He died a happy and tranquil death, resigned to the will of the Lord, which is a source of great satisfaction to us. His wife is very much cast down. He leaves a little daughter the image of her father.

Bettie, you seem to be very anxious for us to move back to S. C. and live near you. To live near you, Bettie, would be a source of great satisfaction to me, for if I know my own heart, I have not a sister whom I love better than I do you and whom I am willing to make greater sacrifices than I would for you. I have but two objections to going back to S. C. The first is leaving all of my folks and the next is, the location of that country. Then why not go to some hilly dry country instead of that flat sultry country. As to my part I would much prefer the hills of Georgia to any other country I know of. Dr. Vann can go and select our homes. What do you say to that? Let us hear from you as soon as you get this for we are always glad to hear from you all.

I have never felt more resigned to moving before in order that Dr. V. may be of benefit to you and children and if we cant make any other arrangement I will consent to come to

S. C. but I think that other arrangements can be made just as well as that. This is the arrangement that Dr. V. and myself has made. You can talk it over with Father V., and your other friends and hear what they have to say on the subject. Kiss those dear little children for me. Our love to all, may the Lord bless you and yours,

Ever,

Your sister,

E. F. VANN

* * * * *

By the middle of May, 1863, Confederate leaders were positive that a full-scale naval attack on Charleston was imminent. Blockaders had roamed at will in Charleston waters for several months. On April 7-8, General G. T. Beauregard reported the approach of "ten iron-clads . . . twenty-seven vessels . . . fifty-five vessels . . . Federal monitors . . . and armed alligators."[63] Secretary of War Seddon wired General Wade Hampton, at Columbia, "Lead your furloughed men and any others eager for the fray to Charleston and God speed you."[64] Milledge L. Bonham, who had returned from fighting in Virginia to become governor of South Carolina, argued that Charleston needed men more desperately than Vicksburg.[65]

The Twenty-First South Carolina Regiment, under Colonel Robert F. Graham, was stationed at Morris Island, about to see war "in all its hideous forms."[66] Even though the attack on the south end of Morris Island was begun on July 10, 1863, Charleston, in spite of constant bombardments, was not evacuated until February 17, 1865.

Of major concern to Sarah Williamson was the welfare of her brother, Wilds Williamson, who, during 1863, was promoted to fourth, and later to third sergeant. Sarah was too distressed over family and local problems to reflect what must have been a joyous reaction to the Confederate victory at the Battle of Chancellorsville on May 1-4. She overlooked the fact that Miss Darby would have been eager for news from the Virginia front, particularly the fighting which involved the Eighth South Carolina Regiment of Kershaw's Brigade, composed largely of men from the Pee Dee area.

⊰{ 173 }⊱

Sarah Williamson, Florence, South Carolina, to Jemima Darby, Ringgold, Louisiana.

Orangedale, May 18 63

Dear Miss Darby

I see by your silence if I do not write you will never write again. It is true I should have written before this. I think you have not been as busy as I. Sister has spent the winter with us. Sick all the time. Soar throat. Fever. Night sweats. Had to mop her throat twice a day. Medicine every two or three hours. A poor little pale babe with colick every evening for three months. Lazy servants to see after. You know such a lazy body as I had enough to do. Sister got well enough to ride. I went home with her the middle of April. Stayed nearly three weeks. Left her some better. I fear she is not long for this world. Her cough is still bad. Is taking cod liver oil. I cant see that it does her any good. Sallie has to be fed. She slept with me all the time. I became very much attached to her. Miss her very much. Have not heard from them in a week today. Jim has an exemption.[67]

I saw Mrs. Vann[68]   Asked about you. Said she heard Lizzie talking about writing you. Is living at the mill yet.[69] Is anxious to have a house built at the plantation.[70] Nails are so high cant build this year. The two oldest boys[71] are going to school to Bettie Nettles. Tom is thought to be very smart. Mr. Vann does not do any better as he grows older. . . . Does not wish her to visit her son's.[72] Says it is a disgrace for her to take a negroe fellow to drive her. Gave her a girl to take with her. She[73] has a child. Cant take her. I hope she will outlive him to have some peace in her life.[74] Mrs. Baker gave him a good talk about it. Said people were talking about it. Would take it up in the church if he did not quit. He has not been to Mrs. F's since.[75] Mrs. B. has gone to Jeff to spend the summer. Has been very busy working for soldiers. Cut up some of her under drapes to make them drawers.

I went to Cheraw when I was with sister. Spent the night with Eliza LaCoste. Had not seen her since she married. She is comfortably fixed. Have a nice little orchard, garden. Plants rye. Has four nice cows. Sells milk at 15 cents a quart. Has Reev and Joe, the negroes Cousin Sallie Ann had.[76] Can weave. Has the same farm. I dont know how many other negroes.

I saw two men. A carriage and horses tooke me over town and to the Depot. Has two nice girls.[77] The oldest very much like Jim.[78] I think her homely. Most persons call her pretty. The youngest is very pretty. Has fair complexion, flaxen ringlets and blue eyes, looks a little like Delle.[79] Florence had her arm broken at the elbow a few days before. Was doing very well. I think the girls[80] are very kind to her. Said they were there as soon as they heard it. Mr. Evans[81] attends to her business. She got a letter from Hannah when I was there. Said they were all well. Had a plenty of work to do. I have not seen them since I came down here. Think I will go to see them when I get to sisters but she is always sick. Never get off. Went to Cheraw to try to get some clothes. Could not get anything. A cotton umbrella for ten dollars. Some coarse calico two dollars and a half a yard. Was light coloured. Did not get any. Flour fifty dollars a barrel. Has fallen to twenty.

As I came down Carrie Smith[82] came on the cars with a young Tom Smith.[83] Lucy McIver[84] has a daughter. Calls her Kate.[85] Robert Edwards gets worse. Miss Charlotte had to leave there. Has been very low. Was better when I heard. Aunt Nancy Dubose had been quite sick when I was at sisters. Have not heard since. Cousin Eliza Evans got back. Came and spent nearly a month with mother. Is as restless as ever. Boards with Rachel.[86] Is going to keep house next year. Cousin Eliza Griffin and Sallie[87] are to live with her. Mrs. Dr. Gregg[88] and Cousin Eliza Griffin spent an evening with mother when I was away. Mother says she is feeble. Mrs. Augustus Law[89] is low. Dont think she will recover. Mrs. Dupree is in usual health. Has a good school. Mr. Dupree preaches at Mechanicsville this year. Have revived the Sunday School.

The Yankees are preparing to attack Charleston again. I hope they have the same luck. Brother Wilds[90] is at home sick. Summer complaint. Cant stand the summer there. Has been trying to get a substitute. I hope he may get one. Are high. 1500 and 2000. Edwin[91] has fattened and been quite healthy until last week. Has diarhea. Was at duty again. Mothers health is as good as she could expect it to be. Attends to the garden. Had beets for dinner today. Andrew's health is poor. Moll is better than last summer. Mother joins me in love. Write soon.

Yours,

SARAH

* * * * *

By July of 1863, South Carolina troops had been assigned to units in localities as far away from home as Gettysburg, Pennsylvania. On the second day of July, "two-thirds of the little band which composed Company F of the Eighth South Carolina Regiment, lay upon the field either cold in death or torn and mangled by wounds." Pee Dee men who were wounded were Captain John K. McIver, Sergeant I. D. Wilson, and Henry Boseman.[92] Leonard Harrell was dead. Dr. James F. Pearce and Dr. James Evans, both of Darlington District, "had been hard at work since daylight, amputating limbs, and relieving the sufferings of the wounded."[93]

But the Federal forces won at Gettysburg, and the Confederate troops were obliged to remain on the defensive until the end of the war. After July 3, the war became a test of endurance.

Vicksburg surrendered on July 4, and Federal forces assumed control of the Mississippi. Southern hopes were revived temporarily after the Battle of Chickamauga on September 19-20, but none of that hope was revealed in a letter which Lizzie Howle received from her friend and customer, Mrs. H. T. LeGrand, of Sumter.

Mrs. H. T. LeGrand, Sumter, South Carolina, to Mrs. Thomas E. Howle, Leavensworth, South Carolina.

Sumter, S. C., Oct. 16, 1863

My dear Lizzie

Your kind letter has been received and would have replied to it immediately but Ada De Lorm expected daily to return and I have been waiting to write by her fearing to trust my receipt from the Express Agent by mail. The money sent you $64.00 did not belong to me but three of my friends who wished mourning dresses. I regret the goods had all been sold and that the money failed to reach you. The delay has caused me much annoyance and no little anxiety. Who is the Express agent at Leavensworth or Dove's? I thought perhaps Charlie De Lorm[94] was and that there would be no difficulty in getting the money to you by this source. Enclosed you will find the receipt. Please get your friend Mr. Wilson[95] to get the money and do keep it until you have an opportunity of sending it by some responsible person. Perhaps such a chance will present itself at the time of your Association which I believe comes off next month. I feel badly about the money and would like to return it as early as possible. Have none of your friends or acquaintances prints they would dispose of? I am anxious to get a dress myself. Only regret that I could not have purchased one while with you. Has Mrs. Harrell[96] sold all she had? Perhaps some of the people in Julia's[97] neighborhood might have one or two dresses to sell. I only hope so.

I regret exceedingly to hear of your feeble health. Earnestly hope you are feeling much better now. Try dear Lizzie to cheer up. God has afflicted us and we should strive to bow with submission to His holy will, for we are assured that "He is too wise to err and too good to be unkind." All things will work together for our good, if we only with faith and confidence draw near and place all our trust in Him. If we are only faithful it will not be long before we shall bid adieux to earth with all its trials and afflictions and take up our eternal abode in our Father's Mansions where we shall meet our precious ones again in the full bloom of eternal glory, never again to be separated or to feel the aching cares and sorrows of this life. Oh! how happy and cheering the thought. How inspiring. God grant that we may realize this priceless and immortal happiness. While we tarry in this vale of tears we are the peculiar object of God's care. How comforting the many precious promises to the widow[98] and fatherless. How kind has our Heavenly Father been since our earthly props have been taken from us. We have lacked for nothing needful. Though our paths have been rough and thorny, yet love and mercy has ever been with us. I feel thankful for all the blessings that have fallen my lot, deeply grateful for even every act of attention and every kind word that has been extended to me and feel encouraged to trust in the Lord to the end of time.

Remember me to your Mother and Father and to all my acquaintances in your neighborhood that may feel an interest in me. Ma desires much love to you.[99] My children send kind regards to your little ones. May God ever bless you and yours and grant you yet many years of peace and comfort in this life and finally reunite you with the loved one gone to Mansions of Eternal Light and Glory, prays

Your sympathizing friend,

H. T. LeGRAND

* * * * *

When the Ninth and Sixth Regiments of the South Carolina Volunteers were reorganized and consolidated, the command became the Sixth Regiment and was assigned to Jenkins's Brigade, Anderson's Division, of Longstreet's Corps. Among the Darlington men who participated in the Battle of Lookout Mountain on October 27-28, 1863, was Captain James Lide Coker, who was seriously wounded, captured by the enemy, and promoted to rank of major.[100] "Now," wrote Dargan, "it was news of Cousin James Coker's terrible wound in the far West, and his mother's long journey and painful nursing, sometimes in the enemy's lines."[101]

The Federals opened the road into Georgia when they drove the Confederates out of Tennessee at the Battle of Chattanooga on November 23-25. Nothing stood in the way of Sherman now; he was ready to begin his march to the sea.

Not even a letter was allowed to travel directly and unmolestedly through strategic Yankee strongholds. Sarah Williamson's letter of January 28, 1864, the last that she was to write to Miss Darby, was sent *Via Arkansas*.

Sarah Williamson, Florence, South Carolina, to Jemima Darby, Ringgold, Louisiana.

> Florence, S. C.
> Jan. 28, 1864

Miss Jemima Darby
　Ringgold, La.
　Via Arkansas

Dear Miss Darby

I have delayed replying to your welcome letter much longer than I should. I received it a month after you wrote. I don't think you received the last one I wrote.

We have all been sick with colds. Mother has a bad cough. I am afraid it will turn to consumption. There are many sad things to tell you. Dear sister died the tenth of August.[102] Suffered a great deal with her throat. Could not talk but very little for some time before. Spent the winter with us. Went home the last of April. Came down twice after. Only lived two weeks after her last visit. Said she felt like she must come and see Mother. She had been complaining all the summer. Couldnt get to see her. Left a daughter nine months old.[103]

Poor little darling did not know her loss. I love her. She has eyes like sister's. Is tall and large. Can talk. Is a perfect little sunbeam in the house. Everyone pets her. She is very smart. Can bring the broom to me. Tries to take off Mother's stocking. Get her shoes. Mother says she is too smart and we all love her too much. I dont think she will be raised. She loves me too much.

Mother had a carbuncle on her back in August and was on the bed six weeks. Suffered a great deal but nothing in comparison with Cousin Thomas Lide.[104] He had one the same time. His was as large as a common-sized waiter. He was confined four months. Did not think he could live. Is so he can go about now. Mr. Chambers[105] died the last of August. Mary had another son[106]   I think I told you she lost four children in two weeks. Mrs. Baker is at Mrs. F's[107]   Jeff[108] is in a hospital at Charlottesville. Linton[109] and Jim[110] are both in the army. Jim stands it better than we thought he would. Dr. Crane[111] has sold his place to refugees. Has rented Jim's house. His sisters dont like it at all. I brought sister's things here to try to take care of them for Sallie if she lives. I hear they talk about it. They may talk. They have no business with what mother gave her. It is nothing more than I expected. I have heard them talking about Margaret and I am no better. I have always been sorry sister married in the family. Think she might have been living now if she had never married.

Lizzie was living at the same place. The old man[112] came to see sister. The old lady's health is poor. Did not come.

Mr. and Mrs. Fort were as well as usual. Aunt Nancy DuBose had a fall but was getting over it. I never hear from there. They dont come down to see Sallie. I have been there once to get the things. Carried the babe to see them.

I hear Miss Rosannah Woods[113] is teaching school near Black Creek. I expect she boards at Wash Lucas. He lives at the old place. Mr. Adams is dead. Cousin Nancy lives with Charlie DeLorme. Mary with Mrs. Dove. All her boys are in the service. We have refugees all around us from the low country. The Wickham house, Goodwin and Cannon are full. Several families in a house. They are constantly running for something to eat. Everything is high. Pork a dollar and a half a pound, butter three, eggs dollar and a half a dozen, corn five dollars a bushel. Taxes are so high dont know what will become of us if the war last much longer.

Brother Wilds was in the bombardment on Morris Island.

Did not get shot; was stunned by a concussion. Had not been home in ten months until last week. Only fifteen days. It seemed like two days. He was very sick after the battle. Is very fat and well now. Left for camp last Wednesday. They are shelling the city every day but do very little damage. I fear they will not work when they get well fixed. William Fountain[114] was wounded and taken by the enemy. Was exchanged and died in Charleston. Dick Howard[115] is a prisoner. They won't exchange any more now. Capt. Coker[116] was wounded at Chickamauga. Cousin Hannah[117] went on to nurse him. The enemy have them now. His wife[118] had an infant a week old. Could not go. Cousin Hannah has suffered a great deal by this miserable war. One son killed[119] and two sons taken.[120] Charlie stayed with John K.[121] He was badly wounded. Since died. DeLeslin Wilson[122] the enemy has and many of our acquaintances. I cant think of all now.

Mrs. Kay Bacot came to her senses a year ago. Was buried last week. I hear she called her family round her, told them good-bye, folded her hands, said she was going to rest, and died. Mr. Jim Sanders died a few weeks past and DuBose Dargan.[123]

Mrs. DuPree has quit teaching. Has some boarders. Mr. DuPree preaches at Mechanicsville. Had a revival there. Many added to the church. There was people that never went to church before joined. Is doing much good there. Charles Andrews went up to be prayed for. Is not satisfied with himself.

Mr. Dargan preaches twice a month at the Hill. Jo King[124] is at Sister Mary Ann's now. The others are well. Jo spent some time with her in the fall. She is a very nice girl. She thought Andrew was away. He got a discharge. Is at home.

Aunt Julia's[125] family are well as usual. Betsy[126] is in an interesting situation. It is very pleasing to Cousin Elizabeth. Brother George's[127] health is not good. Thomas[128] is at school at the Hill. Kate[129] is at Cousin Thomases. Sarah Napier[130] teaches her and Virginia[131] is expected to go back to Limestone. Have no school. Will go to Darlington. Aunt Jane[132] had another spell of paralysis. Is better. Miss Mary has been with her all winter. Dreads going home by herself.[133] Mother joins me in love. Write soon.

Yours,

SARAH

* * * * *

The Twenty-First Regiment, South Carolina Volunteers, remained at Charleston until April 20, 1864, when it was ordered to Wilmington, North Carolina. Lieutenant Colonel Alonzo T. Dargan[134] was in charge of this group of South Carolina men being sent, with General Beauregard, to participate in the campaign on the south side of the James River, to fight the Yankee Butler. They arrived at Petersburg, Virginia, on May 5, spent one night at Drewry's Bluff, and marched the seven miles to Walthall Junction, where they were placed under the command of Colonel R. F. Graham.

In the midst of the first day's fighting, Gus Law[135] and Al DuBose[136] were reported to have said to Colonel Dargan, "Colonel, this is better fighting than Morris Island. We'll soon have them skedaddling."[137] Although the Confederate losses at Walthall Junction were comparatively slight, "Company B was indeed unfortunate in losing Sergt. Wilds Williamson,[138] who was fatally wounded and died at the hospital a few days afterwards."[139] Colonel Dargan was killed the next day "with the colors in his hand, waving them and calling his men to rally."[140]

Sherman completed his march to the sea and took possession of Savannah, Georgia, on December 21, 1864. To General Grant, he proposed his great and final campaign — the march through the Carolinas. His army reached Columbia, the capital of South Carolina, on February 17, 1865, to find it was being evacuated by Wade Hampton.

There has been a great deal of conjecture as to who burned Columbia — Sherman or Hampton. "The fact," wrote William E. Gonzales, "is frequently overlooked that Sherman finally confessed that he burned the city."[141] General Slocum,[142] of the United States Volunteers, believed that "the immediate cause of the disaster was free use of whiskey." At any rate, the town was pillaged, a great portion of the city was burned in the afternoon, and fires spread rapidly as a west wind arose during the night, while "above all, the demoniac and gladsome shouts of the soldiery might be heard."[143] Although actual orders for the burning might not have been given, General Sherman was said to have been pleased with the destruction of Columbia.

The main body of the invading army did not reach Florence, Darlington, or Society Hill. The Fourteenth and Twentieth Army Corps, which had passed west of Columbia, turned east at Winnsboro, and passing through Chesterfield, moved northeast into North Carolina. After leaving Columbia, the Fifteenth Army Corps circled east into Camden and moved northeast into Cheraw. From Columbia, the Seventeenth Army Corps marched through Cheraw, Bennettsville, and Bright's Post Office, all towns within the Pee Dee region where Miss Darby had lived. Devastation marked the progress of the army from Columbia to the northern frontier of the state. The towns of Winnsboro, Camden, and Cheraw were burned, and, according to Brooks, "no single town or village or hamlet within their line of march escaped altogether the torch of the invaders."[144] Captain Oakey of the Second Massachusetts Volunteers reported:

> We marched into Cheraw with music and with colors flying. Staking arms in the main street, we proceeded to supper, while the engineers paid the pontoons across the Pedee River. The railing of the town pump, and the remains of a buggy said to belong to Mr. Lincoln's brother-in-law, Dr. Todd, were quickly reduced to kindling wood to boil the coffee. The necessary destruction of property was quickly accomplished and on we went.[145]

Historians ascribe the dates of January 1 to April 26, 1865, to "The Campaign of the Carolinas." Actually, the Pee Dee region was invaded during the early part of March, with skirmishes at Chesterfield on March 2 and fighting near Cheraw from March 3 until March 5, at which time the Federals moved into North Carolina. On March 4 to March 6 an expedition was sent from near Cheraw to Florence. General Sherman reported that the "expedition of mounted infantry . . . encountered both cavalry and infantry, and returned, having only broken up in part the branch railroad from Florence to Cheraw."[146] Bridges as far down as Darlington were destroyed. Early in March of 1865, church minutes at Black Creek recorded, "No church meeting today in consequence of the presence of Yankee raiders in the vicinity."[147]

Even though Sherman crossed the border to the north and Lee surrendered at Appomattox Courthouse, South Carolina's period of degradation and depression was not finished. Her railroads and bridges were gone; her finances were at a low ebb; the prevalence of crime in remote districts was alarming. Much ill-feeling was kept alive by United States agents searching the country for Confederate cotton and branded mules and horses. Trowbridge, in 1865, found "in South Carolina a more virulent animosity existing in the minds of the common people, against the government and the people of the North, than in any other state." It was only in South Carolina that he was treated with "gross personal insults."[148]

Soon after the war was over, Sarah Williamson died, leaving to her niece, Virginia, now graduated from Limestone College, the task of reporting the final stages of the war to Miss Darby.

Virginia Williamson, Florence, South Carolina, to Jemima Darby, Ringgold, Louisiana.

Florence, July 10, 1867

Miss Jemima Darby
 Ringgold, Louisiana
  Bienville Parish

Dear Miss Darby

I have the melancholy duty to perform of telling you of Aunt Sarah's death. She died the 14th of June 1865.[149] She was sick only a short time, and Oh! how we all missed her. She had been a second mother to us. Grandmother[150] does not seem to get over it at all. She never speaks of her without shedding tears.

I suppose you heard of Uncle Wilds'[151] and Aunt Carrie's[152] deaths. Mrs. DuPre[153] died last year. Her mind had been seriously affected for a year. She had some affection of the brain.

Grandmother's health is not very good. She is confined to the house a great deal. My father, Mr. George W.[154] is now living here with Grandmother. Uncle Sam[155] lived here a while but is now with his son, E[156] Mrs. Council[157] lives here and keeps house for us. Aunt Mollie[158] answered your letter in June but I suppose you did not receive it.

We have been getting on, in the way of servants, etc., very well indeed. The most of father's negroes staid with him, but none of Grandmother's except Julia. We have not had to cook so far, but haven't any idea how soon we may have it to do. The negroes about here are doing very well if the *Yanks* would only let them alone. I believe we would be as well off, if not better off, than before, but they keep them constantly excited about one thing or another giving them more and more privileges and depriving the whites of the same. I don't think I ever saw such dull times. Everybody seems to be disheartened.

We had such constant rains through June that the crops are very much injured, both by rains and grass. There is indeed a great deal of suffering in South Carolina, but the Yankees are giving some rations to the indigent whites and blacks now. There is no garrison at Florence but there is one at Darlington, S. C.

The Yankees[159] did not do much damage in this District. They were repulsed at Florence, consequently did not have time to do much. The main body went through Chesterfield and destroyed *everything*. The people flooded down here by hundreds to get something to eat. I never heard of such destruction. They did very little at Society Hill, but they burnt a good part of Cheraw, that is, the main street.

After the Yankee garrison went to Darlington,[160] the whole of the front square was burnt down, supposedly by them. It is being rebuilt very rapidly and is much prettier than before.

I do not know how Dr. Harlee's family[161] is getting along. Miss Hattie and Sallie are married. S. married Dr. Pierce[162] and H. Mr. Bellamy of Wilmington[163]   Miss Lou[164] is still single.

All of the Kings are gone except Mrs. LaCost and Miss Emily   They are living together in Cheraw. I do not think either of them will live long. They look dreadfully. Miss H.[165] died in March.

Mr. Rice[166] is pastor of the church at Society Hill. I think the people like him very much. Mrs. Gus Law lost her son Gus[167] in the war. She does not know what became of him, but he has never returned, and since the war, her little son Sammie has died. Her three oldest sons are married.[168] Miss E[169] is still single. She looks very much broken.

Father had Uncle Wilds body brought home. It had been buried for two years, but Grandmother insisted on having it opened and much to the surprise of *all* the body seemed to be perfectly sound and the face was natural enough although the back of his head was shot off. His death was almost a death stroke to Aunt S. She never got over it.

Uncle Horace[170] had a very severe spell of typhoid fever in Jan. He came very near dying. His baby did die during his illness and the second child came very near dying. He has only two children out of five.

Aunt Carrie's little girl is still living and is a great pet with us all. She divides her time between here and Aunt Mollie's. She almost idolizes her. She is quite pretty and spoiled of course. I don't know whether you remember me or not. I have but a slight recollection of you but have heard my aunt speak of you often. I must close as I have nothing more worth while. This letter is but a poor apology for Aunt Sarah's, but you must excuse all mistakes, omissions, etc.

Yours respectfully,

VIRGINIA E. WILLIAMSON

Grandmother sends her love to you and says you must not quit writing.

* * * * *

FOOTNOTES

1 *War of the Rebellion,* Series I, Volume XIV, p. 624.

2 *Treasured Reminiscences,* p. 62.

3 "General Orders No. 116, Hdqrs., Army of Northern Virginia, October 2, 1862, R. E. Lee, General, Commanding," *War of the Rebellion,* Series I, Volume XIV, Part II, p. 645.

4 Letter from Bettie Vann Howle, Leavensworth, South Carolina, to Jemima Darby, Ringgold, Louisiana, July 31, 1860.

5 Dargan, *Harmony Hall,* p. 33.

6 "Black Creek Church Book, A.D. 1798," p. 223.

7 "Report of the Battle of Corinth, October 3-12, from U. S. Grant, Major-General, Commanding, to Major-General Halleck, October 5, 1862," *War of the Rebellion,* Series I, Volume XVII, p. 155.

8 "Report of Major-General Earl Van Dorn to the Secretary of War, October 20, 1862," *ibid.,* p. 381.

9 Mrs. Wilson was the mother of Anne Stuart Wilson Williamson (August 12, 1822 — September 13, 1850). Mrs. Wilson's son-in-law was Thomas Charles Williamson, son of Bright and Jane Rogers Williamson. A native of Sumter County, Mrs. Wilson had lived in Darlington, first in 1842, when Frances and Absolem Wilson, Anne Williamson and Sarah Green united with the Presbyterian Church, and again in 1848, when Frances Wilson joined the church.

10 Dr. Horace Williamson, Mechanicsville, was a first cousin to Mrs. Wilson's son-in-law, Thomas Charles Williamson. Since he was a kinsman, as well as the doctor in attendance, she extracted a promise from him to take her body back to Sumter County for burial.

11 Williamsburg was an old community in Sumter County. To go there during wartime involved a long, hazardous trip in a wagon.

12 Thomas Charles and Anne Wilson Williamson had three sons and one daughter, Robert E., Lowndes W., Laurens W., and Janie Williamson. The implication here is that Dr. Williamson and the four children made the trip alone with the corpse.

13 Addie Council was a relative of the Williamson family through the Terrels.

14 Sarah's aunt-in-law, Mrs. Bright Williamson, was the paternal grandmother of Mrs. Wilson's grandchildren.

15 Julia, according to Theodosia Dargan Plowden, Sumter, South Carolina, was not a sister to Theodosia Green who married Dr. Horace Williamson. More likely, she was a daughter of Sarah Green, and a granddaughter of Mrs. Wilson.

16 This uncle was a Green relative for there is no indication of his being related to Mrs. Wilson.

17 There was a young man named Wilson Green who joined the Presbyterian Church at Darlington in 1848. Surely he was Julia's brother.

18 Benjamin W. and Mary Ferguson Chambers's children who died were Mary T. (October 9, 1862), aged two, and Bettie W. (October 16, 1862), aged four.

19 Leavensworth, in the Black Creek neighborhood, was Carrie's home.

20 Theodosia Green Williamson was the wife of Sarah's brother, Horace, of Mechanicsville.

21 Theodosia Green Williamson (April 8, 1857 — July 12, 1946), daughter of Horace and Theodosia Williamson, was five years old.

22 Laurence Benton Prince (June 29, 1819 — January 15, 1899) and his wife, Mary (died October 8, 1848), were buried in St. David's Churchyard, Cheraw.

23 Mrs. William Crosland was Miss Darby's friend from Marlboro. Her son was named George.

24 A. P. LaCoste died at Cheraw in the spring of 1862.

25 Mr. LaCoste had grown, married daughters by his first wife.

26 The Williamsons referred to the Misses King, of Society Hill, as "the girls."

27 Jefferson W. Ferguson (1838-1909) was in Virginia with the army.

28 Martha Lane was the maternal grandmother of the children of Pastor Robert Napier.

29 Ann Fort, wife of Josiah, was "Aunt Nancy" DuBose's daughter, and a sister to Jane DuBose Davis, Society Hill.

30 *War of the Rebellion,* Series I, Volume XIV, p. 624.

31 Subsequently, Sallie's aunts, Sarah Williamson and Mary Ann Charles, were to record meticulously in their letters to Miss Darby each phase of the child's growth and development until her twenty-first birthday.

32 Sarah Williamson went to Leavenwsorth to be present when Carrie was confined. After Sallie's birth, Sarah, Carrie, and the baby returned to the Williamson home, near Florence.

33 Jim Williams had returned to the army.

34 Josiah T. Vann was the "old bachelor" son of William Vann.

35 William Vann had been sick since his trip to Virginia.

36 J. P. Wilson of Leavensworth had promised Tom Howle that he would care for his family.

37 The Howle home was at Leavensworth.

38 Apparently Lewis was an ex-slave. This could well have been the Lewis of whom William Vann wrote to his son, Dr. A. R. Vann, on February 10, 1851, "Lewis is still no better, ... I think it very doubtfull whether he will ever get well or not."

39 Mrs. Bozeman lived in the Swift Creek community.

40 Sallie King, daughter of Henry and Mary Ann Vann King, married William Thomas, who had been reared by a Mr. Privette.

41 Mary Ann King's teen-age daughter, Julia, stayed with Lizzie Howle, her aunt.

42 Lizzie's children were William James, aged nine; Thomas E., Jr., seven; Lawrence Keith, five; Maggie J., two years and a half; Sallie, one year and a half.

43 Ladson Dorrity married Mary Vann, daughter of Mills Vann.

44 Mills Vann was referred to in the church records of 1860 as being "old and infirm."

45 Leavensworth-Auburn-Black Creek were included in the region which Carrie called home.

46 The four Chambers children died within a month: Mary T., aged two, on October 9; Bettie W., four, on October 16; J. F., one, on October 22; and Lelia E., five, on November 9. They were buried in the Chambers family cemetery, near Auburn, South Carolina.

[47] S. B. Wilkins was pastor at Hartsville in 1862.

[48] Charles Wilkins was the son of the pastor.

[49] George Alexander Norwood (1831-1909), son of Joseph and Mary Warren Norwood, married Louisa Wilkins, daughter of S. B. Wilkins, at Hartsville, in 1858.

[50] Richard Furman, son of another minister, Samuel Furman, and grandson of the earliest Richard Furman, married Mary McIver, daughter of James Kolb and Sarah Marshall McIver.

[51] John Culpepper was pastor at Ebenezer Baptist Church.

[52] Thomas Fountain lived at Mechanicsville.

[53] Miss Evans had been at Cooper's Well, Mississippi, for several years.

[54] "Aunt Nancy" DuBose, Society Hill, was the mother of Ann, wife of Josiah Fort, of Black Creek. Jane DuBose Davis, wife of John Davis and mother of John Davis, Jr., was also Mrs. DuBose's daughter.

[55] Kim Lucas married Miss Bell.

[56] Thomas Haywood Kolb, five-year-old son of Dr. and Mrs. A. J. Kolb, died October 11, 1862, and was buried at Providence Cemetery, Ringgold, Louisiana.

[57] Buried originally on the battlefield, Howle's body was returned to Black Creek for permanent interment about five months after his death at Sharpesburg. His and Bettie's graves are in the "old" Black Creek Cemetery, in the woods between the cemetery at the old church site and the Darlington-Society Hill highway (1953).

[58] Walter Brooks Vann was born April 17, 1857.

[59] Dr. Vann had been to South Carolina to attend Thomas Howle's funeral.

[60] Mrs. Vann's brother was John Cannady.

[61] Mrs. Vann's mother was Elizabeth Hockaday Cannady.

[62] The sixth child of the A. R. Vanns, born July 2, 1863, was named Edward Macon for this uncle.

[63] "Telegram from G. T. Beauregard to General S. Cooper, at 11 A.M., April 7, 1863," *War of the Rebellion*, Series I, Volume XIV, p. 887.

[64] "Telegram from J. A. Seddon, Secretary of War, War Department, C. S. A., Richmond, April 8, 1863, to General Wade Hampton, Columbia, S. C.," *ibid.*, p. 890.

[65] "Letter from J. A. Seddon, Secretary of War, War Department, C. S. A., Richmond, to Governor M. L. Bonham, Columbia, S. C., May 14, 1863," *ibid.*, p. 942.

[66] DuBose, *History of Company B, Twenty-First Regiment (Infantry), South Carolina Volunteers*, p. 17.

[67] Jim's exemption from the army was granted because of his wife's poor health.

68 Sarah Jones Vann, William's wife, was fond of Miss Darby.

69 Leavensworth was known as "The Mill."

70 William Vann agreed to deed Lizzie's part of his property to her when she decided to move out.

71 William James (1853-1935) and Thomas Epathraditus (1855-1926) Howle were the oldest sons of Bettie Vann Howle.

72 Abel S. Jones, son of Sarah Jones Vann by a previous marriage, lived at Orangeburg, where he had married and reared a family.

73 The slave had a baby which was too young to travel.

74 Sarah hoped that Mrs. Vann would outlive Mr. Vann.

75 Mrs. Baker, when she threatened to bring Mr. Vann's actions before the church, was staying at the home of her sister, Mrs. Ferguson. Mrs. Baker was not related to Mr. Vann; her right to criticize a neighbor was granted by Baptist doctrine.

76 Sarah Ann King LaCoste, Eliza's sister, was A. P. LaCoste's second wife; the slaves had been hers.

77 Florence was a little over three years; Georgia was two years old.

78 James King (1800-1856) was the father of Eliza, grandfather of Florence and Georgia, and cousin to Miss Williamson.

79 Delle LaCoste Ellerbee was Georgia's half-sister, her father's daughter by his first wife.

80 Mr. LaCoste's daughters were Delle Ellerbee, Ann Eliza Evans, Harriet McIver, and Mary Wilson.

81 John Craig Evans (1822-1886), Cheraw merchant, married Ann Eliza La-Coste (1824-1902), daughter of A. P. and Margaret Dawson Fort LaCoste, October 30, 1845. Mrs. Evans was therefore Eliza LaCoste's stepdaughter.

82 Carrie McIver (Smith) Lucas (1834-1901), the daughter of David Rogerson Williams and Caroline Wilds McIver, was the adopted daughter of her maternal grandmother, who had married Dr. Thomas Smith. She married Major J. J. Lucas in 1861 and lived in the home which she inerited from Dr. Smith until 1892.

83 Thomas Smith Lucas, oldest son of J. J. and Carrie McIver Smith Lucas, was born in 1863.

84 Lucy McIver Watson, daughter of James Kolb and Sarah Marshall McIver, married Colonel R. B. Watson.

85 Kate Watson, daughter of R. B. and Lucy McIver Watson, was named for Lucy's "Aunt Kate," Mrs. Catherine M. Fort.

86 Rachel Holloway Coker was Miss Evans's cousin, who lived at Society Hill.

87 Miss Evans owned her home. Eliza McIver Griffin, widow of Thomas Griffin, and her daughter, Sallie, would move in with her.

88 Mary Ann McIver Gregg, wife of Dr. Reese Gregg, was Mrs. Griffin's niece.

89 Elizabeth McIver Law was Mrs. Gregg's sister.

90 Sergeant J. W. Williamson, with the Twenty-First Regiment, South Carolina Volunteers, was stationed on Morris Island, Charleston, South Carolina.

91 Edwin Williamson, nephew to Wilds and Sarah, was also stationed on Morris Island.

92 Henry Bozeman (1828-1864) lived in the Swift Creek neighborhood, Darlington County.

93 *Treasured Reminiscences,* pp. 68-69.

94 Charlie DeLorme (1835-1907) married Anna Dove in 1856.

95 J. P. Wilson, Leavensworth, was the owner of the store.

96 Mrs. Harrell was a relative of Leonard Harrell who had just died at the front.

97 Julia King Croswell was Mrs. Howle's niece.

98 Obviously, Mrs. LeGrand was a widow also.

99 Mrs. LeGrand knew the Leavensworth-Auburn-Black Creek community well. Evidently she had lived there at one time.

100 *Treasured Reminiscences,* pp. 78-79.

101 Dargan, *Harmony Hall,* p. 32.

102 Caroline M. T. Williamson, wife of James A. Williams, daughter of Thomas and Sarah Wilds Williamson, was born December 19, 1822, and died August 10, 1863. She was buried in the Williams-Chambers family cemetery near Auburn, South Carolina.

103 Sallie Elizabeth (Charles) Williams (October 23, 1862 — May 9, 1895) never married. She is buried in the Williams-Chambers family cemetery near Auburn, South Carolina.

104 Thomas Park Lide (June 10, 1810 — July 23, 1882), son of Hugh and Elizabeth Pugh Lide, married Elizabeth Sparks, first cousin to Mrs. Williamson.

105 Captain Benjamin Wesley Chambers (May 8, 1820 — October 12, 1863) was the husband of Mary Deborah Chambers.

106 Bennie W. Chambers was born August 22, 1863.

107 Elizabeth Williams Ferguson, who was almost blind, was able to ride about over her plantation directing activities.

108 Jefferson W. Ferguson (1838-1909), who never married, was in love with the Miss Nettles who married Mr. Hacker, a refugee during the war.

109 Linton Williams had a discharge but returned to the army.

110 James A. Williams had enlisted, sought a discharge, re-enlisted, obtained an exemption, and now, with his wife dead, was back in the army again.

111 Dr. James B. Crane was a Darlington physician; Jim's house was at Leavensworth.

112 William Vann was Lizzie's father.

113 Rosanna E. Woods was the daughter of Joseph and Hephzibah Dargan Woods.

114 William A. Fountain, Fourth Sergeant, was killed on Morris Island, July 10, 1863.

115 Richard Grandison Howard (March 13, 1832 — September 10, 1898), who married Elizabeth McCall, was Captain, Company I, First South Carolina Infantry, C. S. A.

116 James Lide Coker (January 3, 1837-1918), son of Caleb and Hannah Lide Coker, married Sue Stout of Alabama.

117 Hannah Lide Coker (March 3, 1812 — May 19, 1900) was the wife of Caleb Coker, and the mother of James Lide Coker.

118 Sue Stout of Alabama and James Lide Coker were married on March 28, 1860.

119 Charles Westfield Coker (December 22, 1841 — July 1, 1862) was killed at Malvern Hill.

120 James Lide and William Caleb Coker were captured by Federal forces. William Caleb (June 8, 1839 — April 20, 1907) married (1) Mary McIver, and (2) Lavinia McIver.

121 John K. McIver remained in Virginia.

122 Isaac DeLesseline Wilson, Jr. (August 6, 1836 — April 3, 1894), son of I. D. and Margaret Jane Sparks Wilson of Society Hill, married Sallie Preston (March 20, 1846 — July 26, 1894).

123 DuBose Dargan, son of William E. and Sarah DuBose Dargan, died soon after the war from a resulting illness.

124 Josephine King was the youngest of the King daughters, Society Hill.

125 Julia Terrel Wilds was the widow of Mrs. Williamson's brother, Peter Wilds.

126 Bettie Wilds Lide was the wife of Leighton Lide.

127 George Williamson was Sarah's brother.

128 Thomas Williamson was George's son.

129 Kate Williamson was George's daughter.

130 Sarah Napier was the daughter of Robert Napier, pastor of the Mispah Church.

131 Virginia Williamson was Kate's sister.

132 Jane Rogers Williamson was the widow of Sarah's uncle, Bright Williamson.

133 Mary Rogers, sister of Jane Rogers Williamson, made her home in Alabama with her brothers, Frank Alexander and Thomas Wickham Rogers.

134 Lieutenant Colonel Alonzo T. Dargan (1839 — May 7, 1864), son of Julius and Martha Woods Dargan, married Jennie Quigley. He was killed at Walthall Junction, Virginia.

135 Private E. Augustus Law, Jr., (? — August 21, 1864), son of E. Augustus and Sarah E. McIver Law, Darlington, died at Weldon Railroad, Virginia.

136 First Sergeant Alfred C. DuBose (? — June 29, 1864), Darlington, died near Petersburg, Virginia.

137 DuBose, *History of Company B, Twenty-First Regiment (Infantry), South Carolina Volunteers,* p. 49.

138 Joseph Wilds Williamson (June 16, 1825 — May 6, 1864), son of Thomas and Sarah Wilds Williamson, Orangedale, near Florence, unmarried brother of Sarah Williamson, Mary Ann Williamson Charles, and Caroline Williamson Williams, was buried in Lowther's Hill Cemetery, near Cashaway Ferry, South Carolina.

139 DuBose, *History of Company B,* p. 50.

140 *Ibid.,* p. 52.

141 William E. Gonzales, "South Carolina in the Confederacy," *South in the Building of the Nation,* Volume II (Richmond, 1909), p. 84.

142 Henry Slocum, "Sherman's March from Savannah to Bentonville," *Battles and Leaders of the Civil War,* Volume IV, p. 686.

143 U. R. Brooks, *Stories of the Confederacy* (Columbia, 1912), p. 336.

144 *Ibid.,* p. 332.

145 Daniel Oakey, "Marching through Georgia and the Carolinas," *Battles and Leaders of the Civil War,* Volume IV, p. 675.

146 "Report of Major General William T. Sherman, U. S. Army, Hdqrs. Military Division of the Mississippi, Goldsborough, N. C., April 4, 1865," *War of the Rebellion,* Series I, Volume XLVII, Part I, p. 23.

147 "Black Creek Church Book, A. D. 1798," March, 1865, p. 223.

148 J. T. Trowbridge, *The South: A Tour of Its Battlefields and Ruined Cities* (Hartford, Connecticut, 1866), p. 568.

149 Sarah Wilds Williamson (March 5, 1821 — June 14, 1865), daughter of Thomas and Sarah L. Williamson, was buried in Lowther's Hill Cemetery, near Cashaway Ferry, on the Pee Dee River, South Carolina.

150 Sarah L. Wilds Williamson (August 7, 1793 — March 2, 1871) was the widow of Thomas Williamson.

151 Joseph Wilds Williamson (June 16, 1825 — May 6, 1864) was killed at Walthall Junction, Virginia, and buried in Lowther's Hill Cemetery.

152 Caroline Williamson Williams (December 19, 1822 — August 10, 1863), wife

of James A. Williams, had been buried in the Williams-Chambers family cemetery near Auburn, South Carolina.

153 Sarah Catlett DuPre (June 9, 1809 — February 28, 1867) was, according to her tombstone inscription, the wife of "Elder L. DuPre; she was an ornament to society and an eminently useful member of this church for many years; beloved in life and lamented in death; her end was peace." She is buried in the Baptist Churchyard, Darlington, South Carolina.

154 George L. Williamson (August 25, 1818 — February 18, 1871) was Virginia's father.

155 Samuel Wilds Williamson (November 6, 1811 — April 5, 1877) was a son of Thomas and Sarah Wilds Williamson.

156 Edwin P. Williamson was Samuel's son.

157 Addie Council was Virginia's relative through her mother's family.

158 Mary Ann Williamson Charles was the only remaining Williamson daughter.

159 Sherman marched through South Carolina in 1865.

160 Sickles's Military Command had a post at Darlington in 1867.

161 Dr. Robert Harllee (November 7, 1807 — November 20, 1872), son of Thomas Harllee, married (1) Ann Gurdy, daughter of Joseph Gurdy (no children), and (2) Mrs. Amelia Cannon Howard, the mother of Robert A., Walter C., Harry T., Arthur, Sallie, Louisa, and Hattie.

162 Sallie Harllee (December 8, 1840 — April 28, 1879) married Dr. J. F. Pearce on November 25, 1865, Melrose Plantation.

163 Hattie Harllee (March 17, 1846 — June 1, 1925) married Marsden Bellamy, Wilmington, North Carolina, December 19, 1867.

164 Louisa Harllee was twenty-eight years old.

165 Hannah King, one of "the girls" to the Williamsons, died in March, 1867.

166 W. D. Rice, Society Hill, came from Barnwell County.

167 Private E. Augustus Law, Jr., died on August 21, 1864, at Weldon Railroad, Virginia.

168 The three oldest sons of E. A. and Eliza McIver Law were: Evander McIver, who was born in 1836 and married Jennie Latta on February 3, 1863; Junius Augustus Law, who was born in 1838 and married Blanche Crawford in October, 1866; and John Kolb Law, who was born in 1840 and who married Mary James.

169 Elma Law was thirty-three years old.

170 Dr. Horace Williamson lived at Mechanicsville.

Reconstruction
PART I

"A mute protest of this sombre scenery
and wide-spread destruction and desola-
tion, coupled with the social changes
for the worst . . . speaks to the
traveller more eloquently than the
loudest lamentations."

Edward DeLeon, "Ruin and Reconstruction
of the Southern States," *Southern Magazine*,
XIV (January, 1874).

In the two years which followed the close of the war, no letters went from South Carolina to Miss Darby. Dead were four faithful chroniclers: Mary Ann and Sarah Catlett; Caroline and Sarah Williamson. Pee Dee people were too busy, too wretched, to write.

Through Louisiana newspapers, which brought fragmentary accounts of events in Carolina, Jemima was able to keep abreast of important developments. She knew, for example, that Governor Magrath[1] had been sent, as a prisoner, soon after the war was over, to Fort Pulaski in Savannah, and that there was "no organized State government, no central authority, no militia to which the people might look for the protection of life or property."[2] United States troops had come to garrison the towns and cities that Miss Darby knew so well, and there was a harshness of administration throughout the state.

News of the naming of B. F. Perry[3] as provisional governor on June 13, 1865, was of more than local concern, as was the taking of the governor's oath by James Lawrence Orr[4] on November 27, 1865. Information about Darlington District's participation in the various conventions would have pleased Jemima greatly. She would have been glad to have known that David C. Milling, J. H. Norwood, and J. E. Byrd represented Darlington when the Convention met in the Baptist Church, Columbia, on September 13, 1865, and that E. W. Charles was in the Senate, and F. F. Warley, D. C. Milling, and James Lide Coker were in the House, when the famous "Black Code" was passed.[5]

Announcement of the assignment of General Sickles[6] as commander over Military District No. 2, composed of North and South Carolina, was made by Washington, but it is doubtful if Jemima knew that Governor Orr remained nominal governor only by sufferance of military authority. Citizens of Louisiana were too engrossed in their own problems of Reconstruction to inquire particularly into governmental activities of neighbor states.[7]

When General Sickles assumed command of his district on March 21, 1867, he was told that there were eleven posts within the two states. Williamsburg, Marion, Marlboro, Chesterfield, and Darlington counties were under the administration of the Darlington post until Sickles was relieved of his command on August 31, 1867.[8]

Even though she was seventy-two years old, Jemima would have enjoyed being among her old friends when they planned the first Memorial Day in Darlington in May of 1866.

> They gathered around the graves of their dead heroes, while the earth lay fresh over the forms of many of Darlington's noblest men, and, with tears still undried, they covered the graves with flowers, teaching the children to bring their offerings of love and join in this expression of grateful appreciation of their patriotic service.[9]

This group looked to Mrs. Lavinia Lide[10] for leadership in planning the first memorial program, and elected her to serve as vice-president when the society became the Memorial Association. Miss Lizzie Brearley[11] was the first president of the group.

> To properly appreciate the difficulties and discouragements that confronted the ladies, the political and financial condition of the State must be taken into consideration, and when this is done the apparent hopelessness of their undertaking can easily be appreciated. Despite this they neither despaired nor faltered in the work, and after the lapse of nearly 10 years of hard and patient work their energy and patriotism were crowned with success.[12]

From the Black Creek community, too, Jemima would have appreciated news. The Vanns did not write to tell her about Sarah Jones Vann's death on October 3, 1866, and Lizzie Howle did not tell her cousin that she had received a child's part of the William Vann estate. "I have already conveyed by deed to my daughter Elizabeth Howle a tract of land containing about Three hundred acres, more or less, being a part of my house tract, which I deem her fair share of my land," the old man wrote in his will.[13] With a plantation to manage and five small children to rear, Mrs. Howle had no time to write. She grieved constantly for Tom.

Among the Darby family friends at Society Hill were members of James King's family. By 1867, the only remaining members of this family were Mrs. Eliza LaCoste, of Cheraw, and Emily, the unmarried sister who had gone down to Stony Hill, near Cashaway Ferry, for an extended visit with her distant relative, Mary Ann Williamson, wife of Andrew Charles. During Sarah Williamson's lifetime, "Sister Moll," as she was called by her family, had never written to Miss Darby, but her letter of November 26, 1867, was to be the first in a long series which would extend through the period of South Carolina's reconstruction and on into the Wade Hampton regime. Indeed, Miss Darby's only reports from Darlington District between 1867 and the year of her death, 1884, were to come from Mrs. Andrew Charles.

Mrs. Andrew Charles, Darlington, South Carolina, to Jemima Darby, Ringgold, Louisiana.

Darlington
Nov. 26, 1867

Miss Jemima Darby
    Care of Dr. A. Kolb
    Ringgold, La.

Dear Miss Darby

Your letter of the 21st inst., reached me in due time. I was glad to hear from you again and sorry to hear of your ill health and hope you are all in good health ere this. I am sorry you did not receive the letter I wrote you in reply to one you wrote my dear sister.[14] I will try to answer all of the questions you have asked.

Joe King[15] died a very triumphant death. Hannah[16] also professed conversion. They died of consumption. Emily[17] is with us now and has been down since the first of July. Her health is very feeble. She moved to Cheraw and lives with Eliza.[18] Hannah died one year and a week after Josephine. Emily is telling me all who have died at the Hill that she can think of. Old Mr.[19] and Mrs. Witherspoon[20] old Mrs. McIntosh[21] Miss Nancy McIver[22] Miss Charlotte Kirven[23] Maggie McIntosh[24] Mrs. Sam Evans.[25] These are all of the persons with whom you are acquainted.

Mr. Rice[26] is pastor of the church. I suppose you know him. I think he lived in Sumter when you were here. Emily sold her lot to Mr. Coker.[27] The Hill looks pretty much as it did when you last saw it. The merchants are all at their old stands. Few changes have been made in the buildings. Capt Bobbie Edwards was to have gone off last week.

Lizzie Howle lives at her plantation not far from her fathers. One of Mr. Howle's brothers married one of her nieces Miss King[28] lives with her. I suppose she is getting along as well as most persons. Your cousin Billie[29] was about to be married but concluded that the lady was not good enough for him and flew the track. I do not wish your old relation any harm but I do hope he may never get another wife. He is making himself ridiculous by looking around at the girls.

Mr. DuPre still lives at his old home.[30] He is at this time on a visit to his friends in Illinois. He offers his lot for sale or rent and says it is too large for him. He preaches at Black Creek two Sundays, one at Mechanicsville, the other he is not occupied and sometimes he preaches at our church in the village. We have been without a pastor near a year.[31] Mr. Bealer[32] went to Norfolk, Va., but was forced to come farther south on account of ill health and is not able to preach a good part of his time. I fear his labors are about at an end. He looks dreadfully and is boarding (with his family) at Mrs. Wingate's.

Mrs. Ely Lide[33] has been out on a visit to her friends. Mrs. Noah Bacott[34] (that was) came out and brought Blanch Bell back, who had been on a visit to her and saw her married and took her home to Alabama. They had a nice party. Dr. Dargan's[35] daughters were bridesmaids for her.

There is to be an ordination in our church next Sabbath. Mr. Fred Easton,[36] who is the son of Mrs. Evan Lide. He is a young man of great promise. Mr. R. Fermon, Mr. J. O. B. Dargan, Mr. Bealer,[37] are to perform the ceremonies. I wish you could be transplanted at eleven o'clock next Sunday to a seat in our pugh to witness the scene which you must imagine will be very impressive.

Mr. Brairley[38] still preaches for his congregation. I attended quarterly meeting there Sabbath before last. Mr. Fryerson[39] preached a very fine sermon.

Aunt Julia[40] has been sick but is recovering now. Nancy has seven children.[41] Bettie three.[42]

Aunt Jane Williamson[43] died near a year ago. Miss Mary Rogers[44] could not come out to see her and be with her in her last days on account of ill health.

* * * * *

Mary Ann Charles's second letter[45] to Miss Darby was written during the latter part of 1867 or the early part of 1868 while Emily King was still a guest at Stony Hill, the Charles home. Jemima had made inquiries about Baptist papers published in South Carolina; Mary Ann dashed off a note in reply.

Mrs. Andrew Charles, Stony Hill, Darlington, South Carolina, to Jemima Darby, Ringgold, Louisiana.

I send you the directions of two papers. The Christian Index and Southwestern Baptist United and the Biblical Recorder. Olivia Wingate's husband, you will see, is one of the editors. Manly[46] writes to it, occasionally. I take both papers and like the Index and Southwestern Baptist much the best. There is but one Baptist paper published in this state that I know of that is not worth the name of religious paper. I believe it is published in Greenville or Anderson. I have heard of it, but have never seen a copy.

You asked about Dr. Harlee's[47] family. All are living except one of the sons who was killed in the war.[48] Sallie has married Dr. Pierce.[49] General Harlee[50] has two grown sons and one daughter.[51] About a year ago, Mrs. Sam Wilds died and on the 19th October Cousin Samuel[52] died of rheumatism contracted in camp. He was wounded in the throat on Morriss's Island and at Petersburg where my dear brother fell. He was severely wounded in the hip from which he suffered extremely and came home and returned before he recovered sufficiently. Was pretty soon captured and confined in Fortress Monroe many months after the close of the war. He gradually declined notwithstanding all the medical skill that could be procured. Mother[53] has been quite sick. I saw her on Friday. Left her out of bed. I am sorry that I am so far from her now that I am her only nurse when she is sick. I did not feel so anxious about her when my dear sister was with her. She spoke of you and desired me to write to you. I hope you will receive this letter. Andrew sends kind regards to you. Emily joins me in love and says she hopes you may receive this letter and have day light to read it.

Yours as ever

MARY A. CHARLES

Mary Williamson[54] has married a Texian and gone to her Texas home.

* * * * *

The year 1868 brought to an end all semblance of home rule in South Carolina. Carpetbaggers, scalawags, and Negroes took over. Delegates from Darlington to the Reconstruction Convention of January 14, 1868, at Columbia, were B. F. Whittemore, white; Isaac Brockenton, Jordan Lang, and Richard Humbird, colored.[55] With the state reconstructed under the "Congressional Plan," Robert K. Scott, an Ohio carpetbagger, became governor and Lemuel Boozer, lieutenant governor.[56] During Scott's first term, Darlington was represented in the General Assembly by B. F. Whittemore, white, in the Senate; and by G. Holliman, white, and Jordan Lang, John Boston, Alfred Rush, colored, in the House of Representatives.[57]

Early in 1870, Governor Scott, in a speech in Washington, "depicted the rebellious and bloodthirsty doings of the white people of South Carolina, and declared that the only law for those people was the Winchester rifle."[58] Upon his return to South Carolina, his arming of the Negro militia brought a storm of protest from men who had been leaders in South Carolina politics. Public-spirited citizens like J. L. Coker of Darlington were urged to attend the Convention of March 16, 1870,[59] and use their influence in an effort to re-establish decency and justice, but in spite of their labors, Scott was elected for a second term. Late in 1870, attention became focused once again upon the activities of the Ku Klux Klan, which was hailed as salvation by some South Carolinians and condemned as a menace by others. In the Republican Convention which met in Columbia on August 12, 1872, Franklin J. Moses, Jr., was elected governor.[60] Negroes were now in control of the University of North Carolina; they came in large numbers to sit at the communion table of the whites.[61]

After traveling through South Carolina, J. S. Pike recorded the economic problems faced by a once prosperous people.

> When the war ended, there was nothing left but absolute poverty and nakedness. Famine followed, and suffering beyond computation, the story of which has never been told. Rich planters' families subsisted on corn-bread when they could get it, but often they could not, and then they resorted to a coarse cattle fodder known as cow-peas. . . . There were numbers of large slave-holders and property owners in and about Columbia who went down in the general ruin. Some were immensely wealthy; there were several families owning 500 and 1000 slaves.
>
> But the poor people were stripped as well as the rich. Though they had but little, yet that little was their all. And to lose it was to lose all. And to this was added grievous disappointment. They were hoarding their imaginary money, feeling that they were sure to come out rich in the end. Great was their dismay and their astonishment when they found they had leaned on a broken reed, and their vision of sudden wealth vanished in an instant.[62]

Truly, dark days had come to Miss Darby's native state. It is no wonder that there was little time for letter writing and that postal service required two weeks for a letter to go from Ringgold to Darlington.

But during reconstruction, as during the war, people married and died. Babies were born and the young grew up. Emily King married in 1870; her sister, Eliza LaCoste, died September 3, 1869, and was buried in the LaCoste plot at St. David's, Cheraw. Florence LaCoste, aged twelve, went to Darlington to live with her great-aunt, Serena Bacot Dargan, her Grandmother King's sister; Georgia stayed on in Cheraw with her Aunt Emily.

Sallie Williams, now ten years old, had gone, after her Grandmother Williamson's death in 1871, to live with Mary Ann Charles at Stony Hill. Mary Ann's letter of November 5, 1872, is one of the longest in the series.

Mrs. Andrew Charles, Darlington, South Carolina, to Jemima
Darby, Ringgold, Louisiana.

Darlington, Nov. 5, 1872

Miss Jemima Darby
Ringgold, La.

Dear Miss Darby

Your unexpected letter came to hand in about two weeks
after being postmarked. I need not tell you what a surprise it
was for I had lamented you as dead for I had received no reply
to two letters written you more than two years ago.

First let me answer all your questions. The Kings are all
dead except Emily. About two years ago she married a young
minister, one of the students, sent to supply the Cheraw
Church during vacation. He was twenty-one years old, she
forty-two. He is almost blind, his name is Taylor.[63] Her friends
were shocked at the idea and he has a church at Chesterfield.
Eliza left two girls. Emily kept the youngest. Sarine Dargan has
Florence. She is almost grown and a good likeness of Sarah
Ann.[64]

Mrs. Wilds[65] and all of her family are living. Peter[66] and
Robert[67] are fine young men now. Bob is an active member in
the Baptist Church. Mollie[68] has not married. Bet married
Leighton Lide and has one son and two sweet interesting little
girls.[69] Nancy Coggeshall has nine children.[70]

Mr. DuPre moved to Tennessee near Nashville in about a
year after his wife died.[71] Mr. Vann[72] is in one of the upper
districts of this state. Much liked as a minister. Mr. Mills and
Billie Vann are still living. Mr. Dargan is still pastor of B. C.[73]
church. His sons, Furman,[74] George[75] and John[76] are married.
The latter just through the Theological University of Greenville. Eddie[77] is taking the course. The youngest son[78] Bettie[79]
and Maggie[80] are single. Mr. Beattie is living where you left
him[81] and when I heard from him he was in usual health. Our
Association commences next Friday, which you remember (I
suppose) always commences Friday before the second Sabbath in
November, held with the Bennettsville church. The Convention meets with the Darlington Church Friday before the
third Sabbath. We have as many ministers as when you were
here, I suppose, though some that you knew have died. Yet

others fill their places. Mr. Culpepper[82] spent a night with us last week. Mr. Wilkins[83] still teaches school and preaches.

I must tell you something about Society Hill people. Mrs. Griffin[84] all of her family are living. Peter is to marry Emmie Maldwin[85] who is young enough to be his daughter. She is Hannah McIver's[86] daughter. Cousin Eliza Evans left the Hill five or six years ago. Lives near Greenville. She was here last summer on a visit. The McIntoshes are dying up with consumption. Maggie[87] and Edward[88] have died. Lou[89] is in wretched health. Mr. Burn and family[90] all living. Mr. Sompayrac's family.[91] Mr. Caleb Coker[92] you perhaps have heard died several years back. The store is kept on. Mr. Etsel Adams[93] who married May Gregg became insane, jumped headforemost in an old well on his lot and killed himself. You remember, they live in the old Witherspoon house. Mrs. Sparks[94] has been dead about a year and a half and left her home and came to live with Cousin T. Lide[95] when she died. Emma[96] his only daughter is also dead. She married Terrill Rodgers[97] son of Mr. Ham and Verlina. She left a little boy[98] about a year old, and suppose you have seen a notice of her death in the Baptist paper. A good many very sad deaths have occurred recently among us. Mrs. Gibsons only daughter, who was a pet and caressed by all, married her *first* cousin Andrew Woods who died about two months previous to her death, is dead.

I presume Dr. Kolb has an interesting family.[99] A nice young lady just out is an object of interest to me, as well as the young gentlemen.[100] Bro. Horace's daughter[101] may be near her age (fifteen). She is quite a toast, very much admired, caressed and she makes conquests on all occasions. She is very pretty and intelligent. This will be her second season in Charleston. She is attending the State Fair in Columbia at this time.

On the twenty-fourth of October, we celebrated the tenth birthday of our little darling, Sallie,[102] Sister C's little daughter. We never fail to give a dinner and invite her little friends to dine. They have a merry time of it. She has more birthday and Christmas presents than she could take care of at once. She is sitting by me now drawing with a pencil. I expect to start her to school next year. She is quite an adept at housekeeping. I wish I could send you over a loaf of her light bread and dish of preserves some evening in time for your tea. It would surprise you.

Our district fair came off last week. It was a grand success —

large exhibition of fancy work — some fine specimens of painting and every imaginable article that could be thought of in the household department. The planters were well represented in their line. The machinists also and there was a splendid exhibition of horses, etc. There were over a thousand persons in attendance each day, on one day over two thousand (the ticket office reports). The stockholders realized something over two thousand dollars. The ladies bazaar (Monumental Society)[103] took three hundred dollars, one hundred each day. So you see if we are under radical rule, there is a little life in us yet.

Some of our farmers are making money. Some of our merchants are rich. Yet the circumstances of most of the people are sadly changed. Those that you left rich are the poorest now. Chancelor Dargan's[104] estate is bankrupt. The mansion in Donerail was bought last Monday by Max Gandy. He owns the Dr. McIver house (Hannah Wilsons)[105] on the Hill. She has no home and spends her winters in Charleston and summer at Dovesville with her parents.

You asked me about May Williamson who is Mrs. Brown[106] now. She lives in *Middle* Texas about the crop timbers in Cleburn a little village. She was out on a visit last summer and has no child and health delicate. You know she has always been so.

Our dear mother and brother George have been dead almost two years but G.[107] died about two weeks before Mother.[108] It was a terrible blow to me. I felt as if my last earthly prop had been removed, but G. was very successful in business and left his children exceedingly comfortable. Independent of his estate, they drew from a life insurance company, since his death, ten thousand dollars. Thomas manages the estate well. You know how fond Mother was of giving. She dispensed her charities with her last breath. Julia a servant that she raised performed the last offices around her dying bed and has not since left the children. We have one fine servant who has never left us, and my cook is one of our old servants.

Dear Miss Darby how glad I would be to see you, but it is not possible that we will ever meet in this world, but I hope we may meet in a better where partings are not known. I must bid you good night with the hope of hearing from you very soon. I remain,

Your endeared friend as in days of old,

M. CHARLES

Please present my best wishes and kind regards to Mrs. K. and her children. It would afford me pleasure to make their acquaintance. Andrew desires to be kindly remembered to you.

I will send you a recipe of a favourite pudding of Sallie's to Mrs. K's children. Perhaps you have it. You used to have all sorts stored away. If you have not it, the little folks may like it and call it the (Carolina pudding).

Please if you receive this and reply to it just ask as many questions as you can or would like to have answered. I will answer every one.

Sallie Wilds[109] is the pet of her family. All exert themselves to make life as happy for her as possible. She has never walked nor had any use of her right hand.

* * * * *

By May, 1873, South Carolina had endured four years of Reconstruction government. There were four more difficult years ahead.

From 1868 to 1876, every member of the House of Representatives was a Negro. Through all these years, the senator was B. F. Whittemore, New England carpetbagger, who had been twice expelled from Congress for selling a West Point cadetship for $2000.00 and branded by General John A. Logan, a Union General, as a man of infamous character. Not only was this man repeatedly elected State senator, but he was also sent to the Constitutional Convention in 1868, along with three ignorant blacks, Isaac Brockington, Jordan Lang and Richard Humbird to frame a constitution and make laws for South Carolina.[110]

Mary Ann Charles described unpleasant conditions which existed in Miss Darby's Darlington County on May 29, 1873.

Mrs. Andrew Charles, Stony Hill, Darlington, South Carolina, to Jemima Darby, Ringgold, Louisiana.

Stony Hill[111]
May 29, 1873

Miss Jemima Darby
        Dr. Alexander Kolb
        Ringgold, La.

My dear Miss Darby

I have delayed much longer in writing to you than I would liked to have done, hoping to get the picture and seeds. There is no artist nearer than Sumter and could not get a photograph of myself and have one of Sallie which is not very good. I do not think it is as good looking as she. Her eyes do not show to advantage. They are very fine large dark blue eyes. Mr. Bealer[112] once remarked that a "person could never be considered homely with such splendid eyes as this child has." I could not get any geranium seed and have inquired far and near.

My dear mother[113] died in March of her 77th year. August following was her birth month, August of this year, if she had lived, she would have been 79. She celebrated her last birthday with us which she had been in the habit of doing for a number of years. We gave a nice dinner and invited her old friends to dine with her.

I suppose you have seen a notice of Mr. Culpepper's[114] death in the Herald. Mrs. Sarah Wilson[115] and Mrs. Jesse Keith[116] have died also since I wrote you. Mrs. Zimmermans boys are all dead but William the eldest and Sammie the youngest. John died about a month ago — the fourth since the close of the war.

Mrs. DuPrees[117] house was bought by a Negro, Jack Smith, who occupies it now. You would hardly know the village now. The Yankee garrison burned the square the first year after the close of the war. It is just now being rebuilt. There was another fire about 4 years ago which originated from kerosene oil in a store which used to belong to Mr. P. McCall at the corner as the street turns to go down to Col. Charles.[118] All of his out buildings were burned, his store having been burned in the first fire. His loss was 10 thousand dollars at low figures. The place[119] is very much improved in regard to buildings, but the society unfortunately has not. A great many strangers have moved in, not of the best class, and the colored population have increased almost to innumerable numbers. Numbers of large estates have gone to ruin. Mr. Julius[120] and Chancellor Dargans.[121] Max Gandy[122] bought the Chancellors mansion.

Dr. Player[123] married Elma Law[124] before his wife[125] had been dead eighteen months. Their children have all died[126] but two.[127] Miss Georgia[128] lives with them. She lost everything by the war. Bettie Lide and Leighton[129] live at a place which was left the Lide children by the Grandfather Mr. Sparks[130] that they call Piney Woods place about four miles from the Hill. They are very nicely fixed. Leight is a good planter. It is a very large body of land. It was divided into three parts. Emma Lide who married Terrell Rodgers,[131] Mr. Ham's son took one part. Leight and Alex the other two. Willie[132] took a river plantation.

Mrs. Wilds, Mollie and Sallie[133] were sick when I heard from them. May Brown Williamson[134] is out from Texas. She is in wretched health. Has consumption. Her mother died with it, you remember.

Nancy Coggeshall has nine children and lost her first.[135] Peter gets along remarkably well with such an immense family. Dr. Harlee[136] died this spring. They are very much reduced. The general's[137] large house and splendid gardens were burned recently. Jane Killen that was who married Mr. Nes Smith lives in Marion Village — a widow with two children. Betsy died and left one boy. Mrs. Tish Killen who married Parson Nappier has him. They live at the Coggeshall place near Mr. Bob Rogers.

Emily King Taylor lives in York County now. She wrote to me not long since. Her health is bad. I think I told you that she had married a boy twenty-one years of age. His eye sight prevented his studying at Greenville. He was sent to Cheraw as a supply. Mr. Thomas[138] resigned on account of ill health, I think. His health is not good now, but he still preaches at Bennettsville, and two other churches over there. Jonnie Dargan,[139] Mr. J. D's son lives at Charlie Croslands, preaches two Sabbaths at Bennettsville. Mrs. Dr. Crosland[140] lives there still. Willie and Charlie are married. George[141] is flying around a daughter of Mr. Mose McCall, Emma.[142] Charlie is a Baptist and a very prosperous planter.

Mr. and Mrs. Beattie[143] were in good health when I last heard from them. Mrs. Sam Sparks[144] has been dead about three years I think. Mrs. Keitt[145] and her only daughter live with the old gentleman at the old home. Mr. Sompayrac[146] still has a store on the Hill and has a grown daughter.[147]

Please, Miss Darby, ask me as many questions as you wish about anything out here. I will take great pleasure in answering them.

I must tell you about our little darling Sallie being such a fine student. Her monthly reports are almost perfect. She is particularly fond of the study of history and is a great reader. I could not tell you how many books she has read. She has a fine ear for music. Sings well. Has a strong voice and it will be sweet when properly cultivated. She will commence to take music lessons the next session or perhaps in February. We thought it best not to crowd too many studies at once especially as her health is not good. Her character is like her mother. She is very benevolent and is always trying to do good to others. She is often affected to tears at the sufferings of others. She will now give almost anything that she has if it is to do good and piously inclined. She could not well be otherwise as both her parents were Christians.

Andrew desires to be remembered very kindly to you and our regards to your family with whom you live. I feel as if they are our relations and believe me,

>Yours as ever with feelings of warmest
>affections,

M. CHARLES

* * * * *

A series of destructive yellow fever epidemics swept across the South during the 1870's. The autumn months of 1873, 1878, and 1879 brought plague-like terror to Memphis, Tennessee,[148] and New Orleans, Louisiana.[149] In Shreveport, Louisiana, "the epidemic of September, 1873, resulted in the death of 639 whites and 120 Africans."[150] Miss Darby shared with other citizens of Ringgold their distress for friends and relatives who lived in river ports and large cities, but the epidemic never penetrated the pinehills section of North Louisiana.

Dr. Kolb's children reached school age during the war and reconstruction periods[151] when there were no public schools in Louisiana.[152] To Jemima Darby, at the age of seventy-nine, fell the task of educating her great-nieces. Except for her church school and tutoring experiences, she was not qualified to teach. Yet her experiences had been rich and her lessons were so full of mature wisdom, Baptist dogma and South Carolina hauteur that her three students[153] became conservative, fastidious, and didactic.

Lucy Paxton[154] was born December 27, 1857, at Sparta, Louisiana, and lived there during the war and reconstruction periods. Ella Kolb was born at Ringgold in 1855 and her sister Maria Elizabeth was born in 1859. When Lucy was seventy-three, she wrote her recollections[155] of school days in Bienville Parish, which, in most phases, closely paralleled Ella's and Lizzie's, the main difference being that Jemima Darby served as their "lady of genteel poverty."

During Reconstruction days the Girl was running up like cotton that goes to weed and was attending a private school (there were no public ones). This school was taught by two young ladies of genteel poverty. Indeed, poverty was mostly of the genteel sort, and affluence was almost a badge of dishonor, since few besides the carpet-bagger and the scalawag enjoyed prosperity. In this school pupils studied (as probably at most other schools) Webster's blue back speller, Davies' arithmetic, and Mc. Guffey's reader. Historical information came from Peter Parley, and geographical from an unremembered source. She recalls, however, that some pupils had an old edition in which it was Russian Territory, and a favored few a spick-and-span book in which it was mapped Alaska. School "took in" at eight o'clock in the morning and "let out" at four thirty in the afternoon. . . . At noon the children sat on the protruding roots of the large oaks that shaded the campus and ate sweet potatoes and fat buttermilk bisquit and washed them down with milk. With their chubby and often dirty fingers they punched cavities in the bisquit and filled them with syrup. They brought their lunches in tin buckets, and there was significance in the fact that most of the syrup and milk bottles had been quinine containers. Friday afternoons were given over to supposedly original "compositions" by the girls and delivery of "book speeches" by the boys. At this time the Girl spent most of her Saturdays in the garret of the old home in the company of Godey's and Peterson's "Ladies Books," to which her mother had subscribed before the war. She ate up their sentimental romances with avidity, and they seemed to act as a sort of anaesthetic, so that while she was under their influence she was altogether oblivious of her surroundings but straightway forgot what manner of stories they were. . . .

. . . During one of her summer vacations a girl friend introduced her to Mrs. E. D. E. N. Southworth. Their reading room was a mound under a bunch of sweet-gums in the red-gullied pasture, . . . and they considered it paradise enow to chew the sweet-gum they had garnered from the abraded trunks of the overhanging trees and read the enchanted pages until the sunshine no longer flickering through the palmate leaves and twilight obscured the thrilling pages.

On June 18, 1873, Ella Caroline Kolb, who was almost eighteen years old, prepared an essay on the subject of "Fashions."[156] From Jemima's accounts of what she had observed of South Carolina aristocracy came references to a world of charming ladies and stuffy gentlemen in an elegant Victorian parlor. Ella concluded the exposition with:

Young ladies, throw aside your love for display and your love for admiration gained from the art of dress. If you wish to read, throw away your silly novels and love-sick stories and read something that will cultivate your minds. In so doing you will cultivate your hearts and make your homes a loving resting place for Father, Mother and Brother.

Young gentlemen, if you wish to gain the respect and love of the ladies, remember it is not by having the newest fashions or the most fashionable tailor to do your work, but by a high noble conduct. And let me whisper in your ear. When you talk to the ladies, remember their minds are at least capable of appreciating something better than you generally talk to them about.

If my composition has done no good, I hope it at least has done no harm.

Regardless of her own dislike for Louisiana, Jemima insisted that her nieces observe the same amenities which were observed by young people in the East.[157]

Among her mementoes, Miss Darby preserved one invitation to a social evening in Ringgold. On the envelope, Miss Darby's hostess had written: "Miss J. Darby — Present." The invitation read:

You are respectfully
invited to attend
a Social Party to be given
at Mrs. Jas. Smith's at
7 o'clock P. M.
May 1, 1873.

Mrs. Smith's party was a reminder of social evenings which Jemima had enjoyed in South Carolina. She knew that in spite of all the waste and corruption which characterized government and politics in 1873, her friends in Darlington were concerned with setting good tables and keeping their families well and happy. County fairs had been revived, and members of the Ladies Monumental Society were persistently engaged in securing money with which to erect a fitting monument in honor of their Confederate dead.

Wade Hampton, aristocrat and former soldier, was regarded as the state's most distinguished citizen. People flocked to hear his speeches and sought his leadership while South Carolina grappled with the problems of the period. Women of the Confederacy were deeply impressed with his address before the Southern Historical Society at Richmond on October 29, 1873, in which he said:

Maid, mother, wife, gave freely to that country the most cherished objects of their affection — those far dearer than life itself; and when the cause for which all these sacrifices were made went down in gloom and disaster, they, though impoverished, mourning, desolate, have met their fate with a Christian resignation and a sublime fortitude never surpassed by martyr or hero. Faithful among the faithless, they stand, alike the noblest monuments and brightest exemplars of a just cause. It was wisely done, therefore, to invoke their aid in behalf of our Society; and if they will but give their influence, our success will be assured. . . . It is theirs to teach their children that their fathers were neither traitors nor rebels; that we believed as firmly as in the eternal word of God, that we were in the right; and that we have a settled faith which no trials can shake, that in his own good time the right will be made manifest.[158]

Copies of Bishop Gregg's[159] *History of the Old Cheraws,* first published in San Antonio in 1867, had reached the Pee Dee neighborhood by 1873, and descendants of old families were impressed with the accuracy and scope of the work.

Mrs. Andrew Charles, Darlington, South Carolina, to Jemima Darby, Ringgold, Louisiana.

Darlington
Novm 21, 1873

Miss Jemima Darby
Care of Dr. Alexander Kolb
Ringgold, La.

Dear Miss Darby

Your long looked for letter in reply to the one containing Sallie's photograph has reached me at last. I am very glad to hear from you once more. You spoke of the yellow fever being not very far from you.[160] I hope it has not reached your household.

South Carolina has sympathized deeply with Memphis in her affliction, and contributed largely of her scanty means for its relief. The churches of Charleston, Sumpter and even our monumental society in Darlington have sent on hundreds of dollars. Our Society (Ladies Monumental) have been laboring for several years to raise a sufficient sum to erect a splendid monument to the memory of those who perished in the *war* from this district. We had a nice sum on hand, but I hope it may relieve the wants of some of the poor sufferers.

This District (or county "so called")[161] has been quite healthy this year so far. I have heard of very little sickness.

Our little darling Sallie has returned to her school again. She was obliged to remain at home a month over her vacation on account of having soar eyes. I wish that you could see her in person. She is so very much like her mother.[162] I cannot see the slightest resemblance to Aunt Sarah,[163] but Horace has a pretty daughter[164] just about grown whom, her friends think, looks very much like her Aunt S. She is as fair as a lily, has large blue eyes and a head of the most luxurient dark brown hair. She is very much admired and flattered. I am afraid her "head will be turned." She has been at school at Charleston several winters. Thinks of going north this winter or next.

I do not know whether or not I told you of the death of my niece May Brown.[165] She was out here on a visit, returned home and died about three weeks after reaching her home. Mrs. Council[166] went home with them. She thinks of remaining in Texas until Spring.

Jane has six large healthy looking children,[167] the youngest is at an interesting age, a little over two years old. I named her Estelle. The oldest boy is named Joseph Wilds. The others have fancy names, Leslie is next. Jennie,[168] Anna and Estelle. Aunt Julia's family were well a few days ago. Bettie Lide has a *new* baby,[169] a few days old. She has two boys now and two girls. Nancy has nine.

I received a letter last week from Cousin.[170] Her health is fast failing from what she says. I fear she will not last much longer. She lives in York County, is keeping house this year. She told me that she had raised *ten turkeys* and about one hundred chickens. Mr. Taylor is appointed missionary to the York Association now, and he will be from home so much that they are obliged to break up housekeeping and board. I am glad of it for I think it will be better for Cousin to be where there is a lady in the house. Georgia[171] is in school. Florence[172] is still with Sarina.[173] She is a very sweet girl. I think her a good likeness of her Aunt Sallie Ann.[174]

We are without a pastor. Mr. Eason has gone to take a theological course at Greenville.[175] The new pastor is looked for soon. Mr. Beattie and Wilkins still preach. Mr. Dargan[176] preaches at Black Creek two Sabbaths, two at Florence. His son John[177] lives at Bennettsville, preaches two Sabbaths, alternates with Mr. Thomas.[178] He is very much liked, considered almost equal to Mr. Thomas. Cousin Evan Lide's son Tom[179] is pastor in Marion Village. He is also quite popular.

Miss Darby, please tell me what was the name of Dr. Kolb's father and his grandfather.[180] I sent you the Southerner containing a list of the names of the persons who took premiums at our fair and for what articles. You will doubtless recognize many of the names. There is also a notice of the Cheraw Fair.

Dr. Smith[181] is perfectly helpless now. Has to be lifted about by a servant. Though he is so perfectly helpless he goes to Charleston often and to the Springs in the summer. (I thought of him by remembering that he was at our fair being moved about in a chair.)

I suppose this would look like a new country to you now. The old people are almost all dead that you left and places are so much changed. The young grow old very fast on account of over-taxed bodies and minds, I suppose. Most families have but one servant and numbers have none. From all the information that I can gather from newspapers and other sources, South Carolina is doing about as well as any other state. It is singular to say that the people seem to live as well as they did in antebellum days. They dress a great deal, and go where you will, you see no difference in the keeping of the table. We Carolinians are a wonderful people. You remember about good eating. I have beef, hams, chickens and turkeys in abundance now. Raise as much poultry as I know what to do with. Charles Andrews[182] is with us now. We often have fine fish.

I did not think to tell you that Mr. Eli Gregg[183] died not long ago and all of Dr. Porchers[184] children but the youngest are dead. Julia who married her cousin, Mr. Ashby, from the low country, died this summer leaving six little girls and one boy. I try to tell you about every person that I think you remember and I know that you know almost all in the district.

Please, Miss Darby, tell me your age if you know it.[185] My mother would have been eighty last August. She always thought that you were some older than she. Remember me kindly to your family. Andrew sends his regards to you.

Yours truly,

M. CHARLES

* * * * *

FOOTNOTES

1 A. G. Magrath was governor of South Carolina when the war ended in 1865.

2 John S. Reynolds, *Reconstruction in South Carolina, 1865-1877* (Columbia, 1905), p. 3.

3 Benjamin Franklin Perry (1805-1886), Greenville.

4 James Lawrence Orr (May 12, 1822 — May 5, 1873), Anderson.

5 Reynolds, *Reconstruction in South Carolina, 1865-1877*, p. 20.

6 General Daniel E. Sickles (1825-1914), Gettysburg hero, later became notorious as the "Yankee King of Spain."

7 Louisiana was not readmitted to the Union until June 25, 1868.

8 Reynolds, *Reconstruction in South Carolina, 1865-1877*, p. 64.

9 *Treasured Reminiscences*, collected by John K. McIver Chapter, U. D. C. (Columbia, 1911), p. 14.

10 Mrs. Lavinia Eason, a refugee from Charleston, had come to Harmony Hall during the war. During his visit with Mr. and Mrs. J. O. B. Dargan, she had become the third wife of Mrs. Dargan's brother, Evan J. Lide.

11 Elizabeth Brearley was the daughter of William Brearley, pastor of the Presbyterian Church, Darlington, 1842-1878.

12 Walter D. Woods, "The First Memorial Day, Darlington, South Carolina," *Treasured Reminiscences*, p. 16.

13 William Vann, "Last Will and Testament of William Vann," Year 1878, State of South Carolina, Darlington County, Recorded Wills 12, pp. 76 and 77. Filed March 7, 1887, M. A. Huggins, Judge of Probate.

14 Sarah Williamson died June 14, 1865.

15 Josephine King died in March, 1866.

16 Hannah King died in March, 1867.

17 Emily King and her sisters had worked as seamstresses during the war years.

18 Eliza King LaCoste was a wealthy woman.

19 John D. Witherspoon died November, 1860, at the age of eighty-two.

20 Elizabeth Boykin Witherspoon was murdered by her slaves in September, 1861, at the age of seventy-five. Both Mr. and Mrs. Witherspoon are buried in Trinity Episcopal Churchyard, Society Hill.

21 When Margaret Lucas McIntosh (October 9, 1783 — November 5, 1862), mother of James H. McIntosh, died, her family wrote on her tombstone in Welsh Neck Baptist Churchyard, "So he giveth his beloved sleep."

22 Ann James McIver (March 24, 1785 — July 2, 1860) was the unmarried daughter of Evander and Sarah Kolb McIver.

23 Charlotte Kirven, a member of the Society Hill Church, lived in the Edwards home for many years.

24 Margaret E. McIntosh (September 9, 1842 — July 10, 1864) was the unmarried daughter of James H. and Martha Gregg McIntosh.

25 Alexina Wallace Evans, wife of Samuel W. Evans, died "not long after the war."

26 W. D. Rice came from Barnwell County to be pastor at Welsh Neck Baptist Church, Society Hill.

27 Lewis Maxwell Coker (October 15, 1819 — February 26, 1889), a brother to Caleb Coker, was a merchant in Society Hill.

28 Martha "Pat" (November 11, 1846 — April 13, 1916), daughter of Henry and Mary Ann King, married John D. Howle (November 29, 1838 — December 7, 1897), half brother to Thomas E. Howle, on December 13, 1866.

29 William Vann's second wife, Sarah Jones Vann, had died October 3, 1866. He was seventy-one years old.

30 The DuPre house at 463 Pearl Street, Darlington, was still standing June 1, 1954.

31 From 1865 until 1867, the Darlington Church was pastorless, Brother Bealer having "been called to Norfolk, Virginia."

32 George B. Bealer, former pastor in Darlington, was born in Grahamville, South Carolina, December 7, 1822, and died at Atlanta, Georgia, June 2, 1880.

33 Martha J. Blackwell Lide was the widow of Eli Hugh Lide, who had moved from Darlington District to Alabama and finally died in Texas in 1854.

34 Noah Bacot was a son of Samuel Bacot and a brother to Serena Bacot Dargan, Lissie Bacot Bealer, Caroline Bacot Charles, and Maria Louisa Bacot Dargan.

35 Theodore A. Dargan (August 15, 1822 — September 10, 1881) married Maria Louisa Bacot and they had three daughters: Jessie, Dora, and Lula.

36 With Mrs. Lavinia Eason, a refugee from Charleston, who came to Harmony Hall for a visit during the war, were her two children, Theodosia and Fred. Mrs. Eason married Evan Lide. Fred Eason was pastor of the Baptist Church, Darlington, from his ordination in 1867 until 1873.

37 The three pastors who participated were Richard Furman, J. O. B. Dargan, and George B. Bealer.

38 William Brearley (November 30, 1801 — January 8, 1882), pastor of the Presbyterian Church, Darlington, 1842-1878, married (1) Jane B. English of Sumter County, and (2) Margaret Dick DuBose of Darlington.

39 David E. Frierson was the Presbyterian minister in Florence.

40 Julia Terrel Wilds (June 27, 1813 — October 21, 1876) was the wife of Peter Wilds, brother to Mary Ann's mother.

41 Nancy Wilds Coggeshall (August 7, 1835 — November 8, 1916), daughter of Peter and Julia Terrel Wilds, married Peter Collin Coggeshall II on April 12, 1854, and had seven children by 1867: Anna (1857-1942); Peter Wilds (June 28, 1859 — July 28, 1932); Alva C. (April, 1861 — July, 1932), who married Annie Douglas; Nina (November 28, 1862 — July 11, 1953); Mary (Mamie), born 1864, who married her cousin, Marion Lide; James R. (January 6, 1866 — July 26, 1940), who married Carrie Duncan; Clara, born in 1867. Mrs. Lide and Miss Clara were living at Wilds Hall in 1954.

42 Julia Elizabeth Wilds Lide, daughter of Peter and Julia Terrel Wilds, married Leighton Lide in March, 1861, and had three children by 1867: Marion, who married his cousin, Mamie Coggeshall; Julia; and Bessie.

43 Jane Rogers Williamson, widow of Bright Williamson, died February 7, 1867.

44 Mary Rogers (May 10, 1797 — August 28, 1879), Jane Rogers Williamson's sister, lived in Alabama with their brothers, Frank Alexander and Thomas W. Rogers.

45 The possibility that the second letter is a continuation of the first letter is ruled out by the fact that each is in its own envelope, both bearing Darlington postmarks. The date on the second letter, which is addressed to Miss Jemima Darby, care Dr. Alexander Kolb, Ringgold, La., is not legible.

46 W. Manley Wingate accepted the call of Ebenezer Baptist Church in the January Conference, 1852, but served for one year only, having accepted the call to become president of Wake Forest College, North Carolina.

47 Robert Harllee (November 7, 1807 — November 20, 1872), fifth son of old Thomas Harllee, graduated in medicine and settled at Marion Courthouse, married (1) Ann Gurdy, and (2) Mrs. Amelia Cannon Howard, daughter of Major Cannon of Darlington.

48 Robert Armstrong Harllee (August 10, 1842 — February 28, 1862) attended South Carolina College, 1859-1861, and died at Second Manassas, 1862.

49 Sallie Harllee (December 8, 1840 — April 28, 1879), daughter of Robert and Amelia Harllee, married J. F. Pearce.

50 William Wallace Harllee (1812-1897) married Martha Shackleford (1819-1903).

51 Edward Porcher (August 11, 1843 — February 25, 1878), Charles Stuart (September 29, 1845 — November 14, 1885), and Florence Harllee (1848 — May 6, 1927) were the grown sons and daughters of General and Mrs. Harllee.

52 Samuel Hugh Wilds, son of Jesse and Mary Ervin Wilds, married Anna Ellison. He died October 19, 1867.

53 Sarah Wilds Williamson still lived at her home near Mispah Church between Darlington and Florence.

54 Mary Williamson, daughter of Samuel Thomas and Sarah Terrel Williamson, married Charles Brown of Cleburne, Johnson County, Texas.

55 Reynolds, *Reconstruction in South Carolina, 1865-1877*, p. 76.

56 William Shannon Morrison, "South Carolina, 1865-1909," *The South in the Building of the Nation,* Volume II (Richmond, 1909), p. 99.

57 Reynolds, *Reconstruction in South Carolina, 1865-1877,* p. 106.

58 *Ibid.,* p. 135.

59 *Ibid.,* p. 139.

60 Morrison, "South Carolina, 1865-1909," *The South in the Building of the Nation,* Volume II, p. 99.

61 Reynolds, *Reconstruction in South Carolina, 1865-1877,* p. 233.

62 J. S. Pike, "The Prostrate State," from *Traveling in South Carolina in 1871,* quoted in Walter L. Fleming, *Documentary History of Reconstruction,* Volume I (Cleveland, 1906), p. 15.

63 T. L. Taylor was the twenty-one-year-old Furman University student whom Emily King married.

64 Sarah Ann King LaCoste, sister to Eliza, had been the second wife of A. P. LaCoste, Florence's father.

65 Julia Terrel Wilds (June 27, 1813 — October 21, 1876) was the widow of Peter A. Wilds.

66 Peter Samuel Wilds (May 9, 1849 — August 16, 1922) did not marry; he was widely and affectionately known as "Uncle Pete."

67 Robert Wilds married Eliza Hart.

68 Mary D. Wilds (November 23, 1841 — March 24, 1890) was engaged to Hartwell Hart, who died during the war.

69 Leighton and Bettie Lide had had no children within the five years since Mrs. Charles last wrote in 1867.

70 Since 1867, Peter Collin and Nancy Coggeshall had had two sons, Robert W. (Bert) (August 5, 1870 — July 16, 1945), who married Beulah Walden; and William D. (1872-1923), who married Emma Edwards.

71 Sarah Catlett DuPre, wife of the Baptist pastor Lewis DuPre, died February 28, 1867.

72 "Black Creek Church Book, A. D. 1798," March 15, 1851, p. 153. "The Church met to attend upon examination of Bro. Robert R. Vann, preparatory to his ordination to the Gospel Ministry. Sister Charlotte W. Vann, being present, presented a letter of dismissal from Wateree Baptist Church, in Fairfield District."

73 Black Creek was frequently abbreviated to B. C.

74 James Furman Dargan (1838-1907) married Mary Atmar Smith, Charleston, on July 13, 1870.

75 Timothy George Dargan (1839-1881) married his cousin, Louise Dargan, daughter of T. J. K. and Louisa Wilson Dargan, on November 15, 1866.

76 John Hugh Dargan (1848 — December 6, 1877) married Elizabeth Ann Sloan Townes, Greenville, on June 5, 1872.

77 Edwin Charles Dargan (1852-1930) married Lucy Graves, June 12, 1872.

78 On June 6, 1872, Edwin Charles expressed a desire to enter the ministry at Black Creek Church.

79 Elizabeth Pugh Dargan was thirty years old.

80 Margaret L. K. Dargan was twenty-eight years old.

81 William Q. Beattie (April 12, 1796 — October 29, 1884) married Ann Eliza Terrel (November 26, 1811 — February 22, 1883) and was a lifetime resident of Bennettsville, in Marlboro County.

82 John Culpepper was a Baptist minister.

83 S. B. Wilkins (April 1, 1802 — June, 1879) was the Baptist minister at Hartsville.

84 Eliza McIver Griffin (December 3, 1803 — November 10, 1876) was the widow of Thomas Griffin.

85 Emma Mauldin was the daughter of Joab and Hannah McIver Mauldin.

86 Hannah McIver Mauldin was the daughter of Peter Kolb and Elizabeth Chapman McIver.

87 Margaret E. McIntosh (September 9, 1842 — July 10, 1864), daughter of James H. and Martha Gregg McIntosh, died, according to Mrs. Furman Wilson, "in the bloom of her youth, before her college course was finished, I think."

88 Edward McIntosh, son of James H. and Martha Gregg McIntosh, married Dora Evans, daughter of Captain S. W. Evans. Both of them died in early life.

89 Louisa E. McIntosh was thirty-eight years old.

90 The Reverend J. W. (1808-1880) and Susan Burn (April 13, 1811 — September 19, 1884) lived in Society Hill.

91 Theodore Sompayrac (1824-1911), who married Margaret Douglas (1828-1901), was once a clerk in J. H. McIntosh's store, and after the war owned his own store on the old Gregg property.

92 Caleb Coker (September 14, 1802 — July 17, 1869) married Hannah Lide.

93 E. L. Adams bought the Witherspoon house in 1862.

94 Jeannette McKarrley Sparks (1791 — April 6, 1871) was the widow of Alexander Sparks, Society Hill planter, and the mother of Mrs. Thomas P. Lide.

95 Thomas Park Lide (June 10, 1810 — July 23, 1882) married Elizabeth Sparks, daugher of Alexander and Jeannette McKarrley Sparks.

96 Emma C. Lide Rogers (July 10, 1849 — June 11, 1872), daughter of T. P. and Elizabeth Sparks Lide, married John Terrel Rogers.

97 John Terrel Rogers (October 8, 1847 — January 18, 1912) was born at Browns-ville, South Carolina, and served in Company D, Third Regiment, South Carolina Volunteers, during the war. He married (1) Emma Lide, and (2) Florence Coker, daughter of Hannah L. and Caleb Coker.

98 Thomas Hamilton Rogers, Emma's only child, married Gena Dargan, daughter of John J. and Theodosia Williamson Dargan.

99 In 1872, Dr. Kolb and his wife had six living children: Ella Caroline, seventeen; Maria Elizabeth, thirteen; Mary Harriet, eleven; David Alexander, nine; Lee Jackson, seven; and Edwin Kirtley, four.

100 The implication here is that Ella Caroline Kolb had been introduced to society formally, which was probably Aunt Jemima's hyperbole. What Miss Darby meant was that Ella Kolb had begun to receive some attention from the young men of Ringgold, but her pride would never permit her to accept Mary Ann Charles's accounts of Charleston debuts for Williamson nieces while a Darby relative simply "started courting."

101 Theodosia Green Williamson (April 8, 1857 — July 12, 1946), daughter of Dr. Horace and Theodosia Green Williamson, had a Charleston debut.

102 Sallie Elizabeth Charles Williams (October 23, 1862 — May 9, 1895) was the daughter of James A. and Caroline Williamson Williams.

103 Walter D. Woods, "The First Memorial Day," *Treasured Reminiscences,* p. 18. "The whole cost of the monument and railing enclosing it, $1,650, was raised by hard and persistent work. An arrangement was made with the Fair Company of the county, whereby they [the members of the Monumental Society] could sell refreshments during the annual exhibitions, and outside of the amounts above mentioned, the money was all raised in this way. For the right to sell refreshments, they paid so much each day. This work was begun in 1872."

104 George Washington Dargan (April 3, 1802 — June 12, 1859), son of Timothy II and Lydia Keith Dargan, married (1) Mary Adeline Wilson, and (2) Mrs. Elizabeth Player Wilson.

105 James K. McIver (January 29, 1789 — October 30, 1846), son of Evander McIver, Sr., married Sarah Marshall and lived in the Society Hill home of her father, Judge Marshall. The home eventually became the home of Dr. McIver's only son, John K. McIver, who remodeled the house for his bride, Hannah J. Wilson, whom he married in 1859. Captain McIver was wounded at Gettysburg, and died later of the wounds. After the war, his wife was forced to sell the home. Mr. Gandy was the buyer.

106 Mary Williamson Brown was the wife of Charles Brown, Cleburne, Texas.

107 George L. Williamson died February 18, 1871, and was buried in Lowther's Hill Cemetery, near Cashaway Ferry.

108 Sarah Wilds Williamson died March 2, 1871, and was buried in Lowther's Hill Cemetery. "Asleep in Jesus, blessed sleep," were the words Mary Ann had carved on the stone.

109 Sallie Williamson Wilds (September 27, 1845 — June 19, 1892) was the daughter of Peter A. and Julia Terrel Wilds, both of whom were dead. "Her family" refers to her sister and brother, Mollie and Peter.

110 George R. Pettigrew, *Annals of Ebenezer, 1778-1950* (privately printed, 1952), p. 68.

111 The letter was postmarked Darlington.

112 George B. Bealer (1822-1890) was pastor of the Baptist Church, Darlington.

113 Miss Darby had inquired about the age of Sarah Wilds Williamson.

114 John Culpepper had died late in 1872.

115 Sarah Witherspoon Wilson was the mother of Mary Wilson Player. They lived in Darlington.

116 Jesse L. Keith lived near Darlington.

117 Sarah Catlett DuPre and her sister, Mary Ann Catlett, both friends to Jemima, owned the house at 463 Pearl Street. When Mary Ann died in 1861 and Sarah in 1867, the house went to Pastor L. DuPre, Sarah's husband, who had moved to Tennessee by 1873. Hannah B. Hart and Minnie D. Townsend, in their "Homes of Old Darlington," *Darlington County Historical Records and Papers, 1938-1944*, p. 107, quote Rev. Louis J. Bristow. "The house now occupied by Mrs. Essie Skinner Stogner was known as the DuPre house in the 70's. . . . We moved to Darlington in 1877. . . . My first recollections are associated with the Nettles place. In 1879, our family moved into the DuPre house. Jack Smith owned and occupied the residence on the opposite side of Pearl St. . . . I know this from personal knowledge. It was in *that* house that Jack Smith had Republican gatherings and not in the DuPre house." Since Rev. Bristow did not move into Darlington until 1877, it is assumed that Mary Ann's first-hand account is more authoritative than his. It is likely that Jack Smith lived first at 463, and later moved to the house across the street.

118 Colonel Edgar Welles Charles, signer of the Ordinance of Secession, married (1) Sarah Kolb Lide, and (2) Jane Gray, of Newark, New Jersey.

119 Darlington.

120 Julius A. Dargan (1816 — March 9, 1861), son of Timothy and Lydia Keith Dargan, married Martha Woods.

121 George Washington Dargan (April 3, 1802 — June 12, 1859), son of Timothy and Lydia Keith Dargan, married (1) Mary Adeline Wilson, and (2) Mrs. Elizabeth Player Wilson.

122 Max Gandy, brother to Abel Gandy, was the son of Booker and Delilah Gandy.

123 Dr. William Adger Player (June 6, 1821 — November 9, 1891), a native of Fairfield County, married (1) Adeline Dargan, daughter of Chancellor Dargan, and (2) Elma Law.

124 Mary Elma Law (August 19, 1834 — March 15, 1915) was the daughter of Judge Ezekiel Augustus and Elizabeth McIver Law.

125 Adeline Dargan Player's stone in the Baptist Churchyard, Darlington, bears this inscription:

OUR MOTHER

April 28, 1871

"O Domine Deus, Speravi in Te!"

The quotation is the prayer written by Mary Stuart, Queen of Scots, just before her execution.

126 George Dargan Player (1862 — April 4, 1871); William Dargan Player (1850 — March 15, 1868); Minnie Player (1852 — August 28, 1862) were all buried in the Baptist Churchyard, Darlington.

127 Carrie, who was seventeen in 1873, married James Bradley Law, a brother to her father's second wife; Augusta Corrine (October 4, 1854 — October 1, 1941) was the youngest child.

128 Georgiana H. Dargan (December 22, 1834 — April 11, 1898) was the unmarried daughter of Chancellor G. W. and Mary Adeline Dargan.

129 Mr. and Mrs. Lide lived at Piney Woods for several years before they moved to White Plains.

130 Alexander Sparks (September 27, 1780 — January 29, 1857) was the father of Elizabeth Sparks Lide, Leighton's mother.

131 Emma Lide, daughter of T. P. and Elizabeth Sparks Lide, married John Terrel Rogers and died in 1872.

132 William Kennedy Lide was a son of T. P. and Elizabeth Sparks Lide.

133 Mollie and Sallie were Julia Terrel Wilds's daughters.

134 Mary Williamson Brown, the daughter of Samuel Thomas and Sarah Terrel Williamson, married Charles Brown, Cleburne, Texas.

135 There had been no additions to the Coggeshall family since November, 1872. Julia Wilds Coggeshall (November, 1855 — October, 1859) was the oldest child.

136 Dr. Robert H. Harllee (November 7, 1807 — November 20, 1872), son of Thomas Harllee, settled at Marion Courthouse after graduating in medicine. Dr. Harllee married (1) Ann Gurdy, and (2) Amelia Cannon Howard, and is buried in Hopewell Cemetery near Mars Bluff, Florence County, South Carolina.

137 William Wallace Harllee (1812-1897) married Martha Shackleford.

138 J. A. W. Thomas was pastor at Cheraw and Bennettsville, and later at Society Hill.

139 John Hugh Dargan (October 20, 1848 — December 6, 1877) married Elizabeth Ann Sloan Townes of Greenville on June 5, 1872.

140 Dr. William Crosland (April 23, 1800 — March 23, 1865) married Ann Thorpe (April 12, 1822 — January 30, 1893).

141 George Grosland (May 25, 1847 — April 14, 1908), son of William and Ann

Thorpe Crosland, and his wife, Mary Ann, were buried at Bennettsville, South Carolina.

142 Emma Eliza McCall (February 5, 1847 — May 8, 1909), daughter of Moses Sanders and Mary Elizabeth Gregg McCall, married A. J. W. Bacot.

143 Mr. William Q. Beattie, who had been pastor of the Welsh Neck Baptist Church in 1837, was living in Marlboro County. He had married Ann Terrel.

144 Ann Hurry Sparks (June 22, 1793 — November 13, 1870) was the wife of Samuel Sparks.

145 Sue Sparks Keitt was the widow of Lawrence Keitt and the daughter of Samuel Sparks.

146 Theodore Sompayrac (1824-1911) married Margaret Douglas.

147 Lillie Sompayrac (August 6, 1856 — May 5, 1920), who later married A. A. Gandy, was not quite sixteen.

148 E. Merton Coulter, *The South during Reconstruction. 1865-1877*, Volume VIII (Baton Rouge, 1947), p. 258.

149 Gerald M. Capers, Jr., "Yellow Fever in Memphis in the 1870's," *Mississippi Valley Historical Review*, XXIV (1937-1938), pp. 483-502.

150 *Biographical and Historical Memoirs of Northwest Louisiana* (Chicago, 1890), p. 16.

151 *Scribner's Monthly Magazine*, VII (November, 1873 — April, 1874), p. 27. "The present condition of the educational system of Louisiana is encouraging, although disfigured by the evils arising from political disruption. The State Superintendent of Education is a mulatto gentleman of evident culture, who seems indeed, quite up to the measure of his task, if he had only the means to perform it. He could not tell me how many schools were in operation in the state at the time of my visit, nor indeed, how much the increase had been since the war. . . . There are in Louisiana, 291,000 youth between the ages of 6 and 21, one half being colored. . . . There are but few mixed schools in the State. To the *You must!* of the law, the white man has replied *I will not!*"

152 T. H. Harris, *The Story of Public Education in Louisiana* (New Orleans, 1924), p. 38.

153 Ella was seventeen years old, Lizzie, fourteen, and Mary, twelve.

154 Lucy Paxton Scarborough (December 27, 1857 — April 1, 1951), daughter of Pastor W. E. and Rebecca Wardlow Paxton, married Daniel C. Scarborough, January 4, 1879, Shreveport, Louisiana.

155 Lucy Paxton Scarborough, "So It Was When Her Life Began," *Louisiana Historical Quarterly*, XIII (January — October, 1930), pp. 438-439.

156 School essay written by Ella Caroline Kolb, Ringgold, Louisiana, June 18, 1873.

157 *Scribner's Monthly Magazine*, VI (May, 1873 — October, 1873), p. 241. "We

believe our ladies would dress better if they knew how; that they would not obey the dictates of ignorant inartistic modistes, either men or women, if they had better educated teachers. If they would be fashionable and picturesque both, they would surely prefer it to being fashionable and ugly or fashionable and vulgar. Many of Worth's designs are shockingly ugly and vulgar to ladies of cultivated tastes, and we cannot refrain from wishing that our artists would give a series of lectures to ladies, their best friends and patrons."

158 "Transactions of the Southern Historical Society," *Southern Magazine*, I (January — December, 1873), p. 5.

159 Alexander Gregg (1819-1893) was a native of Society Hill, the first bishop of Texas, and author of *History of the Old Cheraws*, which was reprinted in Columbia by the State Press in 1905.

160 The yellow fever epidemic nearest Ringgold was in Shreveport.

161 "In 1721 what is now Darlington County became a part of Prince George Parish; in 1734, a part of Prince Frederick Parish; in 1757, a part of St. Mark's Parish; in 1768, a part of St. David's Parish. Later in 1768, it became a part of Cheraws District. In 1785, it became known as Darlington County upon the Division of Cheraws into the counties of Chesterfield, Marlboro and Darlington. In 1798, it became Darlington District, and in 1868, it became Darlington County again." J. M. Napier, "Society Hill and Some of Its Contributions to State and Nation," paper read before Darlington County Historical Society, May 8, 1947.

162 Caroline Williamson Williams (December 19, 1822 — August 10, 1863).

163 Sarah Williamson (March 5, 1821 — June 14, 1865).

164 Theodosia Green Williamson (April 8, 1857 — July 12, 1946), daughter of Horace and Theodosia Green Williamson, married J. J. Dargan.

165 Mary Williamson Brown, daughter of Samuel Thomas and Sarah Terrel Williamson, and wife of Charles Brown, Cleburne, Texas, died in June, 1873.

166 Mrs. Addie Council was a relative of Mary Brown's mother.

167 Jane Williamson Wallace (August 4, 1836 — May 26, 1894) and her husband, Thomas Wallace (December 6, 1828 — February 20, 1896), had six children: Joseph Wilds, Leslie, Jennie, Anna, Lottie, and Estelle.

168 Jennie Wallace (June 23, 1865 — August 22, 1923) married Thomas W. Williamson, her second cousin.

169 Leighton and Bettie Wilds Lide's youngest son, Roland, was born in 1873.

170 Mrs. Charles referred to Emily King Taylor as "Cousin."

171 Georgia LaCoste was Mrs. Taylor's niece and ward.

172 Florence LaCoste, Georgia's sister, lived with their great-aunt in Darlington.

173 Serena Bacot Dargan (January 3, 1833 — November 7, 1910) was the widow of Charles Dargan.

[174] Sarah Ann King, sister to the mother of Georgia and Florence, was the second wife of their father, A. P. LaCoste.

[175] Fred Eason, son of Mrs. Evan Lide, was pastor of the Darlington Church from 1867 until 1873, when he enrolled in Furman University, Greenville.

[176] J. O. B. Dargan (August 9, 1813-1882).

[177] John Hugh Dargan (October 20, 1848 — December 6, 1877) married Elizabeth Ann Sloan Townes of Greenville, June 5, 1872.

[178] J. A. W. Thomas, an elderly former pastor at Welsh Neck, was a resident of Bennettsville in 1873.

[179] Thomas P. Lide, son of Evan J. Lide and his second wife, Martha Miller, was pastor of the Welsh Neck Church from 1870 to 1875.

[180] A. J. Kolb's father was Jesse Kolb (July 14, 1788 — June 20, 1850), who married Miss Darby's sister, Elizabeth, April 10, 1810; his grandfather was Jehu Kolb (1758 — May 2, 1844), who married (1) Lucretia —————————, and (2) Angelina ——————————.

[181] Thomas Smith lived in Society Hill.

[182] Charles Andrews was the son of Mrs. Nancy Andrews, kinswoman to the Williamsons.

[183] J. Eli Gregg (1805-1873) was a business man of Society Hill.

[184] Dr. Edwin Porcher, who died July 26, 1871, in the sixty-first year of his age, was buried at Christ Church (Episcopal) near Florence, South Carolina.

[185] Born January 30, 1794, Jemima lacked about two months of being eighty on November 21, 1873; Mrs. Williamson, born August 7, 1793, was almost six months older.

Reconstruction
PART II

Edward DeLeon, traveling in the South at the request of "leading journalists and publishers in the North, who desired accurate and authentic information to lay before their people,"[1] found that "Mississippi, with its negro majority, had fared better than her supposed more fortunate sisters, inasmuch as she, unlike Louisiana and South Carolina, had not a Comus crew of carpet-bag and negro legislators controlling her legislatures, nor a negro Lieutenant-Governor presiding over her Senate."[2] The journalist found South Carolina sitting like a "new Niobe amid the waste places of Charleston never rebuilt, and the ashes of Columbia whose chimney stacks alone marked the sites of beautiful residences,"[3] The freeman, he found, was a sadder, if not wiser man from whom came loud lamentations over the good old times.[4]

In February, 1874, South Carolina taxpayers met once again in convention at Columbia, where they prepared a memorial to the United States Congress protesting deficiencies and expenditures in state government. During 1873, $1,897,544.83 had been wasted, they complained. Governor Moses lived in expensive style, spending $30,000 to $40,000 per year, when his annual salary was $3,500.[5] The federal government chose to ignore appeals from the Convention and proclaimed:

> The gentlemen who have assembled in this Convention constituting themselves the peculiar representatives of the so-called tax-payers, are not what they would have the country believe. They are the prominent politicians of the old regime — the former ruling element of the state — who simply desire to regain the power they lost by the folly of their secession. They are not endorsed by the masses of the sober, thinking white Democrats of the State.[6]

From Darlington went J. J. Lucas,[7] B. F. Williamson,[8] J. A. Law,[9] and E. R. McIver,[10] who, because of old family ties, received endorsements from both the Darby and Williamson families.

In Louisiana, the political situation was unusually tense during 1874. Hatred for Governor W. P. Kellogg ran high.[11] Quantities of arms were being shipped over the state by Black Leaguers, and lawlessness on the part of White Leaguers was spreading. Grant Parish, less than 100 miles from Ringgold, had been the scene of the Colfax Riots in April, 1873. On March 20, 1874, ninety-eight Grant Parish prisoners were indicted, under Ku Klux Klan law, after a seventeen-day trial, ending "the prosecution but not the tribulations of the people, for troops were within calling distance to enforce the mandates of the oppressor and assist in the extortion of exorbitant taxes."[12]

Adding to the alarm of Louisiana citizens was the great flood of 1874, which left 25,000 people homeless.[13] Much livestock was drowned and spring crops in the bottom lands were ruined.

There were three sections in a letter which was postmarked at Darlington on June 13, 1874. Mrs. Charles had begun a letter on May 30, added some news items a few days later, and had written the concluding section in June.

Mrs. Andrew Charles, Darlington, South Carolina, to Jemima Darby, Ringgold, Louisiana.

> Darlington
> May 30, 1874

Dear Miss Darby

Your very welcome letter of the twelfth of April came to hand promptly. I had come to the conclusion that I would never hear from you again, for it is just 6 months since I wrote you last. I was glad to hear from you, that you were not submerged in the deluge which overspread a good portion of your state.[14] We have had an immense quantity of rain and an unusually cool backward spring. I see from our district papers that the planters are despondent about their crops. Cotton killed by frost and no seed to replant with. Our garden is good considering the cold weather. The wet season was favorable to strawberries. Ours never were so fine. We ate and I preserved a nice quantity of them and wish I would send you a jar of them. The prospect for fruit is good except pears were all killed by frost. I wish that you could see my geraniums and hothouse plants. I am getting a nice collection again. A few years ago they were killed by a severe cold snap in February, I think it was. Wish I could put some of the fine little apple geraniums in this letter and they could reach you uninjured. But as I cannot do that, I can send you the seeds which I have procured at last. You can plant them and watch their growth. I will send you some pansy seed too. If you plant them now, they will bloom this summer and if you keep them in a pit or in the house protected, they will bloom in the winter and next spring.

Now to reply to your questions. I only wished that you had asked *hundreds* more. It is a delight to answer them. If you would fill your letter with them I would then know what you would like to hear. The reason I asked the names of Dr. K's parents was because there has been a book written by Bishop Gregg, History of the Pee Dee Country.[15] In it he mentions Lide, Wilds, Dewits, Kolb and all of the settlers of this region of the country. I thought some of them were your connections, but did not know which ones.

I hear from Emily Taylor pretty often. She lives in N. C. Mr. T. is a missionary in that state. They board this year and kept house last. Georgia is off at school. She did not say where. Cousin's health is very bad.

May Sanders (Nick Pigues) lives in Mississippi and has a large family.[16] I think they are well off. May got quite a large sum of money from the estate of G. J. W. McCall[17] since the war.

Write as soon as you receive this. I am anxious to know if you will get the seeds.

Yours affectionately,

M. A. W. C.

* * * * *

Mrs. Andrew Charles, Darlington, South Carolina, to Jemima Darby, Ringgold, Louisiana.[18]

May Lucas married Charles Williams, Linton's son.[19] Mag[20] married Jim White, a brother of the White[21] who married Jane Fort[22] and was killed in battle. Wash[23] has sold out. He is now attending to business for Sarina Dargan on Black Swamp.[24]

His son[25] oversees for Hugh Charles[26] near his father.

Mrs. Baker[27] has been dead years. Baker spent all she had. She came home and died at Mrs. Fergusons.[28] Mrs. F. is still alive. Mr. Mills and Billie Vann[29] are still living. Mr. Dority[30] lives in the Lucas house. They have two grown daughters, one married.[31] The other[32] teaches school at Black Creek Church.

Mr. John Davis died a few months ago.[33] Mrs. Blany Parnell,[34] too. Cousin Evan Lide's wife[35] died recently. He has three sons married and the fourth engaged to Dora Dargan.[36] He is studying Divinity[37] at Greenville. She is several years the elder. The twins[38] are still single.

I think I told you of the death of my niece May Brown. She spent part of last summer here and died in a few weeks after reaching her home in Texas. Mrs. Council went home with her and attended her in her last illness.

Jane has five children. The youngest a little girl. I named her Estelle. She is a very interesting child and a beauty almost. Very fair. Large blue eyes, coral lips. Her hair has never been cut. It is down below her waist. Inclined to curl. Not in ringlets, but curls some.

Cousin Eliza Evans[39] spent a week with us in March. She is the same old seventy six,[40]   very cheerful. I don't think she can hear as well even as she did when you left. She has not lost by the war; has plenty to live comfortably on. Spends her summers up country and winters at the Hill.

Peter Griffin[41] married Hannah Maldwin's[42] daughter. Cousin Eliza Griffin[43] lives in Mr. Elias Gregg's[44] house. Col. Wilson[45] in Mrs. Sparks home. The Hill has changed but little in appearance. If you were dropped down there, you would recognize it as old Society Hill. Mrs. Betsy Edwards[46] is dead. Mrs. Robert Edwards[47] lives at the same place. Hartwell[48] is a talented young minister now. Fannie Coker[49] is in the parsonage as the pastor's wife,[50] Mrs. Stout. A brother to Jimmy Coker's wife.[51] Willie Coker married Mr. Allen McIver's daughter.[52] Mary Emma married Ham Rodgers, son of Ham and Lindy.[53] Darious Gandy's[54] son Jim married Linton Williams daughter, Ella.[55] Two of Mr. Able Gandy's daughters, the youngest, married this spring. Young Frank Williams died of consumption this spring.

The Darlington church has a new Pastor, Strickland,[56] from Augusta. The church seems quite pleased. Mr. Williams has been supplying the church. Mr. Burns[57] preaches at Mechanicsville once a month.

The people complain very much of hard times, but you see no difference in their dress, and none whatever in their tables where I visit. They dance and have picnics and various gatherings just as they did, but it is really surprising how they do it.

We had some ripe peaches on the 28th. Not much larger than a nutmeg. That is the name of this, and very small but delicious and so very early.

* * * * *

Mrs. Andrew Charles, Darlington, South Carolina, to Jemima Darby, Ringgold, Louisiana.[58]

Miss Darby, you always say that you have nothing to write to interest me. Perhaps I could give you a subject that you could fill a part of your letter with. Describe each member of your family, your yard, your house and *your* room and your particular seat for I know you have one, perhaps by a window and how you occupy your time.

Do you cultivate flowers and how large in your village? And in what part of the state? Is it in the Ouachitau country?[59] I have no new map and I do not find it in the old. Do you cook nice things as you did in S. C.? I remember you as having a "Weakness in nice cooking." I have the same propensity if you remember how you assisted me in making plum pickles. I have the same recipe yet.

Sallie is quite a little housekeeper. Makes pickles and preserves and catsup and very nice light bread. She has quite a reputation as a little housekeeper, and is a regular Williamson in her taste for nice food. If there are any recipes of old Carolina dishes that you would like, perhaps I could send them to you. Lettie will have vacation in about four weeks. In her last letter she desired me to send you a tip for her. (I commenced this letter in May but after writing it, I found that I had lost the geranium seeds and had to wait until I could get more). Mollie Wilds sent them to me today.

Please, Miss Darby, fill your letters with questions. I will be pleased to answer as many as you can ask. My kind regards to your family. I wish I could know them. A great deal of love for yourself from your true friend,

M. A. W. C.

* * * * *

Writing in 1874, Mrs. Charles implied that Reconstruction had not produced a new South Carolina, a theory echoed by Morrison when he summarized the period between 1865 and 1909.

Her boundary lines and her physical features remain unchanged. Her population within the dates named has not been affected by either emigration or immigration. Within the past 43 years, marvelous changes have occurred in the social, industrial, political and educational conditions of the state, and South Carolinians have directed all these mighty movements. The same old stock works the same old soil under greatly changed and rapidly changing conditions.[60]

Mrs. Andrew Charles, Darlington, South Carolina, to Jemima Darby, Ringgold, Louisiana.

Darlington
Nov. 20th, 1874

Miss Jemima Darby
Care of Dr. Alexander Kolb
Ringgold, Louisiana

Dear Miss Darby

I received your letter of the 23rd of June. Also the one of the 16th of October and sorry it has happened so that I could not have replied to your first at once. I was in very bad health at the time and Sallie was taken sick very soon. So it was almost out of the question to attend to anything outside of ourselves. I am very, very sorry to hear of your having been so ill and hope the cold weather may brace you up and soon restore you to your former self again. I am glad to hear that your family passed through the measles without suffering from any of the serious results which sometimes follow. Sallie had them in the spring and I was very fearful that she would take cold and it settle on her lungs. They are very weak, but I hope she escaped it.

I will try to answer your questions. Miss Charlotte Doherty[61] married a son of Mr. Evander Byrd. She married remarkably well. Lizzie,[62] it is said, is engaged to a young Blackman. She will do very well, too. He had the misfortune to have one of his eyes put out by a nail flying into it this summer. He offered to release Miss Lizzie from the engagement, but she declined. I don't think that I have seen Mrs. Doherty since you left us. I do not live near Black Creek but within one mile or so of Pee Dee River and about two miles of old Mechanicsville Church. We attend Darlington Church. My membership is there. Our nearest neighbor, Mrs. Garrison, who was a daughter of old Mr. Wiley Goodson, knows Mrs. D's family well. I get my information from her about them, so that I can post you as well as far as possible.

I wish very much that you could get one of Bishop Gregg's[63] books. It was published just after the close of the war. He held them at a high price, consequently failed to sell them successfully. It is a book about thirteen or more inches long. The print is very good and it is pronounced the best history ever written of Old Pee Dee. If I owned a volume I would send it to you with the greatest pleasure. I don't know who has one, but might find out by inquiry. They sold at $2.50 when sent out. It would be a treat to you to get it I know.

I would like to have attended the examination. Not that I am particularly fond of that kind of entertainment but I would like to have seen you once more and like very much to make the acquaintance of your family. Also to visit to Louisiana again. Our relatives live at Bastrop, Mrs. Ross[64] and her sister. We received a letter from them not long since. They are getting old now and have grandchildren.[65]

Perhaps you have seen in the papers of an accident which happened on a railroad in Alabama. Cousin David Lide[66] was among the killed, and his wife was badly wounded, but she may recover.

Mr. DuPree[67] is married. He wrote Col Edwards[68] that he had married a widow. I suppose you remember that he moved to Tennessee just after the war. I saw Miss Lou Harllee[69] not long since. The youngest son Charlie,[70] I think his name is, is a nice looking young man now. The family are very poor now. I think I told you of the death of Dr. Porcher. Died of dropsy of the heart. I have not heard from Emily King Taylor since I wrote you. Florence scarcely ever hears from her.

Old Society Hill stands pretty much as it used to. Perhaps I did not mention the death of Mr. Charles Fort[71]   One of the Bacot's son, Henry,[72] I think was his name, died recently. Mrs. Isaac Wilson[73] has been very ill, but is recovering. Cousin Eliza Evans spent a week with us in February and said she hoped to come back this winter and spend a month. We enjoyed her visit very much. Wish she may come, make a long stay with us. She still is so like her former self, so very entertaining. She reads a great deal and is so full of anecdotes. She is harder of hearing than when you left her. Persons converse with her by writing mostly.

I suppose you have seen by the newspapers that yellow fever is in Charleston. Mr. George McIver[74] and his son Alexander[75] have been ill with it but are recovering. They live in Charleston now. Dell Elerbee,[76] LaCost that was, lost her eldest son, a very promising boy of 14 years, with diptheria. That disease is prevailing with us. Mrs. Dr. Wilson[77] lost a child. There have been forty cases of the disease in Florence but it seems it has been skillfully treated as only two deaths occurred.

Charles Andrews is still living and at our house at night. He desires to be remembered to you. His mother[78] died before the war. He has been spending his time around with his friends since her death.

Our Association met in Marion village this year. There was a fine attendance and a delightful meeting. Tom Lide[79] is pastor of the church. Do you take the religious Herald? Published in Richmond, Va. If not, I would like to send you a copy with the account and proceedings of the Association. Also a Southerner with an account of our county fair. You will recognize many of the names in the premium list.

Sallie is not at home but I will send love to you for her for I am sure she would do it. Her health was so feeble that she could not go back to school, but I hope she will be able to go in February at the beginning of the session.

You forgot my injunction to fill your letters with questions. I could feel in answering them that I was telling you what you would like to know. I write in such a scatter brained manner that I am afraid you get very little to interest you out of such long and tiresome scrawls, they must be to you. I try to tell you what I think you would like to hear and if I fail you will please take the will for the deed. You will not ask me anything.

Andrew sends regards to you. My kindest consideration to Mrs. K., children, and accept kind remembrances and love from your friend,

M. CHARLES

* * * * *

The election of 1874 brought Daniel H. Chamberlain, a cultivated New Englander, to the governor's seat in South Carolina. He was inaugurated on December 1. Early in 1875, state and national papers united in declaring that the Governor sought to perform every promise and redeem every pledge that he made during his campaign.[80] Yet, Negroes and renegade whites continued to obtain important political posts, and South Carolinians remained unhappy, submitting only because of their respect for and fear of the government at Washington. As long as Grant remained President of the United States,[81] conditions were not likely to improve.

In Louisiana a great deal of excitement prevailed when the Legislature convened on January 4, 1875. The Conservatives gained control of the House, but federal troops soon placed the Republicans in control.

> General Sheridan assumed command under his secret orders and made a distorted partisan report in which he suggested that the white people of Arkansas, Mississippi and Louisiana be declared *banditti*. The Federal House of Representatives sent a subcommittee to Louisiana to investigate affairs. . . . The people of Louisiana were truly perplexed as to their course of action by January, 1875.[82]

Regardless of political upheavals, the women of South Carolina and Louisiana found time to consider other matters. At no time did Mrs. Charles's and Miss Darby's interest in the Baptist church wane. Brother Strickland ushered in a new era for Darlington Baptists during his pastorate.[83] With Sallie Williams in school, Mrs. Charles became aware, perhaps for the first time, that schools were a vital part of South Carolina society.

Mrs. Andrew Charles, Darlington, South Carolina, to Jemima Darby, Ringgold, Louisiana.

Miss Jemima Darby
    Care of Dr. Alexander Kolb
    Ringgold, La.

Dear Miss Darby

Your very welcome letter of the 8th December came to hand in due time. We were very glad to hear from you again. In reply to your *few* questions, I commence with our Church. It has had several additions in the past year. Our new pastor[84] is very zealous and seems to be the right man in the right place. Psedo-Baptists flock to our church when they can have just half an excuse. I can tell you how warm he is. So much so that he could not preach in the pulpit. He stands down on the floor. The Church is very much moved recently.

Sallie Wilds[85] professed conversion years ago but has never been immersed. Her friends think she could not stand the shock of the water.

Miss Eliza McIver married Mr. Jonithan Lucas[86] from Charleston. They have several children, their eldest, a girl,[87] ten or twelve years old.

Lizzie Burn[88] married during the war to a nephew of Capt. Hartstein who married Mrs. Burns sister. Miss L. McIntosh[89] is still single and in wretched health. Murry, Margaret and Edward[90] are dead. Mrs. McI[91] died in October. Lucas[92] was married to Miss Rosa Evans a few weeks after his mother's death (a very private marriage). He is a large fleshy man. Suppose he would weigh almost two hundred. Does not look as if he could ever be the least consumptive but appearances are deceitful. You know the family all seem to be going that way.

Robert Wilds[93] married Eliza Hart (Dr H's third daughter) just before Christmas. They have come to live at their plantation near Mechanicsville. They are our neighbors now.

Sallie goes to school in Sumter[94] and boards with (Mary Charles) Haynesworth,[95] that is now. She is too young to send off very far from home. She was but ten years old when she went off.

The school at Limestone[96] was broken up during the War. Dr. Curtis[97] and his father are both dead. Dr. Marks of Barhamville is also dead. That school closed during the war, too.

The High School for boys and girls is at Greenville now.[98] The University you know for young men is still flourishing there.[99] Dr. Judson[100] one of the old professors withdrew to establish a high school for young ladies. The climate is very severe up there[101] in winter. Sallie could not stand it. If she lives to get through the regular course in Sumter, I expect to send her to Charleston. The climate is mild and in spring months, the sea breeze is bracing. Her constitution is very feeble. I must try to take all care of her health as a fine education would do her very little good with worse health than she has now.

Her Pa[102] made us a visit this week. He is beginning to look old. His beard is quite gray. His hair, you will remember, was as black as a raven. He has not changed color in proportion to his beard.

Mrs. Furgerson[103] is in bad health, you know. She has been a martyr to sick head aches. Mrs. Chambers[104] has been a widow since the war. Has one child,[105] a son who is about grown now. He has taken charge of her business this year and has been at the University of Greenville.

There is great complaint of hard times. Notwithstanding, there have been a greater number of marriages taken place this fall and winter than for a number of years previous. South Carolina is very poor and has miserable government but I think we are as proud as ever. I am sorry for Louisiana. There is a portion of our state in a similar condition but I hope things may change soon.

I told you that I would send you the Religious Herald containing an account of the Association. The proceedings were not published. For what reason, I cannot tell. It is their habit to publish it. There was nothing said about the fair either in our district paper. When there is an interesting copy of either or both I will send you one.

Thanks for the copy of your county paper.[106] I must acknowledge that I did not appreciate the lecture for the reason that I could not fully understand it.

I hope your little niece[107] who was sick is quite well again. It is very sad to see a child suffering. Sallie sends regrets to her that she has been so very sick and hopes she is well now and as happy as ever. There has been a very affecting death in our family. May Haynesworth[108] has just lost a most interesting little girl about three years old.

Andrew sends kind regards to you, with mine to your niece and the girls. Sallie joins me in love to all, Kind wishes to you and yours,

Yours truly,

MC

Sallie will go back to school on the 14th of February at which time the session commences. Excuse the blot. It got on after I had written a good part of the letter. I plead laziness to write it over.

Yours as ever,

M. A. W. C.

＊ ＊ ＊ ＊ ＊

Between August 3, 1875, and August 20, 1877, Miss Darby did not write to her friends in South Carolina. She was now past eighty and her health was not good. As the reconstruction period drew to a climax, Jemima Darby, for the first time in her life, admitted to her family that she was old and more than a little weary. Moreover, family matters kept her busy. Now there was a wedding to disturb her. Ella Kolb, at the age of twenty, married James Ashley Cawthon[109] on November 25, 1875. Jemima, assuming a major role in making preparations for an elaborate home wedding, found that the strain tired her greatly. Also, the Kolbs and their aunt were grieved to know that Ella would live in Arkansas; James would farm at Wilson's Bend, near Fulton on Red River. Accompanied by John,[110] Elizabeth,[111] Willie,[112] and Maggie McDaniel,[113] the young Cawthons left Louisiana early in 1877, having buried their first child[114] in Louisiana.

Yet Miss Darby kept in touch with South Carolina through the newspapers.

When General Wade Hampton[115] was nominated for governor at the August, 1876, Convention of South Carolina's Executive Committee, J. A. Law, L. R. Ragsdale, A. F. Edwards, and E. W. Cannon of Darlington were present. During the famous "Red Shirt Campaign," proper steps were taken for the enrollment of colored voters into Democratic clubs officered by colored men, and ample provisions were made for preserving the peace. Individual work among Negroes was unceasing. Whenever a white man had a chance to talk to a Negro, there was an effort to win a vote for Hampton. "Hurrah for Hampton" went out all over South Carolina, and "in that slogan there was a ring of resolution that made it veritably a deathknell of Negro rule in the commonwealth."[116] Women were urged to attend all campaign speeches, and it was said that "ladies attended in such large numbers that the towns were well nigh deserted when the General spoke."[117] Hampton won the election by a small majority and was inaugurated on December 14, 1876, but the Republicans refused to submit. Chamberlain's forces participated in a sham installation and the dual government began and lasted until May 1, 1877. Hampton's greatest contribution toward the restoration of white supremacy in South Carolina was unquestionably his "influence in avoiding a general armed conflict, particularly between the election and the withdrawal of United States troops, when the Democrats were finally permitted to take possession of the government."[118]

So, in 1877, when Carolinians came once more to rule in Carolina, Mary Ann Charles was able to summarize for Miss Darby events during the last two years of reconstruction in Darlington District.

Mrs. Andrew Charles, Stony Hill, Darlington, South Carolina, to Jemima Darby, Ringgold, Louisiana.

Stony Hill
August 25, 1877

Miss Jemima Darby
    Care of Dr. A. Kolb
        Ringgold, Louisiana

Dear Miss Darby

My heart was made glad this afternoon by the reception of a letter from you which reached me in five days after it was mailed. About this hour last night, I said to Sallie, "I have not heard in so long a time from Miss Darby. I fear she is dead, but I will write at once to Mrs. Dr. Kolb to know." I felt assured that she would reply immediately. I cannot tell you how glad we are to hear that you and your dear friends with whom you reside are still living. I think that I have written several letters to you.

In one, I enclosed a notice of Mr. Mills Vann's[119] death and Dr. Smith's[120] death. Col Charles[121] Aunt Julia Wilds[122] and Brother Sam[123] and Charles Andrews[124] have died within a little over a year. The latter dropped dead in our yard of heart disease. In a former letter I told you of Mrs. James McIntosh's[125] death and Aunt Hannah Hart's[126] death. Dr. and Mrs. Harlee[127] and Mrs. Smithy Gregg. Mrs. Mose McCall,[128] Mrs. Eli Gregg. Mrs. Isaac Wilson[129] and a number of others that I cannot think of at present.

The date of your last letter to me (before this of today) is August 3, 1875. It seems a long time since we heard from you. The report that reached you of the exit of the colored population of this State is not true. It would take an immense fleet to transport such a number of beings (forty thousand vessels at least)[130]   And who would bear the expense? They are leaving in small numbers but there is nothing like a general exodus. I think the white population would not sanction such a movement as they are preferred as laborers to any other class.

We have a democratic government and things have taken quite a different turn recently. General Wade Hampton of Columbia is our Governor. You have no doubt seen by the papers. From what I see in the newspapers and hear from all directions, the country has aroused from its long lethargic sleep and everyone seems hopeful and cheerful.

The reports from the crops are generally good, I think. There was a drought in June that did some damage in some sections but I do not hear much of it now. It has been a very dry year altogether though. Fruit has been very fine with us, too. I have preserved, jellied, dryed and am about to finish off by canning.

I hope you had a good meeting and a revival of the spirit among you all. A thing devoutly to be wished for everywhere.

I will inclose a letter of Emily Taylor[131] to you. Florence LaCost[132] is about grown and looks more like her Aunt Sallie Ann,[133] than her mother. Georgia resembles the Lacosts. Floy is still with Serena Dargan. Mrs. Louise[134] Carolina[135] and Sarina[136] are all of that family living. Eugene,[137] Betsy Bealer's only child, went to Texas several years ago to get into business with Mrs. Evrilda Bacot's son, William,[138] who resides there.

James Williams[139] has not married again. Our Sallie is not fifteen yet and is quite a child. Has not near completed her education. I do not want her to come out as a young lady until she is nineteen or twenty, properly educated and fitted for the occupation that she is to occupy.

Dr. Russia Vann[140] still lives in North Carolina. Was down here on a visit to his father[141] and friends last fall. Lizzie Howle[142] has four grown children.[143] One of her sons is said to be very smart. She lives a few miles from her father on her own farm. Mr. Josiah[144] lives with his father. Mr. Robert Vann[145] is in one of the counties of the up country preaching and has not been down this way in a long time.

Mrs. Ferguson[146] is in a low state of health. May Chambers' son[147] married a Greenville girl last year. Jeff is still a bachelor. Mr. Dargan[148] still preaches at Black Creek church. Mrs. May Dorrity lives near the church. Mrs. Jane Davis[149] lived with Mrs. Fort a year or two while her son was at school. She has gone back to her home near Timmonsville.[150] Mr. D.[151] has been dead several years.

I take a leap to Society Hill. Cousin Eliza Griffin[152] died last fall. Peter and Sallie[153] live at Florence. Evander[154] lives with Mr. James Wilson[155] at Leavensworth. Peter married Emmie, the eldest daughter of his cousin, Hannah McIver, of Greenville. Cousin Eliza Evans[156] was very fortunate in not losing her property during the war. She travels about as she did in antebellum days. A number of places on the Hill have changed hands since you left. Willie Coker[157] who married Mrs. Sallie McIver's youngest daughter lives in the old Witherspoon house. Hannah McIver[158] and her two children and her brother John live in Mrs. Spark's house. One of Max Gandy's sons, Tom, lives in the old Dr. McIver house. Mr. and Mrs. Burn[159] and Lizzie live at their same place. I don't know who occupies the house that the Kings lived in. Miss Julia Haws is still living at Rock Spring. Mr. Stout,[160] a young man from Alabama who married Fannie Coker, is pastor of the Baptist church.[161]

Our kindest regards to Mrs. K. and the young ladies and a large share of love to yourself.

Your friend, as ever,

M. A. W. CHARLES

I know nothing of William Prince. Who is he? I will inquire of Cousin Hannah Dabbs. She is the only person who is likely to know.

* * * * *

In the only letter in the series written by Emily King Taylor, which was transmitted to Miss Darby by Mrs. Charles, there is a reference to a sensational best-selling novel, *Rutledge*.[162]

> The heroine of this story . . . is apt to be surly when people do not treat her kindly, and in a fit of injured pride she gets herself engaged to a handsome fellow who turns out to be the illegitimate son of the hero's erring sister and a murderer in the bargain. It was a bad bargain indeed and about ruined the girl's life, but she finally came to an understanding (perversely long delayed) with her middle-aged suitor, the gloomy but well-nigh perfect Mr. Rutledge, of Rutledge. The heroine's troubles are supposed to teach the reader many lessons about the proper deportment of young girls, and especially about the folly of dancing parties (our heroine attended three of them and danced quite too much.)[163]

Mrs. T. L. Taylor, Yorkville, South Carolina, to Mrs. Andrew Charles, Darlington, South Carolina.

Yorkville, So. Ca.,
April the 25th, 1877

Dear Cousin

Your welcome letter is received. It came to hand yesterday, and I cannot tell you how glad I was to hear from you. I had not received a letter from you in nearly three years, and was almost afraid you had forgotten me. My health is generally good, in fact, I think better than it was the last time I saw you.

I should like very much to accept your kind invitation, but do not think I can do so this summer. But I intend to visit Darlington again and when I come, I shall stay with you all long enough to make up for lost time.

We have quit boarding and are housekeeping again. We

are making arrangements to settle permanently near Limestone Springs[164] and expect to move early next fall. I was very
sorry to hear of Aunt Julia's[165] death. I had not heard it until
you wrote. I was also sorry to hear of Cousin Sam's[166] ill health.

It is very late so I must close and go to bed. I would like to
tell you all about ourselves and our surroundings; and will try
and do that next time. Georgia[167] is busy reading "Rutledge,"
but she has taken time to send love to you all, in which I
truly join her. Mr. Taylor sends regards. Do write soon and
let us hear from each other often.

Direct letters to Yorkville and always in care of Rev. T. L.
Taylor. Hoping to hear from you soon, I close by assuring you
that I am, as ever,

Your loving cousin,

EM

* * * * *

FOOTNOTES

1 Edward DeLeon, "Ruin and Reconstruction of the Southern States," *Southern Magazine*, XIV (January, 1874), p. 33.

2 *Ibid.*, p. 35.

3 *Ibid.*, p. 37.

4 *Ibid.*, p. 291.

5 Reynolds, *Reconstruction in South Carolina, 1865-1877*, p. 266.

6 *Ibid.*, p. 260.

7 Colonel J. J. Lucas, Society Hill, Citadel graduate of 1851, was a merchant
in Charleston from 1852 to 1860, a colonel in the Confederate Army, a planter,
who married Carrie McIver, daughter of D. R. W. McIver and his second wife,
Martha Grant.

8 Benjamin F. Williamson, Darlington, married Margaret McIver, daughter of
Evander and Eliza Cowan McIver.

9 Junius A. Law, son of E. A. and Sarah E. McIver Law, married Blanche Crawford.

10 Colonel Evander R. McIver, son of William Cowan and Louise Penn McIver, married Mary Ervin.

11 William Pitt Kellogg was *de facto* governor of Louisiana from 1872-1877.

12 *Biographical and Historical Memoirs of Northwest Louisiana*, p. 499.

13 Coulter, *The South during Reconstruction. 1865-1877*, p. 250.

14 *Harper's New Monthly Magazine*, XLIX (June — November, 1874), p. 297. "A bill was passed by the House, April 28 appropriating $90,000 for the purchase of rations to be distributed among the sufferers from ununndations of the Lower Mississippi. The Senate passed the bill May 1. Another section was added May 7 appropriating an additional sum of $100,000." States which were affected by the flood were: Louisiana, Arkansas, and Tennessee.

15 Alexander Gregg, *History of the Old Cheraws* (San Antonio, 1867; Columbia, 1905).

16 Mary C. Sanders, Cheraw, South Carolina, married Nicholas Bedgegood Pegues, Oxford, Mississippi, in 1853. They had seven children: Thomas, Eliza, Paul, Sallie, Lottie, and the twins, Nick and Joe.

17 George Jay Washington McCall (September 26, 1801 — February 16, 1871) married (1) Harriet Leake Harllee (September 15, 1809 — June 15, 1836), and (2) Luisa C. Huggins.

18 No date is given. This is a continuation of the letter of May 30.

19 A. Linton Williams, son of David and Elizabeth Williams, and brother to James A. Williams, married (1) Martha E. _____, who died in 1851, (2) Martha Harriett Fort, who died in 1858, and (3) Mary A. Norwood.

20 Margaret Lucas was the daughter of Ben Lucas, planter.

21 Evander White married Jane Fort, moved to Cheraw to clerk in a store, went into the Army, and was killed.

22 Jane Fort was the daughter of Josiah and Anne Fort, and a sister to Linton Williams's second wife.

23 George Washington Lucas was now forty-nine years old.

24 Mrs. Serena Dargan lived in Darlington, but owned land on Black Swamp, near the property of Hugh Charles. "Attending to business" meant overseeing the plantation.

25 John Lucas was the twenty-five-year-old son of G. W. and Mary Ann Lucas.

26 Hugh Charles, son of Colonel E. W. Charles, was a brother-in-law to Mary Ann Charles.

27 Deborah S. Williams Dove Baker died February 5, 1865, at the age of fifty-eight.

28 Elizabeth Williams Ferguson, now sixty-seven, owned a place near Auburn.

29 Mills and William Vann were Miss Darby's closest relatives in South Carolina.

30 Ladson Dorrity was the husband of Mills Vann's daughter, Mary.

31 Charlotte Dorrity married a son of Evander Byrd.

32 Lizzie Dorrity, the oldest daughter, was teaching at Black Creek.

33 John Davis, Sr., Society Hill, was the husband of Jane DuBose Davis.

34 Miss Darby had known the Parnells in Society Hill.

35 Evan J. Lide (1802-1882) married three times: (1) Margaret Ervin, (2) Martha Miller, and (3) Mrs. Lavinia Eason. It was Mrs. Lavinia Lide who had just died. Mrs. Martha Miller Lide was the mother of Mr. Lide's children.

36 Dora Dargan (January 16, 1849 — December 23, 1878), daughter of Alonzo Theodore and Maria Louisa Bacot Dargan, became the first wife of Robert W. Lide.

37 Robert W. Lide completed his work at Furman University and became pastor of the First Baptist Church at Darlington.

38 Mary and Elizabeth Lide, Robert's sisters, lived for many years in the old Evan J. Lide home before moving into the town of Darlington.

39 Eliza Evans was sixty-seven years old.

40 "Old seventy-six" was a popular expression. *Harper's New Monthly Magazine,* CCCLIX, Number LX (April, 1880) included a joke: A teacher who was attempting to teach a child the word "Mamma" asked, "What does your father call your mother?" The unexpected reply was "Old seventy-six."

41 Dr. Peter Griffin was the son of Thomas and Eliza McIver Griffin.

42 Hannah McIver Mauldin was the daughter of Peter Kolb and Elizabeth Chapman McIver.

43 Eliza McIver Griffin, now seveny-one years old, was the widow of Thomas Griffin. She was Dr. Griffin's mother.

44 J. Eli Gregg, who died in 1873, owned a home near the Presbyterian Church, Society Hill.

45 Isaac DeLesseline Wilson, Sr., colonel in the militia, married Margaret Jane Sparks, daughter of Mr. and Mrs. Alexander Sparks.

46 "Minutes of the Welsh Neck Baptist Church, Society Hill, South Carolina." On May 12, 1866, it was recommended "that the balance within the Poor Fund ($72.12) be applied to the support of Sister Elizabeth Edwards."

47 Ellen Hartwell Edwards, now forty-six years old, was a widow; Robert Edwards had died July 9, 1869.

48 Hartwell Edwards, son of Robert G. and Ellen Hartwell Edwards, was the

grandson of Jesse Hartwell, who died at Mt. Lebanon, Louisiana, where he had been president of Mt. Lebanon University.

49 Fannie Coker (July 5, 1844 — June 30, 1910), daughter of Caleb and Hannah Lide Coker, married John Stout in May, 1870.

50 John Stout (March 12, 1842 — June 17, 1894), pastor of the Welsh Neck Church from January, 1874-1892, was pastor at Newberry at the time of his marriage.

51 Sue Stout married James Lide Coker, son of Caleb and Hannah Lide Coker, March 28, 1860. John and Sue Stout were natives of Alabama.

52 Mary McIver, daughter of Allen and Sarah Ervin McIver, married William Caleb Coker, January, 1869.

53 Mary Emma Coker, a daughter of Caleb and Hannah Lide Coker, married Paul Hamilton Rogers, son of Ham and Verlina Rogers, December, 1873.

54 Darius Gandy was the son of Booker and Delilah Gandy and was a brother to Abel Gandy.

55 Ella Williams married James Gandy.

56 W. H. Strickland was pastor of the Darlington Baptist Church from 1874 to 1875.

57 Pastor J. W. Burn (1808-1880).

58 No date is given. This is another installment of the letter of May 30.

59 Ouachita.

60 Morrison, "South Carolina, 1865-1909," *The South in the Building of the Nation,* II, p. 92.

61 Charlotte Dorrity was the daughter of Ladson and Mary Vann Dorrity, and granddaughter of Mills Vann, Miss Darby's cousin.

62 Lizzie Dorrity was Charlotte's older sister.

63 Bishop Gregg's memorial on his grave at St. David's, Cheraw, bears this inscription: "In memory of a faithful servant of our Lord Jesus Christ, Rt. Rev. Alexander Gregg; The First Bishop of Texas; born Society Hill, S. C., October 8, 1819; consecrated, Richmond, Va., October 13, 1859; died Austin, Texas, July 10, 1893." Mrs. Gregg was formerly Charlotte Wilson (January 26, 1822 — May 20, 1880).

64 Anne Lide Wilds (January 19, 1823 — April 23, 1893) married Major E. K. W. Ross and is buried in the "Old Cemetery," Bastrop, Louisiana. Anne Wilds was the daughter of Joseph Wilds, Mary Ann's uncle, who died in Louisiana on February 10, 1831.

65 Eli Wilds Ross (January 8, 1846-1899), son of E. K. W. and Anne Lide Wilds Ross, was married at the time. The oldest son of E. K. W. and Anne Wilds Ross, who died at the age of one year, was buried in Lowther's Hill Cemetery,

near Cashaway Ferry, on the Pee Dee River in South Carolina, among his ancestors and kinspeople — Lides, Wildses, Williamsons, and Charleses.

66 David R. Lide, son of James and Jane Holloway Lide, married (1) Frances Miller, sister-in-law to the artist, Scarborough, and (2) Mrs. William Miller, nee DuBose.

67 Lewis DuPre, husband of the late Sarah Catlett, had been a Baptist pastor in Pee Dee churches while Miss Darby lived in South Carolina.

68 Berryman Wheeler Edwards (January 27, 1821 — June 11, 1890), a native of Spartanburg County, married Anna Maria Coker in 1857.

69 Louisa Harllee (June 12, 1839-193__) was the unmarried daughter of Robert and Amelia Harllee.

70 Charles was General Harllee's son; Dr. Harllee's youngest son was Arthur Howard (January 21, 1854 — March 28, 1911).

71 Charles Fort, "Squire Fort" of Society Hill, was a cabinetmaker and wheelwright.

72 Henry H. Bacot (December 1, 1847 — October 15, 1874), son of Dr. Henry H. and Mary McIver Bacot, is buried in the Episcopal Churchyard, Society Hill, South Carolina.

73 Margaret Jane Sparks Wilson was the wife of Colonel I. D. Wilson, Society Hill.

74 George Williams McIver (January 1, 1825 — July 31, 1896) married Harriett LaCoste (July 19, 1826 — September 14, 1903) on October 31, 1845.

75 Alexander Markland McIver (November 3, 1851 — March 21, 1930) married Julia Whilden (November 19, 1852 — September 13, 1926) on July 17, 1873.

76 Dell LaCoste Ellerbee was Mrs. George McIver's sister.

77 In "Memories of Society Hill and Some of Its People," an unpublished manuscript written for her family in 1909 and 1910, Jane Lide Coker Wilson stated: "Our oldest children were born at Society Hill; they are James Lide, John Flavel, an infant who died, William Coker, and Anna Elizabeth."

78 Nancy Andrews (December 20, 1775 — April 5, 1856) was buried with the Williamson and Wilds families at Lowther's Hill Cemetery.

79 Thomas P. Lide was the son of Evan J. Lide and his second wife, Martha Miller.

80 Reynolds, *Reconstruction in South Carolina, 1865-1877*, p. 300.

81 1869-1877.

82 Garnie William McGinty, *A History of Louisiana* (New York, 1949), p. 218.

83 L. W. Coker, *Historical Sketch and Membership Roll* (Darlington, 1945). "Rev. W. H. Strickland was pastor of the Darlington Baptist Church, 1874-1875."

84 W. H. Strickland.

85 Sallie Wilds was the afflicted daughter of Peter and Julia Terrel Wilds.

86 Carrie McIver (1834-1901), daughter of D. R. W. and Caroline Wilds McIver, married J. Jonathan Lucas of Charleston.

87 Fannie McIver Lucas was born in 1864.

88 Elizabeth Burn was the daughter of J. W. and Susan L. Burn.

89 Louisa McIntosh, born July 26, 1834, was forty years old.

90 Edward McIntosh (April 20, 1840 — June 6, 1870), son of James H. and Martha Gregg McIntosh, married Dora Evans (August 28, 1847 — October 20, 1868), daughter of Captain S. W. Evans; Murray McIntosh (November 19, 1850 — January 29, 1871); Margaret McIntosh (September 9, 1842 — July 10, 1864).

91 Martha Gregg McIntosh (January 18, 1812 — October 25, 1874) was the widow of James H. McIntosh.

92 Lucas McIntosh (July 7, 1845 — January 26, 1901) married Rosa Evans (October 15, 1849 — March 21, 1934) in 1874.

93 Robert Wilds, son of Peter and Julia Terrel Wilds, a brother to Mrs. P. C. Coggeshall and Mrs. Leighton Lide, married Eliza Hart, daughter of Dr. R. L. and Eliza A. Flinn Hart of Darlington.

94 According to the *Report of the United States Commissioner of Education* (Washington, 1886), p. 557, Sumter Institute, Sumter, South Carolina, organized in 1866, had an attendance of about a hundred girls.

95 Mary Ann Charles Haynesworth was a sister to Andrew Charles and was the wife of W. F. B. Haynesworth, Sumter.

96 The Charlotte *Observer* of November 16, 1952, reported that Limestone College, Gaffney, South Carolina, was founded by the Baptists as a preparatory school in 1845.

97 Thomas Curtis, D.D., was principal at Limestone.

98 *Report of the United States Commissioner of Education*, p. 572. Greenville College was a Baptist institution, founded in 1854.

99 Furman University was founded in 1851 by South Carolina Baptists.

100 Harvey T. Cook, *The Life Work of James Clement Furman* (privately printed, 1926), p. 268. "Professor Charles H. Judson was the leading spirit at Furman even in 1868 when he was still President of the Female College and Treasurer of the Convention."

101 Greenville.

102 James A. Williams, Leavensworth (September 3, 1825 — February 2, 1886), was Sallie's father.

103 Elizabeth Williams Ferguson (January 16, 1807 — May 6, 1885).

104 Mary Deborah Ferguson Chambers (December 27, 1835 — October 14, 1917), wife of Benjamin Wesley Chambers (May 8, 1820 — October 12, 1863).

105 Ptolemy Philadelphus Chambers (September 5, 1855 — March 26, 1943) was twenty years old.

106 The Sparta *Rural Times* was established in March of 1868 and was published until 1887.

107 Mary Harriet Kolb was thirteen years old.

108 Mary Ann Charles Haynesworth, wife of W. F. B. Haynesworth, Sumter, was Andrew Charles's sister.

109 James Ashley Cawthon (October 20, 1849 — c. 1890), son of Ashley Thomas and Margaret Hunter Vickers Cawthon, married Ella Caroline Kolb on November 25, 1875, in Ringgold, Louisiana.

110 John Franklin McDaniel (April 4, 1837 — October 17, 1917), son of William Warren and Elizabeth Tillman McDaniel, married (1) Sarah Tomlinson on November 30, 1859, in Bienville Parish, Louisiana, and (2) Elizabeth Artemecia Cawthon, February 17, 1875.

111 Betty Cawthon (December 2, 1853 — August 24, 1904), daughter of Ashley Thomas and Margaret Vickers Cawthon, married John Franklin McDaniel.

112 William McDaniel (December 15, 1869-193__) was the five-year-old son of John F. and Sarah Tomlinson McDaniel.

113 Margaret J. McDaniel (January 19, 1876 — February 5, 1961), daughter of John F. and Betty Cawthon McDaniel, was a resident of Columbus, Georgia, at the time of her death.

114 The oldest son of James Ashley and Ella Kolb Cawthon was born October 16, 1876, and died December 26, 1876.

115 Wade Hampton (March 28, 1818 — April 11, 1902), aristocratic, wealthy, leader of the "Old Regime" in South Carolina, was its statesman, soldier, and now governor.

116 Reynolds, *Reconstruction in South Carolina, 1865-1877,* p. 361.

117 *Ibid.,* p. 358.

118 J. Harold Easterby, "Wade Hampton," *Dictionary of American Biography,* VIII (1932), p. 215.

119 Mills Vann (1782-1875), son of William and _____ Hamilton Vann, was ninety-three when he died.

120 Dr. Thomas Smith, Society Hill, married the widow of Judge Wilds.

121 Colonel Edgar Welles Charles, signer of the Ordinance of Secession, married (1) Sara Kolb Lide, and (2) Jane Gray, of Newark, New Jersey.

122 Julia Terrel Wilds (June 27, 1813 — October 21, 1876) was the widow of Peter Wilds.

123 Samuel Wilds Williamson (November 6, 1811 — April 5, 1877) was Mary Ann's brother.

124 Charles Andrews, son of Nancy Andrews, was a cousin of the Charleses.

125 Martha Gregg McIntosh died October 25, 1874.

126 Hannah Lide Hart (November 19, 1796 — October 2, 1875) was the widow of Thomas E. Hart.

127 Robert Harllee (November 7, 1807 — November 20, 1872) and Amelia Melvina Cannon Howard Harllee (August 4, 1810 — February 7, 1877) were buried at "Hopewell" Cemetery, Mars Bluff, South Carolina.

128 Mary Elizabeth Gregg (d. June 23, 1875), daughter of John Gregg, married Moses Sanders McCall.

129 Margaret Jane Sparks Wilson (March 18, 1815 — April 2, 1875) was the wife of Colonel Isaac DeLesseline Wilson.

130 Mrs. Charles had made an attempt to blot out this parenthetical clause.

131 Emily King Taylor was the wife of T. L. Taylor, Baptist minister of Yorkville, South Carolina.

132 Florence LaCoste, aged seventeen, daughter of A. P. and Eliza King LaCoste, was a ward of her great-aunt, Serena Bacot Dargan, Darlington.

133 Sallie Ann King LaCoste (April 23, 1825 — May 10, 1857) was the second wife of A. P. LaCoste, and an aunt to Florence.

134 Louisa Bacot Dargan was the wife of Louis Alonzo Theodore Dargan.

135 Carolina A. Bacot Charles (September 23, 1830 — February 4, 1911), daughter of Samuel and Emilie Leslie Bacot, was the wife of Hugh Lide Charles.

136 Serena Bacot Dargan (January 3, 1833 — November 7, 1910) was the widow of Charles Dargan.

137 Eugene Bealer, born in 1857, was the son of George B. Bealer, former Baptist pastor in Darlington, and Lissie Bacot Bealer.

138 On a tombstone erected to the memory of Henry H. Bacot, son of Dr. Henry and Mary McIver Bacot, in Episcopal Churchyard, Society Hill, there is this inscription: "William D. Bacot, born November 1, 1852; died July 11, 1876. Resting in Louisiana."

139 James A. Williams (September 3, 1825 — February 2, 1886), Leavensworth, was Sallie's father.

140 Alexander Russia Vann (May 5, 1822 — October 22, 1892) was the son of William Vann.

141 William Vann (May 29, 1795 — February 25, 1881) was living with his third wife, Sarah Louise Passmore Vann.

[142] Elizabeth Sarah (Bettie) Vann Howle (November 25, 1833 — January 15, 1913) was the widow of Thomas E. Howle.

[143] William James was twenty-four; Thomas E., Jr., who had married Frances Elizabeth Rhodes on March 9, 1875, was twenty-two; Lawrence Keith was twenty; and Maggie J., eighteen. Sarah Elizabeth (Sallie) was sixteen.

[144] Josiah Thomas Vann (July 29, 1820 — January 7, 1892), son of William and Sarah Goodson Vann, was known as the "old bachelor" by his family.

[145] Robert Vann was ordained to preach by Black Creek Church. Later he became president of Blythewood Female College, Blythewood, South Carolina.

[146] Elizabeth Williams Ferguson (January 16, 1807 — May 6, 1885) was the widow of Alexander Ferguson.

[147] P. P. Chambers, son of Benjamin W. and Mary Deborah Ferguson Chambers, married Ida Cornelia Berry, daughter of Dr. M. J. and Eliza Donaldson Berry, of Greenville, November 21, 1876.

[148] J. O. B. Dargan.

[149] Jane DuBose Davis, widow of John Davis, was Mrs. Fort's sister.

[150] "Minutes of the Welsh Neck Baptist Church, Society Hill, South Carolina," June 21, 1874. "Sister Jane F. Davis has requested a letter of dismissal from us to unite with the Mount Elon Church."

[151] John Davis was the husband of Jane DuBose Davis.

[152] Eliza McIver Griffin, widow of Thomas Griffin, died in 1876.

[153] Dr. Peter Griffin's unmarried sister, Sallie, lived with him and his family.

[154] Evander Griffin was a brother to Peter and Miss Sallie.

[155] James Wilson was owner of the store at Leavensworth, where Evander was clerk.

[156] Eliza Evans (1808-1878).

[157] William C. Coker (June 8, 1839 — April 20, 1907) married Mary McIver, and later Lavinia McIver, daughters of Allen Evander and Sarah Witherspoon Ervin McIver.

[158] Hannah Wilson McIver was the granddaughter of Alexander Sparks. Her brother, John A. Wilson, never married. Her two children were Fannie and John K. McIver.

[159] J. W. Burn (1808-1880), Baptist minister, organized the Hartsville Baptist Church and served as its pastor for thirty years. His wife, Susan, (1811-1884) was buried at Welsh Neck; he at Hartsville.

[160] John Stout (March 12, 1842 — June 17, 1894), who married Fannie Coker in May, 1870, was pastor of the Welsh Neck Church from 1874 to 1892.

[161] Mrs. Charles neglected to give Miss Darby an account of the meeting of the 56th Session of the South Carolina Baptist Convention which was held at Society

Hill on November 22-26, 1876. Among the visitors were Rev. H. A. Tupper, secretary of Foreign Missions and Rev. W. H. McIntosh, corresponding secretary of Home Missions. "The meeting was harmonious, not one unfortunate word was uttered, not an unkind feeling permitted to arise. The meeting was an illustration of 'Behold how good and how pleasant it is for brethren to dwell together in unity,' and when the brethren took the parting hand singing 'Blest Be the Tie That Binds,' few eyes were seen that did not flow with tears." "Minutes of the Welsh Neck Baptist Church, Society Hill, South Carolina," November 26, 1876.

162 Miriam Cole Harris, *Rutledge* (New York, 1860).

163 Frank Luther Mott, *Golden Multitudes* (New York, 1947), pp. 127-128.

164 "Minutes of the Welsh Neck Baptist Church, Society Hill, South Carolina," January 9, 1876. "Letter of dismissal was granted Mrs. Emily King Taylor to join Enon Baptist church in York County."

165 Julia Terrel Wilds was the widow of Peter Wilds.

166 Samuel Wilds Williamson, Mary Ann's brother, had died on April 5, 1877. Mrs. Taylor had not learned of his death when she wrote Mrs. Charles.

167 Georgia LaCoste.

The New South

PART I

"Her soul is stirred with the breath of new life. The light of a grander day is falling fair on her face."

Henry W. Grady, "The New South." Joel Chandler Harris, *Life of Henry W. Grady Including His Writings and Speeches* (New York, 1890), p. 91.

When Rutherford Birchard Hayes was inaugurated President of the United States on March 5, 1877, there were two governors in South Carolina, and two in Louisiana. Having been involved in the nation's "Disputed Election of 1876," the President was in a position to understand, in a very personal way, the problems of leaders in states where dual governments existed. By the end of 1877, Mr. Hayes, former governor of Ohio and distinguished soldier, had adopted a conciliatory policy toward the defeated Confederate states which aided materially in the restoration of home rule in Miss Darby's South Carolina and Louisiana. Governor Wade Hampton lent the prestige of aristocratic lineage and colorful war record to his progressive program of "redemption" in South Carolina; Francis T. Nicholls assumed his duties as governor with demonstrations of great humility and solemn prayers to almighty God for the political redemption of Louisiana. A new era had come to the South.

Mary Ann Charles never lost faith in her South Carolina's ability to survive. Throughout the war and reconstruction, she insisted that "Old South Carolina is not defeated." With the return to power of men like Wade Hampton, Mrs. Charles's faith was reaffirmed. She hailed the redemption of South Carolina with great joy and wrote of her hatred for the Yankees in a long letter to Miss Darby on December 12, 1877.

Mrs. Andrew Charles, Darlington, South Carolina, to Jemima Darby, Ringgold, Louisiana.

Miss Jemima Darby
    Care of Dr. A. Kolb
      Ringgold, La.

Dear Miss Darby

I have delayed answering your letter much longer than I would like to have done for one cause and another, but I will try to make amends by writing you a long one.

First, let me answer your questions. Mr. Dargan[1] still holds meetings at B. C. church, but not always in September. Mr. Dorrity[2] is living but I mentioned *her* name, I suppose, thinking of *her* as your cousin. They live in Mrs. Deby Dove, Baker's whom she was at last,[3] house, near Mrs. Ferguson.[4] Mr. Mills Vann[5] died in his ninety-third year. Mrs. Robert Edwards[6] lives at Hartsville, teaching school. She rents her lot on the Hill and went out there to teach as she could get a large school out there.

James Coker[7] owns the place that belonged to Cousin John Hart.[8] It is quite a village now, store and mill, and last but not least the church[9] which is very flourishing. Mr. Burn[10] is pastor but its prosperous condition could hardly be attributed to him but mainly to James Coker who is a model of energy, piety, and also to some others of the congregation. Hartwell Edwards is quite talented and is now taking an extra course in Theology in Rochester, New York.[11] Janie[12] is rather pretty. I think she resembles her aunt, Mrs. Pressley.[13]

I received a letter recently from Emily Taylor[14] They have bought a place not far from Lime Stone Springs. Mr. T., I think, is doing well and seemed to be very acceptable as preacher up there. Cousin writes cheerfully. Georgia LaCost is still with them. I delivered your message to E‑ and hope she has written to you by this time.

I suppose you remember Mr. Sam Sparks[15] He is still living, ninety-one years old. Mrs. S.[16] has been dead several years. Mr. Danie Sparks[17] is dead. His widow came out here last week from Texas. She has been engaged in a law suit which she has gained and recovered thirty thousand acres of land. Mrs. Sue Keitt[18] lives with her father. She insisted that Mrs. Daniel Sparks come out to spend some months with her father so she, Mrs. K., might go to Staunton, Virginia to spend some time with her daughter who is at school there. Anna[19] is trying to graduate with distinction and wishes her mother to assist her this session.

I do not know where Cousin Eliza Evans is at this time.[20] She is a bird of passage. Dr. Griffin[21] has moved to Columbia. Has charge of the lunatic asylum[22] as physician, gets a salary of three thousand and a nice house free of rent and I think is allowed to practice outside, too. Sallie[23] goes with them. The Dr. has two little boys.[24] Sallie is very much attached to them.

I hope your niece[25] who went to Arkansas has returned to her old home and the bosom of her dear family and friends with the assurance that there is no place on earth so dear and sweet as home, and hope the young ladies[26] enjoyed the Association.[27] One was held with the Black Creek Church and I attended and had a delightful meeting. Mr. Stout (Fannie Coker's husband)[28] is one of the most popular preachers in this part of the country. I do wish that you could be seated in your old pew[29] at Society Hill and hear one of his sermons. It would delight you.

Jonnie Dargan[30] Cousin Jane's third son was buried at the Baptist church last Sabbath. His health had been precarious for a year or more. He was pastor of a large church in Abaville[31] and was quite a distinguished preacher and left a wife and three children.[32] He married a Greenville girl, Lizzie Towns.[33] His family are delighted with her. She is handsome and accomplished.

Our County Fair came off on the two last days in October and the first day of November. It was a grand occasion. Our Governor Hampton honored the people of Darlington with his presence. There were over four thousand persons on the grounds. A grand display of the military, two bands of music. And the Governor was handsomely entertained by the people who did their whole duty to make the occasion a pleasant, happy, galla day. I met Lizzie and Dick Howard[34] at the Fair. I had not seen her since we were at school together. She looks old and broken. Dick looks well. He represented Marion in the Legislature.[35] They have two grown children and I think a large family.[36] Their son graduated at West Point.[37] Is considered very smart. Some of his drawings were on exhibition at the Fair.

I think I told you of the death of Mrs. Dr. Harlee[38] some years back. Harry[39] her son married Mr. Mose McCall's daughter, Mary. Jinette[40] married Sam Nettles[41] last winter. They live not far from us. Betsy and Emma[42] are still single. General Harlee's house was burned (by accident). They moved to Marion Village where they still live.

Mr. John Witherspoon's[43] house was robbed and burned in the latter part of the summer. He and Mrs. W. were visiting their friends in Camden at the time. The burglars were captured and put in the penitentary for life but have made their escape from there. The superintendent is a miserable Yankee and will be removed soon. How I do hate the Yankees. You see, I am not reconstructed yet.

Our household treasure, Sallie,[44] celebrated her fifteenth birthday on the 23rd of Oct by a dinner party at which she had a number of her young friends. She left soon after for Charleston where she is at school.

Mr. George McIver and family[45] live in Charleston now. Removed there at the close of the War. They have been very polite and attentive to her. Mr. and Mrs. McIver's oldest son, Zannie,[46] has recently married Miss Whilden of Charleston. You remember Flora[47] a little dark curly haired girl. She is near-sighted, wears blue glasses, which give her an oldish look. Is not as pretty as when a child. Mr. McIver is one of a firm of Commission merchants who do a large business. They are quite stylish. Mr. Davis[48] who married Cornelia McIver is still there. They have grown daughters.[49] Cornelia has become quite a woman of the world, a "fashionist." Quite a change from the way she was brought up.

Mrs. Katie Fort[50] is still living with Lucy Watson[51] in Edgefield. Mr. Richard Furman[52] lives near there. Three of his sons are in Texas. He paid them a visit last summer and wrote several very interesting letters to the Charleston News and Courier while he was out there. His father, Mr. Sam Furman[53] died this summer past at Ned Edwards[54] in the town of Sumter. Ned is a Baptist preacher. His house was burned a few years ago. The citizens of the town made up a purse and built another for him. I think he lost all of his large fortune in the war. He has a large family and has grandchildren.

Well, Miss Darby, I fear it will be more of an infliction than a pleasure for you to focuse this lengthy epistle, so I will close by sending my kindest regards to Mrs. K., and the young ladies and a quantity of love to yourself.

Yours as ever,

M. A. W. CHARLES

* * * * *

Miss Darby preserved only one letter which was written in Louisiana, a note from Mrs. T. J. Fouts,[55] Sparta, Louisiana, to her niece, Ella Kolb Cawthon, who lived near Fulton, Arkansas, and who was visiting in the Ringgold home of her parents, Dr. and Mrs. Kolb. The Cawthons' second child was to be born early in 1878.[56]

Mrs. Fouts had been asked to buy some lace for Miss Darby in Sparta, a town which had a better selection of such notions. Both the lace and Mrs. Fouts's letter found their way into Miss Darby's possession and the letter was filed away.

The letter from Mrs. Fouts is not dated.

Mrs. Thomas Jefferson Fouts, Sparta, Louisiana, to Mrs. James Ashley Cawthon, Ringgold, Louisiana.

Dear Ella

I send Ma[57] a dress. Tell her to put it on today and walk all about over the house and be well. I am going to send all her flannel. Tell her to give them to Livia.[58] She can use them as lining things for her little children,[59] and Ma will not need them. Tell your Aunt[60] I sent her the widest and all the lace there is here. I got the last piece in Sparta, but it is not the kind your Aunt wanted. I thought I would have been over there[61] before now but couldn't get off. Have been right sick three or four days and other things have prevented my going. Would gladly go every week if I could.

Dick says tell Ma he has to go off sooner than he expected and can't go to see her, but will as soon as he returns if she is not here.

If Jimmy[62] has come you must come over this week and we will have a turkey. I would be so glad to see you rolling up this evening.

Lutie Head[63] married next Thursday night. She is not going to have any there but kinfolks.[64]

Our baby[65] has a dreadful cough and cold. Keeps us from sleep every night. Tom[66] thought of going over to Ringgold today but the weather looked so dark and unfavorable for preaching and he is not well. He thought he would not have any congregation. So he didn't go (as you are aware). Hoping you are all well and better. I will say good-bye.

Affectionately yours,
AUNTY HARRIET

Be sure to send me a note by Pa[67] for you know he won't tell me anything. My love to all especially remember me in much love and affection to *my* poor dear afflicted mother. If she gets worse let us know. If Ma's dress is too high in the neck or sleeves too short, some of you fit it. Make her wear it every day when it is cold.

* * * * *

When Ella Cawthon was able to travel, she, her husband, and infant son returned to Arkansas. Her family in Ringgold grieved to see them go. Maria Elizabeth Kolb, now almost nineteen years old, sought employment as a school teacher near Ringgold.

Reporting on Baptist churches within the Red River Association during the year 1878, the associational clerk wrote: "The general state of the churches is not very encouraging."[68] To Miss Darby, accustomed to Welsh Neck and Black Creek churches, more than a century old, conditions within Bienville Parish churches appeared heathenish.

In New Orleans, Louisiana, Edward Porcher Harllee, son of Miss Darby's old friends, General William Wallace Harllee and his wife, of Marion, South Carolina, had begun to receive recognition for his editorial work on the staff of the *New Orleans Picayune.*[69] Early in 1878, he became seriously ill as the result of overwork, and returned to his father's home.

According to Mrs. Charles, life in Miss Darby's home state was good again. Enthusiasm for Wade Hampton and the redemption of South Carolina was unabated.

Mrs. Andrew Charles, Stony Hill, Darlington, South Carolina, to Miss Jemima Darby, Ringgold, Louisiana.

Miss Jemima Darby
Care Dr. Alexander Kolb
Ringgold, La.

Dear Miss Darby

Your very welcome letter of the 17th at hand. I was just on the eve of dispatching a postal to Mrs. Kolb to know what was the matter that you did not write and thought perhaps my letter had not reached you.

I was glad to hear of the return of your niece,[70] but sorry that she cannot remain with her parents and hope Miss Lizzie[71] may succeed with her school. I dont agree with you in thinking you had almost as well be in a heathen land. I hope you may never get to a worse place for preaching than you are at.[72]

I am sorry Cousin[73] does not write to you. I have not heard from her in almost a year, but I hear sometimes through Florence who lives with Sarina Dargan still.

Dora Dargan[74] who married Robert Lide[75] has moved to Newbern N. C. He was offered a fine salary by the Baptist church there and left Cheraw last fall. I think they have no pastor there, but are supplied perhaps twice a month.

Mr. Stout still preaches at the Hill. Mrs. Robert Edwards has moved back there from Hartsville where she has been teaching a free school.[76] Her son Hartwell graduated in the Theological Seminary at Greenville and is now taking a course at Rochester, New York. He expects to marry Florrie Coker[77] when he graduates there. Mrs. Rachel Coker[78] spends most of her time with Tommie and Ellena.[79] They live in Mr. Elias Gregg's[80] house. I think Cousin Eliza Evans[81] spends most of her time up the country. She owns a house in Greenville. Miss Lou McIntosh[82] has been in poor health for a long time but now Mattie's[83] health is worse than hers. It is feared neither will live long. Mrs. Sompayrac[84] has two or three children grown. Willie Coker[85] bought the old Witherspoon house and lives in it.

I think I told you about Mr. John Witherspoon's house having been burned last fall. They were on a visit to their friends in Camden and lost everything. There were nine family portraits, some of them about a century old.

If you were dropped down at the Depot at the Hill, you would scarcely recognize the place. It is quite a village. Perhaps has more stores and more businesses down there then the old *Hill*. It is built up almost to the river and a very fine *draw* bridge built over the river, which makes Marlborough quite accessible except in time of freshlets and they have become very frequent of late. Mr. and Mrs. Burns and Lizzie live at the same place. Lizzie's husband left during the war and has never come for her. The others of the family are all married and settled off.

I take a jump to Mars Bluff. Edward Harlee[86] son of the General died recently. He had resided in New Orleans for several years and edited the "Picayune." His health failed and he came home and died soon after. He was quite talented.

Mrs. Lizzie Haynesworth[87] married Henry Sanders and went out to Mississippi to visit his family and heir his portion of Theodore's property who died some time last year.

Our old state is looking up and bids fair to be "old South Carolina" once more. Since Hampton has become Governor it seems as if we have all waked up into a new world. It is thought he will be our next Governor. The negroes seem very much pleased with his administration and pour out to hear him speak and cheer him vociferiously. An old woman (colored) came along by the train and yelled at him "Yo stay Governor; yo stay Governor." As far as he could hear her, she screeched at him.

I will tell you a little of our private history. Andrew's health and my own is very good. Sallie is still in Charleston. Will return about the first of June. I have heard through persons who have seen her since I that she is very fine looking from having grown stouter, more fleshy. Suppose her figure has developed. I suppose she needed more flesh. She is tall and has dark brown, glossy hair and large blue eyes. I hope you would think her pretty for everyone who sees her does.

Our garden is pretty, not many vegetables in use yet, but everything is growing beautifully. The fruit prospect is fine, too. I wish you could be with us to enjoy the strawberries with us. I have, or will have, when ripe, enough for our use and for our next neighbors, and have such delightful cream for two. Our cows have the river swamp range. We make more butter than we know what to do with.

I have not succeeded well with chickens on account of the hawks having been particularly troublesome. I have good luck usually with turkeys and Guinna fowls. My flowers got killed (most of them) but I have put out more. I hope to keep them better in the future. Sallie will bring me some from the City. I must close this letter as Andrew is waiting to take it to the office. He joins in kind regards to your family and much love from your old friend,

MARY ANN CHARLES

* * * * *

In the South, life was tranquil during the months between April and October, 1878. Mrs. Charles found nothing of nation-wide significance upon which to comment on October 1. There was, however, a great deal of local news for Miss Darby.

Mrs. Andrew Charles, Stony Hill, Darlington, South Carolina, to Jemima Darby, Ringgold, Louisiana.

Stony Hill
Oct. 1st, 1878

Miss Jemima Darby
    Care of Dr. Alexander Kolb
        Ringgold, La.

Dear Miss Darby

I know you have reason to think that I never intend writting to you again, but you will be convinced that I have not. I am sorry that so long a time has expired since the reception of your letter and it answered. For the first place, I will answer your questions.

I am sorry I have no apple geranium seeds and lost my old plants last winter. I don't know how many persons have applied to me for them. The first I get I will send to you.

Miss Lou Harlee[88] lives with Sallie[89] who married James Pierce.[90] Their old homestead[91] has been sold, but I don't know who bought it. Walter[92] lives with his brother, Harrie[93] who married Mr. Mose McCall's youngest daughter. They have built a nice house on Mary's inheritance of land not far from the old Brockington house on the Pocket road.

I saw Lizzie Howard's[94] daughter not long since and in-

⋅≼ 267 ≽⋅

quired about the people of that region so as to tell you about them. All were in usual health and getting on very well.

Bettie Dargan[95] married a young man by the name of Forrester from Beaufort County. He lived near Mr. Bostick[96] who married Anna McIver, of Cheraw. Mr. Beattie[97] is still living and preaches at the Saw Mill.

I know when you read what I am going to tell you now, you will say "When will wonders cease?" Mr. Lewis Coker[98] and Sallie Griffin[99] married in July and went on to Saritoga.[100] She was living with Dr. Griffin[101] who lives in Columbia and practices in the Asylum. He gets a salary of three thousand. They live in style. Hannah Maldwin[102] and her daughter live with them. The Dr. married her eldest daughter, Emmie. Evander[103] is a partner of Mr. James Wilson[104] and lives with him. Dr. Furman Wilson[105] practices in that neighborhood. Lives where Mr. Linton Williams once lived. Jane[106] looks almost as old as her mother but is still smiling and pleasant. They have, I think, nine children[107] and one grandchild.

Cousin Elizabeth Lide[108] died on the ninth of the month. Cousin Thomas[109] is lonely now. Willie[110] lives at home with him. Hannah McIver[111] and her daughter Fannie[112] are on a visit to them now and suppose they will make a good long visit. Col. Zim Davis[113] failed in business in Charleston and moved his family to the Hill and rented a part of Dr. Pressley's[114] house and left them there and he is seeking business in some western city. I think St. Lewis.

Andrew[115] was at Mr. Dargan's[116] today and heard through them of the death of Mr. DuPre[117]   He got a fall about two months ago which resulted in his death. The whole family moved from Virginia to Nashville just after the war. The old lady[118] is still living. Mr. DuPre received a letter from Mr. Dargan just the day before he died and read "it himself" and seemed so perfectly delighted to do so. He died a triumphant death and bore his long confinement and with great patience and fortitude though he suffered so intensely. Andrew said it was beautiful to behold his perfect calmness and resignation to the will of the Lord.

Mr. James Howle[119] died not long since. He was one of the old men. Mr. Vann[120] still lives and gets about though with difficulty. I think I told you that he married a woman about thirty years old some years ago.[121] Mr. Jack Kirven[122] died a short time before Mr. Howle. A son[123] of Dr. Rush Vann[124] came down from N. Co. last winter and lives at a place that his father once lived at, near his grandfather[125] and this summer he married a daughter of Lizzie Howle, his first cousin.[126] All of Lizzie's children are grown (five). This is the first one married. Mr. Dorety[127] has moved to the neighborhood of Antioch. Mr. Wilkins[128] has just returned from a visit to his son who lives in Illinois. He is very feeble but preaches still. He is going to live with his daughters. Louisa Norwood[129] lives in Charleston. Sallie is quite busy preparing to return to school there as soon as a killing frost comes. She sends love to you, Mrs. K., and the young ladies and says she wishes she could see you all says cant you send us your pictures. We would be very glad to have one of each.

I fear you will have to obtain assistance of all of the eyes and spelling talent of your family to help you in making any sense of this scrawl, but if it does cause trouble, it will be a reminder that we think of you out here. With kind regards and love to all, I remain, ever your friend,

M. CHARLES

* * * * *

Sallie Williams, who was spending the year 1878 at home with her aunt, Mary Ann Charles, shared with other Southerners an enthusiasm for Sir Walter Scott's novels,[130] *Marmion, Ivanhoe, The Heart of Midlothian, Kenilworth, and Quentin Durward.*[131] During the latter part of December, Mrs. Charles wrote to Miss Darby about Sallie's interests and about the family's plans for Christmas, adding a Christmas greeting for all of the Kolbs in Ringgold.

Mrs. Andrew Charles, Darlington, South Carolina, to Jemima Darby, Ringgold, Louisiana.

Miss Jemima Darby
    Care of Dr. A. Kolb
      Ringgold, La.

Dear Miss Darby

I was very glad indeed to receive a letter from you once more. It has been so long since your last. I feared the yellow fever had visited your family, and am very glad that you escaped. I thought of your family when it was raging[132] and read the accounts carefully but did not see your section mentioned at any time and hoped that it would not reach you. We have heard nothing from our relatives[133] about and in Bastrop.[134] The fever and cholera are both very apt to visit that region when it is in New Orleans.

You spoke of the numbers of your acquaintances who have died since you left. Their name is legion. I often think of the scores that I can count since I can recollect who have passed away and wonder why I have been left.

You spoke of the Harlees leaving their beautiful home.[135] They did it not from choice but necessity as hundreds of others were forced to do. None of our family[136] have been forced to the necessity of exchanging their large, comfortable homes for smaller, but numbers have sold them or left them unoccupied and moved on their plantations. I think perhaps I failed to mention in my last letter to you the death of Cousin Elizabeth Lide[137] which occurred on the 5th of September. Speaking of beautiful homes brought that elegant, but now desolate, one to my mind.[138] Cousin Thomas[139] and Willie, his youngest son, live there, so desolate. Bettie and her family[140] come down and stay with them as often as circumstances will admit. The funeral took place at Society Hill and the body laid away in the church yard.[141] The last member of a large family. The occasion was observed with the utmost respect. The stores were all closed and business of all kinds suspended for the day and everybody attended the funeral.

The prominent merchants except Mr. McIntosh[142] are still pursuing their vocations there.[143] Messers Coker[144] Smoot[145] and Sompayrac[146] Mr. Smoot still a bachelor. Mr. Som's oldest daughter (Lily)[147] married a son of Mr. Able Gandy.[148] I heard from Sallie Coker[149] the other day. She and Mr. Lewis[150] seem as happy as it is possible for human beings to be. Cousin Eliza Evans[151] owns a house and lot in Greenville and rents it for her board. She wrote to Sallie since her marriage that she would be down this winter to see her.

Bro. Horace[152] has a granddaughter[153] almost a year old. His eldest child is a daughter[154] and married a son of Mr. Edwin Dargan.[155] They live in the town of Sumter. Jonnie[156] is quite a prominent, young lawyer and was elected to the Legislature from that county this fall. He and family are in Columbia at this time. His[157] second child died, the next, a son, about sixteen is at school. Two little boys died after his birth while teething. They have two little boys living and have had seven in all.

Sallie is at home this winter. I am so glad to have her with us all the time. She is so cheerful and such a good help, too. She is quite happy and well entertained just now with a new magazine. She is an incessent reader almost and has been reading Scott's novels this summer.

December 23rd

Since commencing this letter I have heard of the death of Cousin Eliza Evans. Her remains were brought to Society Hill last week. She died in Greenville.

Sallie says if it were in the range of possibility for a good artist to come to Darlington she would have her photograph taken and send to Miss Lizzie[158] but most of the pictures taken by traveling artists are not worth more than the board on which they are taken. She would send it with pleasure. She did not have one taken while in Charleston. We would be glad to have a picture of every one of your family from yourself to the youngest. Sallie joins me in sending Christmas greetings to all. May you have a Merry and Happy Christmas and many returns of the same. Andrew would join me but he has gone to bed.

We are anticipating a jolly time of it. Sallie has invited a good many of her young friends to be with her. I have been busy all day finishing up the last cakes which were left over from last week. Will make Blanc Mange and Charlotte Russe etc., tomorrow. Have two fat turkeys in the pantry, two hams brought in ready for use, and will have a whole pig. I am finishing this letter for the mail by the man who goes to the Depot for a bit of confectionary.

I feel quite sleepy from my days exercise in flying around so you will excuse me if I give you but little news. I have heard nothing newsy or strange recently. We are having very cold weather at this time. The ground is frozen very hard and ice everywhere but there is water. Our hot house plants are looking well, blooming and fresh. We have some fine cabbages, very nice turnips and lettuce in our garden. I will use some of them day after tomorrow in making chicken salad. All of us are very fond of that dish. Sallie is very fond of such dishes as that.

I have heard nothing from Emily Taylor since I wrote you except through Florence LaCost. She said they were well about two weeks ago.

Mrs. Theodore Dargan's daughter, Dora, who married Robert Lide[159] is extremely ill with diptheria. Their child died with it.[160] The disease was contracted in N. Carolina and is not prevailing here. It is very much to be dreaded. I do hope we may not be visited by it. There is a severe type of cold prevailing now but I hear of no serious results yet. Sallie joins me in love to you all,

As ever,

M. CHARLES

* * * * *

By March, 1879, Mrs. Charles was filling her letters with family news, admonitions regarding church and religion, and discussions of the use of shad[161] for the dining table and guano for the cotton fields. Introduced into the United States in 1842, guano was the only source of phosphoric acid as a soil fertilizer until 1867 when South Carolina rock phosphates were discovered.[162] In 1878, 17,930 tons of guano, valued at $211,239, were brought into the United States from the Peruvian Islands[163] where the fertilizer was produced abundantly by excrement of fowls.[164]

Mrs. Charles and her brother, Horace Williamson, were the only members of the Thomas Williamson family alive in 1879.

Mrs. Andrew Charles, Darlington, South Carolina, to Jemima Darby, Ringgold, Louisiana.

Miss Jemima Darby
    Care of Dr. Kolb
      Ringgold, La.

Dear Miss Darby

    I feel as if I have postponed writing to you too long. Time flies so rapidly to me who finds plenty to occupy it that it passes almost imperceptibly.
    There is a dearth of news at present. I have heard of nothing of more importance than the burning of the old Jack Gee house which was occupied by his second daughter, Mrs. Zimmerman. The fire was accidental, caught on top from a spark.
    The planters are quite busy planting corn, potatoes and some are ready to put in their cotton. They are using an immense quantity of Guano. To show you how lavishly they are using it, I will give you the quantity that one who is not a large planter, Mr. Ras Kirvin,[165] is using. He purchased twenty-seven tons.
    Mr. Billie Vann[166] is still living and gets out to church. Mr. Doraty and family are living near Antioch. One of Lizzie Howle's daughters[167] married some time ago to one of Dr. Rush Vann's sons. They are first cousins, you know. The young man came from North Carolina and took his father's little place[168] near his grandfather's and farmed last year and married. I think they are still there. One of Lizzie's sons went to Texas last year to inspect the Country. Came back the first of the year, satisfied to remain at home. He bought a number of small horses (Marsh tackeys)[169] and sold them and made a handsome profit on them. They are energetic boys; good looking, too.[170] Mrs. Ann Fort[171] is in poor health. Mrs. Ferguson[172] gets almost at death's door sometimes and then rallies again. Mr. Dargan[173] still preaches at Black Creek. Mr. Robert Vann[174] came down not long since to visit his friends in that neighborhood and preached on the Sabbath.
    The Society Hill people are prospering. Cousin Hannah Coker's youngest daughter, Florence, married Terrill Rogers[175] about a month ago. He first married Emma Lide. She died at the birth of their second child. Left a little boy, Tommie

Lide.[176] Terrill bought the David Williams house on the Hill in front of the site of the factory and had the place put in order and it is a beautiful situation and convenient to her mother and sister. Willie Coker[177] and his youngest brother are going to put in operation at the old factory a large flowering mill. Miss Lou McIntosh[178] and Mattie[179] are the only occupants of their old homestead. Both of them are feeble. It was thought last summer that Mattie would not live but a short time but she is still living. She is about to get out to church sometimes. Mrs. Ellen Edwards[180] teaches a free school. Has forty-two scholars. Hartwell[181] preaches at Rock Hill, N. C. Janie[182] is about grown. Small and rather pretty.

The shad fashions have been revived. Shad sells at twenty-five cents. They have not been cheaper than fifty cents since the war. Old Mr. Sandy Bevil died the other day near the Hill. He was very aged. I suppose his age is not known. Mr. Burn[183] still lives at his home there. Lizzie is with them and Eddie. All the others, married and gone. Mr. Wilkins[184] went on a visit last year to his son who lives in Illinois and returned and is living with his daughter Louisa who married George Norwood[185] in Charleston. Mrs. James Hill died recently.

I am very sorry to hear that you are deprived of church privileges. I know it must be hard for you to become accustomed to that way of living but the Sabbath can be well spent in reading good books and entertaining holy thoughts.

I am glad to have Sallie at home but I fear I cannot keep her much longer than fall. She is speaking of going off somewhere to school. She feels as if her education is not completed. She looks very much like her mother from the middle of her face, the upper part; her eyes are large, very dark blue; her brows thick arched like her mothers. She is as tall as I am and large (rather); she has dark brown hair and a good complexion, not so fair as her mother was. She has a good deal of color and at times she is very pretty when in conversation and is antimated. When her countenance is at rest it is pensive and rather sad looking, but she is not moping, but very cheerful. She seems to be a general favorite. She is so kind and considerate of the feelings and rights of others and is always doing what she can to make people comfortable and happy. Just like her mother in that respect. I wish you could all know her. She is sending ever so many messages to you. Says she has one accomplishment that not many ladies can boast of, much less girls of her age. She is quite a marksman with a gun. A young gentleman came up the other day and shot birds with her. He killed twenty and she five birds, only missed two or three times. She is very fond of outdoor sports. Hunting, riding, fishing and cultivating flowers are her favorite amusements. We have encouraged the taste for outdoor amusements as much as we could possibly. I have kept her body well protected with the warmest clothing and thick shoes on her feet. She rides and walks in the coldest weather. She can walk and almost equal the English women. If we had not adopted that course, she would have grown up a feeble hothouse plant. She seems to have as good health as anyone now and appears robust. She has tied a little cluster of white lilac and a bud of the wild crab apple with a thread of her hair to send to you. I hope the lilac may keep fresh that you may see it. It is very delicate and pretty and fragrant. We have some beautiful flowers now. Our vegetable garden is coming on nicely, but it is quite cool tonight. I fear a frost.

We have just written to Jane Wallace[186] inclosing some fine tomato seeds. She has a nice family, two boys who stand first in school. She has four girls, fine looking children, large and healthy looking.[187] Virginia, Kate and Thomas[188] are still single. Brother Horace[189] is quite sick at this time with cold. His wife had measles and the little grandchild and its mother[190] are over from Sumter for a visit. They had measles too. It was fortunate that they happened to be over as little Ethel[191] was teething and having measles too. Was hard for her. She is Horace's idol.

The Wilds[192] are all well. I never hear from Emily but through Florence. She is in Spartenburg still. "Giggie"[193] is in school at Greenville. I hear she is pretty and smart. Andrew and Sallie are in bed but left kind messages for you. Accept a great many from me to you and Mrs. K. and the young ladies.

Your friend as ever,

M. CHARLES

* * * * *

FOOTNOTES

1 J. O. B. Dargan (1813-1882) had been pastor of Black Creek Baptist Church since about 1840.

2 Ladson Dorrity married Mary Vann, daughter of Mills Vann, Miss Darby's cousin.

3 Deborah S. Williams Dove Baker (December 28, 1807 — February 5, 1865) married (1) James Dove, and (2) Sheldon Baker.

4 Elizabeth Williams Ferguson (January 16, 1807 — May 6, 1885) was a sister to Mrs. Baker.

5 Mills Vann (1782-1875).

6 Ellen Hartwell Edwards (April 10, 1828 — July 24, 1902), widow of Robert G. Edwards, owned a home in Society Hill.

7 James Lide Coker (1837-1918), son of Caleb and Hannah Lide Coker, married Susan Stout of Alabama, a sister to John Stout, Society Hill pastor. Major Coker, a graduate of The Citadel and of Harvard, moved to Hartsville from Society Hill after the war, where he became interested in scientific agriculture and where he founded Coker College, a Baptist institution for women.

8 John Lide Hart (1825-1864), son of Captain Thomas E. Hart, was the founder of Hartsville.

9 Mrs. Robert Coker, "Early History of Hartsville," paper read before the Darlington County Historical Society, October 26, 1944. "John, who lived in Hartsville was a very energetic man. He was a sincere church member, giving his time, his means and his talents to the new Baptist church at Hartsville. . . . There is no memorial to him at the church he founded at Hartsville."

10 J. W. Burn (1808-1880) was pastor of the Hartsville Baptist Church for thirty years.

11 "Minutes of the Welsh Neck Baptist Church, Society Hill, South Carolina," May 13, 1877. "Jesse Hartwell Edwards was ordained this day. Brother J. A. W. Thomas preached the Ordination Sermon. First Timothy, 4 Chapter, 15 v. 'Take heed unto thyself and unto thy doctrine.' Brother J. W. Burn offered the prayer; and Pastor Stout delivered the Charge."
J. Hartwell Edwards, son of Robert G. and Ellen Hartwell Edwards, married Kate Watson, daughter of R. B. and Lucy McIver Watson, and was a Baptist minister in Virginia, North Carolina, and South Carolina.

12 Janie Edwards, daughter of Robert G. and Ellen Hartwell Edwards, married Mr. Remsburg, Fayetteville, North Carolina.

13 Jane Edwards Pressley, first wife of Dr. S. H. Pressley, Society Hill, was Robert G. Edwards's sister. She died July 27, 1851.

14 Emily King Taylor had indicated that they planned to move to near Limestone Springs in her letter of April 25, 1877.

15 Samuel Sparks, who was born March 21, 1787, was not quite ninety-one.

16 Ann Hurry Sparks, who was born June 22, 1793, died November 13, 1870.

17 Daniel Sparks, son of Samuel and Ann Hurry Sparks, moved to Louisiana, married there, then became a Texas resident with considerable land holdings.

18 Sue Sparks Keitt was Samuel Sparks's only daughter.

19 Anna Keitt, daughter of Lawrence and Sue Sparks Keitt, was attending Augusta Female Seminary, Staunton, Virginia.

20 Eliza Evans owned a home in Society Hill, a home near Greenville, and spent quite a time with her brother's family in Cooper's Well, Mississippi. Moreover, she visited among her kinfolk in all sections of South Carolina.

21 Dr. Peter Griffin, son of Thomas and Eliza McIver Griffin, had studied medicine in Paris, had been a medical officer during the war, and was a practicing physician until he received the appointment to the state hospital.

22 South Carolina State Hospital, Columbia, was established in 1821.

23 Sallie Griffin (October 9, 1828 — June 1, 1884) was Dr. Griffin's unmarried sister.

24 Walter and Harry Griffin were the two sons of Peter and Emma Griffin.

25 Ella Kolb, who married James Ashley Cawthon on November 25, 1875, moved with him to Wilson's Bend, on Red River, near Fulton, Arkansas, early in 1877. She was making plans late in 1877 to return to Ringgold for the birth of her second child early in 1878.

26 Maria Elizabeth Kolb was now eighteen; Mary Harriet was sixteen.

27 Red River Association met in September, 1877.

28 John Stout (March 12, 1842 — June 17, 1894) was pastor of Welsh Neck Baptist Church.

29 Jane Lide Coker Wilson (Mrs. Furman E.), *Memories of Society Hill* (Pee Dee Historical Society, 1909-1910), p. 9. "The pews in this building were rented, a custom quite general in those days in town and city churches, the rents being applied to the salary of the pastor, supplemented by other contributions. . . . There were free seats for those who could not rent and owners of pews always welcomed visitors to share their seats."

30 John Hugh Dargan (October 20, 1848 — December 6, 1877) married Elizabeth Ann Sloan Townes, Greenville, on June 5, 1872.

31 Edwin Charles Dargan, *Harmony Hall* (Columbia, 1912), p. 51. "It must have been in 1875 that John and sister Lizzie removed to Abbeville County in the upper part of the state, where he served as pastor of Damascus and Mt. Moriah Baptist churches until his lamented death in 1877."

32 John's children were Frank Townes, Evan Pugh, and Ella Dargan.

33 Dargan, *Harmony Hall*, p. 51. "John completed his theological course at

Greenville in 1872 and in June of that year married Miss Elizabeth Townes of that city, to whom he had been engaged since his college years some years before."

34 Richard Grandison Howard (March 13, 1832 — September 10, 1898), son of Charles B. and Amelia M. Cannon Howard, married Elizabeth Ann McCall (December 1, 1832 — May 2, 1911) at Marion, South Carolina, January 20, 1852.

35 Richard Howard represented Marion County in the South Carolina Legislature, 1858 — 1862.

36 William, Robert, Armstrong Jolly, Fitzhugh Lee, Amelia, Bessie, and Mell were the names of Mr. and Mrs. Howard's children.

37 William Howard graduated from the United States Military Academy as a lieutenant in the artillery.

38 Amelia Melvina Cannon, who first married Charles Brown Howard and who later married Dr. Robert Harllee, was Richard Howard's mother. She died February 7, 1877.

39 Henry Thomas (Harry) Harllee (June 13, 1851 — March 10, 1918) married Mary Hart McCall, on December 29, 1873, in Darlington County, with Dr. W. T. Thompson, Presbyterian minister, officiating.

40 Sarah Jeanette McCall (January 1, 1841 — May 6, 1914), daughter of Moses Sanders and Mary Elizabeth Gregg McCall, married Samuel James Nettles.

41 Samuel James Nettles (December 21, 1838 — February 5, 1879) and his wife were buried in Grove Hill Cemetery, Darlington, South Carolina.

42 Emma Eliza McCall (February 5, 1847 — May 8, 1909), daughter of Moses and Mary E. Gregg McCall, married A. J. W. Bacot; there is no record of a Betsey (or Elizabeth) among Moses McCall's daughters.

43 John Witherspoon, Jr. (September 29, 1818 — February 27, 1902), son of Elizabeth Boykin Witherspoon, married Mary S. C. Williams (October 30, 1821 — September 13, 1887), daughter of Colonel J. N. and Serena Chesnut Williams. They were buried in Episcopal Churchyard, Society Hill, South Carolina.

44 Sallie Williams, daughter of James A. and Caroline Williamson Williams, was the ward of Mrs. Charles and her husband.

45 George Williams McIver (January 1, 1825 — July 31, 1896), son of Alexander Markland and Mary Hanford McIver, married Harriet LaCoste on October 31, 1845.

46 Alexander Markland McIver (November 3, 1851 — March 21, 1930) married Julia Whilden, Charleston, July 17, 1873.

47 Flora McIver (February 24, 1859 — June 2, 1886) never married; she was killed in a train accident. Harvey T. Cook, *The Life Work of James Clement Furman* (privately printed, 1926), p. 321. "It was on the families of Dr. Wilson, of Cheraw, and Brother McIver of Charleston, that the terrible blow fell, which deprived them so suddenly and so grievously of two lovely daughters. Rushing with railway speed, from a home in Charleston to another home in Cheraw, in a

moment in the twinkling of an eye, these young ladies with four other victims, are in the midst of a horrible railroad crash, which leaves nothing to be told but the grim message 'the girls are dead.' Had the wires that conveyed that intelligence been themselves intelligent, they might well have shrunk, chilled and incapable from bearing tidings so exquisitely distressing. . . .

'Many die as sudden, few so safe.'

From their graves sweet memories spring. . . . May Flora and Hannah continue to live on, even on earth, in your improved lives of piety and usefulness."

48 Colonel Zimmerman Davis, Charleston, married Cornelia McIver, daughter of James Kolb and Sarah Marshall McIver.

49 Lucy, Hannah, and Cornelia Davis were the three Davis daughters.

50 Catherine Botsford Fort, daughter of the Reverend Mr. Edmond and Catherine McIver Botsford, was the widow of Moses Fort. After the death of Sarah Marshall McIver, Mrs. Fort and James Kolb McIver became engaged to be married, but Mr. McIver died, leaving his daughters in the care of Mrs. Fort.

51 Lucy McIver Watson, daughter of James Kolb and Sarah Marshall McIver, was the wife of Colonel R. B. Watson, Edgefield.

52 Reverend Richard Furman was the son of Reverend Samuel Furman and grandson of the first Reverend Richard Furman. He married Mary McIver, daughter of James Kolb and Sarah Marshall McIver and a sister to Lucy McIver Watson and Cornelia McIver Davis. Wilson, *Memories of Society Hill*, p. 9. "When Rev. Samuel Furman left us, we were blest in having Rev. Richard Furman, his son, as pastor. He was more universally loved than any former pastor. His preaching was tender, earnest, impressive, often eloquent, and impassioned. At the same time, it was instructive, well-prepared and logical and while strong and pungent was never harsh or denunciatory. He spoke the truth in love. Children loved to hear him; the colored people came in throngs and delighted to listen and to sing."

53 Reverend Samuel Furman was the son of Reverend Richard Furman I, and brother to Reverend James C. Furman, first president of Furman University.

54 Edward Edwards, son of Thomas and Margaret Marshall Edwards, married Julia Furman, daughter of Samuel Furman.

55 Mary Harriet Brinson (October 25, 1834 — November 16, 1894), daughter of Philip P. and Maria T. Nelson Brinson, married Thomas Jefferson Fouts, April 18, 1861. Mrs. Fouts was a sister to Mrs. Cawthon's mother.

56 James Alexander Cawthon, second son of James Ashley and Ella Kolb Cawthon, was born March 6, 1878, Ringgold, Louisiana, and married Maggie Mae Dance of Athens, Louisiana, January 18, 1905. He died July 6, 1961.

57 Maria Theresa Nelson (December 8, 1793 — December 29, 1878), daughter of John and Nancy Ware Hunter Nelson, married Philip P. Brinson, October, 1829, Natchitoches, Louisiana.

58 Olivia Watkins (1846 — July 23, 1920) married Haywood Brinson, son of Philip P. and Maria T. Nelson Brinson.

59 In 1878, the Haywood Brinsons had at least twelve of their fourteen children: Alexander, who married Mattie Simmons; Haywood, who died young; Olivia, who married Louis Raybon; Mollie (May 29, 1866 — April 26, 1935), who married George L. Beard; William, who married Laura Pullig, daughter of Sam Pullig of Bienville Parish; Cornelia, who married Charlie Henson; John Hunter, who died young; Thomas, who died young; Emma (1871-1940), who married Pemberton W. Miles; Virgil, who married Mary Sanders of Texas; Augustus W. (born April 3, 1874), who married Annie Lou Lester; Philip E., who married Geneva Van Zant of Bienville Parish.

60 Miss Darby.

61 Sparta was about 13 miles east of Ringgold.

62 James Ashley Cawthon (October 20, 1849-c. 1890), who married Ella Kolb in 1875, would come to Ringgold from Fulton, Arkansas, by steamboat. Ella had arrived earlier for a longer visit.

63 Lutie Head, daughter of the Honorable James Robert and Sophronia Prothro Head, married Parks M. Hammett (1857-1936) early in 1878.

64 If all the relatives came, there was a large crowd at the wedding. Mr. and Mrs. Head had five sons, Reverend D. F., Joshua P., James Douglas, George E., W. P., and five daughters, Mary A. Head Moody, Mittie Head Hightower, Alice Louise Head Tarver, Fannie Head Crowson, and Sophronia Head Mays. Most of Lutie's brothers and sisters had families by 1878.

65 Earl Fouts was the youngest Fouts child in 1878.

66 Dr. T. J. Fouts (February 14, 1834 — April 7, 1901), married (1) Harriet M. Brinson, April 18, 1861, and (2) Mrs. Pittman, of Athens. He was a Baptist minister, as well as a doctor. He belonged to the Red River Association; his name is mentioned frequently in Associational proceedings.

67 Philip Purser Brinson (December 31, 1802 — May 24, 1882), son of James Brinson, married Maria Theresa Nelson, October, 1829. Mr. Brinson divided his time among his daughters, Mrs. Kolb, in Ringgold, Mrs. Fouts, in Sparta, and his son, Haywood Brinson.

68 W. E. Paxton, *A History of the Baptists of Louisiana* (St. Louis, 1888), p. 332.

69 William C. Harllee, *Kinfolks* (New Orleans, 1934), p. 806.

70 Ella Kolb Cawthon had returned to Fulton, Arkansas, after a long visit in Ringgold.

71 Maria Elizabeth Kolb (May 30, 1859 — January 10, 1935), daughter of Alexander J. and Amanda Melvina Brinson Kolb, married Henry Jones Tooke.

72 R. B. Howell and W. U. Richardson, *Bienville Parish, Louisiana* (New Orleans, 1885), p. 1. "There are various denominations in Bienville Parish, but the Methodist Episcopal South and the Missionary Baptist are most flourishing."

73 Emily King Taylor had promised to write to Miss Darby.

74 Dora Dargan Lide (January 16, 1849 — December 23, 1878), daughter of Louis Alonzo Theodore and Maria Louisa Bacot Dargan, married Robert W. Lide.

75 Robert W. Lide was the son of Evan J. and Martha Miller Lide.

76 "Minutes of the Welsh Neck Baptist Church, Society Hill, South Carolina," January 20, 1878. "Sister E. E. Edwards and daughter Janie were received by letter from Hartsville. They had removed to that neighborhood two years previously and were now returning."

77 Florence Coker, daughter of Caleb and Hannah Lide Coker, married John Terrel Rogers; J. Hartwell Edwards, son of Robert and Ellen Hartwell Edwards, married Kate Watson.

78 Rachel Holloway Coker, daughter of Jesse and Rachel McIver Holloway, married Thomas Coker in 1843. She was left a widow with an infant son in 1846.

79 Thomas Coker, son of Thomas and Rachel Holloway Coker, married Ellena Hart. Mr. Coker's mother made her home with them in Society Hill.

80 Elias Gregg was a brother to David Gregg and Mary Gregg Marshall.

81 Eliza Evans (1807-1878).

82 Louisa McIntosh (July 26, 1834 — May 21, 1883) was an unmarried daughter of James H. and Martha G. McIntosh.

83 Martha McIntosh (September 29, 1848 — October 16, 1922), daughter of James H. and Martha G. McIntosh, married Theodore Perry Bell.

84 Margaret Douglas Sompayrac (1828-1901), daughter of Archibald Douglas, married Theodore Sompayrac.

85 William Caleb Coker (June 8, 1839 — April 20, 1907), son of Caleb and Hannah Lide Coker, married Mary and Lavinia McIver.

86 Edward Porcher Harllee (August 11, 1843 — February 25, 1878), son of William Wallace and Martha Shackleford Harllee, never married. He was buried in the family cemetery, Hopewell, Mars Bluff, South Carolina. In March, 1878, the *New Orleans Picayune* quoted General Harllee's letter which announced: "The spirit of our beloved Edward left its earthly tenement today at one PM. We are overwhelmed with the calamity."

87 Elizabeth Hannah McCall (October 4, 1826 — February 13, 1909), daughter of James Sanders and Eliza Ellison Lucretia Muldrow McCall, married (1) Thomas Baker Haynesworth (February 3, 1816 — April 3, 1861), and (2) Henry E. P. Sanders.

88 Louisa Harllee (June 12, 1839-193_) was an unmarried daughter of Dr. Robert and Amelia Melvina Cannon Harllee.

89 Sarah Elizabeth (Sallie) Harllee (December 8, 1840 — April 28, 1879) married James Furman Pearce, November 25, 1865.

90 Dr. James Furman Pearce (March 28, 1836 — August 28, 1917) married (1) Sarah Elizabeth Harllee, and (2) Louisa Harllee.

91 Melrose Plantation was near Mars Bluff, South Carolina.

92 Walter Cannon Harllee (March 18, 1850 – July 14, 1931), who married Mary Ann Young on April 24, 1895, was not married in 1878.

93 Henry Thomas (Harry) Harllee (June 13, 1851 – March 10, 1918) married Mary Hart McCall, December 29, 1875, Darlington County.

94 Elizabeth McCall (December 1, 1832 – May 2, 1911) was the wife of Richard Howard, a half brother to the Harllees.

95 Elizabeth Pugh Dargan (1842-1883), daughter of J. O. B. and Jane Lide Dargan, married Eldred Forrester, a Baptist minister, on May 15, 1878.

96 The Reverend Mr. J. M. Bostick married (1) Helen McIver (July 7, 1837 – August 29, 1867), and (2) Anna Rogerson McIver (November 15, 1828 – December 14, 1869). The Misses McIver were daughters of Alexander Markland and Mary Hanford McIver.

97 W. Q. Beattie, a Baptist minister, from Marlboro County, married Ann Terrel in 1828. He was about eighty-five years old in 1878.

98 Lewis M. Coker (October 15, 1819 – February 26, 1889), son of Caleb and Hannah Lide Coker, married Sarah Griffin in July, 1878.

99 Sarah Griffin (October 9, 1828 – June 1, 1884), daughter of Thomas and Eliza McIver Griffin, was fifty years old.

100 Saratoga Springs, New York, was a fashionable resort.

101 Dr. Peter Griffin, Sallie's brother, lived in Columbia, South Carolina.

102 Hannah McIver Mauldin, daughter of Peter Kolb and Eliza Chapman McIver, married Joab Mauldin and had three daughters: Emmala, who married Dr. Griffin; Dora, who married Rev. G. W. Greene; and Elizabeth, who married George Walter McIver.

103 Evander Griffin was the unmarried son of Thomas and Eliza McIver Griffin.

104 James P. Wilson was the plantation owner and storekeeper at Leavensworth.

105 Dr. Furman Edwards Wilson (February 17, 1826 – January 31, 1897), son of John F. and Hannah Kolb Evans Wilson, married Jane Lide Coker, June 20, 1850.

106 Jane Lide Coker Wilson (August 16, 1831 – November 22, 1920) was the daughter of Caleb and Hannah Lide Coker. Hannah Lide Coker, born on March 3, 1812, was sixty-six. She lived until May 19, 1900.

107 Dr. and Mrs. Furman Wilson had eight children: James Lide, who married Alice Bailey; John Flavel, who married Mary D. Evans; Anna Elizabeth, who married Robert W. Lide and was living in December, 1953; Marian Evans, who did not marry and died October 31, 1939; William Coker (1856-1953), who married Adeline Selby; Frances Pugh, who did not marry and died May 29, 1937; Edward Furman, who married Lily Kloman; Sue Stout, who was living in Society Hill, South Carolina, on August 10, 1953, at which time she answered questions about her family in a letter to John A. Cawthon, Russellville, Arkansas.

108 Elizabeth Sparks Lide (December 8, 1812 — September 8, 1878), daughter of Alexander and Jeanette McKarrley Sparks, married Thomas P. Lide.

109 Thomas P. Lide (July 10, 1810 — July 23, 1882) was the son of Hugh and Elizabeth Pugh Lide.

110 William Kennedy Lide was Thomas Lide's son.

111 Hannah Wilson McIver was the widow of Captain John K. McIver.

112 Fannie McIver, daughter of John K. and Hannah Wilson McIver, later married Colonel H. T. Thompson.

113 Colonel Zimmerman Davis married Cornelia McIver.

114 Dr. S. H. Pressley, Society Hill, married Sarah McIver, sister to Mrs. Zimmerman Davis.

115 Andrew Charles (July 10, 1827 — February 15, 1891), son of Colonel E. W. and Sarah Kolb Lide Charles, was Mrs. Dargan's nephew.

116 J. O. B. Dargan (1813-1882), long-time minister of Black Creek Baptist Church, married Margaret Jane Lide (1815-1886), Mr. Charles's aunt.

117 Reverend Lewis DuPre's first wife was Sarah T. Catlett, Darlington. She and her sister, Mary Ann, were close friends of Miss Darby.

118 Mrs. DuPre, mother of Lewis DuPre, was known in Darlington District, where she had visited her son and his wife, Sarah, in 1856.

119 James Howle (1799-1878) married: (1) Margaret A. Keith, November 21, 1824, (2) Mary Jane Kirven, May 19, 1836, and (3) Penelope Parrott McNeese, November 25, 1858.

120 William Vann was eighty-three years old.

121 William Vann's third wife, whom he married on December 19, 1867, was Louise Passmore.

122 John Kirven (July 18, 1791 — April 2, 1878) married (1) Nancy ——————— (July 18, 1792 — May 18, 1857), and (2) Parmelia ——————— (February 29, 1818 — July 4, 1886). All are buried at the old cemetery at Black Creek.

123 Josiah T. Vann was a son of Dr. A. R. and Fannie Cannady Vann.

124 Dr. Alexander Russia Vann (May 5, 1822 — October 22, 1892), son of William and Sarah Goodson Vann, married Fannie Cannady, March 29, 1850.

125 William Vann's place was near Auburn, South Carolina.

126 Maggie J. Howle (April 24, 1859 — November 13, 1937), daughter of Thomas E. and Lizzie Vann Howle, married her cousin, Josiah Thomas Vann, March 4, 1878.

127 Ladson Dorrity married Mary Vann, daughter of Mills Vann.

128 S. B. Wilkins (1802-1879) was once pastor at Welsh Neck Church.

129 Louisa Norwood, daughter of S. B. Wilkins, married George Norwood on March 28, 1858.

130 Frank Luther Mott, *Golden Multitudes* (New York, 1947), p. 68. "The Scott madness, far from being confined to eastern cities, raged as well in the South. . . . Indeed, it is probable that Southern readers loved Scott more devotedly than the people of any other region outside of Scotland itself."

131 William E. Dodd, *The Cotton Kingdom* (New Haven, 1919), p. 81. "Scott's romanticism and hero-worship suited their tastes and braced their social system, and he furnished matter enough for the longest of the idle days of a lonely cotton plantation."

132 E. Merton Coulter, *The South during Reconstruction. 1865-1877* (Baton Rouge, 1947), p. 258. "Then in the 1870's New Orleans was visited by a series of yellow fever epidemics, the worst being in 1878."

133 Anne Lide Wilds Ross (January 19, 1823 — April 23, 1893), wife of Major E. K. W. Ross, was Mrs. Charles's first cousin.

134 Bastrop, the seat of government in Morehouse Parish, is located in northeastern Louisiana, near the Arkansas line, almost 300 miles from New Orleans.

135 Harry Harllee, who married Mary Hart McCall, was living at Melrose Plantation, Florence County, when Harry Lee was born September 27, 1876, but had moved to DeWitt Hill Plantation, also in Florence County, when Robert was born in December of 1877.

136 Williamson and Charles.

137 Elizabeth Sparks Lide (December 8, 1812 — September 5, 1878), daughter of Alexander Sparks, married Thomas P. Lide.

138 Mrs. Ezra P. Lide, "White Plains, Springville," *Darlington County Historical Society Records and Papers, 1938-1944*, October 28, 1941, p. 138. "White Plains was the home of Thomas P. and Elizabeth Sparks Lide. The house was first built in 1822 by Elisah DuBose. Lide had the place from James DuBose who married Harriet Pegues. It was known locally as the Baptist Hotel. The home had the first piano in Society Hill."

139 Thomas P. Lide (June 10, 1810 — July 23, 1882), son of Hugh and Elizabeth Pugh Lide, married Elizabeth Sparks.

140 Leighton Wilson and Julia Elizabeth Wilds Lide lived at the Piney Woods place which Leighton had inherited from his Grandfather Sparks.

141 Mrs. Lide was buried in Welsh Neck Baptist Churchyard, Society Hill.

142 James H. McIntosh died before Miss Darby left South Carolina, on October 24, 1858.

143 Mrs. Charles referred to Society Hill.

144 Lewis M. Coker, now almost sixty years old, had just married Sallie Griffin.

145 Stephen Allison Smoot (September 23, 1817 — February 28, 1880) was the son of David and Sarah Thomas Smoot.

146 Theodore Sompayrac (1824-1911) married Margaret Douglas.

147 Lillie Sompayrac (August, 1853 — May, 1920), daughter of Theodore and Margaret Douglas Sompayrac, married A. A. Gandy (November, 1853 — August, 1932).

148 A. A. Gandy was a son of Abel Gandy, Sr.

149 Sallie Griffin, who had just married Mr. Lewis M. Coker, was a distant cousin to Mrs. Charles, and the families had always been good friends.

150 Lewis M. Coker (October 15, 1819 — February 26, 1889).

151 When Sallie Griffin was a child, her mother's cousin, Eliza Evans, had "adopted" her and had taken her to Mississippi for a long visit.

152 Dr. Horace Williamson married Theodosia Green, of Sumter County.

153 Ethel Dargan, oldest daughter of John J. and Theodosia Williamson Dargan, was born in 1877. She became the wife of Augustus Stanyarne Flud.

154 Theodosia Green Williamson (April 8, 1857 — July 12, 1946), daughter of Dr. Horace and Theodosia Green Williamson, married John J. Dargan.

155 William Edwin Dargan and his wife, Sara DuBose, had three sons, George William, William Edwin, Jr., and John Julius.

156 John Julius Dargan (October 10, 1848 — March 8, 1925) married Theodosia Williamson.

157 Here Mrs. Charles goes back to her brother, Dr. Horace Williamson, in order to describe the other members of his family.

158 Maria Elizabeth Kolb (May 30, 1859 — January 10, 1935) married Henry Jones Tooke, March 2, 1881.

159 Dora Dargan (January 16, 1849 — December 23, 1878), daughter of Louis Alonzo Theodore and Maria Louisa Bacot Dargan, married Robert W. Lide.

160 Leslie Bacot Lide (August 23, 1876 — December 1, 1878), son of Robert W. and Dora Dargan Lide, died when he was a little more than two years old. Pastor Lide was living at New Bern, North Carolina, but he brought the bodies of his wife and son back to Darlington to bury them in the Baptist Churchyard.

161 Shad is a food fish which is obtained from the large rivers along the Atlantic coast of North America. Fannie M. Farmer, *Boston Cooking School Book* (Boston, 1896), p. 182. "Shad always sold by the piece irrespective of size, which varied from 18 to 28 inches."

162 *Yearbook of the United States Department of Agriculture* (Washington, 1900), p. 337.

163 *Ibid.*, p. 278.

164 Lucius L. Van Slyke, *Fertilizer and Crops* (New York, 1912).

165 Erasmus Eugene Kirven (1858-1933) married Emma Blackwell (1867-1931).

166 William Vann (May 29, 1795 — February 25, 1881) was Miss Darby's cousin.

167 Maggie J. Howle (April 24, 1859 — November 13, 1937) married Josiah T. Vann, March 4, 1878.

168 According to the State of Carolina, Darlington County Grantor Index, Book V, 1806-1898, p. 498, William Vann deeded to A. R. Vann 308 acres, near Big Cypress and adjoining Fraser's land, on August 20, 1867.

169 In Texas, small wild Spanish horses were known as "mustangs"; in South Carolina, Georgia, and Florida, they were known as "Marsh Tackeys." *South in the Building of the Nation* (Richmond, 1909), Volume X, p. 137. "All of these horses were descendants of estrays from the Spanish horses or from captures made by Apaches and Comanches."

170 William James Howle, twenty-six, married Nettie Gandy December 24, 1879; Thomas E. Howle, Jr., twenty-four, married Frances E. Rhodes, March 9, 1875; and Lawrence Keith Howle, twenty-two, who later married Mary Ella Campbell, was single.

171 Ann Fort, the wife of Josiah E. Fort and the sister of "Aunt Nancy" DuBose of Society Hill, died in 1883.

172 Elizabeth Williams (January 16, 1807 — May 6, 1885) married Alexander Ferguson.

173 J. O. B. Dargan.

174 Robert R. Vann, son of Mills Vann, was ordained to preach at Black Creek Church in 1851 and left soon afterwards to preach in the northern part of South Carolina.

175 John Terrel Rogers (October 8, 1847 — January 18, 1912) married (1) Emma Lide, and (2) Florence Coker, daughter of Caleb and Hannah L. Coker.

176 Thomas Lide Rogers.

177 William Caleb Coker (June 8, 1839 — April 20, 1907), son of Caleb and Hannah L. Coker, married (1) Mary McIver, and (2) Lavinia McIver, her sister.

178 Louisa E. McIntosh (July 26, 1834 — May 21, 1883) was the unmarried daughter of James H. and Martha Gregg McIntosh.

179 Martha McIntosh, who married Theodore Percey Bell, lived until October 16, 1922.

180 Ellen C. Hartwell Edwards (April 10, 1828 — July 24, 1902) was the widow of Robert G. Edwards.

181 Pastor Hartwell Edwards married Kate Watson, daughter of R. B. and Lucy McIver Watson, Spring Ridge.

182 Jane C. Edwards later married a Mr. Remsburg, Fayetteville, North Carolina.

183 Rev. J. W. Burn (1808-1880) and Susan L., his wife (1811-1884), were the parents of Lizzie and Edward C. Burn. Edward, the youngest son, built a small

home near his father's old home, which is described by Mrs. Jane Lide Coker Wilson, *Memories of Society Hill,* p. 41.

184 Pastor S. B. Wilkins (April 11, 1802 — April 11, 1879).

185 George A. Norwood (October 23, 1831 — September 18, 1909), son of Joseph and Mary Warren Norwood, married Mary Louisa Wilkins, eldest daughter of S. B. Wilkins, on March 28, 1858.

186 Jane Williamson (August 4, 1836 — May 26, 1894), daughter of Mrs. Charles's brother, Samuel, married Thomas Wallace (December 6, 1828 — February 20, 1896).

187 Mr. and Mrs. Wallace had six children: Joseph Wilds, Leslie, Jennie, Anna, Estelle, and Lottie. Jennie Wallace married her second cousin, Thomas W. Williamson.

188 Virginia, Kate, and Thomas Williamson were the children of Mrs. Charles's brother, George, and his wife, Catherine Williams Williamson; they were Sallie Williams's double first cousins.

189 Dr. Horace Williamson lived at Mechanicsville, South Carolina.

190 Theodosia Green Williamson (April 8, 1857 — July 12, 1946) married John Julius Dargan.

191 Ethel Dargan, oldest daughter of John Julius and Theodosia Green Williamson Dargan, married Augustus S. Flud.

192 Sallie Williamson Wilds (September 27, 1845 — June 19, 1892) and Mary D. Wilds (November 23, 1841 — March 24, 1890) were the unmarried daughters of Peter and Julia Terrel Wilds. Sallie was afflicted; Mollie had been betrothed to her cousin, Hartwell Hart, who was killed during the War between the States. Peter Wilds was their unmarried brother.

193 Georgia LaCoste was called "Giggie."

The New South

PART II

To Mrs. Charles, the task of chronicling events of the Pee Dee region for Miss Darby in 1879 was a task which had "no beginning and no end." She would have preferred talking to writing. She could have "talked a month almost incessently" about growing things and pastors, about old people and maturing youth.

Babies born just prior to and at the beginning of the war were now young people, preparing to go away to college, and old enough to talk of love. Sallie Williams's best friends and beaux were the children of Mary Ann's kinfolks and Miss Darby's old acquaintances, the Williamsons and the Coggeshalls.

Mrs. Andrew Charles, Stony Hill, Darlington, South Carolina, to Jemima Darby, Ringgold, Louisiana.

Stony Hill
August 29, 1879

Dear Miss Darby

You have reason to think me a lazy correspondent. I had no idea that it had been so long as it has since your very welcome letter was received. Sallie reminded me that I had delayed answering your letter a very long time. When I sit down to write to you, I don't know where to begin or where to end. I feel as if I have so much that I wish you to know that I can scarcely have patience to write. I feel as if I could talk a month almost incessently.

Nothing unusual has transpired in our immediate families since I wrote. Nothing new or startling has taken place that I have heard of. The health of the country is good up to this time but if the weather should become very dry I suppose it might become sickly as we have been deluged with rain since the first of July. The early part of the summer was very dry and the "heated term" was long and unprecidentedly hot.

We have had very little fruit except melons. They were fine. We have a great quantity of grapes now. We will miss the peach preserves, apple jelly etc. We had bushels of plums in July, a fine salmon colored kind of Damson which never fails. I preserved and jellied a quantity of them and some water melon rind and tomatoes, a poor variety. Now I will make some grape and crabapples after frost and we will have to make the best of them. Andrew is very fond of sweet meals of any kind. I am sorry to have so small a variety on his account.

I am glad you saw the proceedings of the Convention[1] and the names of some of your old acquaintances[2] still among them. I hope you have your new minister established and that you may all be pleased and he may be a fixture in your church and build it up.

We have a good preacher at the church in the village, Mr. Alexander,[3] a graduate of Furman University. Mr. John Dargan[4] at Mechanicsville. Mr. Nappier[5] still preaches at Mizpah. On the first Sabbath of this month, he held a protracted meeting and twelve were added to his church. The baptizing took place in Black Creek, just above the bridge, called Rogers Bridge. I know you know the very spot and perhaps you have seen baptizings at the spot. You can imagine the scene. I did not hear of it in time to attend. I knew of the meeting in progress, but did not hear on what day the baptizing would take place.

Mr. Wilkins[6] died in June at his daughters in Charleston (Louisa)[7] who married a son of Mr. Joseph Norwood. They have eight children,[8] one married and has two children. Mr. Norwood is quite prosperous   does a large business as commission merchant. James Coker[9] is his partner. He has also moved to Charleston.

Cousin Hannah[10] Mamie[11] and Eddie[12] are all of the Coker family left at the old home, all married and gone. Eddie, it is said, fancies Fannie McIver,[13] daughter of Hannah Wilson. Col. Wilson[14] lives at the mill with his brother James.[15] Evander Griffin[16] is partner in the store and carries on the business. Mr. Wilson has given up to him pretty much.   Mrs. Dority[17] lives near Antioch.

Sallie is on a visit to two of her friends, who are to go off soon to school. Nancy Coggeshall's daughter[18] will go to Greenville,[19] Mamie Williamson,[20] daughter of Cousin Frank and Margaret McIver. Their oldest daughter, Annie,[21] is said to be the beauty of Darlington. Miss Mary Rogers[22] is still living in Alabama; has had a cancer on her breast for several years. May Haynesworth[23] has been on a visit to us all. She has two daughters[24] graduated at the high school in Sumter and her eldest son, Edgar Charles Haynesworth, will finish his course at Greenville[25] next June.

The old Sam Sparks[26] house burned down by accident. Took fire on top. Mrs. Keitt[27] and her daughter were in it but they could save but few things. They have been staying with Cousin Thomas Lide[28] since. I think they speak of going to Washington or Charleston to live now.

Sallie has grown quite tall and is rather large too, but she is not robust.[29] We are afraid to send her from home again as she was so ill in Charleston. She has a good Education, sings beautifully, performs well on the piano and is an almost incessent reader. I try to keep her visiting and having her friends with her and keep her from reading too much. Jane and Mr. Wallace[30] have been up. Leslie[31] just left this week. Nancy's oldest son[32] was to see Sallie the other day. He is desperately in love with her.

I have not heard from Emily Taylor in a long time.[33] Florence hears from them fairly regularly. F. is in Cheraw now on a visit to her sisters,[34] Mrs. Evans[35] Wilson[36] and Elerbee.[37] Mrs. George McIver[38] moved to Charleston soon after the war. They have but three children. I suppose you remember them, Zannie[39] Walter[40] and Flora.[41] The eldest is married. Mr. M. bettered his condition greatly by the move to the city. They were very attentive to Sallie last winter. She saw a great deal of them.

Robert Lide[42] preaches twice a month at Cheraw. Mr. Stout[43] is still at the Hill. The Union meeting commences at his church today. The church is in a flourishing condition. Mr. Dargan[44] preaches at Black Creek. There is to be a protracted meeting there before long. Mr. Billie Vann[45] is quite feeble. Mrs. Ferguson[46] is an invalid, confined to her bed frequently. James Williams[47] is a great sufferer, too, has lumbago or some afflication of the back (stoops as he walks and beard very gray). Lizzie Howle[48] seems to get along very well. One of her daughters[49] married a son of her Uncle, Russia Vann. He came down from N. C., lived at his father's place near his grandfather's. I think they still live there. Robert Vann[50] came on a visit to his friends last summer and preached at B. Creek while there.

* * * * *

As the 1870's came to a close, Mary Ann Charles was sensitive to significant changes which were occurring in South Carolina agriculture, industry, transportation, and politics.

Since 1869, J. L. Coker had been discussing the manufacturing of local products with the Darlington County Agricultural Society, whose meetings, during the 1870's, had been given over to improvement of field, orchard, and garden crops and of farm implements.[52] Cotton was being produced in vast quantities and was selling at nine cents a pound. In Florence County, Frank M. Rogers had already begun to investigate the possibility of reviving tobacco culture in the Pee Dee region. The Grange had been established in South Carolina in 1871, and, in a few years, the Farmers' Movement,[53] organized and led by Benjamin R. (Pitchfork Ben) Tillman, would make a vigorous entry into politics.

In 1876, Henry P. Hammett opened the era of modern industrialization in the state with a new textile mill, the Piedmont, which operated 10,000 spindles.[54] With the general expansion of industry, a number of new cotton seed oil mills were erected and developed.

Outside capitalists, as well as South Carolinians, were investing money in transportation at the beginning of the 1880's. The Southern Railway ran lines through the upper Piedmont section and took over many small lines which had been destroyed during the war and reconstruction periods. The Atlantic Coast Line and Seaboard followed a similar policy.[55]

Wade Hampton's term of office, which ended in 1879 when he was elected to the United States Senate, had been one of "unexampled activity and prosperity."[56] Lieutenant Governor William D. Simpson served as governor for only a few months before being named chief justice, and Thomas B. Jeter, president of the senate, took over as governor. In 1880, Johnson Hagood, "a Democrat, was elected Governor,"[57] and "much attention was given to agriculture, fence laws, the credit system, education and practical matters generally."[58]

In Louisiana, "agriculture had recovered considerably and crops were almost up to the prewar level."[59] The entire Democratic state ticket, headed by Louis A. Wiltz and Samuel D. McEnery for governor and lieutenant governor, won by a large majority late in 1879, and a new constitution condemning gambling as a vice and overhauling the educational system had been approved by Jemima before it was submitted for ratification on December 8, 1879.

But Miss Darby's major concern was with affairs of the Baptist Church. She was delighted to report that a satisfactory pastor had come to the Ringgold Church,[60] and that she had attended an old-fashioned Association,[61] where there was good preaching.[62]

Mrs. Andrew Charles, Darlington, South Carolina, to Jemima Darby, Ringgold, Louisiana.

Darlington
November 29, 1879

Miss Jemima Darby
    Care of Dr. A. Kolb
    Ringgold, La.

Dear Miss Darby

I have been too slow in replying to your very much welcome letter and when I do commence a letter to you I have so much that I want to tell you that I do not know what to say first or where to leave off saying. I will commence by answering your questions after looking over your letter. In reading over your letter, I find one question: "Who Mary Malloy married?" David Coit[63] who died in about four weeks after their marriage. Jimmy Coit,[64] the elder brother, married Sallie McLean. They are quite prosperous and have a nice family.[65] John McLean married Miss Godfrey who died some years ago and he has since married a daughter[66] of Mr. Sam Evans of Society Hill. Old Mrs. Godfrey died about a year ago.

Old Cheraw is recuperating fast. There is a Telegraph line to Charleston and a railroad almost completed to Salsbury, N. C., and more cotton sold there than at any time in antibellum days. Our old State is alive again and wide awake. Wonderful improvements in farming have been made. There are numbers of planters who make over a bale of cotton to every acre planted. That is wonderful for these lands. A son of Mr. Augustus Law[67] who moved to California just after the War has been on a visit to his friends and the home of his childhood. He said he would advise no one to leave this State and go there. He is prospering but not by farming. He has a lucrative office in a large town, forty or fifty miles from San Francisco, at which place, he and his wife, May James that was,[68] took passage on a palace car for New York where they met his mother,[69] and his sister Elma Player.[70] Their trip out here and back to their home cost them just one thousand dollars.

I heard through Jamie Williams[71] yesterday from the neighborhood of Black Creek. Mr. Billie Vann[72] has been confined to his bed for almost eight months and is nothing but a living skeleton. Mrs. Furgerson[73] is very feeble, in bed at times and up for a while. Mrs. Fort[74] is very feeble, too. Cousin Thomas Lide[75] is fast passing away, too. He totters as he walks. A dreadful accident happened to his son, Leighton, Bettie Wilds's husband.[76] His horse took fright and threw him from his buggy against a tree. There may be concussion of the brain. He had not spoken articulately in four days. His condition was exceedingly critical when we last heard.

About the same time, a serious accident happened to Furman Dargan.[77] He had a leg broken. He was on his way home to see his friends and while in Greenville, it occurred. Mr. Richard Furman,[78] his wife, Sarah and his youngest son are on their way to Texas where they expect to make their home in the future. Two of his sons live in Fort Worth and the other is in some town not very distant. Mr. F. cannot preach now (in very feeble health). Mr. James Furman[79] is still professor at the University at Greenville. Emily Taylor is in that part of the country. I never hear from her now. I saw Florrie LaCoste not long since but did not think to ask her about them. Georgia[80] was at the Female College, Greenville, last year. I suppose is there still.

Bettie Lide[81] told me to remember her most kindly to you and said that you were associated with her old home in Springville and with her Ma.[82]

I must tell you about the Harlees. Sallie Pierce[83] died in the spring. She was in ill health and sometimes became a monomaniac on the subject of religion. Miss Lou[84] lives with the Dr. at her sister's request and has charge of her children (two or three)[85] I saw Mrs. Mary McLeningham the other day and did not know her at first. She is much changed. Looks old.

I must rejoice with you on your having a fine young pastor at your church and your having had an old fashioned Association. I can imagine how you enjoyed the good preaching. Only those who have been deprived of the privilege can have any idea what a treat it is to hear good preaching and while in Carolina you were singularly blessed in that respect. I do hope that your pastor may never leave that church and that his usefulness may never cease. The Peony leaf reached me perfectly and I laid it away between the leaves of my Bible where I will see it as I turn over its pages and think of you each time that I see it.

Sallie is on a visit to her Pa now. She expects to be back before Christmas and have a Merry time as she expects to have some of her young friends with her then. Last year she had a dozen to spend it with her. Some of her Sumter friends will come this time. I think of you when I am preparing for these little parties. What a nice hand you were to make cake and pies, etc. I have a recipe now that you gave me that Mrs. Harlee made her plum pickles by. We like it better than any other because it calls for more vinegar in the making. They are not so sweet as others.

I fear I have wearied you with this long letter. If so you must excuse me for I want to tell you all I can. Our kith and kin are all in usual health. Very little sickness anywhere that I hear from.

Remember me to the family and love for yourself.

Yours as ever,

M. C.

Andrew would send a message to you but he has retired. Is always in bed early when we are out of something interesting to read. We take by turns to read a bunch and have finished up for this week.

* * * * *

In a short letter on April 24, 1880, Mrs. Charles described a sitting room scene in her home. With roses on the table and a new copy of *Harper's Magazine*[86] before them, the Charles family had only a bitter, but remote memory of war and reconstruction.

The April issue of *Harper's Magazine*[87] featured articles about English music and musicians, and Irish fishing villages. William Black's story "White Wing — A Yachting Romance," and Phebe Yates Pember's "Mr. Witherton's Romance" were included among the short stories. "Mary Anerley" was running serially. There was a lengthy scientific exposition called "Home Studies in Nature," and a travel story about the Far West entitled "La Valle Real de Santa Fe." Sallie Williams, who loved poetry as much as her Uncle Andrew, probably enjoyed the selections from the April issue of *Harper's*.

If members of the Charles family were interested in public affairs, they read an editorial regarding the army's determination to protect the Indians, and noted that the Pope[88] had recommended that the rite of marriage be removed from all civil jurisdiction. Sallie, the family musician, had an opportunity to look at pictures of the popular violinist, Madame Norman-Neruda,[89] and the pianist who accompanied her, Charles Halle.[90] There were no articles with religious themes in the April issue of *Harper's*, but Mrs. Charles provided readings about church affairs by subscribing to Baptist magazines and newspapers.

Mrs. Andrew Charles, Stony Hill, Darlington, South Carolina, to Jemima Darby, Ringgold, Louisiana.

Stony Hill
April 24, 1880

Miss Jemima Darby
    Care of Dr. A. Kolb
    Ringgold, La.

Dear Miss Darby

I have delayed writing to you from time to time with the determination to write the next day and I hope never to postpone answering your letter so long again. I have nothing of particular interest to relate. Andrew and Sallie are by the table looking over Harpers Magazine and I am endeavoring to entertain you with a very dry letter for there is a dearth of news at this time.

Sallie attended the Sunday School Convention which met at Black Creek Church this spring. They had a large attendance and an interesting meeting. The object of the Convention is to devise ways and means to increase interest in Sunday schools. All denominations have been quite alive on the subject for a good many years past.

You would not know where you were if you were to drop down in the new church at Black Creek now. The old people have passed away, most of them, and the congregation is composed of young people and very different looking from the former congregation. They have an organ and Tollie Chambers wife,[91] who was a Greenville lady, performs on it. Mrs. Furgerson[92] was in usual health. Mr. Billie Vann has rallied a little. Is able to roll about the house in a chair. Mrs. Dority's[93] family were at church. Mrs. Ann Fort[94] is very feeble. Miss Carrie Kirven was married in B. C. Church a short time since.[95] It took place at night and was attended with a great deal of ceremony.

Miss Lou and Mattie McIntosh[96] attended the Convention. They are very feeble. Mr. Alison Smoot[97] died since I wrote you. He was engaged to be married and the lady went north to visit her friends and he died in her absence, leaving the bulk of his property to his Sister Bettie (Mrs. Winters.)[98]

Leighton Lide[99] recovers slowly. Bettie was to see us not long ago. She inquired particularly about you and sends her kindest remembrances to you.

I heard from Emily Taylor through Florrie LaCost. She lives in Spartanburg. Mr. T. has a school and preaches. Georgia is at the Female College at Greenville.

I told you about the death of Sallie Pierce.[100] Miss Lou Harlee lives with the Dr. at the dying request of her sister and takes charge of the two children which she left. Sarah Johnson who was Miss McCall has been dead more than a year. I saw a son of hers last October. He is a handsome young man.

The spring weather has brought out the beautiful roses, etc. I wish you could see the vase of flowers that sits just in front of me as I write. I know it would delight you as you have always had an eye and appreciation for the beautiful in nature.

Sallie joins in love to you and kindest regards to all.

Your affectionate friend,

M. W. CHARLES

Our prospect for fruit is good at this time. I suppose we can safely hope to realize a good crop. Our hot house plants are looking very nicely since the warm weather.

* * * * *

In the spring of 1880, Miss Darby recalled that she had been away from South Carolina for twenty years. She wondered if she would recognize any of her friends back in Darlington.

Her nephew's children had grown up. Ella was married and lived in Arkansas. Early in the year, Lizzie and Mary[101] boarded a steamboat[102] and traveled for seven days before reaching Fulton,[103] the home of their sister and her family.[104]

Mrs. Andrew Charles, Stony Hill, Darlington, South Carolina, to Jemima Darby, Ringgold, Louisiana.

Stony Hill
July 19th, 1880

Miss Jemima Darby
Ringgold, La.

Dear Miss Darby

I was very glad to receive your letter last week. The time seemed long before you replied. I had no thought of retaliation in writing a short letter for I always write you everything that I can think of at the time I write, but if my last letter was short I must make up for what was wanting in length in this.

I will reply to your letter before giving you the general news. I am glad indeed that the young ladies[105] had a pleasant visit to their sister's. It is very pleasant to take a trip from home now and then, to freshen up, and then we appreciate home so much more when we return.

There was a new Baptist church[106] built in Darlington while Mr. Bealer[107] was pastor during the War. It is the handsomest church in the County, built on the plan of City churches. The fount is under the pulpit, carpeted throughout. The pews all have very comfortable, morocco cushions. Chandeliers, sofas, marble top tables, etc. It has been repainted and the yard improved recently. The lawn is growing rapidly.

We have had a disasterous drought. The corn crop is a failure. Small grain was very much injured too. The fruit is injured by the dry weather. A plenty of peaches and apples but none good. The late fruit may be better. We had a plenty of nice plums. I made a plenty of sweet pickles and preserves and jelly. We prefer the plums for making jelly cake to any other for the reasons that it is more acid than jelly made from other fruits.

I hope you had a pleasant visit from Mr. Lee.[108]

I scarcely ever see Mrs. Doraty.[109] I go to Black Creek only to our Association now and then. I think they attend Antioch Church now.

Sallie has been from home almost three weeks. I will deliver Mary's[110] message. We all feel as if we are acquainted with Dr. K's family but it would be difficult to correspond with any member of the family (and make the correspondence interesting). We know little about the country and nothing about the people outside of your household and they know nothing about this country or the people. I know that Sallie would be pleased to correspond with Mary if she could make the letters interesting, but she dislikes very much to write, and really, I must say, that she is not happy in her expressions with her pen. She talks well, and has been a good deal complimented on her conversational gifts, but she certainly is not gifted in letter writing. So I am afraid you would form a poor opinion of her from her letters. Please say to Mrs. K. that I would gladly send my picture[111] if I had one or could meet with a good artist.

I have never had but one picture of myself taken. Lou Williamson[112] has that in Sumter. I would be very glad to receive Mrs. K's likeness. An *old* one would be acceptable. If I had any picture whatever of myself I would send it. You spoke of the possibility of not knowing us. I think you would recognize many of us though we have changed. My teeth are out and I cannot have the courage to have the roots removed and a new set made. Dr. Ropp, Mattie McCowns husband, is a fine dentist living in Florence. He made a set for Bettie Lide[113] which fits nicely. Miss Lou Harlee has married Dr. Pierce[114] her brother-in-law. They were married and took the train   went north on a bridal tour. Dr. P. is in poor health. Sallie left two children and gave them to Lou and so she concluded to adopt the Dr. too. Harry Harlee[115] has built a nice house on the "pocket road" in sight of the old Brockington house. Walter[116] lives with him. H. is prospering. Walter is not steady. Mell Howard[117] and Mr. Whitna[118] live in Florida and have an orange grove. Lou Stephenson owns and keeps a large boarding house in Aiken, S. C. She was on a visit to her friends (the Millings)[119] in Darlington a few weeks since.

Sallie came home sooner than I expected and will write

Mary. I commenced this letter three days ago. Since that time I have heard that Mr. Burn[120] is at the point of death.[121] His health has been feeble for a long time.[122]

Mr. Max Gandy[123] died a short time since. Mr. Phelps[124] "turned up" at the Hill the other day asking to be restored to the church.[125] He went off and was not heard from in a long time and when heard from had joined the Presbyterians and when heard from again had changed to the Episcopal religion. He was destitute of employment, money and friends. The church made up a purse for him and he left for parts unknown.

May Haynesworth[126] is over and we will have a visit from her and her two daughters who have just completed their education. One of them looks very much like her mother. I suppose you remember how she looked when a girl. Both of the girls are quite pretty. Fannie and Lula. We will give a party on Monday evening and have a company of young girls to meet them. Sallie is just ready to write the invitations and desires to be remembered with love to you and the family and says to Mary that she will write before very long, but she will find her a slow and poor correspondent. I fear you will find this letter dull for I feel as if I have told you very little of interest. So I will close by bidding you good night. With love to all, I remain,

Yours affectionately,

M. W. CHARLES

Andrew is on a visit to Edwin Dargan[127] He would send a message. Enclose a few Apple Geranium seeds. We are having a plenty of melons, peaches and apples, but none good. The weather has been too dry. The garden has suffered for rain. Only a few vegetables good. We have had very little rain since April. Nothing like what the farmers call a season. Only light showers occasionally.

* * * * *

When Miss Muggie Lockett, of Ringgold, married Herman F. Scheen, a merchant of Sparta, Louisiana, in the fall of 1880, her father, James M. Lockett,[128] entertained with a reception at his home. Miss Darby was invited to both the reception on November 11 and the wedding on November 18. On November 9, she received this invitation to the party.

J. M. Lockett
presents compliments
to Miss J. Darby and solicits the
pleasure of her company on
Thursday Eve   the 11th Inst.,

Ringgold, La.,
Nov. 9th, 1880.

A week later, Miss Darby received a note inviting her to the wedding.

Mr. J. M. Lockett requests the pleasure
of your company at the marriage of his daughter
MUGGIE
to Mr. Fritz Scheen
Thursday Eve., Nov. 18, 1880.

A duplicate of the invitation to the wedding was addressed to "Misses L. and M. and Messers D. and L. Kolb." Both invitations were in Mr. Lockett's handwriting.

Miss Lockett's fiance, Herman Frederick (Fritz) Scheen,[129] was praised by an unnamed biographer for his business acumen:

He has been a resident of Sparta since 1871, is doing an excellent business, which is constantly on the increase and is a gentleman highly favored and respected in the community. He is a native of Handover, Germany, was born near the city of Osnabrunck, Prussia, Feb. 8, 1852. . . . Miss Muggie Lockett who became his wife November 18, 1880, was born in Louisiana and was possessed of a fine classical education being a graduate of the Ringgold High School.[130]

Miss Darby's reasons for retaining these mementoes of her life in Ringgold must remain a matter of conjecture. Perhaps she thought that Mr. Lockett, who could afford a classical education for his daughter, whom he gave in marriage to one of the richest men in the parish, was a symbol of improving cultural conditions. Perhaps she was beginning to admit that the rawness of the Louisiana frontier was disappearing.

While Miss Darby and members of her family were enjoying social activities consequent to the Scheen-Lockett wedding in November, there were unpleasant illnesses among members of the Charles family. Christmas had not been a festive occasion, but when Mrs. Charles was well enough to travel, she went for a visit to Springville[131] where she spent some time in the home[132] of Thomas P. Lide[133] where his daughter-in-law, Bettie,[134] was in charge of the household.

Mrs. Charles's letters of February 28 and March 7, 1881, were actually two parts of one letter mailed in the same envelope. The letter of March 7 was a lengthy postscript to the letter of February 28. The cordial greetings which Mary Ann sent to Melvina Kolb in her letter of March 7 must have been regarded with very little enthusiasm by Miss Darby's harassed niece-in-law. On March 2, 1881, there was a double wedding at the Kolb home. Maria Elizabeth Kolb married Henry Jones Tooke;[135] Mary Harriet Kolb married a widower, William Gibson McGinty.[136] As soon as the wedding was over, Mary and Mr. McGinty moved to California,[137] and Mrs. Kolb hurried away to Arkansas for the birth of Ella Kolb Cawthon's child about the middle of March. Both Mrs. Cawthon and her daughter, Flora, died on the day that the baby was born, March 18. After burying Ella and the infant at Fulton, James Cawthon and his two sons, James and Hunter, accompanied Miss Mell back to Ringgold.

Mrs. Andrew Charles, Darlington, South Carolina, to Jemima Darby, Ringgold, Louisiana.

Dear Miss Darby

It has been a long time since your letter came to hand but owing to sickness and other hinderances of less importance, I have delayed. In November Andrew took a severe cold and was threatened with pneumonia and before he recovered I was affected the same way. Sallie was on a visit to her friends and had to come home to nurse me and pretty soon she was attacked similarly and was sick a long time and got up and had a relapse and is just out of bed for the last two days. None of us was well enough to enjoy Christmas. We received some nice presents. I received a set of dinner knives, a pretty shawl and some other things. Sallie got a gold watch and chain, a beautiful cup, a pair of bud stands, a book of poems and some other things. I hope you and your family had a happy Christmas.

I have just returned from a visit to some of our friends in Springville. Bettie Lide has moved down to Cousin Thomas Lide's. He is very feeble and was living all alone and thought it was better for them to move to his than for him to go to them. Bettie inquired about you and sent her love and said tell you that she has kept up your sister's grave.[138] Just before she moved[139] she went to it and dressed it off again and planted some more flowers around it. The graveyard is being put in nice order.[140] Mr. Stout still preaches at the church very acceptably. I don't know that I told you of the death of Mr. Allison Smoot.[141] He left a legacy to the church. Cousin Eliza Evans left a thousand dollars also.[142] The town that you knew as on the hills looks pretty much as it did when you left it, but the business place is down at the depot. Quite a village has sprung up there.

Sallie received a letter from her cousin in which he mentioned Mr. Vann.[143] The old gentleman is still living but confined to his bed most of the time. Mr. Doraty[144] expected to move from Antioch down to Palmetto, the half-way station between Darlington and Florence to attend to business for Mr. Augustus Edwards.[145] Addie, their last daughter,[146] married some time ago to a young man by the name of Miller. She married well. All of them did equally well. Mrs. Fort[147] is very feeble, scarcely ever gets to church. Mrs. Davis, her sister, looks well. Jonnie,[148] her son, is married and lives with her at their home near Sully.

* * * * *

Mrs. Andrew Charles, Darlington, South Carolina, to Jemima Darby, Ringgold, Louisiana.

Darlington
March 7th, 1881

I see by the Charleston News and Courier that Lue Crawford's husband, Dr. Stephenson, died last week. She is in very bad health and has four children. Keeps a boarding house in Aiken, S. C.

Mr. Billie Vann was buried on the 27th Feb. I think I told you that he had been confined to his bed for almost a year. Quincy Dabbs[149] was buried the day before Christmas. He left two sons almost grown.[150] They are industrious, fine boys. Old Mrs. Hool, Mrs. Dabbs'[151] mother lives with them. Cousin Hannah[152] is the only remaining member of the family. She still lives, as for some time, with Cousin Jane Dargan.[153]

I am very glad you have a good minister[154] and that you enjoy his preaching and hope he may remain a long time. We have an excellent preacher[155] and flourishing Sabbath School.

Miss Susan Orr[156] is the oldest living member of our church. She never gets out now since the fall she got in the latter part of the summer. I think she fell a few steps down the stairsteps. It was thought for a while that some bone was broken but there was not. She is able to sit up and crochet pretty things and is very cheerful.

Mrs. Backhouse[157] is very feeble. She lives alone in the house that Mr. Wilkins[158] lived in near Cousin Evan Lide's.[159] The place belongs to her. She rents the out house and land. The woman who rents waits on her for part of the rent. She seems quite comfortable, has a great many kind friends to visit and see after her.

I heard from Emily Taylor through Florrie LaCost. She is in usual health living in York County. Mr. Taylor has a high school and preaches. Georgia is still in school at Greenville. Florrie has not seen her for a number of years. She told me that she had a good picture of their Auntie and Giggie.[160] I would like to see them. I was looking at Sarina Dargan[161] the other day and thinking that one who had lost sight of her for a while would scarcely recognize her. She is so broken. Her hair is almost white. Her health is good now. Mrs. Theodore Dargan[162] looks about as well as ever.

Nancy's son[163] who is so infatuated with Sallie is to go off to New York or Ohio to study medicine, I think, or some profession. Bettie Lide has two sweet, pretty daughters,[164] not grown yet. Her eldest is a son[165] and youngest a beautiful little boy[166] about six years old. Peter,[167] Mollie[168] and Sallie Wilds[169] live at the old homestead. In the division it fell to Peter. Robert[170] is building a nice home at his place about two miles from us. He has two little boys.[171]

Miss Darby please tell me in your next letter in what year you left Carolina.[172] I would prize a bulb of your peony from association with your family. We receive them by mail and express from New York and other places. You could seal up anything of the kind in a small paper box and put it in the mail. I would receive it as promptly as a letter.

I hope you may be able to spell out all I have written. My eyesight is beginning to be very dim. I usually write at night. Sallie would send kind messages to you and all of your family if she were present. Andrew joins in kind regards to you and your friends and accept a large share of my best wishes for your welfare in this world and an eternity of bliss beyond this life.

Your friend, as ever,

M. CHARLES

I send you a few flower seeds. If they grow, name one for Andrew, one for Sallie and one for me. A few tomato seeds The *Acme*. You may have them but call these the *"Charleston Tomato."* Andrew sends kind regards. Sallie joins in love to you and all yours,

As ever,

M. CHARLES

Please give my love to Mrs. K. and to the girls.[173] Say to Mary that Sallie will write to her before long. I told her I wanted to write to you first so as not for both to write at once.

* * * * *

Early in February, 1882, Miss Darby, who had just recovered from a long illness, announced to Mrs. Charles that she had passed her eighty-eighth birthday on January 30. She told, too, of the death of Ella Kolb Cawthon's young son. This event was reported by Pastor T. J. Fouts[174] to the *Rural Times.*

Died on the 20th of November, 1881, of Diphtheric Croup, after an illness of six days, Hunter Cawthon, infant son of Jas. A. and E. C. Cawthon, and grandson of Dr. A. J. and Mrs. A. M. Kolb, aged one year and ten months.

Just eight months since (March 18, 1881) the mother of this bright little boy was removed by death from earth to rest with the Saviour — then little Hunter was taken to the home of an idolizing grand-father and grand-mother, where he was the pet and joy of the household and was daily entwining himself around their hearts, and growing more and more interesting. But death, it is said, loves a shining mark, and comes alike to all sexes and ages, has again visited this household and borne away in his ruthless embrace, this little jewel; and now that little prattling tongue is hushed, the little footsteps are still, the little high chair no more occupies its place by the table of grandmother; and oh! what sadness reigns around the household. . . . Death is but the gate to endless joys, and little Hunter now rests with mother, whom he so soon followed, in the presence of our Lord Jesus. Wherefore comfort ye, one another.[175]

Mrs. Charles, who was an expert at extolling longevity in the Christian service and experienced in comforting the bereaved, answered immediately.

Mrs. Andrew Charles, Darlington, South Carolina, to Jemima Darby, Ringgold, Louisiana.

Miss Jemima Darby
Care Dr. A. Kolb
Ringgold, La.

Dear Miss Darby

I am sorry that you had not received my long letter that I wrote immediately on receipt of yours. I was just about to write to you again thinking that you could not have received my last. I am truly glad to hear that you have recovered from a long and tedious confinement. Cousin Thomas Lide[176] was similarly affected a few years ago. He was in bed about the same length of time or Andrew says that he was confined in his bed about six months. He is in a very low state of health now. His friends think him near his end.

And you have passed your eighty-eighth birthday. There are few indeed who can say that they have passed so long a life and one as well spent as yours has been. You have met with great kindness and attention throughout and to the present time.

I do sincerely sorrow with you all in the loss of your little darling boy[177] for I know how the affections of a household can be centered on one little object of the kind. We had one idol, too. Sallie's little brother[178] took convultions and died on his first birthday.

I do hope that Mrs. McGinty[179] may get home in March never to return to the land of gold and snow. Glad that David[180] found out that home is the best place.

The weather is beautiful and springlike. I have been out gardening again today. Have a good many seeds up. Sallie was walking by and looking over the asparagus bed and was surprised to find several long shoots up. I don't think that I have ever noticed a sprout in February before. I do hope that we may have fruit this year. I have been quite taken up for some time putting out grape vines and having the scaffoling extended to vines that are growing. They bore bushels and bushels of grapes on them. I make wine for our domestic uses.[181] I would like to send you some, if it were possible.

I will remember your message to Bettie Lide[182] She is closely confined at home now. Cousin Thomas is in bed now almost entirely. Mr. Dargan[183] is approaching his end too. He has been in bed for six months (most of the time). He has the family disease, Consumption. Mr. and Mrs. Beattie[184] are very feeble living at the same place.

I have heard nothing from Emily Taylor since last summer. I know that she is in usual health or Florry would let me hear from her. Georgia LaCost graduated with distinction at the Greenville Female College. Mr. Taylor has educated her. She is to become an assistant in his high school which he has established in Spartanburg. He has done nobly in that respect.

I have been contemplating a visit to Society Hill, but have been too unwell to undertake the trip, but my health is better now and I may go if I keep so well as I am now. I am thinking of visiting Sallie Griffin Coker[185] Ellen Edwards[186] and Mrs. Sallie McIver[187] who lives with her daughter[188] who married Willie Coker.[189]

Sallie says please ask some of the family to say to Mary that she has been hoping for a letter from her for about a year (but in vain does she look). Sends kindest regards to you, Mrs. K. and Lizzie. I hope that this letter may reach you in good time. I write immediately to dispell the thought from your mind that I was remiss in answering your letter.

M. CHARLES

My love to Mrs. K. and Lizzie and congratulations and a name for her little girl[190] — Estelle Charles. C. is a pretty middle letter.

Your affectionate friend,

M. CHARLES

* * * * *

Postal cards were introduced into the United States from Europe in 1873.[191] Mrs. Charles mailed only one card to Miss Darby; it was dated October 3, 1882.

Mrs. Andrew Charles, Darlington, South Carolina, to Jemima Darby, Ringgold, Louisiana.

                                          Darlington
                                          Oct. 3, 1882

Miss Jemima Darby
      Care of Dr. A. Kolb
      Ringgold, La.

Dear Miss Darby

It has been a long time since I heard from you. I hope you are still in health. Our family have all been sick and indeed almost every family have had sickness and a good many deaths have occured since I last wrote you. When I hear from you, I will write a long letter to tell you all that I think will interest you. All join in kind regards to you and family.

                    Yours as ever,

                    M. C.

* * * * *

Throughout her stay in Louisiana, Jemima Darby, who was almost eighty-nine years old, had professed a great fondness for her great-nieces and nephews and their mother, but her strongest affection was reserved for her nephew.

Dr. Kolb practiced medicine in Ringgold for twenty-nine years; his aunt lived with him twenty-four years. She exercised a strong influence over him, particularly in matters of religion. During his young manhood, he had practically laid religious thoughts aside, but, in 1874, partly because of his aunt's strict adherence to Baptist principles, he joined the Ringgold Baptist Church by letter from the church at Eufaula, Alabama.

His granddaughter, in an effort to preserve recollections of Dr. Kolb, wrote of him:

His home was a mecca for preachers of all denominations. The churches then were not supplied with resident pastors, often, but mostly by those who traveled from church to church. Hardly a week passed that there was not a minister of some church in his home, and in addition to caring for his own immediate family, he helped to care for his wife's aged parents, a sister-in-law, Miss Julia Brinson, and his own aunt, Miss Jemima Darby.

His practice of medicine covered many miles of territory through all kinds of weather and hardships even knowing many times there would be no compensation whatever for his services. Yet his larder was kept filled with good things to eat by those who cared and had no other means to pay.

His traveling was done by buggy and horse or horseback. There were many times when the weather was so severe with ice, sleet and snow that he had to send his Negro manservant ahead to clear the way for him. My mother has often told me of the hardships he had to undergo to serve the people.[192]

The people of Bienville Parish, whom Dr. Kolb served, were "Southern in character, hospitable, patriotic in sentiment and extended a welcome to the civilized immigrant from every land."[193] There were 5,455 whites and 4,987 Negroes in Bienville Parish in 1880. With the exception of twenty-one "foreign borns," all residents of the parish were born in Southern states: Louisiana, Mississippi, Alabama, Virginia, Georgia, South Carolina, Texas, Kentucky, North Carolina, and Tennessee. Of the 10,422 inhabitants, 407 listed South Carolina as the state of their nativity. In religion there were various denominations, but the parish was predominantly "Methodist Episcopal Church, South, and Missionary Baptist"; in politics, the citizens were "largely Democrats."[194] Sparta, Ringgold, and Liberty Hill sustained good schools. Dr. Kolb had reason to feel a kinship with such a population.

Indeed, the parish was advertised as a land of desirable contrasts:

To fully comprehend its beauties and advantages, and contrast them with its defects and disadvantages, one should ascend from the alluvial regions of the great rivers to the high lands of which Bienville is part. Here he will find productive hills as well as fertile valleys; bold springs as well as stagnant bayous; the stout oak as well as stately magnolias; dense pine forests as well as moss-fringed cypress brakes; and fragrant fields of corn as well as beautiful fields of cotton.

He will also find snow and ice in winter as well as excessive heat in summer.[195]

Fruit, game, and fish flourished in the parish:

> . . . plum is a fruit common in every household . . . figs do well with a little care . . . the grape, especially the scuppernong, thrives well . . . every farmer has an orchard of peach trees.[196]

Bienville has a liberal share of game consisting mainly of deer, turkey, wolves, ducks and now and then a straggling bear or panther, catamounts, foxes, beavers, otters, raccoons, opossums, minks, squirrels, rabbits, partridges, snipes, hawks and owls.[197]

Principal kinds of fish in the parish waters are trout, buffalo, catfish, suckers, gar-fish, bass and a variety of perch such as white, red and goggle-eye. . . .[198]

In Ringgold, there were places of mercantile business[199] where "merchants enjoy a fair share of the patronage of their respective locality."[200] There were three weekly newspapers in the parish, but the *Rural Times,* published in Sparta, was the most popular in Ringgold. Transportation was no problem because Lake Bistineau "rendered intercourse with the markets of the Southwest easy and rapid."[201]

State and parish government officials were not strangers to the people of Ringgold. Governor S. D. McEnery's home was in Ouachita Parish. The official directory of Bienville Parish included:

Representative	Dr. I. P. Webb
Sheriff	B. M. Manning
Clerk	A. J. Moore
Assessor	W. B. Colbert
Treasurer	Dr. T. J. Fouts
Surveyor	G. N. Clampitt
Coroner	Dr. R. F. Harrell
President, Police Jury	H. F. Scheen
President, Board of School Directors	J. T. Boone
Parish Superintendent of Education	W. U. Richardson[202]

Ben Manning,[203] the sheriff, had bought the homestead of Jim Cawthon's grandparents, near Springhill Church, six miles from Ringgold. Tom Fouts was Dr. Kolb's brother-in-law. The president of the police jury was Fritz Scheen,[204] of Sparta, to whose wedding the entire Kolb family had been invited in 1880. Judge John Thomas Boone, Mount Lebanon;[205] Superintendent Richardson, Sparta;[206] W. B. Colbert, Gibsland; Dr. Robert Fuller Harrell, Mount Lebanon; Dr. I. P. Webb, Mount Lebanon;[207] and George Clampitt, Arcadia,[208] were all Kolb's friends.

Yet, to Miss Darby and Dr. Kolb, Ringgold was not home. She, looking backward, pined for a South Carolina which was now altered beyond recognition; he, looking forward, fixed his eyes upon Texas and awaited his opportunity to go West.

FOOTNOTES

[1] The Southern Baptist Convention met in Atlanta, Georgia, on May 8-12, 1879. William Wright Barnes, *The Southern Baptist Convention, 1845-1953* (Nashville, 1954), p. 69. "The end of their reconstruction era came with the Atlanta Convention." Hereafter, there would continue to be a Southern Baptist Convention and a Northern Baptist Convention.

[2] The principal speaker for the Convention was Dr. James Clement Furman, one-time pastor at Welsh Neck and the son and brother of ministers whom Miss Darby knew also.

[3] L. W. Coker, *Historical Sketch and Membership Roll* (Darlington, First Baptist Church, 1945), p. 6. "In April, 1876, Rev. W. J. Alexander took charge as pastor and served five years when he resigned to accept a professorship in South Carolina College. Dr. Alexander was described as a man of gentle spirit, pure life, spotless character and strength of intellect."

[4] John Orr Beasley Dargan was serving as pastor at both Black Creek and Mechanicsville when his health gave way in 1881.

[5] George R. Pettigrew, *Annals of Ebenezer, 1778-1950* (privately printed, 1952), p. 61. "Rev. Robert Napier . . . lived near Mars Bluff, 18 or 20 miles remote . . . but he was punctual in meeting his appointments at Ebenezer via horse and buggy." He declined to serve at Ebenezer after 1876, but served out his years as pastor at Mispah.

6 Harvey T. Cook, *A Biographical Sketch of George Alexander Norwood* (privately printed, 1911), p. 39. G. A. Norwood's "father-in-law, who spent his last days under his roof, and whose unobstrusive piety and unselfishness made a lasting impression upon him, caused him to cherish lofty ideals for ministers. He was inclined to think that the good man's presence under his roof was the cause of his prosperity."

7 Mary Louisa Wilkins, eldest daughter of S. B. Wilkins, married George Alexander Norwood at her father's home in Leavensworth, March 28, 1858.

8 George Alexander Norwood (October 23, 1831 — September 18, 1909) and his wife had eight children: George A., Jr., who married Louise Hart; J. Wilkins, who married Vina Patrick; Sam W., who married (1) Lidie Goodlett, (2) Fannie Conyers, and (3) Marian Pack; Joseph, who married (1) Fannie Edwards, and (2) Albertina Buck; Sallie, who married Reverend D. W. Key; Lula, who married Henry Mullins; Clara, who married W. F. Watson; and Annie, who married Adam H. Moss.

9 Cook, *A Biographical Sketch of George Alexander Norwood*, p. 11. Mr. Norwood moved to Charleston, where he was in partnership with Bardin, Parker, and Company, commission merchants, investing the $25,000 which he had saved at Effingham. His partnership with J. L. Coker, Darlington, continued until 1881, when Mr. Coker withdrew. Mr. Coker had attended the Norwood wedding in 1858 at Leavensworth and was present at the fiftieth anniversary in 1908.

10 Hannah Ann Lide Coker (March 3, 1812 — May 19, 1900), widow of Caleb Coker, was the mother of Mamie and Eddie.

11 Mary Lide Coker (January 18, 1847 — November 21, 1929), daughter of Caleb and Hannah Lide Coker, was never married.

12 Edward Thomas Coker (April 17, 1850 — April 3, 1933) married Mary Wilson (June 17, 1861 — February 19, 1923).

13 Fannie McIver, daughter of John K. and Hannah Wilson McIver, married Col. H. T. Thompson.

14 Colonel Isaac DeLesseline Wilson, son of John F. and Elizabeth DeLesseline Wilson, married Margaret Jane Sparks, daughter of Alexander Sparks.

15 James P. Wilson, son of John F. and Elizabeth DeLesseline Wilson, was Colonel I. D. Wilson's own brother; Elizabeth Wilson Adams, John Jamison, who married Mary LaCoste, and Dr. Furman E., who married Jane Lide Coker, were his half sister and half brothers, their mother having been Hannah Kolb Evans.

16 Evander Griffin, son of Thomas and Eliza McIver Griffin, was a distant cousin of Mr. Wilson.

17 Mary Vann Dorrity, daughter of Mills Vann, was Miss Darby's second cousin.

18 Anna Coggeshall (1857-1942), daughter of Peter Collin and Nancy Wilds Coggeshall, never married.

19 Greenville Female College was operated under the control of Furman University and the Baptist Convention of South Carolina.

20 Mary Rogers Williamson (January 2, 1864 — ?), daughter of Benjamin F. and Margaret McIver Williamson, married C. B. Edwards.

21 Anne Eliza Williamson (November 24, 1859 — ?), oldest daughter of Benjamin F. and Margaret McIver Williamson, never married.

22 Mary Rogers (May 10, 1797 — August 28, 1879) was a sister to Mrs. Bright Williamson and a great-aunt to Mamie and Annie. Miss Rogers died the day before Mrs. Charles wrote to Miss Darby, but the news had not reached Darlington.

23 Mary Ann Lide Charles, daughter of Colonel E. W. and Sarah Lide Charles, was married to W. F. B. Haynesworth, of Sumter.

24 Fannie and Lula were Mrs. Haynesworth's daughters.

25 Edgar Charles Haynesworth graduated at Furman University.

26 Samuel Sparks, husband of Ann Hurry, died at the age of ninety-one on September 19, 1878.

27 Sue Sparks Keitt was the daughter of Samuel Sparks and the widow of Lawrence Keitt.

28 Thomas Lide's wife was Elizabeth Sparks, a first cousin to Mrs. Keitt.

29 Sallie Williams was almost seventeen years old.

30 Thomas Wallace (December 6, 1828 — February 20, 1896) was the husband of Mrs. Charles's niece, Jane Williamson Wallace.

31 Leslie Wallace, second son of Thomas and Jane Wallace, was Mrs. Charles's great-nephew.

32 Peter Wilds Coggeshall (1859-1932), son of Peter Collin and Nancy Wilds Coggeshall, never married.

33 Emily King Taylor was the only surviving member of the family of James and Hannah Bacot King, Miss Darby's old friends.

34 Florence LaCoste had only one own sister, Georgia, called "Giggie," who lived with Mrs. Taylor. Their father, A. P. LaCoste, had four other daughters by his first wife, Margaret Dawson Fort.

35 Ann Eliza LaCoste married Captain John C. Evans.

36 Mary C. LaCoste married Dr. John J. Wilson.

37 Delle LaCoste married Mr. Ellerbee.

38 Harriett LaCoste (July 19, 1826 — September 14, 1903) married George Williams McIver on October 31, 1845. Mr. and Mrs. McIver are buried in St. David's Cemetery, Cheraw, South Carolina.

39 Alexander (Zannie) Markland McIver (November 3, 1851 — March 21, 1930) married Julia Whilden on July 17, 1873.

40 George Walter McIver (September 18, 1853 — September 13, 1933) married Elizabeth Mauldin, January 13, 1880.

41 Flora McIver (February 24, 1859 — June 2, 1886) never married. Louise McIver McMaster, "Roderick McIver and His Family," p. 38. "Flora McIver met a very tragic death. In 1886, there had been some heavy rains on the Northeastern Railroad and when a train was crossing some of the benches on the north side gave way. Some of the coaches were pitched head end into the swamp and a number of persons were killed. Among these was Flora McIver." Hannah Wilson, daughter of Dr. John J. and Mary C. LaCoste Wilson, was also killed.

42 Robert W. Lide was the son of Evan J. Lide and his second wife, Martha Miller.

43 John Stout (March 12, 1842 — June 17, 1894) was born in Mobile, Alabama, and died in Dallas, Texas, but was buried in Welsh Neck Churchyard beside his wife, the former Fannie Coker of Society Hill.

44 J. O. B. Dargan (August 9, 1813-1882) was pastor at Black Creek until his death.

45 William Vann (May 29, 1795 — February 25, 1881) was eighty-four years old.

46 Elizabeth C. Williams Ferguson (January 16, 1807 — May 6, 1885) was seventy-four years old, and blind.

47 James A. Williams (September 3, 1825 — February 2, 1886) married Caroline Williamson, a sister to Mrs. Charles. He was Sallie Williams's father.

48 Lizzie Vann Howle (November 25, 1833 — January 15, 1913) married Thomas E. Howle on November 19, 1852. Captain Howle was killed at Sharpsburg, September 17, 1862, and Mrs. Howle had remained a widow.

49 Maggie J. Howle (April 24, 1859 — November 13, 1937) married Josiah T. Vann, March 4, 1878.

50 Robert Vann was the son of Mills Vann and the nephew of William Vann.

51 The letter is unsigned, but it is obvious that Mary Ann Charles was the writer.

52 J. M. Napier, *Historical Sketch of the Darlington County Agricultural Society, 1846-1946* (privately printed, 1946), p. 12.

53 Work Projects Administration, *South Carolina, A Guide to the Palmetto State* (New York, 1941), p. 61.

54 *Ibid.*, p. 70.

55 James Wood Davidson, *School History of South Carolina*, Revised edition (Columbia, 1894), p. 317.

56 *Ibid.*, p. 297.

57 *Ibid.*, p. 299.

58 *Ibid.*, p. 300.

[59] Garnie William McGinty, *A History of Louisiana* (New York, 1949), p. 230.

[60] Paxton, *A History of the Baptists of Louisiana*, p. 333. "The excellent practice of printing in the minutes the names and addresses of the ordained ministers has been neglected by the clerk for some years past; but the following list I give from the minutes and from personal recollections: John DuPree, J. F. Hinson, Wm. McBride, N. W. Warren, W. H. McGee, G. W. Singleton, J. W. Carswell, T. J. Fouts, W. H. Chandler, J. A. Walker, L. P. Lowry, J. A. Harrell, W. C. Moreland, and F. Courtney."

[61] *Ibid.*, p. 333. "Red River Baptist Association met with Pleasant Grove Church, Bienville Parish, September 27, 1879."

[62] Paxton listed several participants in the 1879 Association. John A. Harrell (1817 — ?), who came to Louisiana in 1848, preached at Sparta from 1854 until 1866 and at Ringgold from 1866 until 1871. In 1879, when he preached "the introductory" at the Pleasant Grove Association, he had been pastor at Saline, in Bienville Parish, for nineteen years. Moderator of the Association was Robert H. Burnett (1812 — ?), who was born in Edgefield District, South Carolina. In 1879, he was a deacon in Gilgal Baptist Church, Claiborne Parish. Later he became president of the Louisiana State Convention. D. H. Head, the oldest son of James Robert and Sophronia Prothro Head, was educated at Mt. Lebanon and at Georgetown Theological College, and finally moved to Ouachita Parish. In 1879, he was a prominent minister of Arcadia, Louisiana, and served as clerk of the Association.

[63] Dr. David Coit (June 6, 1829 — July 21, 1865) married Mary Malloy (March 3, 1837 — September 6, 1890), only daughter of Duncan and Mary A. Malloy. They were buried at St. David's, Cheraw. John Adger Law (ed.), *Citadel Cadets, The Journal of Cadet Tom Law* (Clinton, 1941), p. 165. "Dr. David Coit, Cheraw, taught school at Hartsville; was a surgeon, 8th South Carolina Regiment."

[64] James C. Coit (1832-1908) married Sarah E. McLean.

[65] The mother of David and James Coit was, before her marriage, Mariah Campbell, who, according to legend, was courted by Sam Houston. D. D. McColl, *Sketches of Old Marlboro* (Columbia, 1916). "Mariah Campbell, as a beautiful young woman, was well known in Washington society during the time that her brother Robert B., served in Congress. There Sam Houston, then youthful and gallant, met her and laid his fortunes at her feet." Miss Campbell married (1) David G. Coit, lawyer from Cheraw, and (2) James H. McQueen, Richmond County, North Carolina. She was buried in the old Stewartsville graveyard.

[66] Agnes Evans, daughter of Samuel W. and Alexina Wallace Evans, married John McLean.

[67] John Kolb Law, son of E. Augustus and Elizabeth McIver Law, Darlington, married Mary James.

[68] Mary James was the daughter of William Elias James, Sr., Darlington.

[69] Elizabeth McIver (April 3, 1815 — June 28, 1885), daughter of Evander and Eliza Cowan McIver, married E. Augustus Law (July 3, 1809 — July 27, 1882).

[70] Elma Law Player, daughter of E. Augustus and Elizabeth McIver Law, was the second wife of Dr. William Player, Darlington.

71 James A. Williams, Mrs. Charles's brother-in-law, had evidently come to take Sallie home for a visit.

72 William Vann (May 29, 1795 — February 25, 1881) was remembered by his granddaughter, Sallie Howle Campbell, as "extremely skinny and ugly."

73 Elizabeth C. Williams Ferguson (January 16, 1807 — May 6, 1885) was the widow of Alexander Ferguson.

74 Ann, the wife of Josiah Fort, had not been well since her son, Eddie, died during the war; she died in 1883.

75 Thomas P. Lide (June 10, 1810 — July 23, 1882) had just resigned his position as president of the Darlington County Agricultural Society after serving for twenty-two years.

76 Leighton Wilson Lide (October 8, 1838 — August 24, 1910) was never well after this accident.

77 James Furman Dargan (April 1, 1838 — June 6, 1907), son of J. O. B. and Jane Lide Dargan, married Mary Atmar Smith of Charleston.

78 Reverend Richard Furman was the son of Samuel Furman and the grandson of Richard Furman I. He married Mary McIver, daughter of James Kolb and Sarah Marshall McIver.

79 James Clement Furman (December 5, 1809 — March 3, 1891), son of Richard and Dorothea Maria Burn Furman, married (1) Harriet Davis, and (2) Mary Glynn Davis, daughters of Pastor Jonathan Davis. Mr. Furman was pastor of Welsh Neck Church, Society Hill, 1833-1844, president of Furman University, 1852-1879, and professor of ethics and metaphysics at Furman, 1881-1891.

While Dr. and Mrs. Furman were living at Society Hill, their young daughter died, and they wrote these words on her marker in Welsh Neck Churchyard:

Here lie the mortal parts
of
A beloved and lovely child
ELIZABETH WILLIAMS SMITH FURMAN
Who died 31 August, 1840
Aged 5 years, 7 mos., 5 days.

80 Georgia LaCoste was preparing to be a teacher.

81 Julia Elizabeth Wilds (June 24, 1839 — January 11, 1915) was the wife of Leighton Lide.

82 Julia Terrel Wilds (June 27, 1813 — October 21, 1876) was the wife of Peter A. Wilds.

83 Sarah Elizabeth Harllee (December 8, 1840 — April 28, 1879) married James Furman Pearce, November 25, 1865.

84 Louisa Harllee (June 12, 1839-193___) was still living in 1933, aged ninety-four.

85 The children of Dr. J. F. and Sallie Pearce were Robert Harllee, Annie, and Louisa.

86 William E. Dodd, *The Cotton Kingdom* (New Haven, 1919), p. 80. "But while *North American Review* and *Knickerbocker Magazine* seldom gained a place on Southern tables, *Harper's Magazine* . . . found many readers in the South."

87 *Harper's New Monthly Magazine,* CCCLIX, Number LX (April, 1880).

88 Pope Leo XIII (February 20, 1878 — July 20, 1903).

89 Madame Wilma Maria Franziska Norman-Neruda (1839-1911), Moravian violinist, married Ludwig Norman, but divorced him in 1869. In 1888, she married her accompanist, Sir Charles Hallé.

90 Karl Hallé (1819-1895) was a distinguished Westphalian pianist and conductor, who in 1888 became the husband of Madame Norman-Neruda.

91 Ida Cornelia Berry (February 23, 1860 — May 13, 1951), daughter of Dr. M. J. Berry and Eliza Donaldson Berry, Greenville, South Carolina, married Ptolemy Philadelphus (Tollie) Chambers on November 21, 1876.

92 Elizabeth C. Williams Ferguson (January 16, 1807 — May 6, 1885) was almost blind and her general health was poor.

93 Mary Vann Dorrity and family had moved into several different communities since Miss Darby left South Carolina.

94 Ann Fort was the wife of Josiah Fort.

95 Carrie Kirven, the daughter of Erasmus and Mary King Kirven, married Coit Wilson.

96 Louisa McIntosh, aged forty-four, and Martha McIntosh, thirty-two, lived at Society Hill, but never lost an opportunity to participate in church activities of the Association.

97 "Minutes of the Welsh Neck Baptist Church, Society Hill, South Carolina," February 28, 1880. "The Church and Community were saddened by the sudden death of Brother Allison Smoot which occurred on this Day, Feb. 28. Our Pastor being absent, his funeral was conducted by Rev. J. W. Burn on the day following."

98 Elizabeth Smoot Winters (1835 — July 14, 1915), daughter of David and Sarah Thomas Smoot, married J. G. Winters (1831-1910).

99 Leighton Lide, husband of Bettie Wilds Lide, had been injured in a buggy accident in 1879.

100 Sarah Elizabeth Harllee (December 8, 1840 — April 28, 1879), daughter of Dr. Robert Harllee, married James Furman Pearce, November 25, 1865. Louisa Harllee (June 12, 1839-193__) was her sister.

101 Maria Elizabeth Kolb was almost twenty-one years old; Mary was soon to be nineteen.

102 C. D. Morrison and Company, *Shreveport City Directory* (Marshall, Texas, 1878), p. 56. "Distances on Red River from Shreveport. New Orleans and Red River Transportation Company. James H. Jordan, Agent, No. 20, Levee, Shreveport.

Scopina Cut-off _____ 30 miles
Reuben White's _____ 55 miles
Coushatta _____ 140 miles."

103 Washington, Arkansas, *Southwestern Press*, February 18, 1880, p. 1. There were two boats, the Frank Willard and the Caddo Bell, which were making the regular run from Louisiana to Fulton.

104 James and Ella Kolb Cawthon had two children: James Alexander, two years old, and Hunter, born February 6, 1880.

105 Lizzie and Mary Kolb had returned from their visit to Ella Kolb Cawthon and her family in Fulton, Arkansas.

106 *Historical Sketch and Membership Roll* (Darlington, First Baptist Church, 1945), p. 8. "In 1857 the house, the frame of which was used in our present Sunday School building, was erected at a cost of $6,000."

107 G. B. Bealer served as pastor of the Darlington Church from 1851 to 1865, which period included the war, but Mrs. Charles was mistaken about the house having been built during the war.

108 Elder Starling Cato Lee (September 2, 1826 — April 3, 1886) was born in Wilson County, Alabama. Paxton, *A History of the Baptists of Louisiana*, p. 572. Mr. Lee was "editor of the *Baptist Messenger,* at Farmerville, later at Arcadia, Louisiana, a paper which by 1880, had attained a circulation of 1,200, and was published weekly." Elder Lee and his wife, Mattie M., were buried at Arcadia, Louisiana.

109 Mary Vann Dorrity had been reared in Black Creek neighborhood, and she and her husband had moved to the Antioch neighborhood soon after the war. They were within easy driving distance of Black Creek and frequently came back there to special services.

110 Mary Harriet Kolb, Dr. Kolb's third daughter, was born August 12, 1861; Sallie, who was born October 24, 1862, was a year younger.

111 Jemima had had her own photograph made in 1880 and had suggested an exchange of pictures between her family and the Charles family.

112 Martha Louisa (Lou) Rembert (June 12, 1831 — August 5, 1899), daughter of Colonel James English and Sarah George Martin Rembert, of Sumter, married Lucius Alexander Williamson, son of Bright and Jane Rogers Williamson, Darlington. She was, therefore, the wife of Mary Ann's first cousin. Mr. Williamson died in May, 1881; his widow later married the Reverend Mr. William Mood.

113 Julia Elizabeth Wilds (June 24, 1839 — January 11, 1915) married Leighton Lide. They now lived at White Plains, the Lide home in Springville.

114 Louisa Jane Harllee (1839-193__) married her brother-in-law, Dr. James Furman Pearce (March 28, 1836 — August 28, 1917) at Melrose on July 1, 1880, with Pastor W. D. Kirkland, Methodist minister, officiating.

115 Henry Thomas (Harry) Harllee (June 12, 1851 — March 10, 1918), brother to Mrs. Pearce, was married to Mary Hart McCall (July 20, 1851 — August 31, 1929) on December 29, 1875, by Dr. W. T. Thompson, Presbyterian minister in Darlington County.

116 Walter Cannon Harllee (March 18, 1850 — July 14, 1931) married Mary Ann Young on April 24, 1895. In a letter dated December 2, 1883, Mrs. Charles wrote that Walter was "a frequent visitor at our house." It is assumed that Mrs. Charles later considered Walter Harllee "steady."

117 Amelia Melvina Howard (February 4, 1834 — January 13, 1888) married Joseph N. Whitner, November 14, 1855, Mars Bluff, South Carolina. She was the daughter of Amelia Cannon Howard Harllee and her first husband, Charles Brown Howard. Richard Grandison Howard was Mrs. Whitner's brother.

118 Joseph Newton Whitner (November 14, 1831 — July 19, 1881) had been a soldier in the Confederate Army.

119 Members of the David C. Milling family, Darlington, were Lou Stephenson's friends.

120 J. W. Burn (1808-1880), first pastor of the Hartsville Baptist Church, lived in Society Hill.

121 "Minutes of the Welsh Neck Baptist Church, Society Hill, South Carolina," August 1, 1880. "Though not a member of this church, Rev. J. W. Burn was for twenty-five years identified with us and it is deemed proper to insert this minute of his death as a token of our respect for his memory. On the fourth Sunday in August, the pastor preached a memorial discourse with reference to Mr. Burn."

122 At his own request, Mr. Burn was buried at the church in Hartsville. His wife, Susan, was buried at Welsh Neck Church.

123 Max Gandy was the son of Booker and Delilah Gandy.

124 Miss Darby knew Pastor John Cheston Phelps well. He, a Northerner, had been pastor at Welch Neck during the pre-war days, 1855-1860, and had found it difficult to adjust to South Carolina ways. In 1862, people in Society Hill heard that he had married a "rich old maid."

125 "Minutes of the Welsh Neck Baptist Church, Society Hill, South Carolina," July 11, 1860. "The Pastor explained the visit of Mr. Phelps, former pastor, who wished to be restored to the fellowship of the church and be granted a license to preach again. He was examined by a committee composed of the Pastor, the Deacons and Brother J. H. Edwards, who declined to recommend him."

126 Mary Ann Charles, Andrew's sister, married W. F. B. Haynesworth, Sumter.

127 Edwin Charles Dargan (November 17, 1852 — October 26, 1930), son of Pastor J. O. B. and Jane Lide Dargan, was Andrew Charles's first cousin, and friend from their boyhood days. Dargan, *Harmony Hall*, p. 102. "He was a fre-

quent visitor to our home as long as he lived. . . . Dear Cousin Andrew. He was a gentle and jovial soul and is affectionately remembered."

128 James M. Lockett (August 15, 1826 — February 6, 1901) was born in Morengo County, Alabama, and is buried in Springville Cemetery, Coushatta, Louisiana.

129 Herman F. Scheen (February 8, 1852 — May 2, 1925) married (1) Muggie Lockett, and (2) Mattie Gowen.

130 *Biographical and Historical Memoirs of Northwest Louisiana* (Chicago, 1890), p. 199.

131 Robert Ervin Coker, "Springville: A Summer Village of Old Darlington District," *South Carolina Historical Magazine*, LIII, Number 4 (October, 1952), p. 190. "Springville probably originated when someone from the Mechanicsville section of Darlington District discovered the advantages of an elevated pineland with sandy soil that would not hold water in puddles, that had uncounted springs of pure mineral waters, and a fine large creek with cool, clean water and firm sandbars for bathing. . . . As Springville was never incorporated, it had no precise boundaries. It was simply the region east of Black Creek from about Hood's Bridge, a couple of miles from Darlington, S. C., northward to about a mile beyond Lide's Bridge; and thence westward across Black Creek to include the residences of T. P. Lide. . . . and others."

132 *Ibid.*, p. 209. "The T. P. Lide home was called White Plains. . . . The . . . home was bought by Isaiah DuBose, who built in 1822 the large home now standing . . . the glass enclosed cupola on top was removed a long time ago, as well as the detached 'Library' at the side of the large front yard. A broad veranda, or piazza, extends across the front, and along most of the two sides. The pleasing front door under a glass 'fan', the French windows, the ornamental porch railing, the eaves brackets and the chimneys, show the thought in architectural design. Within, were paneled wainscoting, mahogany-railed stairway, neatly molded mantels and trim of doors and windows, and plaster cornicing."

133 *Ibid.*, p. 208. "Although not a preacher, Mr. Lide, in the strongly religious communities with which he was associated, was particularly active and prominent in church work, as well as in public affairs. At Furman University . . . he is reputed to have been an effective speaker, distinguished for both humor and seriousness in the presentation of earnest convictions."

134 *Ibid.*, p. 210. Henry DuBose "sold the place to Mr. T. P. Lide, from which it passed to his son, Leighton and wife, Bettie Wilds Lide, and then to their children. Mrs. Bettie Lide, so widely esteemed for her exceptional poise, intelligence and charm, besides keeping a beautiful home and garden, seemed to read widely and to be always alert to what went on out-of-doors with the flowers and birds."

135 Henry Jones Tooke (June 21, 1854 — August 26, 1934), son of John and Anna Nixon Vickers Tooke, was born near Ringgold soon after his parents migrated to Louisiana from Thomas County, Georgia.

136 William Gibson McGinty (July 21, 1852 — June 17, 1939) had three small children by his first wife, Emma Smith: a daughter, Genevria; and two sons, Eugene, former mayor of Salt Lake City, Utah, and Oliver.

137 Mr. and Mrs. McGinty were living in Rosita, Custer County, California, when their first child, Vivian Kolb McGinty, was born on December 19, 1881.

138 Mary Darby (January 6, 1796 — July 18, 1858) was buried in Welsh Neck Baptist Churchyard, Society Hill, South Carolina.

139 Leighton and Bettie Wilds Lide lived near Society Hill before their move to White Plains.

140 "Minutes of the Welsh Neck Baptist Church, Society Hill, South Carolina," July 11, 1880. "It was resolved to put the cemetery in order and a committee composed of Pastor Stout, the Deacons, P. Hamilton Rogers, Miss Louisa McIntosh, and Mrs. L. M. Coker was named."

141 Ibid. "W. C. Coker, executor of the estate of A. Smoot, informed the church that the will provided that $400.00 be transferred to the church for the purposes of keeping the cemetery in order, the interest only to be used." Allison Smoot, a bachelor, was the son of David and Sarah Thomas Smoot.

142 Ibid., February 28, 1880. "A committee was named as trustees of the fund left to the church by Sister Eliza Evans, composed of L. M. Coker, W. C. Coker, Dr. S. H. Pressley, J. T. Rogers, and Allison Smoot."

143 William Vann died on February 25, before Mrs. Charles's letter reached Miss Darby.

144 Ladson A. Dorrity married Mary Vann, daughter of Mills Vann.

145 Augustus F. Edwards married Bettie Hart on December 29, 1858.

146 Addie Dorrity, daughter of Ladson and Mary Dorrity, married Mr. Miller.

147 Ann DuBose Fort, widow of Josiah Fort, died in 1883.

148 Mrs. Charles must have meant Charles Davis; John Davis, Jr., died in Virginia at the beginning of the war.

149 J. Quincy Dabbs (1825-1880), the son of Samuel and Sarah L. Grove Dabbs, married Eufronia Hoole.

150 James H. Dabbs (1865-1885) was buried beside his father in the Presbyterian Churchyard, Darlington.

151 Eufronia Hoole married J. Quincy Dabbs.

152 Hannah Elizabeth Dabbs (1814-1893) was a sister to J. Quincy Dabbs. Dargan, Harmony Hall, p. 16. "This estimable lady was a distant kinswoman and devoted friend of Jane Lide. . . . She never married, but was always mother number two at Harmony Hall. She was one of the most unselfish, affectionate and loyal of women. During my father's frequent absences, during sickness, and for hundreds of little household details, her company and help were an invaluable aid to the busy and overburdened mother."

153 Margaret Jane Frances Lide (November 10, 1815 — March 16, 1886) married J. O. B. Dargan June 13, 1837. She was the daughter of Hugh and Elizabeth Pugh Lide.

154 Dr. T. J. Fouts of Sparta, Melvina Kolb's brother-in-law, preached at Ringgold during this period.

155 W. J. Alexander was pastor of the Darlington Baptist Church from 1876 until 1881.

156 Susannah E. W. Orr was a signer of the Covenant of the Baptist Church at Ebenezer, in Darlington District, in January, 1823. She was granted a letter of dismissal to unite with the Darlington Church early in 1838.
Hannah B. Hart and Minnie D. Townsend, "Homes of Old Darlington," *Darlington County Historical Society Records and Papers, 1938-1944*, October 28, 1941, p. 96. "For years there lived in the Woods home a very old lady, Miss Susan Orr, a devout Christian. She organized and was first president of the local Baptist Missionary Society. She died in November, 1883."

157 Edith M. A. Woods Bacchus (spelled Backhouse, Baccus, Bakehouse, and Bacchus), widow of Pastor J. A. Bacchus, was the aunt of Peter Brunson's sons, being the sister of their mother, Susanna Pamela Woods Brunson. Robert E. Coker, "Springville: A Summer Village of Old Darlington District," p. 194. "Later the Wilkins home was occupied by Mrs. Bacchus, widow of a Baptist minister. In my boyhood it was known locally as the 'Bacchus place,' a small house had then replaced the original one that had burned."

158 Pastor S. B. Wilkins had died in Charleston April 11, 1879.

159 Evan James Lide (March 18, 1802 — September 9, 1882), son of Hugh and Elizabeth Pugh Lide, married (1) Margaret Ervin, (2) Martha Miller, and (3) Mrs. Lavinia Eason.

160 Emily King Taylor and Georgia LaCoste.

161 Serena Leslie Bacot Dargan was forty-eight years old.

162 Louisa Bacot Dargan, wife of Dr. Theodore Dargan, was Mrs. Serena Dargan's sister.

163 Peter Wilds Coggeshall (1859 — July, 1932) never married.

164 Julia and Bessie Lide.

165 Marion Lide married his cousin, Mary Coggeshall.

166 Roland Lide.

167 Peter Wilds, who never married, was known to the community as "Uncle Pete."

168 Mary D. Wilds (November 23, 1841 — March 24, 1890) never married.

169 Sallie Williamson Wilds (September 27, 1845 — June 19, 1892) never married.

170 Robert Wilds, youngest son of Peter and Julia Terrel Wilds, married Eliza Hart.

171 Terrel and Robert Hartwell Wilds were the sons of Robert and Eliza Hart Wilds; their daughter, Annie, was the second wife of Arthur H. Rogers.

172 Jemima Darby left Leavensworth, South Carolina, early in April, 1860.

[173] Mrs. Charles seemed not to have known that "the girls" had married on March 2.

[174] Dr. Thomas Jefferson Fouts (February 14, 1834 — April 7, 1901) married (1) Harriet M. Brinson, and (2) Mrs. Pittman, of Athens. Mrs. Harriet Fouts was young Hunter Cawthon's great-aunt, and Dr. Fouts was the pastor at the Ringgold Baptist Church.

[175] Sparta, Louisiana, *Rural Times,* December, 1881.

[176] Thomas P. Lide (June 10, 1810 — July 23, 1882) married Elizabeth Sparks.

[177] Hunter Cawthon (February 6, 1880 — November 20, 1881) was buried at Providence Cemetery, Ringgold, beside his brother, who died in 1876.

[178] James Leon Williams (November 18, 1860 — November 5, 1861), who died before Sallie was born, would have been twenty-one years old if he had lived.

[179] Mary Kolb McGinty and her family were living in Custer County, California.

[180] David Alexander Kolb (July 1, 1863 — March 20, 1916), son of Dr. and Mrs. A. J. Kolb, married Celina Valois, Marksville, Louisiana, in 1894.

[181] *Historical Sketch and Membership Roll,* Darlington, First Baptist Church, 1945, "Church Covenant," p. 9. "We also engage to . . . abstain from the sale and use of intoxicating drinks as a beverage." Domestic uses of wine by Mrs. Charles probably meant medicinal uses.

[182] Bettie Wilds Lide was busy at White Plains with an ill father-in-law and a husband who had not recovered from a buggy accident.

[183] Pastor J. O. B. Dargan, who was sixty-nine, died in 1882.

[184] W. Q. Beattie and Ann Terrel Beattie, of Marlboro County, who had been married in 1828, were old friends of Miss Darby. Mr. Beattie had been pastor in Darlington in 1831-1834 and again in 1837-1838. *Historical Sketch,* p. 4. "Mr. Beattie was well equipped for the work and he is described as a gentle, lovable man who was greatly blessed in his ministry. . . . While he was pastor in 1832, there was a great revival in Darlington and many joined the Baptist, Methodist and Presbyterian churches, the pastors of the Psedo-Baptist churches immersing their candidates also."

[185] Sarah Griffin Coker (October 9, 1828 — June 1, 1884) was the wife of Lewis Coker.

[186] Ellen Hartwell Edwards (April 10, 1828 — July 24, 1902) was the widow of Robert G. Edwards.

[187] Sallie Ervin McIver (June 30, 1826 — October 30, 1897) was the widow of Allen McIver.

[188] Mary McIver Coker died in 1883.

[189] William Caleb Coker (1839-1907) married (1) Mary McIver, and (2) Lavinia McIver.

190 Mary Ella Tooke was born January 22, 1882. The suggestion for a name came from South Carolina too late. The Tookes had already named the baby for Mary Kolb McGinty and for Ella Kolb Cawthon. She was called Ella, and married David K. Thomas on June 23, 1908. Mrs. Thomas was living in Ringgold in 1965.

191 Richard B. Morris (ed.), *Encyclopedia of American History* (New York, 1953), p. 431.

192 Ida G. Tooke, "Some North Louisiana Pioneers," November 20, 1952.

193 Howell and Richardson, *Bienville Parish, Louisiana*, p. 4.

194 *Ibid.*, p. 5.

195 *Ibid.*, p. 3.

196 *Ibid.*, p. 13.

197 *Ibid.*, p. 15.

198 *Ibid.*, p. 17.

199 F. H. Tompkins, *North Louisiana* (Cincinnati, 1886), p. 149. "The trade of the place is large and largely absorbed by J. A. Sledge, a merchant of means and a self-made man. . . . He has a handsome brick store."

200 Howell and Richardson, *Bienville Parish, Louisiana*, p. 6.

201 *Ibid.*, p. 8.

202 *Ibid.*, p. 26.

203 Ben M. Manning (October 20, 1834 — October 31, 1918) was a sergeant in Company C, Fourth Louisiana Cavalry, C. S. A. His wife, Mary Meek, died December 27, 1899, at the age of fifty-nine. They were buried at Providence Cemetery, Ringgold.

204 Herman Frederick Scheen (February 8, 1852 — May 2, 1925) married Muggie Lockett, Ringgold, November 20, 1880. Their oldest son, Henry, born November 10, 1881, was buried at Sparta on September 11, 1883. Muggie L. Scheen died in 1886, and on February 15, 1887, Mr. Scheen married Mattie Gowen (June 9, 1860 — February 5, 1929) at Arcadia. Mr. Scheen and his second wife are buried at Camp Ground Cemetery, near Bienville, Louisiana.

205 John Thomas Boone (December 28, 1840 — January 23, 1913) married Celesta L. Shipp (November 30, 1847 — May 1, 1899).

206 W. U. Richardson was still living in Sparta when his wife, the former Alice Tarver (February 6, 1853 — March 10, 1890), died. She is buried at the Sparta Cemetery.

207 Dr. I. P. Webb (January 25, 1833 — January 5, 1911) and his wife, Frances N. (October 23, 1838 — December 1, 1903), are buried at Mt. Lebanon, La.

208 Pastor George N. Clampitt (September 7, 1813 — March 4, 1896) and his wife, Mary N. (February 4, 1822 — May 4, 1907), lived, died, and were buried at Arcadia, Louisiana.

A Thousand Miles from South Carolina

"And some there be which have no
memorial. . . ."

Ecclesiasticus XLIV.

Sam Williamson's daughter, Mary, who married Charles Brown, was buried in Cleburne, Texas;[1] marsh tackeys bought in Texas brought a handsome profit to Lizzie Howle's son;[2] Eugene Bealer, whose mother was a Bacot,[3] was in business in Texas; General Harllee's sons[4] were living in Texas, married to Texas women; Mr. Richard Furman,[5] who married a McIver, went there; but Mary Ann Charles could not understand why anyone should elect to go to Texas. She felt no enthusiasm for a land of northers and unwholesome climate, and now, late in 1882, Miss Darby had written her that Mr. McGinty[6] planned to move to San Antonio.

Mrs. Andrew Charles, Stony Hill, South Carolina, to Jemima Darby, Ringgold, Louisiana.

Dec. 7, 1882[7]
Stony Hill, South Carolina

Dear Miss Darby

Your letter of Oct. 12 came to hand in due time. I am sorry it so happened that I have not replied earlier. I have been confined to bed part of the time   my health poor. You mentioned in your letter of having had a good deal of sickness in your country. It has been a remarkedly sickly year here too. A good many of the old land marks are being removed. I think I mentioned Mr. John Dargan's[8] death in one of my letters to you. Cousin Evan Lide[9] has died too. Every member of that family of Lides are dead except Cousin Jane Dargan.[10] She is going to move to Alabama soon to live with her daughter[11] whose husband has been pastor of the Baptist Church at Celma, Alabama.[12] We regret to have her leave at this time of her life but Maggie[13] is with her now and would be so lonely here. All of Cousin Evan Lide's family[14] are married except the twins and Ezra. Evan married last week to one of our and his kin-folk — Miss Reeves of Marion. The marriage took place in the church and was a grand affair. We were invited but did not attend. I was too unwell. Will go to call on them soon as they will be our neighbors. Mrs. Louisa Dargan[15] died a short time since. Carolina[16] and Sarina[17] are all that remain of that family. Miss Lou's eldest daughter, Jessie, is a widow with three children. Lula,[18] her youngest, married a son of Mr. and Mrs. Bill Evans, Devonal. Dr. Theodore[19] died in the spring. Every one of that family are dead.

Our State Convention met at Darlington on November 23, and was largely attended and had fine weather from the opening to its closing.[20] Mr. James Furman[21] and Mr. J. A. W. Thomas[22] were the only ministers there that you know. Mr. Richard Furman[23] moved down from Sumter to Texas. He was in ill health and his mind was impaired. His sons moved out some years previous and induced their parents to go as their father could not preach and was dependent upon them for support. Sarah[24] is still single. A daughter of Mr. James Furman by his last wife,[25] Miss LaNough[26] is to marry a nephew of Mae Charles' husband,[27] Harry Haynesworth, very soon. She is the beauty of Greenville.

You spoke of Mr. McGinty's having moved to San Antonio. I am afraid that climate will not suit his constitution any better than California for the "nothers" which that part or perhaps all of the state are subject to are very trying on newcomers, and particularly those whose lungs are not strong. They must come to *Middle South Carolina,* or Florida.

I have not heard from Emily Taylor since I wrote you last. Florrie LaCost still lives with Sarina. Georgia[28] is teaching school at Spartanburg, assisting Mr. Taylor. She graduated with distinction at Greenville Seminary. Florrie[29] is very much beloved by those who are so fortunate as to know her. Sarena keeps her at home very closely. She is more like Sallie Ann[30] than her mother, Eliza.[31] "Giggy," as Florrie calls her, is like her father, short and fat and was pretty when I last saw her.

You spoke of the possibility of my not being able to read your letter. I read *every* word with *no* trouble *whatever. Every word* is *perfectly* distinct. We never fail to remark on how well you write. Andrew and Sallie join in love to you and all the family.

Your affectionate friend as ever,

M. CHARLES

* * * * *

Along with New Year's greetings for 1883, Mary Ann Charles sent answers to a long list of questions which Miss Darby had asked about her South Carolina acquaintances.

Mrs. Andrew Charles, Darlington, South Carolina, to Jemima Darby, Ringgold, Louisiana.

Darlington
Jan. 8th, 1883

Miss Jemima Darby
    Care of Dr. A. Kolb
    Ringgold, La.

Dear Miss Darby

Your very welcome letter to hand. A happy new year greeting to you all. The holidays passed very pleasantly with us. On Tuesday night after Christmas we had a gathering of young people and had a lively time. I wish I could have sent you some of the "old Carolina" nice things, especially a large slice of white mountain cake. I think I sent you a recipe for it. I think it second best cake that we make; a ten-pound fruit cake (only) is better.

I will answer your questions. Cousin Thomas Lide[32] died. Leighton and family[33] live and own his house and lands. Bettie has two sons and two daughters.[34] Very bright, attractive children. Julia, their older daughter, is considered the prettiest girl in Darlington. Mr. and Mrs. Beattie[35] are still living at their same home in Marlborough. Two sons are all that are living of their children. They are remarkably kind and attentive to their parents. They have a nice white lady to keep house and attend to their parents. The boys are fine planters and make an abundance to live on. I mentioned the death of Cousin Evan Lide.[36] The church sustains a great loss in his death. He was so punctual in his attendance and always ready

◄{ 333 }►

to give liberally to all benevolent objects. We do not take the *Tennessee Baptist,* but some nearer home. The *Baptist Courier* published in Greenville, S. C., and the *Herald*, a Richmond paper. I told you about Emily Taylor[37] being in bad health. I hope she may not be so near the end as her friends think her. Florrie[38] is not robust; Georgia[39] seems more so and like her father.

I see a notice in the Darlington paper of the marriage of a daughter of Mr. John Evans,[40] of Cheraw, to a gentleman from Virginia and also of the marriage of the second daughter of Mr. Sompayrac,[41] of Society Hill to a man from Florida. You remember Mr. Theodore Sompayrac as a beau of Sallie King,[42] don't you? Who afterward married Margaret Douglas.

Hannah McIver[43] and her son Jonnie[44] and daughter Fannie[45] have moved to Darlington. F. is to marry the son of the Governor of our State — Thompson.[46] She will live in Charleston when married. Her mother will remain in Darlington with her son. They have long since joined the Episcopal church. Col. Wilson[47] lives at the Mill[48] with the bachelor James.[49]

Mrs. Charles Fort[50] lives in the same house all alone. Victoria[51] lives at Darlington. Her daughter stays with her grandmother during the school term and goes to Mrs. Ellen Edwards[52] who teaches at her house. Her son, Hartwell,[53] has charge of a church near Greenville, S. C. Janie[54] is about grown, her only daughter. Jim[55] married a Miss Wilson from Sumter, a maiden lady. Miss Susan Orr[56] is living still, but has been confined to her bed for more than a year from a fall. Sallie would send love but she is on a visit to her Pa who has lately married a nice lady. We are all pleased with his selection of a wife. Dear Miss Darby, please give my love to Mrs. K. and the girls.[57] Accept a share from your friend,

As ever,

M. C.

* * * * *

Twenty years had passed since Jemima Darby withdrew her letter from Welsh Neck Baptist Church in order to make her home in Louisiana. When Mrs. Charles related contemporary conditions in the Society Hill church and community, Miss Darby's memories focused on the forty years when she had been a member of the congregation. It seemed not so long ago that:

The brethren were invited to state the present condition of their religious feelings. This was done by all present in a frank and feeling manner. It was a season of solemn and affecting interest; and although as a church we are not as we should be, many complaining of coldness and the want of enjoyment in religion, yet we can but regard it as the DAWN OF A NEW DAY.[58]

In those days, Luther Rice[59] preached in Miss Darby's hearing,[60] and there had been "the solemn and interesting service of dedicating to God the New House of Worship" on January 4, 1843,[61] when Dr. Thomas Curtis preached from Mal. 1:11. She remembered the pastorates of the various Furmans. When Professor Mims of Furman University was ordained on July 16, 1843, Dr. James C. Furman preached the ordination sermon, Richard Furman offered the prayer and gave the right hand of church fellowship, and J. O. B. Dargan gave the charge.[62] Dr. J. C. Furman's farewell sermon on December 22, 1844,[63] was from the Ps. 119:19, "I am a Stranger in the Earth," and Reverend J. Lewis Shuck[64] had brought a native Chinese preacher to address the people of the Welsh Neck Church.[65]

Now, in her letter of February 5, 1883, Jemima invited Mrs. Charles and her family out to Louisiana for a visit. Having passed her eighty-ninth birthday on January 30, Miss Darby had become reconciled to the fact that she would never see South Carolina again, but she was not willing to die without one last visit from friends from home. Besides, there was all of this talk about the McGintys and Texas.

Mrs. Andrew Charles, Darlington, South Carolina, to Jemima Darby, Ringgold, Louisiana.

Darlington
February 15, 1883

Dear Miss Darby

Your letter of the fifth to hand. We are glad to hear from you. We would be delighted to take a trip to see you but it is a long ways and we would be obliged to go out that way in winter and might get stuck in the mud. You know I have been there and in winter, too.[66]

I have not heard from Emily[67] since I wrote you. Mrs. Whitna[68] is in Darlington now. She is a widow and has one daughter with her. I do not know whether she has any more children or not.[69] If you would like to write her, direct your letter to Florence, care of Mr. Hary Harlee.[70] I know she would be very glad to hear from you. I hear she is to remain with her friends in Darlington a few weeks longer. I have told you about Dr. Pressley[71] a number of times. I think you must have missed some of my letters.[72] He is still practicing at Society Hill and lives at his same house. Sarah[73] looked well when I saw her last. Sallie Griffin[74] married Lewis Coker[75] and lives at his house behind the store which he still runs. Mr. Beattie[76] is about ninety years old. Mrs. B.[77] is at the point of death now. When I last heard she was kept alive on brandy. Mrs. Valina Rogers[78] who was her sister was buried last Sunday. Mrs. Wick Rogers[79] is the only survivor of that large family.

I told you of Cousin Jane Dargan's[80] move to Alabama. Andrew[81] received a long letter from her. She seems to be very pleasantly situated. Mr. Forrester[82] is pastor of the church at Selma. They have a large congregation and a large membership and fine material and a working church too. The church is just a few steps from their door, convenient for Cousin Jane.

Robert Lide,[83] a son of Cousin Evan, is pastor of Black Creek Church now. His second wife is Jane Coker Wilson's daughter.[84] His first was Dora Dargan,[85] Mrs. Lou, Theodore's daughter.

Lizzie Vann (Howle)[86] has two sons and two daughters married.[87] Josiah[88] lives at the old home. Russia[89] lives near Wake Forest, N. C. He comes down now and then to see his friends. I told you that James Williams[90] had married a Miss Wilson from Sumpter. She is a maiden lady. We are all pleased with his choice.

I will take a jump again to Society Hill. Mr. Stout[91] preaches very acceptably to the congregation there. Mrs. Ellen Edwards[92] is one of his co-workers. Miss Lou[93] and Mattie McIntosh[94] are very active, too. Mrs. Charles Fort[95] lives the same place, I suppose. Alone part of the time. Both of her daughters[96] are married and gone. She tried to keep some of her grandchildren with her but when they are at home, she is alone. Mrs. Katie Fort[97] is still alive. Lives with Lucy Watson[98] up the country. Hannah (Wilson) McIver's son John[99] and daughter

Fannie moved to Darlington the first of this year. Fannie[100] married the other day, the son of our governor.

Col. Wilson[101] lives at the Mill with the old bachelor. Mrs. Fergerson[102] is still living but is almost blind. Jeff[103] is not married.

Sallie is on a visit to Nancy Coggeshall[104] and family. I know she will send love to you, Mrs. K. and Lizzie.[105]

Andrew sends kind regards, too, and accept a great deal of love from your friend as of old,

Yours as ever,

M. C.

I heard the other day that Mrs. Backhouse[106] is near her end. She owns Mr. Wilkins old place in Springville. Lives alone there.

* * * * *

Throughout the period when Mary Ann Charles and Miss Darby exchanged letters, there was a great deal of talk about cooking and gardening. On May 7, 1883, Mrs. Charles reported the latest news from family friends, but for the most part, her letter dealt with recipes and vegetables.

The Kolbs, in the meantime, had set a specific time to go to San Antonio for their visit with Mary Kolb McGinty and her family.

Mrs. Andrew Charles, Stony Hill, Darlington, South Carolina, to Jemima Darby, Ringgold, Louisiana.

Stony Hill, May 7, 1883

Dear Miss Darby

Your very welcome letter received in due time. I am sorry to hear of Dr. K's ill health. I hope a little relaxation from constant worry and care and anxiety may benefit his health and I know Mary[107] will be delighted to see them.

I will answer your questions. Mrs. Whitna[108] came on a visit and I think has gone home. She is a widow now. I think I mentioned it to you.

I am very glad you all were pleased with the recipes I sent and while I think of it, I will tell you what you can make a delightful yeast from if you cannot get hops. Take five or six fig leaves and boil a strong tea and mix a smooth stiff batter of wheat flour and then put in a spoonful of brewer's yeast or a dissolved yeast cake and set it to rise in a warm place and in the morning mix in corn meal just so that you can make it out like thin biscuit and lay them in a cool place to dry and then you can keep them for several months. Take one cake, dissolve in water, put in a spoonful of lard or butter, one of sugar, mix and sponge at night and set it in a warm place to rise. Then work and set to rise again. When it begins to crack a a little, bake (make the sponges into rolls or a loaf) as you like. Corn fodder can be used as well as the fig leaves in the same way.

The fruit crop has been almost destroyed here though we will have a plenty of plums and apples. We have had strawberries once and will have a great quantity of them soon. I bought the plants last year and they are in perfection now. The bed has been properly kept and I never have seen so many on the bushes. Our garden is not so good. The weather has been too cool and rains almost every day. Too much for everything except strawberries. We luxuriate on asparagus. We planted a bed as soon as we came here[109] and have had it fine for twenty years. The same bed. Our hot house plants are pretty. Blooming beautifully.

Caroline Charles,[110] Sarine Dargan[111] and Florrie LaCoste have been on a pleasure trip to Charleston and Columbia. It is the first trip that Florrie has ever taken farther than Cheraw.[112]

Miss Susan Orr[113] keeps cheerful but cannot walk. Mrs. Backhouse[114] is very feeble. She will live alone and have a colored woman who rents some of her land. Her nephews, Mr. Peter Bronson's[115] sons do all in their power to induce her to live with them but she seems to prefer her own house. They are very kind, attentive to her.

Mrs. Furgerson is almost blind. The lady James Williams married[116] is no relation of his. His uncle adopted her and gave her his name. She is a niece of Mr. Wilson and her real name is Anderson. She is a fine woman and Jim is comfortably situated now. Mrs. Chambers[117] has but one child[118] and two grandchildren.[119] Tolly is an energetic, fine man. Robert Lide[120] is pastor of B. Creek Church. Have good congregations there still. Mr. Stout[121] at Society Hill. Dr. Pressley[122] practices yet. Mrs. Nelly Fort[123] still lives in the valley and Mr. Mays the same place. Miss Lou[124] and Mattie[125] McIntosh are there too. Sallie joins me in love to you, Lizzie. Andrew sends kind regards.

Your friend as ever,

M. C.

I send you some very pretty Balsam seeds — double white and red and purple spotted.

* * * * *

Having no regular pastor at the Darlington Baptist Church gave Mrs. Charles cause for unhappiness. After Mr. Alexander[126] left in 1881, there was no resident pastor until the spring of 1883 when Mr. Moore[127] arrived. Dr. Moore, who was "greatly admired for his Christian character and intellect,"[128] preached in Darlington until 1891 when he accepted a professorship at Furman University, Greenville.

Dr. and Mrs. Kolb made their visit to Texas between May and September, 1883, and had returned to Louisiana when Miss Darby reported to Mrs. Charles late in September.

Jemima wanted very much to see Mrs. Charles and other South Carolina friends. Mary Ann was fairly certain that she and Miss Darby would never meet again. Yet, she reminded her friend in Louisiana of a song,[129] "Shall We Meet," which they had sung together in Baptist meetings in South Carolina.[130]

Mrs. Andrew Charles, Darlington, South Carolina, to Jemima Darby, Ringgold, Louisiana.

Dear Miss Darby

Your letter reached me after having taken the rounds somewhere. I was just ready to write to know what was the matter
with you. I am glad to hear that all of you are still in the land
of the living.

We are in usual health now. Sallie was in feeble health the
first of the summer but since her trip up the country, her health
has been better. She is vy feeble naturally and cannot get
through the summers down here, and has to go to the mountains or elsewhere every summer.

I hope Dr. and Mrs. K's trip has been a real benefit to them.
I suppose it would take some time for them to recover from
the fatigue of the trip and feel the benefit of the change.

We have had a good deal of sickness, through the country
this summer. The weather has been so excessively warm and
dry, with the almost total absence of thunder and lightning,
which are said to be conducive to health. There is great complaint of short crops and the gardens have been very poor.
Most persons did not have even tomatoes. Had a nice dish for
dinner today.

The Church at the Hill still has its fine pastor, Mr. Stout,[131]
but is in great grief at this time for the loss of two of its most
valued members. Mrs. Ellen Edwards,[132] has moved to Mississippi to live with her son[133] who has charge of a church
there. Mrs. Willie Coker[134] died after an illness of several
months, leaving seven children,[135] an infant of a few weeks old.
I think I mentioned to you that Cousin Maria Pouncy (Lide
that was)[136] had come to live with her sister, Cousin Hannah
Coker.[137] Her daughters[138] also came. Cousin M has taken charge
of May's infant.[139]

Sallie Coker Griffin[140] has just returned from their trip
North. Dr. Pressley[141] practices still. Mrs. Sompayrac[142] has
several children married.

We have been without a pastor for a long time but secured
one[143] at last. I do hope he may be the right man. All seem
pleased with him so far. The church is about to build a parsonage, a need which has been long felt.

I have not heard from Emily[144] since I wrote you. She cor-
responded with me a long time but finally quit. Flory[145] says

she writes to her at long intervals. Mr. Taylor educated Georgia.[146] She is teaching now.

Dear Miss Darby, I would be delighted to meet you once more in the flesh. Let us hope and pray to meet "beyond the river where the surges cease to roll." Andrew has just retired & desired to be remembered to you. Sallie is busy practicing.[147] She performs prettily on the piano and organ. She calls out "Give my love to Miss D." & I join in love to you & all yours.

As ever,

M. C.

* * * * *

From the public press and Baptist periodicals, Miss Darby learned that the two hundredth anniversary of the First Baptist Church, Charleston, was to be celebrated in connection with the sixty-third session of the State Convention of the Baptist denomination of South Carolina on November 21-25, 1883. B. W. Edwards,[148] of Darlington, was president of the Convention that year, and plans were made for historical speeches and inspirational sermons. From the Charleston *News and Courier,* she read:[149]

The annual sermon before the Convention was preached last night by Rev. Charles Manly, D. D.,[150] of Greenville. The church was filled by a large and brilliant congregation, and the services throughout were deeply impressive and earnest. The music was conducted by Professor G. O. Robinson of Augusta, who presided at the organ, and was assisted by an improvised choir of fine singers. The Rev. A. J. S. Thomas,[151] pastor of the church; the Rev. L. H. Shuck, D. D.,[152] and Dr. Manly occupied seats in the pulpit. The opening prayer was offered by Dr. Shuck.

Dr. Manly's sermon was based upon John IV, 36 — "And he that reapeth receiveth wages and gathereth fruit unto life eternal; that both he that soweth and he that reapeth may rejoice together." The discourse was an eloquent plea for greater consecration of the Christian to the work of the Master, and a clear setting forth of the mutual joys and labors of those who are sowing and those who are reaping in the kingdom of God.

On Thursday, November 22, at 11:00 A.M.,[153] Rev. Basil Manly[154] and Rev. H. A. Tupper[155] delivered addresses on the history of Baptist churches in South Carolina. That evening, Dr. J. C. Furman, speaking on "The Church's Connection with the Causes of Education and Missions," referred frequently to Pee Dee churches and citizens:[156] Evan Pugh and his descendants, the Lides and Dargans; Jesse Hartwell; Robert Napier; Manly Wingate. Miss Darby knew that William G. Whilden prepared, as part of the anniversary celebration, the genealogies of some of the early ministers of the Baptist churches in South Carolina,[157] and that the Darby name appeared among the descendants of William Screven's[158] sister-in-law, Elizabeth Cutt Elliot, along with such familiar lines as Williams, McIver, Bostick, Hart, and Frierson.

Still, the Kolbs of Louisiana could not understand their aunt's unyielding attachment to her South Carolina Baptist heritage.

Distressing, too, was the news that Mary and Mr. McGinty had tried to persuade Dr. and Mrs. Kolb to move to Texas permanently, arguing that the climate in San Antonio was preferable to that of North Louisiana. Mrs. Charles shared Miss Darby's doubts about the wisdom of such a move.

Mrs. Andrew Charles, Darlington, South Carolina, to Jemima Darby, Ringgold, Louisiana.

Darlington, S. C.
Decem. 2, 1883

Miss Jemima Darby
Ringgold, La.

Dear Miss Darby

I am sorry it has been so that I could not reply sooner to your letter. I have had rheumatism in my right hand so badly that I almost lost the use of it. I was truly glad to hear that you keep in such good health and that Dr. K's health improved by his trip to Texas. I would be too glad if Mary could have her parents near her but it is late in life for them[159] to break up and move to a new country to start life anew.

You spoke of the Hardshell Convention or Association.[160]

There are a very few of that religious sect[161] in this country that I know of. Our annual Convention met in Charleston, on the same day that it used to when you attended here, commencing on Wednesday before the second Sabbath in November. They open on Wednesday and close on Sunday. The weather was charming and the attendance very large. Not withstanding the short crop, there was a large amount of money secured for benevolent purposes. Our pastor's name is Moore.[162] He is from Virginia, a young man with a nice wife and infant.

Darlington is improving. New streets are being evened out and we have a bank[163] and are building a factory. It is to be on the hill where Mrs. Emily Hunter[164] used to live. Numbers of cottages are to be erected for the operators, which will make a little village of themselves. Miss Susan Orr[165] died the last of November. Mrs. Ann Fort[166] died about the same time. Jeff Furgeson[167] was here yesterday. Said his mother[168] was in usual health. Bettie Dargan Forrester[169] died in Selma, Alabama. The remains were brought on — buried in the family grounds at Darlington.[170] She left two little girls,[171] one three weeks old.[172] Cousin Jane and Maggie[173] have lived with them a year. Bettie died of "Bright's Disease." I have not heard from Mrs. Edwards and Janie[174] since they went to Oxford. Mary Sanders who married Pegues[175] lives in Oxford. They are Presbyterians, though. Mr. Forrester has been called to the Hartsville Church and I see from the Richmond *Herald* that he has been elected to a church in Virginia.[176] I hope he may come to Hartsville. Cousin Jane has but three children, Furman[177] is in Alabama and Eddie[178] in Virginia, pastor of a church in Petersburg.[179]

Bettie Lide[180] Nancy Coggeshall[181] and Jane Wallace[182] inquire about you. All send love to you.

Walter Harlee[183] is a frequent visitor at our house. He clirks in a store at Mechanicsville. It has become a place of considerable importance. Hundreds of bales of cotton are bought there. Walter says he must have been too small to remember you. He spent a year with Mell Whitna[184] in Florida. Had a delightful visit.

Florrie LaCost has been down. She is a charming girl.[185] She had been to see Emily and Georgia. They live in Union County. Georgia is teaching school. Gets fifty dollars per month. She has invested some money in land. Mr. T. has built a large house and seems to be doing well. Florrie says he will not stay at any place long.[186] He has two churches. E- has a nice horse and buggy.

Andrew sends kind regards to you, your folks and love from your old friend,[187]

M. C.

Sallie[188] is anticipating a Merry Christmas. We all expect to spend the time with Jane.[189] They are to have a party there. Jenny Wallace[190] is to spend her vacation at home. She is at school in Charleston.

My kindest regards and Christmas greetings to you all.[191]

* * * * *

William Gibson McGinty liked San Antonio, "a great place to visit, a great place to live."[192] Business was humming. Railroads were being completed; industries were encouraged. Farms and ranches increased in South Texas, and San Antonio must supply windmills, plows, saddles, wagons, and harnesses. A telephone exchange was opened; banking facilities grew. Hotels, saloons, livery stables, opera houses, breweries, woodyards, newspapers, tourists — San Antonio had everything that an up-and-coming American city needed. Gib urged the Kolbs to join him and Mary.

McGinty was a carpenter[193] but he could not meet the demands of all his customers. Everybody wanted a house built. Jim Cawthon could find plenty to do; he was skillful with tools, too.[194] Why didn't the whole family come?

Gib's urging included Lizzie and Jones. There was work for all. Hadn't the girls always been together? Didn't they all marry in the same wedding? Vivian and Ella were approximately the same age. No need to stay in the same place. Bienville was sluggish; old Bexar was waking up.

Dr. Kolb was sick; his sons were adolescents. Already a wanderer at twenty, David no longer lived at home regularly. Edwin was fifteen, Lee a little older. They had heard of the rip-snorting Texas town and had begged to go out to live with Sister Mary. Cowboys came in from the roundup and shot up the town. Fun was plentiful and Brother Gib would show them around.

Mary wanted her mother in Texas; Lizzie lived in Louisiana. Both of Mrs. Kolb's daughters were expecting babies that year.[195] Ella's little Jimmy would go where his father went. Miss Darby did not argue; her menfolks would have to decide. She remembered departing from Carolina in 1860, the admonitions and sound advice. A fool she was, they told her, to travel at sixty-six, and now she was ninety and most of her friends were dead. If Mell and Alexander wanted to travel, she would not be a hindrance.

And, in January of 1884, they all went — Miss Darby; Dr. Kolb and Miss Mell; Ella's youngster and his father; Lizzie, Jones, and two-year-old Ella. In Texas, the clan would be united. With young Vivian, McGinty and Mary waited. David, Lee, and Edwin, who had gone on before, were anxious for the reunion with their parents and other relatives. In the first segment of the only letter by Miss Darby which has been preserved, she announced her plans to her most faithful South Carolina correspondent, Mary Ann Williamson Charles.

Miss Jemima Darby, Ringgold, Louisiana, to Mrs. Andrew Charles, Darlington, South Carolina.

Ringgold, January the 8, 1884

Mrs. Charles

My dear friend   I received your very much appreciated letter in due time. Was sorry to hear of your suffering with rheumatism. Hope you are entirely well before this time and that you all had a pleasant Christmas at your niece's in Cheraw.[196] Our Christmas was very dull owing to sickness in the family. Mel[197] and Lizzie's little Ella[198] was very sick at the time. Mel has been on the bed nearly eleven weeks. She is a little better now but don't sit up but very little.

I was glad to hear from Mary Sanders[199] and Hannah[200] but you did not say anything about Henrietta.[201] I had not heard anything from them since I parted with them in Cheraw. I was surprised to hear that Emily had moved to Georgia.[202] I am glad that Eliza LaCoste's two daughters are doing so well.

I was sorry to hear of Betty Dargan's death.[203] It was fortunate that her mother[204] was with her at the time of her death

I suppose she will come back if her son-in-law[205] comes to Hartsville.

Walter Harlee[206] was a little babe when I came from South Carolina   Tell Sallie his frequent visits look *suspicious*. His is a very rare privilege.

Dear Mary   I must now tell you that Alexander[207] has decided to move to San Antonio and I expect we will start next week although Mel is yet in bed and it is freezing cold. She is over anxious to start. Two weeks ago she said she would be glad to start right then. She tells him not to wait a minute on her account. Her three youngest children[208] are there and the other two will go with us. I dread it on her account and don't know what the consequences will be. If all was well I would not mind it. She will have to lie down all the way.

* * * * *

Dr. Kolb and his family entrained at Shreveport, using two cars to accommodate eight people and their belongings. Westward progress on railroads out of Shreveport had been slow, but by 1884 regular service over the Texas and Pacific road had been established.[209] Trains departed from Shreveport for Marshall at 7:45 A.M. and at 5:15 P. M., and moved on west toward Dallas from Marshall at 3:10 A.M. and at 11:55 P.M., each day.[210] At Dallas, travelers again changed trains before heading south toward San Antonio.

The long trip wearied Miss Darby greatly. She particularly disliked the long periods of waiting between trains at layover stations. Train officials and members of her family, seeing her fatigue, urged her to rest, but her reply was, "A lady does not lie down in public places."[211]

Upon their arrival in San Antonio, the Kolbs went first to the home of the McGintys, a house at the corner of Camden and Brooklyn avenues in Ward Two.[212] W. G. McGinty had four children, three by his first wife, and Mary's son, Vivian. Thus there were six children and eleven adults, counting the teen-agers, under one roof, a situation which could not remain satisfactory for a long period of time. Mrs. McGinty's baby was due in a few weeks; Dr. Kolb was in poor health; Miss Darby's strength had been drained away by the trip.

The Kolbs and Tookes sought out a "House Renting

Agency"[213] from which they rented living quarters within the Ward Two neighborhood. James Cawthon, who was working with McGinty, remained a boarder at that home, but his son went to live with his grandparents, Dr. and Mrs. Kolb. All of the men with the exception of Dr. Kolb secured employment. Even young Edwin obtained work as a clerk at a downtown fruit stand.[214] Miss Darby moved into the house with her nephew and his wife.

Soon after her arrival in San Antonio, Miss Darby wrote a brief account of her trip to the western edge of the Cotton Kingdom. In spite of her ninety years, Jemima Darby was a perceptive observer and an enthusiastic reporter of the journey. The recipient of her hurried note, Mary Ann Williamson Charles, had no way of knowing that this would be the final letter from her "ever affectionate friend, Jemima Darby."

Miss Jemima Darby, San Antonio, Texas, to Mrs. Andrew Charles, Darlington, South Carolina.

January the 28

We bid adieu to Ringgold last Tuesday. Had to lay over Wednesday waiting for the boat. Took the cars at 4 Thursday afternoon. Past Marshall and Long View in the night so I can't give you any description of those cities. The next city was Austin a large and beautiful city on the Colorado River. The next was Round Rock[215] not of much importance except for the rock to make fences. We then past another large city,[216] can't give you the name of it now. We were passing curiosities all the time.

We are now at the depot at San Antonio. We hired a hack and drove about three hundred yards to Mr. McGinty's. Mary was on the watch and just made one leap to the carriage. We had a joyous meeting. Found all well and overjoyed but the yellow flag was hanging out but they said the small pox had all disappeared.

I don't think the face of the country pretty at all but it is said to be a great place to make money and that is the object of most people. San Antonio is a very pretty city and growing rapidly. It is already four miles square. Mary's is a very pretty house and I expect that we will take the joining lot and improve it. Is a mountainous country where the city is.

I don't expect you will appreciate this hurried and bloched

up letter but I will try to do [better] after a while when I can get out and see something of the city. We started on Tuesday, lay over one day and got here Saturday at four o'clock in the evening. If we had not been detained we would have made the trip in three and a half days. Give my best love to all enquireing friends and tell them I am gone about 23 hundred miles from where I was born and raised. I will give you Mary's address so you will please write to me and direct your letter to Mary until we know certain where our office will be. Mel stood the trip better than we expected. She and Lizzie and Mary all send love to you and Sallie   Give my love to Sally
    Kind regards to Mr. Charles
    Do write soon, to your ever affectionate friend

JEMIMA DARBY

Mrs. M. H. McGinty
Box 587
San Antonio
Tex.

* * * * *

By the middle of February, the Kolbs realized that Miss Darby was seriously ill. What had begun as a common cold during the trip had developed into pneumonia. Dr. Kolb was not satisfied with his own treatment of his aunt. He sent for a San Antonio doctor, who offered very little encouragement for the tired old lady. She lapsed into a coma about the middle of the week, and on Thursday, February 21, she died without regaining consciousness. On Friday morning, the San Antonio *Light* reported: "Miss R. J. Darby, aged 90 years, died of pneumonia, in the Second Ward, on the 21st."[217] Telegraphic service brought front page news to the *Light*. A tornadic wind had struck in the Carolinas on the twenty-first.[218]

Faced with the problem of burying his aunt in a strange city, Dr. Kolb found that the City Cemetery at the north end of Paso Hondo, east of Pine Street, in San Antonio,[219] was the burial ground for rich and poor. It was not too different, he was told when he went out to investigate, from community cemeteries such as were found in towns like Ringgold and Darlington. Two days earlier, Franklin L. Paschal,[220] a former mayor of the city, was

◄{ 348 }►

buried with a great deal of pomp in a lot reserved for him and his wife. There in the row, a short distance away, was the new grave of John Burns.[221] The grave that was being dug was for a little girl, Violet Rose.[222] Miss Darby would lie next to her.[223]

Since their arrival in San Antonio, the Kolbs had been too busy, too sick, to go to church, and church people had not known to call. So it was that Jemima came to die with no prayerful Baptist pastor beside her. Nor was the pastor of the First Baptist Church[224] available to preach her funeral service.[225] A layman from the Baptist chapel,[226] a few neighbors, and the family went out Paso Hondo to hold graveside services for Miss Darby.

A light drizzle and cold wind came up before the little cortege reached the cemetery. Dr. Kolb and the women would not leave the carriages; David, Edwin, Lee, Cawthon, and McGinty followed the coffin across the cemetery. And Maria Elizabeth Kolb Tooke, hearing the hollow sound of Texas earth hitting the wooden box, wished that she could think of some way to perpetuate the memory of Jemima Darby of South Carolina.[227] For Mary Harriet Kolb McGinty there remained the task of notifying South Carolina friends of her great-aunt's death.

Mrs. William Gibson McGinty, San Antonio, Texas, to Mrs. Andrew Charles, Darlington, South Carolina.

426 Moralas St.
San Antonio Tex.
Oct. 19th, 1884

Mrs. Mary Charles

Dear Friend,

I received your letter to our dear Aunt two weeks ago, and it is with great sorrow that I tell you of her death. She was taken sick a few days after she arrived in San Antonio and died after an illness of four weeks. She had Pneumonia. For several days before she died we could not understand anything she said   she seemed to know us all and would try to talk. It was so distressing that we could not understand her. Her greatest desire before leaving La was to come to San Antonio and seemed to be in a hurry to get off. It was very sad to have to give her up though we knew there could not be many more years for her in this world   She was ninety a few days before she died   she lived a long and useful life.

Father[228] & Mother[229] are not as much improved in health as we would like but are better than when they came Mother could not walk without assistance when they came, but now can walk from her house to mine, the distance of one block

She has been in bed two days with fever but is better this eve.

You asked who Sister Lizzie married   her husband's name is Jones Tooke.[230] They have two children a girl[231] and boy[232] the baby is two months old. We have another little boy seven months old.[233]

I will close for this time as I have other letters to write. We would be glad to hear from you again, it seems that we have known you always. Our regards to yourself & family.

Lovingly,

MARY McGINTY

* * * * *

Time, as man marks time, had ended for Jemima Darby. Her long journey was over.

FOOTNOTES

1 Mary Williamson Brown, daughter of Mrs. Charles's brother, Samuel Williamson, died in Cleburne, Texas, in 1874, shortly after her return from a visit to Darlington County.

2 William James Howle, son of Thomas E. and Lizzie Vann Howle, was twenty-six years old when he made his trip to Texas in 1879.

3 Eugene Bealer, son of George and Lissie Bacot Bealer, was twenty years old when he went out to Texas in 1877 to join his cousin.

4 Charles Stuart Harllee (September 29, 1845 — November 14, 1885) married Makle Barbara Jones (August 29, 1854 — June 23, 1887). He was buried in Oakdale

Cemetery, Austin, Texas, and his wife was buried in the cemetery at Nixon, Texas. James Shackleford Harllee (June 9, 1857 — ?) married Frances Susan Rogers and was living in Corsicana, Texas, in 1934.

5 Richard Furman, son of Samuel Furman, both former pastors at Welsh Neck, Society Hill, married Mary McIver, daughter of James Kolb and Sarah Marshall McIver. Mr. and Mrs. Furman were on their way to Texas on November 29, 1879.

6 William Gibson McGinty (July 21, 1852 — June 17, 1939) married Mary Harriet Kolb on March 2, 1881, and moved her and his three children to California, where Vivian Kolb McGinty was born at Rosita, Custer County, on December 19, 1881.

7 On this same date, the youngest daughter of Miss Darby's cousin, Sarah Elizabeth Howle, gave birth to her first child, Meta Elise Campbell. Mrs. Charles did not report the baby's birth, nor had she announced Sarah Elizabeth Howle's (called "Carolina Secession" by Dr. Crane at her birth in 1861) marriage to William T. Campbell on March 15, 1881. Meta Campbell married Alfred Eugene Davis, April 15, 1900.

8 John Orr Beasley Dargan (August 9, 1813-1882), son of Timothy and Lydia Keith Dargan, joined Ebenezer Baptist Church in October, 1831, and married Jane Lide on June 13, 1837. He was pastor of Black Creek Baptist Church for forty years, and was buried in the churchyard of the Baptist Church at Darlington, South Carolina.

9 Evan James Lide (March 18, 1802 — September 9, 1882), son of Hugh and Elizabeth Pugh Lide, married (1) Margaret Ervin, (2) Martha Miller, and (3) Mrs. Lavinia Eason. Edwin Charles Dargan, Harmony Hall (Columbia, 1912), p. 97. "He kept up his reading and was a man of culture. . . . He was successful as a planter and accumulated considerable wealth. . . . He was for many years a beloved and revered deacon of the Darlington Baptist Church."

10 Margaret Jane Frances Lide (November 10, 1815 — March 16, 1886) married J. O. B. Dargan on June 13, 1837. She was the daughter of Hugh and Elizabeth Pugh Lide and the sister of Evan J. Lide.

11 Elizabeth Pugh Dargan (1842-1883), daughter of J. O. B. and Jane Lide Dargan, married Eldred J. Forrester on May 15, 1878, and moved with him to Fort Deposit, Lowndes County, Alabama. When the Alabama State Convention met in Troy on July 13, 1881, Mrs. Forrester was selected to be chairman of a woman's central committee to facilitate the mission work among women in Alabama.

12 B. F. Riley, History of the Baptists of Alabama from 1808 until 1894 (Birmingham, 1895), p. 382. "During the year [1882] Rev. E. J. Forrester became pastor of the church at Selma to succeed Dr. Cleveland, who was now editor-in-chief of the Alabama Baptist."

13 Margaret Lydia Keith Dargan (1844-1911), the only unmarried daughter of J. O. B. and Jane Lide Dargan, was living in Alabama with her sister's family, making it necessary that her mother go there also.

14 Evan J. Lide was married three times, but all his children were by his second wife, Martha Miller Lide (December 10, 1818 — September 5, 1857), who was a sister-in-law to William H. Scarborough, the artist. Their children who lived to be

grown were John Miller Lide; the twins, Mary and Elizabeth Lide; Ezra Lide; Thomas Lide; Evan P. Lide; William Lide; and Robert W. Lide, long pastor of the First Baptist Church, Darlington.

15 Maria Louisa Bacot Dargan was the wife of Theodore Dargan and a sister to Serena Bacot Dargan and Mrs. Hugh Charles.

16 Caroline Bacot Charles, wife of Hugh Lide Charles, Darlington, was Mary Ann Charles's sister-in-law.

17 Serena Bacot Dargan (January 3, 1833 — November 7, 1910), widow of Charles A. Dargan, cousin to Theodore Dargan, was a sister to Mrs. Hugh Charles.

18 Theodore and Louisa Bacot Dargan had seven children: Jessie; Dora, who married Robert Lide; Charles; Lucian; Lula, who married Devonal Evans; Alphonse, called "Rab"; and Alonzo.

19 Dr. Theodore Dargan (born August 15, 1822) died on September 10, 1881, not in the spring of 1882.

20 L. W. Coker, *Historical Sketch and Membership Roll* (Darlington, First Baptist Church, 1945), p. 8. "The church has entertained the Baptist State Convention five times, as follows: in 1844, 1863, 1872, 1882, 1898."

21 James Clement Furman (December 5, 1809 — March 3, 1890), son of Richard and Dorothea Maria Burn Furman, was pastor of Welsh Neck Church from 1833 to 1844 while Jemima was a member there.

22 J. A. W. Thomas and J. C. Furman had also been principal speakers at Welsh Neck Association's Semi-Centennial celebration on November 9, 1882, when Mr. Thomas delivered the historical sketch and Mr. Furman the missionary sermon.

23 Richard Furman, son of Samuel Furman, and husband of Mary McIver, died in Fort Worth, Texas, October 24, 1886.

24 Sarah Furman was the unmarried daughter of Richard and Mary McIver Furman.

25 Mary Glenn Davis (1824 — January 9, 1911) married J. C. Furman, her sister's widower, in June, 1856.

26 According to Harvey T. Cook, *The Life Work of James Clement Furman* (privately printed, 1926), pp. 229 and 233, Professor J. L. Lanneau of Furman University was Dr. Furman's co-worker during their money-raising campaigns of the war and reconstruction years. It was likely that the daughter born during the period was named Annie Lanneau. She is, however, called Annie Furman Haynesworth by Cook, pp. 323-324, in the account of Mr. Furman's writing on the death of his daughter: "On the 16th of Sept. [1887] we were taking part in religious services at Woodruff, in connection with the centennial anniversary of Bethel church. We had promised to be present, but we went with some reluctance, for we were leaving a beloved daughter quite sick. . . . On reaching Greenville members of the family met us at the depot, the first words we heard, in answer to our anxious inquiry 'Father, our dear Annie is in Heaven . . .' God had given her a singularly lovely person; and with that, an exquisite taste, so that she deeply enjoyed all beautiful things. The flowers 'her sisters were' and scenes of material

nature found a responsive chord of admiration in her sensitive heart. . . . Yet if she ever felt a consciousness of her own beauty no change of countenance ever betrayed the consciousness. . . . In the family, in the school, in the humblest walk of life, she was loved by all who knew her."

27 William F. B. Haynesworth, Sumter, married Mary Ann Charles, sister to Andrew, Mary Ann Williamson Charles's husband.

28 Georgia LaCoste, daughter of A. P. and Eliza King LaCoste, was the ward of her aunt, Emily King Taylor, and Mr. Taylor, a Baptist minister, of Spartanburg, South Carolina.

29 Florence LaCoste, the daughter of A. P. and Eliza King LaCoste, was the ward of her great-aunt, Serena Bacot Dargan, Darlington.

30 Sallie Ann King, daughter of James and Hannah Bacot King, was the second wife of A. P. LaCoste, the father of Georgia and Florence.

31 Eliza King, daughter of James and Hannah Bacot King, was the third and last wife of A. P. LaCoste.

32 Thomas P. Lide (June 10, 1810 — July 23, 1882) married Elizabeth Sparks (December 8, 1812 — September 8, 1878). They were buried at the Welsh Neck Baptist Churchyard, Society Hill, South Carolina.

33 Leighton Wilson and Elizabeth Wilds Lide lived at White Plains, Springville, former home of Thomas P. and Elizabeth Lide.

34 Leighton and Elizabeth Lide had four children: Marion, who married Mary Coggeshall; Julia, who did not marry; Bessie, who married Ezra Lide; and Roland, who did not marry.

35 W. Q. Beattie, Baptist minister, and Ann Terrel Beattie lived in Marlboro County.

36 Evan James Lide (March 18, 1802 — September 9, 1882), son of Hugh and Elizabeth Pugh Lide, whose third wife, Lavinia Eason Lide, survived him, was for many years a deacon in the Darlington Baptist Church.

37 Emily King Taylor, Spartanburg, South Carolina.

38 Florence LaCoste, Darlington, South Carolina.

39 Georgia LaCoste, Spartanburg, South Carolina.

40 Captain John Craig Evans (1832-1886) married Ann Eliza LaCoste (1824-1902), a daughter of A. P. LaCoste and a half sister to Florence and Georgia.

41 Theodore Sompayrac (1824 — April 12, 1911) married Margaret Douglas (1828 — October 7, 1901).

42 Sallie King (April 23, 1825 — May 10, 1857) was the second wife of A. P. LaCoste, who, after her death, married her sister, Eliza, the mother of Georgia and Florence.

43 Hannah J. Wilson married John Kolb McIver, son of James Kolb and Sarah Marshall McIver, 1859. Captain McIver died of wounds received at the Battle of

Gettysburg. According to Louise McIver McMaster, "Roderick McIver and His Family" (mimeographed family history, December, 1952), p. 16, "He was a typical southern gentleman, a graduate of Furman University, and of a special course at the University of Virginia. No truer patriot ever shed his blood for his country's rights. The U. D. C. Chapter in Darlington is named in his honor."

44 John K. McIver, son of John K. and Hannah Wilson McIver, married Louise Boyd.

45 Fannie McIver, daughter of John K. and Hannah Wilson McIver, married Henry T. Thompson.

46 Hugh Smith Thompson (January 24, 1836 — November 20, 1904) was a school teacher and professor before becoming governor of South Carolina, 1882-1886. Later he became assistant secretary of the United States Treasury, a member of the Civil Service Commission, and finally comptroller of the New York Life Insurance Company.

47 Colonel Isaac DeLesseline Wilson, who married Margaret Jane Sparks, was the father of Hannah McIver. He died April 3, 1894.

48 Leavensworth.

49 James P. Wilson (December 6, 1808 — November 3, 1891) never married.

50 Jane Lide Coker Wilson, *Memories of Society Hill* (Pee Dee Historical Society, 1909-1910), p. 43.

51 Victoria Fort Defee lived in Darlington.

52 Ellen C. Hartwell Edwards (April 10, 1828 — July 24, 1910), daughter of Jesse and Margaret Hartwell, married Robert G. Edwards, who died in 1869.

53 Hartwell Edwards, son of Robert and Ellen Hartwell Edwards, married Kate Watson, daughter of R. B. and Lucy McIver Watson, of Ridge Springs, South Carolina.

54 Jane C. Edwards, daughter of Robert and Ellen Hartwell Edwards, married Mr. Remsburg, Fayetteville, North Carolina.

55 James A. Williams (September 3, 1825 — February 2, 1886) married (1) Caroline M. T. Williamson, Mary Ann Charles's sister and Sallie's mother, and (2) Agnes Wilson, Mayesville, South Carolina. The second Mrs. Williams was an adopted daughter of Jim's uncle, Mr. Wilson; her real name was Anderson.

56 Susannah E. W. Orr, who had been a member of the Darlington Church since 1838, died in November, 1883.

57 Mrs. Henry Jones Tooke, Ringgold, Louisiana, had one daughter, Ella; and Mrs. William Gibson McGinty, San Antonio, Texas, had one son, Vivian, and three stepchildren.

58 "Minutes of the Welsh Neck Baptist Church, Society Hill, South Carolina," September 3, 1844.

59 Luther Rice (March 25, 1785 — September 25, 1836) had returned from his missionary work in India and had been invited by Reverend Richard Furman, Sr., Charleston, to explain the mission program to churches in the South.

60 "Minutes," November 5, 1831.

61 *Ibid.*, January 4, 1843.

62 *Ibid.*, July 16, 1843.

63 *Ibid.*, December 22, 1844.

64 J. Lewis Shuck and his wife, Henrietta Hall Shuck, were missionaries to China when Mrs. Shuck died in Hong Kong about 1840. Mr. Shuck continued his work with the aid of native preachers.

65 "Minutes," July 5, 1846.

66 Mrs. Charles had visited her cousin, Anne Lide Wilds Ross and Major Ross, in Bastrop, Louisiana, before the war.

67 Jemima and Mary Darby had been close friends of the King family in Society Hill. Jemima made frequent inquiries about them; and Mary Ann mentioned them often. For many years, Emily King Taylor had been the only surviving member of her family.

68 Amelia Melvina Howard (1834-1888), daughter of Charles Brown and Amelia M. Cannon Howard, married Joseph Newton Whitner in 1855, and moved to Florida, where Mr. Whitner died in 1881. She had returned to Darlington County for a visit with her relatives.

69 Mrs. Whitner's children were: Joseph Newton (May 2, 1857 — March 2, 1917); Charles Howard (September 12, 1858 — January 5, 1910); Richard Howard (October 25, 1861 — April, 1911); and Elizabeth Harrison "Elise" (January 31, 1865 — July 15, 1896), who married Alfred S. Foster, September 19, 1895.

70 Henry Thomas Harllee (1851-1918), son of Robert and Amelia Melvina Cannon Howard Harllee, was Mrs. Whitner's half brother. He married Mary Hart McCall in 1875. Mrs. Whitner was making her headquarters at the home of Mr. and Mrs. Harllee while visiting in the homes of other relatives.

71 Dr. S. H. Pressley, Society Hill, married (1) Jane Draughon Edwards (October 16, 1821 — July 27, 1851), daughter of Peter Kolb and Jane Draughon Edwards, and (2) Sarah McIver (July 20, 1831 — January 29, 1899), daughter of James Kolb and Sarah Marshall McIver. Dr. Pressley died February 18, 1885, after having served Welsh Neck Church as clerk for more than forty-five years.

72 It had been approximately twenty years since there had been a specific reference to Dr. Pressley.

73 Sarah McIver Pressley was a sister to John Kolb McIver, who married Hannah J. Wilson, and to Mrs. Richard Furman, Mrs. Zimmerman Davis, and Mrs. R. B. Watson. Mrs. Pressley died at Ridge Springs, South Carolina, January 29, 1899, and her body was brought back to Welsh Neck for burial.

74 Sarah Griffin Coker (October 9, 1828 — June 1, 1884), daughter of Thomas and Eliza McIver Griffin, married Lewis Maxwell Coker. She was a cousin to Mrs. Pressley.

75 Lewis Maxwell Coker (October 15, 1819 — February 26, 1889), son of Caleb and Hannah Lide Coker, was a Society Hill merchant.

76 W. Q. Beattie, Marlboro, was pastor at Darlington in 1831-1834 and again in 1837-1838.

77 Ann Terrel married W. Q. Beattie in 1828.

78 Valina Terrel Rogers was the wife of Hamilton Rogers and the mother of John Terrel Rogers, who was born in Brownsville, South Carolina, October 8, 1847.

79 Bettie Terrel Rogers, wife of Thomas Wickham Rogers, lived in Alabama.

80 Jane Lide Dargan (November 10, 1815 — March 16, 1886), widow of Pastor J. O. B. Dargan, was living in Selma, Alabama, with her daughter, Mrs. Forrester.

81 Dargan, *Harmony Hall,* p. 102. "Cousin Andrew . . . was a frequent visitor to our home as long as he lived. He was deeply devoted to my mother and loved to come to see her and talk to her, whether for the morning or to spend the day."

82 E. J. Forrester was Mrs. Dargan's son-in-law.

83 Robert Ervin Coker, "Springville: A Summer Village of Old Darlington District," *South Carolina Historical Magazine,* LIII, Number 4 (October, 1952), p. 195. "Evan J. Lide was the father of . . . the greatly beloved Robert W. Lide, long pastor of the First Baptist Church in Darlington. The Reverend Robert Lide died not so long ago in Florence; his children have gone far and wide from Florence to Korea and China."

84 Anne Elizabeth Wilson, daughter of Furman and Jane Coker Wilson, married Robert W. Lide.

85 Dora Dargan (1849-1878), daughter of Theodore and Louisa Bacot Dargan, married Robert W. Lide.

86 Elizabeth Sarah Vann (November 25, 1833 — January 15, 1913), daughter of William and Sarah Jones Vann, married Thomas E. Howle.

87 Thomas E. Howle, Jr., married Frances E. Rhodes on March 9, 1875; Maggie J. Howle married Josiah T. Vann, son of Dr. A. R. and Fannie Cannady Vann, on March 4, 1878; William James Howle married Nettie Gandy, daughter of John Gandy, on December 24, 1879; and Sarah Elizabeth Howle married William Timmons Campbell, March 15, 1881.

88 Josiah T. Vann (July 29, 1820 — January 7, 1892) married Sallie C. Byrd on October 21, 1886.

89 Alexander Russia Vann (May 5, 1822 — October 22, 1892) married Elizabeth Frances Cannady, March 29, 1850.

90 James A. Williams (September 3, 1825 — February 2, 1886) married (1) Caroline Williamson, and (2) Agnes Wilson.

91 John Stout (March 12, 1842 — June 17, 1894) married Frances Coker.

92 Ellen Hartwell married Robert Edwards.

93 Wilson, *Memories of Society Hill,* p. 68. "Miss Louisa McIntosh, the eldest daughter, who died not long after her mother's death, lovely in person and character, was a most active, devoted member of our church."

[94] *Ibid.* "So was the youngest daughter, Miss Martha McIntosh, who is now Mrs. T. P. Bell of Atlanta, and as useful and consecrated a church and mission worker as she was when here, where she is still missed and loved."

[95] Nelly Gandy Fort, wife of Charles Fort, lived between the Episcopal Church and Main Street, Society Hill.

[96] Mr. and Mrs. Fort had two daughters, Mrs. Victoria Fort Defee, Darlington, and Mrs. Fannie Fort DeWitt, wife of Robert DeWitt.

[97] Catherine Botsford Fort, daughter of Edmond and Catherine Edwards Botsford, lived with Lucy McIver Watson, Ridge Springs, South Carolina. McMaster, "Roderick McIver and His Family," p. 16. "She was like a mother to the children of Dr. McIver and after the marriage of the youngest daughter, Lucy (Watson), she lived in Ridge Springs, dying there at an advanced age."

[98] Lucy McIver Watson, daughter of James Kolb and Sarah Marshall McIver, married R. B. Watson.

[99] John Kolb McIver, son of John Kolb and Hannah Wilson McIver, married Louise Boyd.

[100] Fannie McIver, daughter of John Kolb and Hannah Wilson McIver, married Henry T. Thompson, son of Governor Hugh S. Thompson of South Carolina.

[101] Colonel Isaac DeLesseline Wilson died April 3, 1894.

[102] Elizabeth Williams Ferguson (1807-1885) lived at Leavensworth.

[103] Jefferson W. Ferguson (January 7, 1838 — September 4, 1909) was the son of Elizabeth Williams Ferguson. He never married.

[104] Nancy Wilds Coggeshall (August 7, 1835 — November 8, 1916), daughter of Peter and Julia Terrel Wilds, married Peter Collin Coggeshall II. Her daughters were: Anna, twenty-six; Nina, twenty-one; Mary, nineteen; and Clara, sixteen.

[105] Mrs. Henry Jones Tooke, Ringgold, Louisiana.

[106] Edith M. A. Woods Bacchus, widow of the Baptist minister, J. A. Bacchus, lived alone on the "Wilkins place," in Springville.

[107] Morrison and Fourmy's *General Directory of the City of San Antonio, 1883-1884*, p. 225. "William G. McGinty, carpenter, residence: Camden and Brooklyn."

[108] Amelia Melvina Howard (1834-1888) was living in Sanford, Florida, when her husband, Joseph Newton Whitner, died in 1881, and came to Darlington County in 1883 for a visit with her brother and half brothers.

[109] On December 14, 1860, Sarah Williamson reported that Andrew and Mary Ann Charles had just moved into their new home at Stony Hill. Hence they had been living at this same place for almost twenty-three years.

[110] Caroline Bacot Charles, wife of Hugh L. Charles, was Mary Ann's sister-in-law and Mrs. Dargan's sister.

[111] Serena Bacot Dargan, widow of Charles Dargan, was the great-aunt of Florence LaCoste, her ward.

112 Florence LaCoste, daughter of A. P. and Eliza King LaCoste, was born at Cheraw in 1860. When her father, and soon after, her mother, had died, she came to Darlington about 1870 to live with her mother's aunt, Serena Bacot Dargan. She had gone to the northern part of South Carolina to visit her sister, Georgia, who lived with their aunt, Emily King Taylor, and to Cheraw to visit her half sisters.

113 Susannah E. W. Orr, oldest member of the Baptist Church, Darlington, died in 1883.

114 Edith M. A. Woods Bacchus was the sister of Peter Alexander Brunson's wife, Susanna Pamela Woods Brunson. Mrs. Bacchus and Mrs. Brunson were daughters of Joseph and Hepzibah Dargan Woods.

115 Peter Brunson married Susanna P. Woods (July 4, 1809 — May 27, 1843).

116 Agnes Wilson Williams was the second wife of James A. Williams.

117 Mary Deborah Ferguson Chambers (December 27, 1835 — October 12, 1917), daughter of Alexander and Elizabeth Williams Ferguson, was the wife of Benjamin Wesley Chambers (May 8, 1820 — October 12, 1863).

118 Ptolemy Philadelphus Chambers (September 5, 1855 — March 26, 1943) married Ida Cornelia Berry (February 23, 1860 — May 13, 1951), of Greenville, on November 21, 1876.

119 Eunice Chambers, Card from Hartsville, South Carolina, to John A. Cawthon, Russellville, Arkansas, February 9, 1953. "My parents' oldest son, Benjamin W. Chambers, son of P. P. and Ida Cornelia Berry Chambers, was born Aug. 29, 1880, and died April 21, 1902. He was a senior at V. P. I. when he died." Eunice Chambers, Letter from Hartsville, South Carolina, to John A. Cawthon, Russellville, Arkansas, December 3, 1953. "Their oldest child was Mary Elise Chambers (Aug. 16, 1878 — Sept. 23, 1880). Elise, as you see, was the oldest child and Benny was the second child."

120 Robert W. Lide was the son of Evan and Martha Miller Lide. His second wife was a daughter of Furman and Jane Coker Wilson.

121 John Stout, pastor at Welsh Neck Baptist Church, Society Hill, was the husband of Frances Coker Stout.

122 S. H. Pressley, Society Hill, married (1) Jane Draughon Edwards, and (2) Sarah McIver.

123 Nelly Gandy Fort of Society Hill was a sister to Abel Gandy.

124 "Minutes of the Welsh Neck Baptist Church, Society Hill, South Carolina," May 21, 1883. "With much sorrow we record the death of one of our most devoted and useful members, Miss Louisa McIntosh. She cherished her life and health that she might use them for the Glory of God, but rendered them up cheerfully at His call."

125 Ibid., October 14, 1922. Mrs. Martha McIntosh Bell died at Ridge Crest, North Carolina. She was baptized in 1864 and married Dr. T. P. Bell, corresponding secretary for the Sunday School Board of the Southern Baptist Convention, in 1896. Mrs. Bell was the first president of the Baptist Missionary Union.

126 W. J. Alexander served as pastor of the Darlington Church from 1876 until 1881 when he accepted a professorship at South Carolina College.

127 Gordon B. Moore was pastor at Darlington from 1883 until 1891.

128 L. W. Coker, *Historical Sketch and Membership Roll* (Darlington, First Baptist Church, 1945), p. 6.

129 Horace Lorenzo Hastings, "Shall We Meet?" Number 143 in Robert H. Coleman and W. W. Hamilton, *The Evangel* (Philadelphia, 1909).

130 John Foster Kirk, *Supplement to Allibone's Critical Dictionary of English Literature and British and American Authors* (Philadelphia, 1899), Volume II, p. 784. Horace Lorenzo Hastings's most productive years were between 1852 and 1886, when he published approximately twenty-five volumes, all dealing with the subject of religion and being, in most cases, connected with hymnology.
John Julian (ed.), *Dictionary of Hymnology* (London, 1915), p. 494. Hastings's best known hymn "Shall We Meet," was written in New York City in 1858.

131 John Stout (1842-1894) was a native of Mobile, Alabama. He married Frances Coker in 1871. When he died in Dallas, Texas, in 1894, while attending the Southern Baptist Convention, his body was brought to Welsh Neck Churchyard for burial.

132 Ellen Hartwell Edwards (April 10, 1828 — July 24, 1902) had lived in Louisiana during the 1860's; the "West" was not new to her.

133 Hartwell Edwards married Kate Watson.

134 Wilson, *Memories of Society Hill*, p. 15. "In August, 1883, Brother William's lovely and beloved wife, Mary McIver Coker died, leaving seven young children, the youngest an infant of a few months. Their care devolved on their grandmother and aunt and they received from them devoted care, though their mother's death was a sore bereavement."

135 In reporting William Caleb Coker's death on April 20, 1907, a Darlington newspaper listed seven surviving children: "*viz.* Prof. Edward C. Coker, of Winthrop College; Allen M. Coker, of Society Hill; Frank Coker, of Columbia University, New York; Robert E. Coker, Callao, Peru; and Misses Sallie, Mary and Lavinia Coker, of Darlington." E. C. Coker became professor of mathematics and astronomy at the University of South Carolina; Francis W. Coker (Frank) became professor of government, emeritus, at Yale; Robert E. became Kenan professor of zoology, University of North Carolina; and Dr. Sarah E. Coker (Sallie) became medical director, child welfare service, New Mexico, according to Robert E. Coker, "Springville," *South Carolina Historical Magazine*, October, 1952, p. 200.
Listed in *Who's Who in America*, 1954-1955, Volume 28, p. 517, are Francis W. Coker, Hamden, Conn., Born Nov. 1, 1878, married Helene Ruth Patton, July 6, 1916; and Robert E. Coker, Chapel Hill, North Carolina, born June 4, 1876, married Jennie Coit, Oct. 11, 1910.

136 Maria Lide Pouncy, daughter of James and Jane Holloway Lide, married Josiah Pouncy. According to Wilson, *Memories of Society Hill*, p. 15, "Dear Aunt Maria Pouncy left us in 1901 to join the ever enlarging family circle in the Heavenly Home."

137 Hannah Lide Coker (March 3, 1812 — May 19, 1900), wife of Caleb Coker, was a sister to Mrs. Pouncy.

138 Maria Lide Pouncy and her three daughters, Janie H. P. (November 12, 1847 — November 19, 1914), Anna M. (May 21, 1851 — November 9, 1921), and Minnie (Mary C.) (October 8, 1855 — September 25, 1934), were received by letter from Center Ridge Baptist Church. "Minutes of the Welsh Neck Baptist Church, Society Hill, South Carolina," November 5, 1882.

139 Lavinia Coker, youngest child of William Caleb and Mary McIver Coker, became the third wife of Arthur H. Rogers, son of Paul H. and Emma Coker Rogers. Mr. and Mrs. Rogers lived at the Rogers home, Society Hill.

140 Sallie Griffin (October 9, 1828 — June 1, 1884) married Lewis M. Coker, aged fifty-nine, in 1878, when she was fifty.

141 S. H. Pressley, Society Hill, was a prominent member of Welsh Neck Church.

142 Margaret Douglas Sompayrac (1828-1901) was the wife of Theodore Sompayrac.

143 Dr. Gordon B. Moore was employed as pastor in the early months of 1883.

144 Emily King Taylor.

145 Florence LaCoste was Mrs. Taylor's niece.

146 Georgia LaCoste, Florence's sister, lived with Mr. and Mrs. Taylor until she began to teach.

147 It is possible that Sallie's music brought to Mrs. Charles's mind the suitability of Hastings's words to her sentiments about death and the future life.

148 Colonel B. W. Edwards married Anna Maria Coker in 1857.

149 H. A. Tupper (ed.), *Two Centuries of the First Baptist Church of South Carolina, 1683-1883* (Baltimore, 1889), p. xiii.

150 Rev. Charles Manly, the son of Rev. Basil Manly, Sr., was pastor of the Baptist Church and in charge of Central Female College, Tuscaloosa, Alabama, prior to his removal to Greenville, South Carolina, where he became president of Furman University.

151 Rev. A. J. S. Thomas was pastor at Charleston from January 7, 1883, until July 3, 1887.

152 Lewis H. Shuck, son of J. Lewis and Henrietta Hall Shuck, was born while his parents, missionaries to China, were on their way to the Orient. He was educated in Virginia and at Wake Forest College, North Carolina, and served as pastor of First Church, Charleston, from December, 1869, until November, 1882.

153 Tupper, p. 3.

154 Rev. Basil Manly, Jr., son of Basil Manly, Sr., was a professor at Southern Baptist Theological Seminary, Greenville.

155 Henry Allen Tupper, Sr., son of Tristram and Eliza Yoer Tupper, was living in Richmond, Virginia. He was corresponding secretary of the Board of Foreign Missions, Southern Baptist Convention, from 1872-1893.

156 Tupper, p. 195 ff.

157 Tupper, p. 19 ff.

158 Rev. William Screven (born in Somersetshire, England, in 1629; died in Georgetown, South Carolina, October 10, 1713) was the first pastor of the Charleston Church. He married Bridget Cutt, daughter of Robert Cutt, member of the British Parliament. When Robert Cutt died in 1675, his widow married Captain Francis Champernown, a kinsman of Sir Walter Raleigh and Sir Humphrey Gilbert.

159 Dr. Kolb was sixty-three; his wife was fifty-one.

160 Minden, Louisiana, *Webster Review*, August 8, 1950, p. 1. "The Primitive Baptist Church (New Providence) of Ringgold has just completed observing its 100th anniversary." Thus, the "Hardshell" or Primitive Baptist Church at Ringgold was thirty-three years old in 1883, and was enjoying greater prosperity and growth than the Southern Baptist Convention church to which Miss Darby belonged.

161 Henry C. Vedder, *A Short History of the Baptists* (Philadelphia, 1897), p. 275. "There are also a number of Calvinistic Baptist bodies that for one reason or another decline fellowship with the Regular Baptists — Holding a hyper-Calvinistic theology, they are opposed to missions, Sunday Schools and 'all contrivances which seem to make the salvation of men depend on Human effort.' They call themselves Primitive Baptists and have been known as 'Anti-Mission' and 'Hardshell' Baptists. They have churches in twenty-eight states — In the South, they seem to be not merely holding their own, but increasing."

162 Dr. Gordon B. Moore was pastor at Darlington from 1883 until 1891.

163 Sue Flinn James, "His Springville," *Darlington County Historical Society Records and Papers, 1938-1944*, p. 67. "Mr. Laurens Williamson (son of Thomas Charles and Ann Williamson) married Miss Adele Dargan . . . and was, for years, the respected cashier in the old Bank at Darlington."

164 Andrew and Emilie Bacot Hunter, Darlington, were the parents of Ida Hunter, who married George W. Dargan. Mrs. Hunter was a sister to Mrs. Serena Dargan, Mrs. Caroline Charles, Mrs. Louisa Dargan, and Mrs. Lissie Bealer.

165 Susannah Orr was the oldest member of the Darlington Baptist Church at the time of her death.

166 Ann DuBose Fort, Black Creek community, was the wife of Josiah Fort.

167 Jefferson W. Ferguson (January 7, 1838 — September 4, 1909), son of Elizabeth Williams Ferguson, never married. Eunice Chambers, Letter from Hartsville, South Carolina, to John A. Cawthon, Russellville, Arkansas, February 5, 1953: "Mr. Wilson told me yesterday that a girl certainly played a dirty trick on Uncle Jeff. He was engaged to a Miss Nettles whom he loved so very much. He went to war and they were to be married upon his return. He was delayed in returning (a year) and she ups and married Mr. Hacker. Mr. Wilson said, 'The BUM! He should have been in the war instead of refugeeing up there in Charleston.' Uncle Jeff never married and I remember him well. He was a great person and devoted to all of us. Mother was his favorite."

168 *Ibid.*, "Mrs. Ferguson had two children: Mary Deborah who was Pammie, my grandmother . . . and Jefferson W. Ferguson."

169 Elizabeth Pugh Dargan (May 3, 1842-1883) married Eldred Forrester, May 15, 1878.

170 Mrs. Forrester was buried in the Dargan lot in the churchyard of the Baptist Church at Darlington.

171 Maude Dargan Forrester married Emmett H. Williams, April 15, 1902.

172 Elizabeth Dargan Forrester married William Lucien McLeod.

173 Margaret L. K. Dargan (September 16, 1844 — April 29, 1911) married her sister's widower, Eldred Forrester, January 6, 1885.

174 Ellen Hartwell Edwards and her daughter, Janie, had gone to Mississippi to live with Hartwell and Kate Watson Edwards.

175 Mary Sanders Pegues, a native of Cheraw, South Carolina, was the wife of Nicholas Bedgegood Pegues, of Oxford, Mississippi. Mr. Pegues, also a native of South Carolina, was born January 1, 1821.

176 B. F. Riley, *History of the Baptists of Alabama, from 1808 until 1894* (Birmingham, 1895), p. 384. "Rev. E. J. Forrester resigned the care of the Selma Church during the latter part of 1883."

177 James Furman Dargan (April 1, 1838 — June 6, 1907) married Mary Atmar Smith, Charleston, July 13, 1870.

178 Edwin Charles Dargan (November 17, 1852 — October 26, 1930). Porter Routh, *Meet the Presidents* (Nashville, 1953), p. 39. "At 21 he was a graduate of Furman University, Greenville, S. C.; at 25, he was a graduate of the Southern Baptist Theological Seminary, then located at Greenville. Honorary degrees were later conferred upon him by Baylor University and also by Washington and Lee University. After serving several small churches in Virginia, Dr. Dargan felt the urge to go West and accepted the pastorate of the Baptist church in Dixon, California."

179 *Who Was Who in America, 1897-1942*, Volume I (Chicago, 1942), p. 294. Dr. and Mrs. E. C. Dargan were living in Barboursville, Virginia, when Edwin Preston Dargan was born on September 7, 1879.

180 Julia Elizabeth Wilds Lide, wife of Leighton Lide, lived at White Plains, Springville.

181 Nancy Wilds Coggeshall, wife of Peter Collin Coggeshall, lived at Wilds Hall, Springville.

182 Jane Williamson Wallace, wife of Thomas Wallace, lived near Cashaway Ferry.

183 Walter Cannon Harllee (March 18, 1850 — July 14, 1931), son of Robert and Amelia Melvina Cannon Howard Harllee, married Mary Ann Young in 1895.

184 Amelia Melvina Howard Whitner, widow of Joseph Newton Whitner, was a half sister to Walter Harllee, who was thirty-three years old. He was ten years old when Miss Darby left Darlington.

185 Florence LaCoste, now about twenty-three years old, had led a sheltered life in the home of her great-aunt, Mrs. Charles Dargan, Darlington. Only recently had she begun to visit in the homes of friends.

186 When Emily King married T. J. Taylor in 1872, she was forty-two; he was twenty-one. In 1883, she was sickly and old at fifty-three while he was only thirty-two.

187 Mary Ann Charles was only fifty-four years old, but her health was poor and her eyesight bad. She regarded herself an old woman.

188 Sallie Williams, born in 1862, was now about twenty-one years old.

189 Jane Williamson Wallace was Mrs. Charles's niece, but she was only seven years her junior.

190 Jenny Wallace, daughter of Thomas and Jane Wallace, married her second cousin, Thomas W. Williamson, and became one of Sallie Williams's heirs, according to her will of July 7, 1893. Actually her husband and his sisters, Virginia and Kate, were Sallie's double first cousins.

191 The Kolb family was composed of Dr. and Mrs. Kolb and their sons: David Alexander (July 1, 1863 — March 20, 1916), who married Celina Valois, Marksville, Louisiana, in 1894; Lee Jackson (August 31, 1865 — November 19, 1885), who never married; and Edwin Kirtley (March 13, 1868 — June 1, 1925), who married (1) Pearl Williams in 1892, and (2) Myrtle Williams Lee in June, 1898. James Alexander Cawthon, five-year-old son of James Ashley and Ella Kolb Cawthon, was also a member of the Kolb household. James Ashley Cawthon was an intermittent visitor. Henry Jones and Maria Elizabeth Kolb Tooke and their daughter, Ella, lived within the neighborhood.

192 Boyce House, *City of Flaming Adventure, The Chronicle of San Antonio* (San Antonio, 1949), p. 172.

193 Morrison and Fourmy's *General Directory of the City of San Antonio. 1883-1884,* p. 225. "Wm. G. McGinty, Carpenter, Camden and Brooklyn."

194 Morrison and Fourmy's *General Directory of the City of San Antonio. 1885-1886,* p. 100. "James A. Cawthon, Carpenter, boards, W. G. McGinty, 426 Morales, between Leona and Frio."

195 Charles Gibson McGinty (March 17, 1884 — February 8, 1886) and Edwin Parramore Tooke (August 11, 1884 — April 12, 1944) were both born in San Antonio.

196 Mrs. Thomas Wallace (Jane Williamson).

197 Amanda Melvina Brinson Kolb.

198 Mary Ella Tooke was born January 22, 1882.

199 Mary Sanders Pegues, wife of the Reverend N. B. Pegues.

200 Elizabeth Hannah McCall Sanders, daughter of James Sanders and Elizabeth Muldrow McCall, married (1) Thomas B. Haynesworth, and (2) Henry E. Sanders. She lived in Mississippi also.

201 Henrietta was referred to in a letter from Sarah Williamson, March 6, 1862, when Miss Williamson reported a visit by Mrs. James (assumed to be Mrs. James Sanders) and Martha Sanders "who has a fine large daughter, [who] looks very much like Henrietta."

202 Reverend and Mrs. Taylor (Emily King) and Georgia LaCoste, Mrs. Taylor's niece and ward, lived in Union County, South Carolina, where Miss LaCoste was a teacher.

203 Elizabeth Dargan Forrester died in Selma, Alabama, in 1883.

204 Jane Lide Dargan (November 10, 1815-1886), daughter of Hugh and Elizabeth Pugh Lide, married the Reverend J. O. B. Dargan in 1837. Betty was their daughter.

205 Eldred J. Forrester was a Baptist minister in Selma, Alabama, who had been called to the church in Hartsville.

206 Walter Cannon Harllee married Mary Ann Young in 1895.

207 Dr. Alexander James Kolb.

208 David Kolb, twenty-one, Lee Kolb, eighteen, and Edwin Kolb, sixteen, had gone out to San Antonio to live with Mary Kolb McGinty. Planning to make the trip with their parents and aunt were Maria Elizabeth Kolb Tooke and her family and James Ashley Cawthon and his son, James Alexander.

209 Morrison and Fourmy's *General Directory of the City of Shreveport. 1882-1883*, p. 15.

210 *Ibid.*, p. 40.

211 Maria Elizabeth Kolb Tooke, Interview in Koran, Louisiana, September 5, 1934.

212 Camden Street in Ward Two was the fourth street northwest of the San Antonio River. It began at Jones and extended southwest to Acequia or Main Avenue. Brooklyn Avenue in Ward Two was the fifth avenue northeast of Acequia. It began west of the San Antonio River and extended to the Upper Labor Ditch.

213 Means and Slaskin, 33 Soledad, advertised as "House Renting Agency," in the San Antonio *Light*, Volume IV, Number 46 (February 22, 1884), p. 2.

214 Morrison and Fourmy's *General Directory of the City of San Antonio. 1883-1884*, p. 204. "Edwin Kolb, Clerk, J. Devine Fruit Stand, 217 Flores St., Home: A. J. Kolb, 2nd Ward."

215 Actually, they had reached Round Rock before they passed through Austin.

216 San Marcos.

217 San Antonio *Light*, Volume IV, Number 46 (February 22, 1884), "Deaths," p. 4.

218 *Ibid.*, p. 1. "Raleigh. Feb. 21. The number of lives lost in North Carolina by cyclone is about 50 and an equal number wounded. Much property has been destroyed."

[219] Morrison and Fourmy's *General Directory of the City of San Antonio. 1883-1884,* p. 92.

[220] "Franklin L. Paschal, Veteran of 1836, Died February 18, 1884, Aged 74 Yrs.," is the inscription on a tombstone in the northeastern side of the cemetery, near the gate of the National Cemetery, on the north end of Paso Hondo, east of Pine Street.

[221] *Light,* February 22, 1884, p. 4. "John Burns, aged 46, died on February 19th in the Second Ward of consumption and paralysis."

[222] *Ibid.,* p. 4. "Miss Violet Rose, aged 4 yrs., and 4 mos., died on the 21st., from typhoid fever."

[223] "Record of Burials by City Sexton, City Cemetery No. 1," 1884, February 22. Name — Miss R. J. Darby. Age — 90 Yrs. Sex — Female. Marital Status — Single. Nativity — U. S. Color — White. Grave — 76.

[224] The First Baptist Church was located at the southeast corner of Travis and Jefferson Streets in 1884; W. H. Dodson was the pastor.

[225] Mrs. W. H. Russell (Church secretary, First Baptist Church, San Antonio, Texas), Letter to John A. Cawthon, Russellville, Arkansas, August 25, 1953. "We have your letter of August 9th in regard to the record of Jemima Darby. We are unable to locate any name like that on any of the old records that we have."

[226] The Baptist Chapel at the southeast corner of Hidalgo and North Frio streets had no regular pastor.

[227] On August 19, 1953, there was no evidence of a grave with a Darby marker. The sexton's record for City Cemetery No. 1 showed that Jemima Darby had been buried in Grave No. 76, but the sexton was unable to point out the exact location of these early rows. He felt reasonably sure that the grave was in the vicinity of Mr. Paschal's grave; beyond that, he was not able to venture a guess.

[228] Dr. Kolb died May 6, 1886.

[229] Mrs. Kolb lived to return to Louisiana and died there May 23, 1890.

[230] Henry Jones Tooke (June 21, 1854 — August 26, 1934) married Maria Elizabeth Kolb March 2, 1881, in Ringgold, Louisiana.

[231] Mary Ella Tooke, born January 22, 1882, married David K. Thomas June 23, 1908, in Koran, Louisiana.

[232] Edwin Parramore Tooke was born in San Antonio, August 11, 1884, and died in Tulsa, Oklahoma, April 12, 1944. He married Lela Viola Dees December 10, 1910, in Shreveport, Louisiana.

[233] Charles Gibson McGinty was born in San Antonio on March 17, 1884, and died February 8, 1886. Mrs. McGinty's other child was Vivian Kolb McGinty, who was born December 19, 1881, Rosita, Custer County, California, and died June 20, 1953, in Phoenix, Arizona; he married (1) Helen Watkins on August 20, 1902, in Salt Lake City, Utah, and (2) Ethel M. Hunter, March 8, 1923, in Oakland, California.

Bibliography

BOOKS AND PAMPHLETS

Ames, J. S. *The Williams Family of Society Hill*. Issued by Pee Dee Historical Association. Columbia: State Company, 1910.

Barnes, William Wright. *The Southern Baptist Convention. 1845-1953*. Nashville: Broadman Press, 1954.

Battles and Leaders of the Civil War. New York: Century Company, 1884, 1888. 4 vols.

Biographical and Historical Memoirs of Northwest Louisiana. Chicago: John Morris Company, 1890.

Bratton, Virginia Mason. *History of the South Carolina Daughters of the American Revolution. 1892-1936*. South Carolina Daughters of the American Revolution. Columbia: The R. L. Bryan Company, 1937.

Brooks, U. R. *Stories of the Confederacy*. Columbia: State Press, 1912.

Burroughs, P. E. *Honoring the Deaconship*. Nashville: The Sunday School Board of the Southern Baptist Convention, 1929.

Cassel, Daniel Kolb. *A Genealogical History of the Kolb, Kulb, or Culp Family and Its Branches in America, with Biographical Sketches of Their Descendants from the Earliest Available Records from 1707 to the Present Time*. Norristown, Pennsylvania: Morgan R. Wills, Publishers, 1895.

Chesnut, Mary Boykin. *A Diary from Dixie*. Ed. by Ben Ames Williams. New York: Houghton Mifflin Company, 1949.

Christian, John T. *A History of the Baptists of Louisiana*. Shreveport: Executive Board of the Louisiana Baptist Convention, 1923.

Coker, L. W. *Historical Sketch and Membership Roll*. Darlington: First Baptist Church, 1945.

Coker, W. C. "Sketch of the Organization of the Darlington Companies in the Eighth Regiment, S. C., Volunteers of the Confederate Army." *Treasured Reminiscences.* Collected by John K. McIver Chapter, U. D. C. Columbia: State Press, 1911.

Coleman, Robert H., and Hamilton, W. W. *The Evangel.* Philadelphia: American Baptist Publication Society, 1909.

Cook, Harvey Toliver. *A Biographical Sketch of George Alexander Norwood.* Privately printed, New York: DeVirre Press, 1911.

_____. *The Life and Legacy of David Rogerson Williams.* Privately printed, New York: 1916.

_____. *The Life Work of James Clement Furman.* Privately printed by Alister G. Furman, 1926.

Coulter, E. Merton. *The South during Reconstruction. 1865-1877.* Vol. 8. Baton Rouge: Louisiana State University Press, 1947.

Cubberley, Ellwood P. *Public Education in the United States.* New York: Houghton Mifflin Company, 1919.

Daniel, Robert Norman. *Furman University, A History.* Greenville: Furman University, 1951.

Darby, R. C., ed. *Genealogy of the Darby Family.* Privately printed, 1912-1914.

Dargan, Edwin Charles. *Harmony Hall.* Columbia: State Press, 1912.

Dargan, John J. *School History of South Carolina.* Columbia: State Press, 1906.

Davidson, James Wood. *School History of South Carolina.* Columbia: Duffie and Chapman, 1869.

_____. *School History of South Carolina.* Rev. ed. Columbia: W. J. Duffie, 1894.

Davis, Jefferson. *The Rise and Fall of the Confederate Government.* Richmond: Garrett and Massie, Inc. Memorial edition prepared by United Daughters of the Confederacy, 1939. 2 vols.

DeBow, J. D. B. *Industrial Resources Etc., of the Southwest.* New Orleans: Office of DeBow's Review, 1852-1853. 3 vols.

Dodd, William E. *The Cotton Kingdom.* New Haven: Yale University Press, 1919.

DuBose, Henry Kershaw. *History of Company B, Twenty-First Regiment (Infantry), South Carolina Volunteers.* Columbia: R. L. Bryan Company, 1909.

DuBose, John Witherspoon. "The Witherspoons of Society Hill." *Bulletin* of Pee Dee Historical Association. Hartsville, South Carolina: Hartsville Publishing Company, 1910.

Durham, John Pinckney, and Ramond, John S., ed. and comp. *Baptist Builders of Louisiana.* Privately printed, Shreveport: 1934.

Easterby, J. Harold. "Wade Hampton." *Dictionary of American Biography.* Vol. VIII. Ed. by Dumas Malone. New York: Charles Scribner's Sons, 1932.

Ervin, Julia. *History of the Darlington Presbyterian Church.* Privately printed, 1952.

Evans, Clement A., ed. *Confederate Military History.* Atlanta: Confederate Publishing Company, 1899. 12 vols.

Farmer, Fannie M. *Boston Cooking School Book.* Boston: Little, Brown and Company, 1896.

Fleming, Walter L. *Documentary History of Reconstruction, Political, Military, Social, Religious, Educational and Industrial, 1865 to the Present Time.* Cleveland: Arthur H. Clark Company, 1906. 2 vols.

Funk and Wagnall's Encyclopedia. Ed. by Joseph Laffan Morse. New York: Unicorn Publishers, 1952. 36 vols.

Furman, Wood. *A History of the Charleston Association of Baptist Churches.* Charleston: J. Hoff, No. 6, Broad St., 1811.

Gonzales, William E. "South Carolina in the Confederacy." *The South in the Building of the Nation.* Vol. II. Richmond: Southern Historical Publication Society, 1909.

Grady, Henry W. "The Old South and the New." *The World's Famous Orations.* Vol. X. New York: Funk and Wagnall's Company, 1906.

Gregg, Alexander. *History of the Old Cheraws.* San Antonio: 1867. (Reprinted, Columbia: The State Press, 1905.)

Harllee, William. *Kinfolks.* New Orleans: Search and Pfaff Ltd., 1934. 3 vols.

Harper, Robert Henry. *Louisiana Methodism.* Washington, D. C.: Kaufman Press, 1949.

Harris, Joel Chandler. *Life of Henry W. Grady Including His*

Writings and Speeches. New York: Cassell Publishing Company, 1890.

Harris, Miriam Cole. *Rutledge.* New York: Derby and Jackson, 1860.

Harris, T. H. *The Story of Public Education in Louisiana.* New Orleans: Delgado Trades School, 1924.

Hart, T. W. *Robert Sanders.* New York: Irving Company, 1897.

Henning, Helen Kohn. *William Harrison Scarborough, Portraitist and Miniaturist: A Parade of the Living Past.* Columbia: R. L. Bryan Company, 1937.

History of Old Ebenezer Church and Genealogy of Dargan, Woods and Other Families. Bulletin of Pee Dee Historical Society. Weldon, North Carolina: Harrell's Printing House, 1909.

House, Boyce. *City of Flaming Adventure: The Chronicle of San Antonio.* San Antonio: Naylor Company, 1949.

Howell, R. B., and Richardson, W. U. *Bienville Parish, Louisiana.* New Orleans: F. F. Hansell and Company, 1885.

Johnson, Guion Griffis. *Ante-Bellum North Carolina, A Social History.* Chapel Hill: University of North Carolina Press, 1937.

Julian, John, ed. *Dictionary of Hymnology.* London: John Murray Company, 1915.

Julien, Carl, and Dabbs, James McBride. *Pee Dee Panorama.* Columbia: University of South Carolina Press, 1951.

Kirk, John Foster. *Supplement to Allibone's Critical Dictionary of English Literature and British and American Authors.* Philadelphia: J. B. Lippincott Company, 1899. 2 vols.

Law, John Adger, ed. *Citadel Cadets, The Journal of Cadet Tom Law.* Clinton: P. C. Press, 1941.

McColl, D. D. *Sketches of Old Marlboro.* Privately printed in Bennettsville, South Carolina. (Reprinted, Columbia: State Company, 1916.)

McDaniel, George W. *The People Called Baptists.* Nashville: Sunday School Board of the Southern Baptist Convention, 1919.

McGinty, Garnie William. *A History of Louisiana.* New York: Exposition Press, 1949.

Macartney, Clarence Edward. *Highways and Byways of the Civil War.* Pittsburg: Gibson Press, 1938.

Malone, Dumas, ed. *Dictionary of American Biography*. New York: Charles Scribner's Sons, 1933. 20 vols.

Memorial Record of Alabama. Madison, Wisconsin: Brant and Fuller, 1893. 2 vols.

Miller, Francis Trevelyan. *The Photographic History of the Civil War*. New York: Review of Reviews, 1911. 10 vols.

Milling, Chapman J., ed. *Colonial South Carolina*. Columbia: University of South Carolina Press, 1951.

Morris, Richard B., ed. *Encyclopedia of American History*. New York: Harper and Brothers, 1953.

Morrison and Fourmy's *General Directory of the City of San Antonio, 1883-1884*. Marshall, Texas: Jennings Brothers, 1883.

_____. *General Directory of the City of San Antonio, 1885-1886*. Marshall: Jennings Brothers, 1885.

_____. *General Directory of the City of Shreveport, 1882-1883*. Marshall: Jennings Brothers, 1882.

Morrison, C. D., and Company. *Shreveport City Directory*. Marshall: Jennings Brothers, 1878.

Morrison, William Shannon. "South Carolina, 1865-1909." *The South in the Building of the Nation*. Vol. II. Richmond: Southern Historical Publication Society, 1909.

Mott, Frank Luther. *Golden Multitudes*. New York: Macmillan Company, 1947.

Oakey, Daniel. "Marching through Georgia and the Carolinas." *Battles and Leaders of the Civil War*. Vol. IV. New York: Century Company, 1884, 1888.

Odum, Howard W., Yeuell, Gladstone H., and Summersell, Charles G. *Alabama Past and Future*. Chicago: Science Research Associates, 1941.

Olmsted, Frederick Law. *The Cotton Kingdom*. Ed. by Arthur M. Schlesinger. New York: Alfred A. Knopf, 1953.

Owsley, Frank Lawrence. *Plain Folk of the Old South*. Baton Rouge: Louisiana State University Press, 1949.

Page, Thomas Nelson. *The Old South*. Chatauqua, New York: Chatauqua Press, 1892, 1919.

Paxton, William E. *A History of the Baptists of Louisiana*. St. Louis: C. R. Barns Publishing Company, 1888.

Pettigrew, George R. *Annals of Ebenezer, 1778-1950*. Privately printed, 1952.

Phillips, Ulrich Bonnell. *A History of Transportation in the Eastern Cotton Belt in 1860*. New York: Columbia University Press, 1908.

Pike, J. S. "The Prostrate State." From *Traveling in South Carolina in 1871*, quoted in Fleming, Walter L., *Documentary History of the Reconstruction*, Vol. I. Cleveland: Arthur H. Clark Company, 1906.

Pollard, Edward Alfred. *The Lost Cause: A New Southern History of the War of the Confederates*. New York: E. B. Treat and Company, 1866.

Population of the United States, 1860. Washington: U. S. Census Office.

Randall, J. G. *The Civil War and Reconstruction*. Boston: D. C. Heath and Company, 1937.

Report of the United States Commissioner of Education for the Year 1884-1885. Washington: Government Printing Office, 1886.

Reynolds, John S. *Reconstruction in South Carolina, 1865-1877*. Columbia: State Press, 1905.

Riley, B. F. *History of the Baptists of Alabama from 1808 until 1894*. Birmingham: Roberts and Son, 1895.

Routh, Porter. *Meet the Presidents*. Nashville: Broadman Press, 1953.

Sessums, Roy T. *Bienville Parish: Resources and Facilities*. Baton Rouge: Department of Public Works, Planning Division, 1952.

Slocum, Henry. "Sherman's March from Savannah to Bentonville." *Battles and Leaders of the Civil War*. Vol. IV. New York: Century Company, 1884, 1888.

The Society, Daughters of Colonial Wars in the State of South Carolina. *South Carolina Colonial Soldiers and Patriots*. Comp. by Leonardo Andrea. Columbia: R. L. Bryan Company, 1952.

The South in the Building of the Nation. A History of the Southern States Designed To Record the South's Part in the Making of the American Nation; To Portray the Character and Genius, To Chronicle the Achievements and Progress and To Illustrate the Life and Traditions of the South's People. Richmond: Southern Historical Publication Society, 1909. 12 vols.

South Carolina Daughters of the American Revolution. *Roster and Ancestral Roll.* Comp. by Mrs. G. Duncan Foxworth. Columbia: R. L. Bryan Company, 1954.

Taylor, Walter Carroll. *History of Limestone College, Gaffney, S. C.* Privately printed by W. C. Taylor, 1937.

Tompkins, F. H. *North Louisiana.* Cincinnati: A. H. Pugh Printing Company, 1886.

Townsend, Leah. *South Carolina Baptists.* Florence, South Carolina: Florence Printing Company, 1935.

Treasured Reminiscences. Collected by John K. McIver Chapter, U. D. C. Columbia: State Company, 1911.

Trowbridge, J. T. *The South: A Tour of Its Battlefields and Ruined Cities.* Hartford, Connecticut: L. Stebbins, 1866.

Tryon, Warren S., ed. and comp. *A Mirror for American Life and Manners in the United States 1790-1870 as Recorded by American Travelers.* Chicago: University of Chicago Press, 1952. 3 vols.

Tupper, H. A., ed. *Two Centuries of the First Baptist Church of South Carolina, 1683-1883.* Baltimore: R. H. Woodward and Company, 1889.

United States Department of Agriculture. *Yearbook.* Washington: Government Printing Office, 1900.

Van Ness, J. J. *Training in Church Membership.* Nashville: Baptist Sunday School Board, 1908.

Van Slyke, Lucius L. *Fertilizer and Crops.* New York: Orange, Judd Company, 1912.

Vedder, Henry C. *A Short History of the Baptists.* Philadelphia: American Baptist Publication Society, 1897.

War of the Rebellion: A Compilation of Official Records of the Union and Confederate Armies. Prepared under the direction of the Secretary of War by Bvt. Lieut. Col. Robert N. Scott. Series I: Volumes I, II, VI, XIV, XV, XVI, XVII, XXVI, and XLVII. Washington: Government Printing Office, 1880.

    Beauregard, G. T. Letter to Hon. L. P. Walker, Secretary of War, April 13, 1861, from Charleston. Series I, Volume I, p. 309.

    Beauregard, G. T. Letter to Hon. L. P. Walker, Secretary of War, April 14, 1861, from Charleston. Series I, Volume I, p. 309.

Whitting, W. H. C. Report from Headquarters Provisional Forces, C. S. A., Charleston, April 15, 1861. Series I, Volume I, p. 309.

"Report of Col. A. P. Hill, 13th Virginia Infantry," June 19, 1861. Series I, Volume II, pp. 130-131.

"Report of Col. E. B. C. Cash, Eighth South Carolina Infantry, of Operations, July 18 and 19, 1861." Series I, Volume II, pp. 531-533.

Orders of R. S. Ripley, Brig. Gen., Commanding, Headquarters, Provisional Forces, Sept. S. C., Fulafinny, S. C., to Col. William E. Martin, Commanding Mounted Regiment, November 16, 1861. Series I, Volume VI, p. 34.

"Report of M. Lovell to Hon. J. P. Benjamin, Secretary of War, from Headquarters Dept. No 1, New Orleans, La.," November 19, 1861. Series I, Volume VI, p. 769.

Orders of T. W. Sherman, Brig. Gen., Commanding, Headquarters, Expeditionary Corps, Port Royal, S. C., December 3, 1861. Series I, Volume VI, p. 201.

Report of T. W. Sherman to General Meigs, Washington, D. C., December 10, 1861. Series I, Volume VI, p. 202.

Report of T. W. Sherman, Port Royal, S. C., to General George B. McClellan, December 23, 1861. Series I, Volume VI, p. 210.

General Orders No. 9, Headquarters, Expeditionary Corps, United States Army, Hilton Head, S. C., February 6, 1862. Series I, Volume VI, p. 222.

Report of Col. Henry Moore, 47th New York Infantry, Edisto Island, February 15, 1862, to L. Thomas, Adjutant General, Washington. Series I, Volume VI, pp. 89-90.

Correspondence from Headquarters, Military District, South Carolina, R. S. Ripley, Brig. Gen., Commanding, Charleston, February 18, 1862, to Capt. W. H. Taylor, Assistant Adjutant-General, Savannah, Georgia. Series I, Volume VI, p. 391.

"Notes Relative to an Attack — Charleston Harbor," prepared by D. F. Woodbury for General J. G. Barnard, Army of the Potomac, February 18, 1862. Series I, Volume VI, pp. 227-235.

Report of Adjutant-General's Department, State of South Carolina, to Hon. James Chesnut, Jr., Chief of Military Department, Executive Council of South Carolina. Series I, Volume VI, p. 404.

Special Orders No. 20, Hdqrs., Dept., S. Carolina, Georgia, etc. Pocataligo, April 10, 1862, by order of Major-General Pemberton: J. R. Waddy, Assistant Adjutant General. Series I, Volume VI, p. 433.

Proclamation, Headquarters, Department of the Gulf, New Orleans, May 1, 1862. Series I, Volume VI, p. 717.

General Orders No. 28, Hdqrs., Department of the Gulf, New Orleans, May 15, 1862, by command of Major General Butler. Series I, Volume XV, p. 426.

Report of Lieut. Col. Ellison Capers, Twenty-Fourth South Carolina Infantry, Camp 24th S. C. Volunteers, Regt., Advance Forces, James Island, S. C., June 10, 1862. Series I, Volume XXVI, p. 29.

Report of Lieut. Orran H. Howard, Acting Signal Officer, U. S. Army, Signal Station, Beaufort, S. C., June 23, 1862. Series I, Volume XXVI, p. 27.

General Orders No. 116, Hdqrs., Army of Northern Virginia, October 2, 1862, R. E. Lee, General, Commanding. Series I, Volume XIV, p. 645.

Report of the Battle of Corinth, October 3-12, from U. S. Grant, Major-General, Commanding, to Major-General Halleck, October 5, 1862. Series I, Volume XVII, p. 155.

Report of Major-General Earl Van Dorn to the Secretary of War, October 20, 1862. Series I, Volume XVII, p. 381.

Beauregard, G. T. Telegram to General S. Cooper, April 7, 1863, at 11 A.M. Series I, Volume XIV, p. 887.

Seddon, J. A. Telegram to General Wade Hampton, Columbia, from Secretary of War, War Department, C. S. A., Richmond, April 8, 1863. Series I, Volume XIV, p. 890.

Seddon, J. A. Letter to Governor M. L. Bonham, Columbia, from Secretary of War, War Department, C. S. A., Richmond, May 14, 1863. Series I, Volume XIV, p. 942.

Report of Major General William T. Sherman, U. S. Army, Hdqrs. Military Division of the Mississippi, Goldsborough, N. C., April 4, 1865. Series I, Volume XLVII, Part I.

Wellman, Manley Wade. *Giant in Gray*. New York: Charles Scribner's Sons, 1949.

Welsh, Spencer Glasgow. *A Confederate Surgeon's Letters to His Wife*. Marietta, Georgia: Continental Book Company, 1954.

Who's Who in America, 1954-1955. Chicago: A. N. Marquis Company, 1954.

Who Was Who in America, 1897-1942. Volume I. Chicago: A. N. Marquis Company, 1942.

Wilson, Jane Lide Coker , (Mrs. Furman E.). *Memories of Society Hill*. South Carolina: Pee Dee Historical Society, 1909-1910.

Work Projects Administration. *Louisiana: A Guide to the State*. New York: Hastings House, 1941.

Work Projects Administration. *South Carolina, A Guide to the Palmetto State*. New York: Oxford University Press, 1941.

CHURCH RECORDS

"Black Creek Church Book, A. D. 1798." Greenville: Furman University Library, Baptist Collection.

"Church Book, Records, 1756-78, Cashaway Neck Pee Dee South Carolina." Greenville: Furman University Library, Baptist Collection.

"The History of Mispah Baptist Church (1834-1934)." Greenville: Furman University Library, Baptist Collection.

Minutes of Welsh Neck Association, 1832-1871. Greenville: Furman University Library, Baptist Collection.

"Minutes of the Welsh Neck Baptist Church, Society Hill, South Carolina."

"Mispah Baptist Church Book. 1834-1862." Greenville: Furman University Library, Baptist Collection.

DOCUMENTS

Catlett, Sarah T. Will of February, 1834. Recorded in Will Book 10, p. 29, Darlington County Wills, *County Wills of South Carolina*. Columbia: University of South Carolina Library, 1939.

Charles, Mary Ann Williamson. Will of January 5, 1889. State of South Carolina, Darlington County. Probated May 18, 1895.

Darby, Jemima. Deed to James King, November 15, 1836. State of South Carolina, Darlington County Deed Book N, 1806-1898, p. 267.

Darby, Mary. Deed to James King, October 1, 1838. State of South Carolina, Darlington County Deed Book N, 1806-1898, p. 213.

Darby, Owen, Heirs of. Records of sale of land, March 11, 1807 — October 1, 1838. State of South Carolina, Darlington County Grantor Index A — E, 1806-1898.

Darby heirs. Deed to Samuel Bacot, January 4, 1823. State of South Carolina, Darlington County Deed Book H, 1806-1898, p. 209.

Kolb, Angelina. Acceptance of Widow's Pension Award, October 24, 1855. Washington: Files of the Government Pension Records.

Kolb, Angelina. Application for Widow's Pension (Revolutionary War Soldiers), South Carolina, May 30, 1853. Washington: Files of the Government Pension Records.

Kolb, Jehu. Application for Pension for Revolutionary War Service, South Carolina, October 21, 1829. Washington: Files of the Government Pension Records.

Kolb, Jehu. Application for Pension for Revolutionary War Service, South Carolina, October 14, 1832. Washington: Files of the Government Pension Records.

Kolb, Jesse and Elizabeth. Deed to Samuel Bacot, November 8, 1808. State of South Carolina, Darlington County Deed Book H, 1806-1898, p. 208.

Kolb, Jesse and Elizabeth. Deeds to (1) Jordan Sanders, September 9, 1822, and (2) Samuel Bacot, November 8, 1822. State of South Carolina, Darlington County Deed Book H, 1806-1898, pp. 202 and 208.

"Record of Burials by City Sexton, City Cemetery No. 1." San Antonio, Texas.

State of South Carolina, Darlington County Grantor Index, Book V, 1806-1898, August 20, 1867.

Survey of Alexander Craig, District Surveyor, February 24, 1786. Recorded in Book No. 1, p. 288, Bundle 103, Plat No. 198. Columbia: South Carolina Historical Association Files.

Vann, William. "Last Will and Testament of William Vann."

Year 1878, State of South Carolina, Darlington County, Recorded Wills 12, pp. 76 and 77. Filed 7th March 1887, M. A. Huggins, Judge of Probate.

Williams, Elizabeth Witherspoon. Will of October 10, 1830, Recorded January, 1841. Darlington County Wills Collection. Darlington: Public Library.

LETTERS AND INTERVIEWS

Campbell, Sarah Elizabeth Howle. Interview in Darlington, South Carolina, May 30, 1953.

Campbell, Edith. Letter from Darlington, South Carolina, to John A. Cawthon, Russellville, Arkansas, May 21, 1953.

Chambers, Eunice. Card from Hartsville, South Carolina, to John A. Cawthon, Russellville, Arkansas, February 9, 1953.

Chambers, Eunice. Letter from Hartsville, South Carolina, to John A. Cawthon, Russellville, Arkansas, February 5, 1953.

Chambers, Eunice. Letter from Hartsville, South Carolina, to John A. Cawthon, Russellville, Arkansas, December 3, 1953.

Coggeshall, Beulah Walden (Mrs. Robert). Letter from Darlington, South Carolina, to John A. Cawthon, Russellville, Arkansas, October 22, 1952.

Coggeshall, Beulah Walden (Mrs. Robert). Letter from Darlington, South Carolina, to John A. Cawthon, Russellville, Arkansas, November 17, 1952.

Coggeshall, Beulah Walden (Mrs. Robert). Letter from Darlington, South Carolina, to John A. Cawthon, Russellville, Arkansas, November 30, 1952.

Coggeshall, Beulah Walden (Mrs. Robert). Letter from Darlington, South Carolina, to John A. Cawthon, Russellville, Arkansas, February 19, 1953.

McFarland, J. F. Letter from Mansfield, Louisiana, to John A. Cawthon, Russellville, Arkansas, October 17, 1952.

Rose, Eleanor Vann. Letter from Franklinton, North Carolina, to John A. Cawthon, Russellville, Arkansas, December 16, 1952.

Rose, Eleanor Vann. Letter from Franklinton, North Carolina, to John A. Cawthon, Russellville, Arkansas, February 9, 1953.

Rose, Eleanor Vann. Letter from Franklinton, North Carolina, to John A. Cawthon, Russellville, Arkansas, February 21, 1953.

Russell, Mrs. W. H. (Church secretary, First Baptist Church, San

Antonio, Texas). Letter to John A. Cawthon, Russellville, Arkansas, August 25, 1953.

Sinclair, T. J. (Manager, School and College Service, Public Relations Department, Association of American Railroads). Letter from Washington 6, D. C., to John A. Cawthon, Russellville, Arkansas, January 26, 1953.

Tooke, Ida G. Letter from Koran, Louisiana, to John A. Cawthon, Baton Rouge, Louisiana, November 14, 1934.

Tooke, Ida G. Letter from Ringgold, Louisiana, to John A. Cawthon, Russellville, Arkansas, September 17, 1952.

Tooke, Ida G. Letter from Ringgold, Louisiana, to John A. Cawthon, Russellville, Arkansas, September 28, 1952.

Tooke, Ida G. Letter from Ringgold, Louisiana, to John A. Cawthon, Russellville, Arkansas, October 27, 1952.

Tooke, Ida G. Letter from Ringgold, Louisiana, to John A. Cawthon, Russellville, Arkansas, December 7, 1952.

Tooke, Maria Elizabeth Kolb. Interview in Koran, Louisiana, September 5, 1934.

Wilson, Sue Stout. Letter from Society Hill, South Carolina, to John A. Cawthon, Russellville, Arkansas, August 10, 1953.

MAGAZINES

Capers, Gerald M., Jr. "Yellow Fever in Memphis in the 1870's." *Mississippi Valley Historical Review,* XXIV (1937-1938), 483-502.

Coker, Robert Ervin. "Springville: A Summer Village of Old Darlington District." *South Carolina Historical Magazine,* LIII, Number 4 (October, 1952).

DeLeon, Edward. "Ruin and Reconstruction of the Southern States." *Southern Magazine,* XIV (January, 1874).

Harper's New Monthly Magazine, VI (December, 1852 — May, 1853).

Harper's New Monthly Magazine, XLIX (June — November, 1874).

Harper's New Monthly Magazine, CCCLIX, Number LX (April, 1880).

Johnson, Marie White. "The Colfax Riot of April, 1873." *Louisiana Historical Quarterly,* XIII (January — October, 1930), 391-427.

Prichard, Walter, ed. "A Tourist's Description of Louisiana in 1860." *Louisiana Historical Quarterly,* XXI, Number 4 (October, 1938), 1110-1214.

Sass, Herbert Ravenel. "South Carolina Rediscovered." *The National Geographic Magazine,* CIII, Number 3 (March, 1953), 281-321.

Scarborough, Lucy Paxton. "So It Was When Her Life Began." *Louisiana Historical Quarterly,* XIII (January — October, 1930), 438-439.

Scribner's Monthly Magazine, VI (May, 1873 — October, 1873).

Scribner's Monthly Magazine, VII (November, 1873 — April, 1874).

Souder, John D. "The Life and Times of Dielman Kolb, 1691-1756." *The Mennonite Quarterly Review,* III, Number 1 (January, 1929), 33-41.

"Transactions of the Southern Historical Society." *Southern Magazine,* I (January — December, 1874).

NEWSPAPERS

"Black Creek Church, Dovesville." *The Baptist Courier,* Volume 85, Number 47 (December 3, 1953), p. 13.

Charlotte, North Carolina, *Observer,* November 16, 1952.

Darlington, South Carolina, *News and Press,* June 11, 1953.

Jones, Mary Scanland. "Secession Day in Louisiana." Shreveport, Louisiana, *Times,* January 26, 1939.

Longino, Luther. "Travel: Yesterday, Today and Tomorrow." Minden, Louisiana, *Signal-Tribune,* Historical Edition, Volume 70, Section 2, December 31, 1934.

McClure, Lilla. "Old Military Road Once Vital to U. S. Defense." Shreveport *Times,* May 3, 1953.

Minden, Louisiana, *Webster Review,* August 8, 1950.

New Orleans, Louisiana, *Picayune,* March, 1878.

San Antonio, Texas, *Light,* Volume IV, Number 46 (February 22, 1884).

"Slabtown, Ringgold . . . and Now." Ringgold, Louisiana, *Press News,* Progress Edition, July 28, 1950.

Sparta, Louisiana, *Rural Times,* December, 1881.

Sparta, Louisiana, *Rural Times,* May 24, 1882.

Washington, Arkansas, *Southwestern Press,* February 18, 1880.

UNPUBLISHED MANUSCRIPTS

Charles, W. E. "Sketch of the Darlington Guards." Unpublished manuscript prepared in 1901 and preserved by Beulah Walden Coggeshall (Mrs. Robert), Darlington, South Carolina.

Coker, Edward D. "County History — Sketch of the Early History of Society Hill." Paper read before Darlington County Historical Society on April 4, 1938; preserved by Darlington County Circulating Library.

Coker, Mrs. Robert. "Early History of Hartsville." Paper read before the Darlington County Historical Society, October 26, 1944.

Darby family records from Jemima Darby's Bible, in possession of Ida G. Tooke, Ringgold, Louisiana.

Ervin, Julia. "Old Houses in Leavensworth." *Darlington County Historical Society Records and Papers, 1938-1944.* October 28, 1941.

Hart, Hannah B., and Townsend, Minnie D. "Homes of Old Darlington." *Darlington County Historical Society Records and Papers, 1938-1944.* October 28, 1941.

James, Sue Flinn. "His Springville." *Darlington County Historical Society Records and Papers, 1938-1944.*

Kolb, Ella Caroline. School essay. Ringgold, Louisiana, June 18, 1875.

Lide, Mrs. Ezra P. "White Plains, Springville." *Darlington County Historical Society Records and Papers, 1938-1944.* October 28, 1941.

McMaster, Louise McIver. "Roderick McIver and His Family." Mimeographed family history, December, 1952.

Mathematics Drill Book. Prepared by "David C. Kolb, 1827, Marlborough District, S. C., November 23rd, 1826, April 17; David C. Kolb was born July 27, 1811." In possession of Annis Cawthon, Ruston, Louisiana.

Napier, J. M. "Society Hill and Some of Its Contributions to State and Nation." Paper read before Darlington County Historical Society, May 8, 1947.

Tooke, Ida G. "Some North Louisiana Pioneers." Unpublished manuscript, Ringgold, Louisiana, 1952.

Wilson, Jane Lide Coker. "Memories of Society Hill and Some of Its People." Unpublished paper written for her family, 1909-1910.

Wilson, Thomas Evans. "Kolb Family Chart." Darlington, South Carolina, July, 1932.

Index

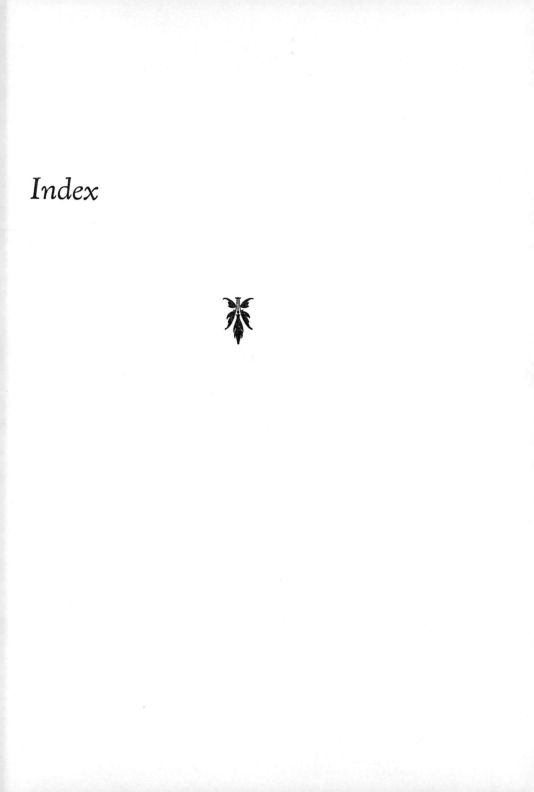

Darby family, 20, 22, 148, 199, 231, 342
Darby, Artemus Burnham, 22
Darby, Benjamin, 3, 9
Darby, Honor, 5
Darby, Jacob, 3, 9
Darby, James, 22
Darby, James Carel, 3, 9
Darby, Jeremiah, 3, 9
Darby, Margaret Elliott (Mrs. James), 9, 22
Darby, Mary, xiv, xvi, 3, 6, 7, 9, 10, 12, 13, 14, 15, 16, 20, 22, 24, 32, 33, 34, 41, 42, 43, 44, 45, 49, 52, 69, 95, 305, 324, 355
Darby, Mary Eugenia Thompson (Mrs. Artemus B.), 9, 22
Darby, Mary Vann (Mrs. Owen), 3, 5, 9, 45
Darby, Owen, 3, 5, 6, 9, 21, 45
Darby, Peggy, 5
Darby, Rebecca, 3, 9
Darby, William Henry, 3, 9
Dargan family, xvi, 8, 157, 342
Dargan, Alonzo, 352
Dargan, Colonel Alonzo T., 78, 95, 181, 192
Dargan, Alphonse (Rab), 352
Dargan, Charles, 352
Dargan, Charles A., 50, 226, 254, 352, 357
Dargan, Dubose, 180, 191
Dargan, Edwin Charles, 75, 79, 204, 221, 277, 302, 322, 343, 362
Dargan, Edwin Preston, 362
Dargan, Elizabeth Ann Townes (Mrs. John Hugh), 221, 224, 227, 261, 277, 278
Dargan, Elizabeth M. Player (Mrs. George W.), 86, 222, 223
Dargan, Ella, 277
Dargan, Evan Pugh, 277
Dargan, Frank Townes, 277
Dargan, Chancellor George W., 58, 86, 206, 209, 222, 223, 224
Dargan, George William, 110, 113, 121, 124, 285, 361
Dargan, Georgianna H., 209, 224
Dargan, Ida Louise Hunter (Mrs. George W.), 110, 113, 121, 124, 361
Dargan, J. A., 107
Dargan, James Furman, 141, 157, 204, 220, 296, 319, 343, 362

Dargan, Jane Lide (Mrs. J. O. B.), xvi, 90, 146, 155, 157, 159, 160, 217, 261, 282, 283, 306, 319, 322, 324, 331, 336, 343, 345, 351, 356, 364
Dargan, Jennie Quigby (Mrs. Alonzo T.), 95, 192
Dargan, Jessie, 218, 352
Dargan, John Hugh, 204, 209, 215, 221, 224, 227, 261, 277
Dargan, John Julius, 94, 222, 226, 271, 285, 287
Dargan, Rev. John Orr Beasley, xvi, 68, 72, 74, 75, 79, 80, 90, 93, 103, 105, 139, 146, 150, 155, 156, 157, 159, 169, 170, 180, 200, 204, 215, 217, 218, 227, 245, 255, 260, 268, 273, 276, 282, 283, 286, 292, 293, 310, 314, 317, 319, 322, 324, 326, 331, 335, 351, 356, 364
Dargan, Julius Alfred, 39, 47, 95, 112, 122, 192, 209, 223
Dargan, Louisa Dargan (Mrs. George), 155, 220
Dargan, Louisa L. Wilson (Mrs. T. J. K.), 25, 220
Dargan, Lucian, 352
Dargan, Lucy Graves (Mrs. Edwin C.), 221, 362
Dargan, Lula, 218
Dargan, Lydia Keith (Mrs. Timothy), 24, 25, 47, 122, 222, 223, 351
Dargan, Maria Louisa Bacot (Mrs. Theodore Alonzo), 24, 121, 218, 244, 249, 254, 272, 281, 285, 307, 325, 332, 336, 352, 356, 361
Dargan, Martha Woods (Mrs. Julius A.), 47, 95, 122, 192, 223
Dargan, Mary Adeline Wilson (Mrs. George W.), 86, 222, 223, 224
Dargan, Mary Atmar Smith (Mrs. James Furman), 157, 220, 319, 362
Dargan, Sarah Dubose (Mrs. William E.), 113, 121, 124, 191, 285
Dargan, Serena Bacot (Mrs. Charles), 41, 43, 50, 203, 204, 215, 218, 226, 233, 244, 248, 254, 265, 307, 325, 332, 338, 352, 353, 357, 358, 361, 363
Dargan, Dr. Theodore Alonzo, 24, 109, 121, 200, 218, 249, 254, 281, 285, 325, 332, 336, 352, 356
Dargan, Theodosia Green Williamson (Mrs. John J.), 76, 85, 94, 99, 168, 186, 205, 214, 222, 226, 271, 275, 285, 287

Fort, Augustus, 43
Fort, Catherine M. Botsford (Mrs. Moses), 77, 113, 119, 125, 146, 150, 159, 179, 189, 245, 255, 262, 279, 336, 357
Fort, Charles, 237, 251, 357
Fort, J. Edwards, 116, 118, 128, 130, 136, 154, 319
Fort, Mrs. John, 77, 81
Fort, Josiah A., 26, 72, 92, 128, 130, 136, 154, 179, 187, 188, 248, 286, 319, 320, 324, 361
Fort, Margaret Norwood (Mrs. Albert), 50, 77, 142, 157
Fort, Moses, 125, 279
Fort, Nelly Gandy (Mrs. Charles), 334, 336, 339, 357, 358
Foster, Alfred S., 355
Foster, Elizabeth (Elise) Harrison (Mrs. Alfred S.), 355
Fountain, Elizabeth, 84, 99, 104, 119
Fountain, Fannie, 99, 119
Fountain, Mary, 99, 119
Fountain, Sarah, 99, 119
Fountain, Tom, 170, 188
Fountain, Mrs. Tom, 85
Fountain, William, 180, 191
Fountain, Mrs. William, 84, 99
Fouts, Earl, 263, 280
Fouts, Harriet Brinson (Mrs. T. J.), xv, 66, 263, 264, 279, 280, 326
Fouts, Dr. Thomas Jefferson, 66, 263, 279, 280, 306, 308, 313, 314, 318, 324, 326
Fouts, Mrs. T. J. (formerly Mrs. Pittman), 280, 326
Fraser family, 286
Fraser, Elizabeth James Witherspoon (Mrs. Thomas Boone), 124
Fraser, Hannah Boone (Mrs. Ladson), 124
Fraser, Ladson, 124
Fraser, Martha McCutcheon (Mrs. William), 124
Fraser, Thomas Boone, 124
Fraser, William, 124
Frazier, John, 116, 128, 143, 158
Frazier, William H., 11, 113, 128
Freer, Mrs., 168
French, Miss, 109
Frierson family, 342

Frierson, Adaline Albrooks McCall McIntyre (Mrs. David E.), 116, 127, 138, 155
Frierson, Rev. David E., 116, 127, 155, 200, 218
Frierson, Flora McIver (Mrs. William), 57, 86
Frierson, Dr. George P., 86
Frierson, Mary A. Scriven (Mrs. George P.), 86
Frierson, Dr. William, 57, 86
Furman family, xvi, 47, 335
Furman, Dorothea Maria Burn (Mrs. Richard I), 319, 352
Furman, Elizabeth Williams Smith, 319
Furman, Harriet Davis (Mrs. James C.), 319
Furman, Dr. James Clement, 24, 98, 126, 157, 279, 296, 314, 319, 332, 335, 342, 352
Furman, Josiah B., 123
Furman, Mary Glynn Davis (Mrs. James C.), 319, 332, 352
Furman, Mary McIver (Mrs. Richard II), 188, 279, 296, 319, 331, 351, 352, 355
Furman, Richard I, 188, 279, 319, 352, 354
Furman, Rev. Richard, 98, 126, 170, 188, 200, 218, 262, 279, 296, 319, 331, 332, 335, 351, 352
Furman, Rev. Samuel, 188, 262, 279, 319, 351, 352
Furman, Sarah, 296, 332, 352

G

Gains, Samuel, 108
Gandy, Abel A., 80, 91, 96, 99, 125, 128, 222, 223, 225, 234, 250, 270, 285, 358
Gandy, Abel A., Jr., 270, 285
Gandy, Booker, 96, 223, 250, 322
Gandy, Darius, 234, 250
Gandy, David, 116, 128
Gandy, Delilah (Mrs. Booker), 96, 223, 250, 322
Gandy, Elizabeth Smoot (Mrs. Lafayette), 85, 99, 114, 125, 128
Gandy, Ella Williams (Mrs. James), 234, 250
Gandy, James, 234, 250
Gandy, John, 72, 91, 356

Harllee, Mary Ann Young (Mrs. Walter Cannon), 282, 322, 362, 364
Harllee, Mary Hart McCall (Mrs. Henry Thomas), 261, 267, 278, 282, 284, 322, 355
Harllee, Peter, 127
Harllee, Dr. Robert, 127, 184, 193, 201, 209, 219, 224, 244, 251, 254, 278, 281, 320, 355, 362
Harllee, Robert, 284
Harllee, Robert Armstrong, 193, 201, 219
Harllee, Thomas, 127, 193, 219, 224
Harllee, Walter Cannon, 193, 267, 282, 301, 322, 343, 346, 362, 364
Harllee, General William Wallace, 127, 201, 209, 219, 224, 251, 262, 264, 266, 281, 331
Harrell, John A., 318
Harrell, Leonard, 176, 190
Harrell, Mrs., 177, 190
Harrell, Dr. Robert Fuller, 313, 314
Harrison, Anna Symmes (Mrs. William Henry) (1775-1864), 26
Harrison, William Henry (1773-1841), 26
Hart family, 342
Hart, Elizabeth A. Flinn (Mrs. Robert), 155, 252
Hart, Hannah Fountain (Mrs. John Lide), 84, 99, 119
Hart, Hannah Lide (Mrs. Thomas E.), 121, 126, 157, 254
Hart, Jesse Hartwell, 110, 121, 142, 157, 220, 287
Hart, John Lide, 99, 114, 125, 260, 276
Hart, Dr. Robert Lide, 137, 155, 240, 252
Hart, Thomas E., 121, 126, 157, 254, 276
Hartstein, Captain, 240
Hartwell, Eliza H. Jewett (Mrs. J. Boardman), 51
Hartwell, Jesse, 86
Hartwell, Dr. Jesse, 51, 57, 86, 91, 99, 124, 250, 342, 354
Hartwell, J. Boardman, 44, 51
Hartwell, Margaret F. (Mrs. Jesse), 51, 57, 85, 87, 99, 113, 124, 125, 354
Haws, Julia, 245
Hayes, Rutherford Birchard (1822-1893), 259
Haynesworth family, 9

Haynesworth, Annie Lanneau Furman (Mrs. Harry), 332, 352
Haynesworth, Edgar Charles, 293, 316
Haynesworth, Fannie, 293, 302, 316
Haynesworth, Harry, 332
Haynesworth, Lula, 293, 302, 316
Haynesworth, Mary Ann Charles (Mrs. William F. B.), 40, 48, 240, 241, 252, 253, 293, 302, 316, 322, 332, 353
Haynesworth, M. S., 118, 130
Haynesworth, Thomas Baker, 130, 281, 363
Haynesworth, Mrs. Tom, 118, 130
Haynesworth, William F. B., 48, 252, 253, 316, 322, 332, 353
Head, Rev. D. F., 280, 318
Head, George E., 280
Head, James Douglas, 280
Head, Hon. James Robert, 280, 318
Head, Joshua, 280
Head, Sophronia Prothro (Mrs. J. R.), 280, 318
Head, W. P., 280
Henning family, 141
Henson, Charles, 280
Henson, Cornelia Brinson (Mrs. Charles), 280
Hightower, Mittie Head, 280
Hill, General Ambrose Powell (1825-1865), 152, 153, 162
Hill, Bettie, xv, 133, 134
Hill, Mrs. James, 274
Hill, Quincy, 168
Hinson, John F., 318
Hogg, Mr., 104
Holliman, G., 202
Holloman, Ann Mahala Vann, 16, 25
Holloway, Jesse, 124, 281
Holloway, Sarah Rachel McIver (Mrs. Jesse), 96, 124, 281
Hoole, Captain A. J., 105
Hooper, Captain, 67
Houston, Sam (1793-1863), 38, 318
Howard, Amelia, 278
Howard, Armstrong Jolly, 278
Howard, Bessie, 278
Howard, Charles Brown, 278, 322, 355
Howard, Elizabeth Ann McCall (Mrs. Richard G.), 191, 261, 267, 278, 282
Howard, Fitzhugh Lee, 278
Howard, Mell, 278
Howard, Lieutenant Orran H., 160

Howard, Richard Grandison, 180, 191, 261, 278, 282, 322
Howard, Robert, 278
Howard, William, 278
Howells, Hannah Davis, 279
Howle family, 26, 31, 57, 76
Howle, Elizabeth (Bettie or Lizzie) Vann (Mrs. Thomas E.), xv, xvi, 11, 16, 18, 20, 23, 25, 37, 43, 46, 50, 67, 69, 71, 73, 75, 79, 80, 81, 91, 92, 97, 103, 105, 111, 112, 116, 118, 120, 127, 136, 138, 139, 143, 152, 153, 158, 166, 167, 170, 171, 172, 174, 176, 177, 179, 185, 187, 188, 189, 190, 191, 198, 199, 200, 245, 255, 269, 273, 283, 293, 317, 331, 336, 350, 351, 356
Howle, Frances Elizabeth Rhodes (Mrs. Thomas E., Jr.), 255, 286, 356
Howle, James F., Sr., 16, 23, 26, 139, 156, 268, 283
Howle, James F., Jr., 17, 26, 72, 120, 139, 156, 166
Howle, John D., 218
Howle, Lawrence Keith, 43, 50, 71, 91, 187, 255, 286
Howle, Margaret A. Keith (Mrs. James, Sr.), 26, 120, 283
Howle, Martha (Pat) (Mrs. John D.), 200, 218
Howle, Mary Ella Campbell (Mrs. Lawrence Keith), 50, 286
Howle, Mary House (Mrs. James F.), 26, 156
Howle, Mary Jane Kirven (Mrs. James, Sr.), 26, 120, 283
Howle, Nettie Gandy (Mrs. William James), 286, 356
Howle, "Old Grandmother," 104, 120
Howle, Penelope (Mrs. James, Sr.), 120, 283
Howle, Thomas E., Sr., xv, xvi, 16, 17, 18, 20, 23, 25, 26, 35, 36, 37, 46, 50, 60, 68, 70, 71, 72, 73, 79, 80, 90, 91, 95, 96, 97, 106, 114, 116, 117, 118, 120, 126, 127, 133, 134, 136, 138, 139, 143, 144, 145, 149, 151, 152, 153, 154, 156, 159, 166, 167, 170, 171, 187, 188, 199, 200, 218, 255, 283, 317, 350, 356
Howle, Thomas E., Jr., 37, 46, 71, 91, 174, 187, 189, 255, 286, 356
Howle, William James, 16, 18, 20, 25, 37, 71, 91, 187, 189, 255, 286, 331, 350, 356

Hubbard, Flora Burn, 113, 124
Humbird, Richard, 202, 207
Hunter, Andrew, 50, 59, 87, 121, 124, 361
Hunter, Dr., 59
Hunter, Emilie Bacot (Mrs. Andrew), 43, 50, 87, 121, 124, 343, 361

J

Jackson, Andrew (1767-1845), 148
Jackson, Thomas J. (Stonewall) (1824-1863), 66, 148, 149, 152, 153, 161, 165
James family, 8, 99, 126
James, Mr., 84, 115
James, "Old Mrs.," 84
James, Robert Ervin, 137, 142, 150, 154, 157, 162
James, William Elias, Sr., 121, 150, 154, 157, 162, 318
James, William E., Jr., 110, 121, 162
Jamison family, 9
Jeter, Thomas B. (1827-1883), 294
Jinks, George and Tom, 168
Johnson, Dr. Marion, 58
Johnson, Rosannah Culpepper, 84, 99, 103, 104, 119
Johnson, Sarah McCall, 299
Jones, Abel S., 174, 189
Jones, Elizabeth Mercer (Mrs. Jeremiah), 23
Jones, Jeremiah, 23
Jossey, Carolina (Mrs. J.), 40, 69, 91
Jossey, Rev. J., 91
Judson, Professor Charles H., 241, 252

K

Keith, Mrs. Jesse, 208, 223
Keitt, Anna, 261, 277
Keitt, Lawrence, 255, 277, 316
Keitt, Sue Sparks (Mrs. Lawrence), 210, 225, 260, 277, 293, 316
Kellogg, William Pitt (1830-1918), 248
Kemper, Captain Del, 136
Kersham, Colonel J. B., 135
Key, Rev. D. W., 315
Key, Sallie Norwood (Mrs. D. W.), 315
Killins, Mrs. Fisher, 108, 147, 160
King family, xvi, 41, 49, 50, 51, 80, 81, 82, 83, 84, 99, 108, 113, 117, 118, 137, 142, 154, 186, 245, 355

McDaniel, Elizabeth A. Cawthon (Mrs. John F.), 242, 253
McDaniel, Elizabeth Tillman (Mrs. W. W.), 253
McDaniel, John Franklin, 242, 253
McDaniel, K. P., 64, 89
McDaniel, Margaret J. (Maggie), 242, 253
McDaniel, Sarah Tomlinson (Mrs. John F.), 253
McDaniel, Susan W. (Mrs. K. P.), 89
McDaniel, William (Willie), 242, 253
McDaniel, William Warren, 253
McDowell, Irvin (1818-1885), 152
McEnery, Samuel D. (1837-1910), 294, 313
McFarland, J. F., 65, 89
McGee, William H., 318
McGinty, Charles Gibson, 350, 363, 365
McGinty, Emma Smith (Mrs. W. G.), 323
McGinty, Ethel Hunter (Mrs. V. K.), 365
McGinty, Eugene, 323
McGinty, Genevria, 323
McGinty, Helen Watkins (Mrs. V. K.), 365
McGinty, Mary Harriet Kolb (Mrs. W. G.), 66, 125, 222, 225, 241, 253, 261, 277, 300, 301, 302, 303, 304, 307, 309, 310, 320, 321, 323, 326, 327, 334, 337, 342, 344, 345, 346, 347, 348, 349, 350, 351, 354, 364, 365
McGinty, Oliver, 323
McGinty, Vivian Kolb, 323, 344, 345, 346, 351, 354, 365
McGinty, William Gibson, 304, 323, 331, 332, 335, 342, 344, 345, 346, 347, 349, 351, 357, 363
McIntosh family, 205
McIntosh, David Gregg, 130, 137, 154
McIntosh, Dora Evans (Mrs. Edward), 221, 252
McIntosh, Edward, 130, 205, 221, 240, 252
McIntosh, James H., 44, 52, 130, 217, 218, 221, 252, 270, 281, 284, 286
McIntosh, Dr. James H., Jr., 130
McIntosh, Louisa, 205, 221, 240, 252, 265, 274, 281, 286, 299, 320, 324, 336, 339, 356, 358
McIntosh, Lucas, 240, 252

McIntosh, Margaret E., 200, 205, 218, 221, 240, 252
McIntosh, Margaret Lucas, 44, 52, 130, 200, 217
McIntosh, Martha Gregg (Mrs. James H., Sr.), 52, 118, 130, 218, 221, 240, 244, 252, 254, 281, 286
McIntosh, Murray, 240, 252
McIntosh, Rosa Evans (Mrs. Lucas), 240, 252
McIntosh, Rev. W. H., 256
McIntyre, Richard F., 127
McIver family, Society Hill, S. C., 8, 342
McIver family, Kingston, La., 48, 342
McIver, Abel, 124
McIver, Alexander, 8, 22, 98, 161, 278
McIver, Alexander Markland, 161, 238, 251, 262, 278, 282, 293, 316
McIver, Allen Evander, 58, 90, 162, 234, 250, 255, 326
McIver, Ann James (Aunt Nancy), 49, 74, 80, 92, 96, 97, 200, 218
McIver, Caroline Wilds (Mrs. D. R. W.), 21, 48, 52, 86, 126, 252
McIver, Rev. D. R. W., 8, 21, 22, 48, 52, 57, 86, 115, 126, 247, 252
McIver, Eliza Cowan (Mrs. Evander), 108, 113, 120, 123, 247, 318
McIver, Eliza Mauldin (Mrs. George Walter), 282, 317
McIver, Elizabeth Chapman (Mrs. Peter Kolb), 221, 249, 282
McIver, Evander (the elder), 49, 92, 96, 218, 222
McIver, Evander, 120, 123, 247, 318
McIver, Colonel Evander R., 231, 248
McIver, Flora, 161, 262, 278, 279, 293, 317
McIver, George Walter, 161, 282, 293, 317
McIver, George Williams, 24, 150, 161, 238, 251, 262, 278, 316
McIver, Hannah Wilson (Mrs. John K.), 130, 162, 205, 222, 245, 255, 268, 283, 292, 315, 334, 336, 353, 354, 355, 357
McIver, Harriett LaCoste (Mrs. George W.), 24, 150, 161, 189, 251, 278, 293, 316
McIver, James Kolb, 130, 159, 188, 222, 279, 319, 351, 353, 355, 357
McIver, John, 21, 86
McIver, John H., 8, 22

McIver, John J., 106
McIver, Captain John Kolb, xv, 41, 106, 117, 125, 130, 151, 152, 162, 176, 180, 191, 206, 222, 245, 255, 283, 315, 353, 354, 355, 357
McIver, John Kolb, Jr., 334, 336, 354, 357
McIver, Julia Whilden (Mrs. Alexander M.), 251, 262, 278, 316
McIver, Louise Boyd (Mrs. John K., Jr.), 354
McIver, Louise Penn (Mrs. William Cowan), 248
McIver, Martha Elizabeth Screven Grant (Mrs. D. R. W.), 48, 86, 247
McIver, Mary Ann Williams (Mrs. John), 21, 86
McIver, Mary Ervin (Mrs. Evander R.), 248
McIver, Mary Hanford (Mrs. Alexander), 22, 98, 161, 278, 282
McIver, Peter Kolb, 221, 249, 282
McIver, Rachel Love (Mrs. Abel), 124
McIver, Sarah (Sallie) Witherspoon Ervin (Mrs. Allen Evander), 58, 90, 150, 162, 245, 250, 255, 310, 326
McIver, Sarah Bacot (Mrs. Thomas), 41, 160
McIver, Sarah Kolb (Mrs. Evander, the elder), 92, 96, 218
McIver, Sarah Marshall (Mrs. James Kolb), 130, 159, 188, 222, 279, 319, 351, 353, 355, 357
McIver, Colonel Thomas Edwards, 41, 160
McIver, William Cowan, 248
McKee, W. J., 62
McLean, Agnes Evans (Mrs. John), 295, 318
McLean, John, 295, 318
McLean, Mrs. John (nee Godfrey), 295
McLeningham, Mary, 296
McLeod, Elizabeth Dargan Forrester (Mrs. William L.), 343, 362
McLeod, William Lucien, 362
McQueen, James H., 318
McQueen, Mariah Campbell Coit (Mrs. James H.), 318
Magrath, A. G. (1813-1893), 197, 217
Malloy, Catherine (Mrs. Charles), 46
Malloy, Charles, 46

Malloy, Duncan, 46, 318
Malloy, Mary Ann Malloy (Mrs. Duncan), 38, 46, 318
Manly, Rev. Basil, Sr., 342, 360
Manly, Rev. Basil, Jr., 360
Manly, Rev. Charles, 341, 360
Manning, Ben M., 313, 314, 327
Manning, John L. (1816-1889), 14, 111
Manning, Mary Meek (Mrs. Ben M.), 327
Marks, Dr., 240
Marshall, Adam, 86
Marshall, James G., 57, 86
Marshall, John J., 57, 86
Marshall, Maria Hawes (Mrs. John J.), 86
Marshall, Mary Gregg, 281
Marshall, Oliver H., 57, 86
Martin, Colonel William E., 156
Mauldin, Hannah McIver (Mrs. Joab), 205, 221, 234, 245, 249, 268, 282
Mauldin, Joab, 221, 282
Mays, Sophronia Head, 280
Meigs, General Montgomery Cunningham (1816-1892), 156
Miles, Emma Brinson (Mrs. P. W.), 280
Miles, Pemberton W., 280
Miller, Addie Dorrity, 305, 324
Miller, Stephen D., 8
Milling, David C., 197, 301, 322
Mims, Lieutenant A. J., 148
Mims, Professor, 335
Monroe, James, 63
Mood, Lou Rembert Williamson (Mrs. William), 43, 50, 301, 321
Mood, Rev. William, 321
Moody, Mary A. Head, 280
Moore, A. J., 313
Moore, Rev. Gordon B., 339, 340, 343, 359, 360, 361
Moore, Colonel Henry, 144, 158
Moreland, W. C., 318
Morrison, Elizabeth Woods (Mrs. John), 39, 47
Morrison, John, 47
Moses, Franklin J., Jr. (1838-1887), 202, 231
Moss, Adam H., 315
Moss, Annie Norwood (Mrs. Adam H.), 315
Muldrow, Elihu, 110, 121
Muldrow, Samuel, 121
Muldrow, Ursula W. (Mrs. Samuel), 121

Sompayrac, Margaret Douglas (Mrs. Theodore), 221, 225, 265, 281, 285, 334, 340, 353, 360
Sompayrac, Theodore, 205, 210, 221, 225, 270, 281, 285, 334, 353, 360
Southworth, Mrs. E. D. E. N. (1819-1899), 212
Sparks family, 9, 234
Sparks, Alexander, 8, 22, 97, 209, 221, 224, 249, 255, 283, 284, 315
Sparks, Ann Hurry (Mrs. Samuel), 209, 225, 260, 277, 316
Sparks, Daniel, I, 22
Sparks, Daniel, 260, 277
Sparks, Mrs. Daniel, 260
Sparks, Jeannette McKarrley (Mrs. Alexander), 82, 97, 205, 221, 245, 249, 283
Sparks, Samuel, 210, 225, 260, 277, 293, 316
Stanland, J. B., 63
Stephens, Rev. John, 98
Stephenson, Dr., 306
Stephenson, Lou Crawford, 301, 306, 322
Stevens, General Isaac Ingalls (1818-1862), 147
Stogner, Mrs. Essie Skinner, 223
Stokes, William, 142, 145, 159
Stout, Fannie Coker (Mrs. John), 234, 245, 250, 255, 261, 317, 356, 358, 359
Stout, Rev. John, 234, 245, 250, 255, 261, 265, 276, 277, 293, 305, 317, 324, 336, 339, 340, 356, 358, 359
Strickland, Rev. W. H., 234, 239, 240, 250, 251, 252
Swinton, Mrs. William, 73, 92

T

Tarver, Alice Louise Head, 280
Taylor, Emily King (Mrs. T. L.), xv, 41, 42, 44, 48, 50, 51, 82, 85, 97, 124, 145, 157, 171, 184, 199, 201, 202, 203, 204, 209, 215, 217, 220, 226, 233, 237, 244, 246, 247, 254, 256, 260, 265, 272, 275, 276, 280, 293, 296, 299, 306, 310, 316, 325, 332, 334, 336, 340, 343, 344, 345, 353, 355, 358, 360, 363, 364
Taylor, Margaret Smith (Mrs. Zachary) (1788-1852), 26

Taylor, Rev. T. L., 204, 215, 220, 233, 247, 254, 260, 299, 306, 310, 332, 341, 343, 344, 353, 360, 363, 364
Taylor, W. H., 158
Tedder, Betty, 104, 170
Teel, Christopher, 4
Terrel family, 125, 186
Terrel, Ann Allison (Mrs. John), 39, 47
Terrel, John, 47
Theus, Mary Ann (Mrs. Simeon), 89
Theus, Simeon, 64, 89
Thomas, Rev. A. J. S., 341, 360
Thomas, D. K., 64
Thomas, David K., II, 327, 365
Thomas, Rev. J. A. W., 147, 160, 209, 215, 224, 227, 276, 332, 352
Thomas, James Bryant, 63, 88
Thomas, Jeremiah, 146
Thomas, Lorenso (1804-1875), 158
Thomas, Margaret Spears (Mrs. J. A. W.), 160
Thomas, Mary Ella Tooke (Mrs. David K., II), xiii, xviii, 310, 327, 344, 345, 350, 354, 363, 365
Thomas, Sallie King (Mrs. William), 170, 187
Thomas, Telitha Ann Missouri Nix (Mrs. James B.), 88
Thomas, Tristram, 160
Thomas, William, 187
Thomas, Rev. Zachariah, 63, 64, 88
Thompson, Fannie McIver (Mrs. Henry T.), 255, 268, 283, 292, 315, 334, 337, 354, 357
Thompson, Henry T., 283, 315, 334, 337, 354, 357
Thompson, Hugh Smith (1836-1904), 334, 337, 357
Thompson, Rev. W. T., 278, 322
Tillman, Benjamin R. (Pitchfork Ben) (1847-1918), 249
Tooke family, 88
Tooke, Anna Nixon Vickers (Mrs. John Arthur), 88, 323
Tooke, Edwin Parramore, 350, 363, 365
Tooke, Henry Jones, 89, 280, 285, 304, 323, 344, 345, 346, 350, 363, 365
Tooke, Ida Gertrude, xiii, xiv, xv, xvii, xviii, 20, 89, 311
Tooke, John, 88
Tooke, John Arthur, 63, 64, 88, 89, 323
Tooke, Lela Viola Dees (Mrs. E. P.), 365

Tooke, Maria Elizabeth Kolb (Mrs. H. J.), xiii, xvii, 62, 89, 99, 125, 211, 222, 225, 261, 264, 265, 271, 277, 280, 285, 300, 303, 304, 310, 312, 320, 321, 326, 334, 337, 339, 344, 345, 348, 349, 350, 354, 357, 363, 364, 365
Tooke, Mary (Polly) Jones (Mrs. John), 88
Tullis, Mrs., 42, 49
Tullis, Thomas E., 49
Tupper, Eliza Yoer (Mrs. Tristram), 360
Tupper, Rev. Henry Allen, 256, 342, 360
Tupper, Tristram, 360
Tutwiler, Henry, 123

V

Van Dorn, General Earl (1820-1863), 166, 167, 185
Vann family, xvi, 69
Vann, Dr. Alexander Russia, xv, xvii, 11, 12, 13, 14, 17, 19, 23, 24, 25, 31, 32, 33, 34, 35, 36, 37, 46, 61, 68, 70, 71, 78, 86, 87, 95, 171, 172, 173, 187, 188, 245, 254, 268, 273, 283, 286, 293, 336, 356
Vann, Charlotte W. (Mrs. Robert), 16, 25, 220
Vann, Clementina Wright (Mrs. Mills), 11, 43, 50, 92
Vann, Edward Macon, 188
Vann, Elizabeth Frances Cannady (Mrs. Alexander Russia), xiv, xv, xvi, xvii, 11, 12, 14, 16, 18, 19, 20, 23, 25, 26, 31, 33, 35, 37, 45, 46, 78, 171, 172, 173, 188, 283, 356
Vann, Josiah T., 11, 15, 16, 23, 31, 32, 37, 45, 46, 61, 70, 71, 78, 86, 87, 95, 104, 119, 169, 170, 187, 245, 255, 336, 356
Vann, Josiah Thomas, II, 33, 34, 45, 46, 71, 91, 268, 269, 273, 283, 286, 293, 317, 356
Vann, Louise Passmore (Mrs. William, II), xvi, 11, 254, 268, 283
Vann, Maggie J. Howle (Mrs. Josiah Thomas, II), 91, 187, 255, 269, 273, 283, 286, 293, 317, 356
Vann, Margaret H., 11, 23
Vann, Mills, 11, 12, 15, 24, 25, 50, 92, 119, 122, 126, 130, 187, 204, 234, 244, 249, 250, 253, 260, 276, 286, 315, 317, 324
Vann, Robert R., 16, 25, 204, 220, 245, 255, 273, 286, 293, 317
Vann, Sallie C. Byrd (Mrs. Josiah T.), xvi, 23, 356
Vann, Samuel Cannady, 12, 13, 16, 18, 20, 23, 25, 32, 34, 46
Vann, Sarah Ann, 11, 23
Vann, Sarah Goodson (Mrs. William, II), xvi, 11, 25, 255, 283
Vann, Sarah Jones (Mrs. William, II), xvi, 11, 12, 15, 23, 116, 118, 130, 136, 154, 170, 174, 177, 179, 189, 198, 218, 356
Vann, Thomas, 11
Vann, Walter Brooks, 172, 188
Vann, William, 10, 11, 23, 24, 46, 253
Vann, Mrs. William (nee Hamilton), 23, 24, 253
Vann, William, of Orangeburg, S. C., 15, 25
Vann, William, II, xv, xvi, 10, 11, 12, 13, 15, 16, 19, 23, 24, 25, 32, 35, 36, 37, 46, 69, 72, 80, 114, 116, 118, 126, 127, 130, 142, 154, 170, 173, 174, 177, 179, 187, 189, 191, 198, 200, 204, 217, 218, 234, 245, 249, 254, 255, 268, 269, 273, 283, 286, 293, 296, 299, 305, 306, 317, 319, 324, 356
Vann, William Wyatte, 12, 23
Vaughn, Colonel J. C., 153
Vickers, James Jackson, 64, 89
Vickers, Jane Thomas (Mrs. John L.), 89
Vickers, John L., 64, 89

W

Walker, John Andrew, 318
Walker, Leroy Pope (1817-1884), 129
Wallace family, 126
Wallace, Anna, 215, 226, 287
Wallace, Estelle, 215, 226, 234, 287
Wallace, Dr., 118
Wallace, Jane Williamson (Mrs. Thomas S.), 76, 78, 82, 93, 95, 97, 114, 118, 125, 130, 215, 226, 234, 275, 287, 293, 316, 343, 344, 345, 362, 363